P9-EDZ-905

becoming a

physical education teacher

contemporary and enduring issues

Richard
Tinning

Doune
Macdonald

Jan
Wright

Chris
Hickey

becoming a
physical
education
teacher

contemporary and enduring issues

Prentice
Hall

Copyright © 2001 Pearson Education Australia Pty Limited

Pearson Education Australia
Unit 4, Level 2
14 Aquatic Drive
Frenchs Forest NSW 2086

All rights reserved. Except under the conditions described in the Copyright Act 1968 of Australia and subsequent amendments, no part of this publication may be reproduced, stored in a retrieval system or transmitted in any form or by any means, electronic, mechanical, photocopying, recording or otherwise, without the prior permission of the copyright owner.

Senior Acquisitions Editor: Catherine Godfrey
Managing Editor: Susan Lewis
Copy Editor: Linda Morris
Cover and text design: Carol Hudson Graphic Design
Cover photograph: Nicholas Canosa
Typeset by Midland Typesetters, Maryborough
Printed in Malaysia

1 2 3 4 5 05 04 03 02 01

National Library of Australia
Cataloguing-in-Publication Data

Becoming a Physical Education Teacher: Contemporary and enduring issues.

Bibliography.
Includes index.
ISBN 0 7248 0341 6.

1. Physical education teachers—Training of—Australia. 2. Physical education and training—Study and teaching—Australia. I. Tinning, Richard, 1946– .

372.860994

Every effort has been made to trace and acknowledge copyright. However, should any infringement have occurred, the publishers tender their apologies and invite copyright owners to contact them.

Prentice Hall is an imprint of Pearson Education Australia

contents

AUGUSTANA UNIVERSITY COLLEGE
LIBRARY

section one

chapter one

objectives

By the end of this chapter you should be able to:

- discuss the purpose of this book and the value position that informs what is written;
- understand the meaning of reflection and the significance of becoming a reflective teacher of physical education;
- identify yourself in the context of the 'options generation';
- explain how we use the terms pedagogy, curriculum and discourse.

The logic

There is a logic which we have followed in this book. Basically we try and connect you and your experiences in becoming a (health and) physical education teacher with a progressively widening and analytic view of the world of physical activity, young people, schooling and the world beyond the school gate.

We assume that you already know a lot about being a young person, about the joys and pleasures of participation in physical activity, and about living a life (your life) in this particular period of time—namely the beginning of the 21st century. We also assume that you will become (health and) physical education teachers in the new millennium and that there will be particular challenges to our profession in these new times.

A word on the title of the book

We have chosen this title for very specific reasons. First, we believe that in your time at university you are beginning the *formal* part of 'becoming a physical education teacher'. Formal in the sense that you are studying for a degree which will certify you to teach physical education. But there are also informal aspects of becoming a teacher: some of them took place while you were at school and others will continue as you begin a career of teaching. We will talk more about this later but it is important to recognise that you are in the *process* of becoming a teacher and this book will help you to understand that process and *become* a better teacher.

Of course this title also begs the question 'What exactly does it mean to teach physical education?'. As you will see throughout this book, teaching physical education can mean different things depending on the contextual circumstances. For example, it might mean teaching hurdling to a class of year 9 girls out on the school oval, or it might mean teaching a mixed class of year 12 students the biomechanics of rotational activities like diving in the classroom situation. The (often artificial) distinction between practical and theoretical physical education is a significant issue and we will return to it later in the book. For the moment, however, we want to register that the focus of this book is with teaching physical education in the middle school context—namely years 7–10. What takes place as physical education in the middle school varies in schools across Australian states and territories and in New Zealand. It is, however, appropriate to say that in the main there is a practical physical activity orientation to the subject, which will often include some classroom-based theory work. Also, more and more it will be 'connected' to health education as part of the key learning area called Health and Physical Education in Australia and New Zealand.

It was the educational researcher Philip Wexler (1992) who claimed that *becoming somebody* was the main mission for most young people in secondary school. In other words, young people in school (as many of you were very recently) are in the process of constructing identities for themselves. As you engage on your teacher education course you will be continuing that process. In this case you will be constructing an identity as a physical education teacher.

It won't be your only identity but it will be a significant one relating to your occupational life. In this sense we can think of all of us as having multiple identities, of which being a PE teacher is but one.

The second part of the title is also deliberate. Physical education in schools in the new century has to confront and deal with many issues that have been around since the beginning of the last century. These are the enduring issues that do not seem to go away and must be dealt with in the daily life of teaching physical education. Also, there are many issues that demand consideration and attention that are contemporary—they did not exist even 30 years ago, they are issues of today and are born of the current educational, political and social context.

A book for all semesters

What we have done in this book is to recognise that you do not become a physical education teacher in the time span of a one semester course on 'How to teach physical education'. Bit by bit all the experiences that you have throughout your university course will contribute to the sort of teacher you become. Buying a textbook for one unit can be frustrating if it sits on the shelf for the rest of your course. In this book we have assumed that you will use this text throughout your degree or graduate diploma program, not only for set work for a particular unit but also for reference as you progress towards your degree. Accordingly, this book should be part of your professional library from the first semester of your course.

We also recognise that textbooks like this one do not need to be read cover to cover like a novel. You will dip in and out of the pages as the circumstances of your course change. In terms of order, the fact that Chapter 2 comes before Chapter 3 does not mean that they must be read in that order. We have tried to make connections and cross references between chapters but you will not lose the plot if you chop and choose your order of reading. We do say, however, that it is necessary to read *this* chapter first, as it sets out the intentions and agenda of the book.

Becoming a 'reflective' teacher

Becoming a physical education teacher begs one important question: What sort of PE teacher do you want to be? You probably have in your own mind an image of a PE teacher whom you admired and on whom you would like to model yourself. Perhaps you have had a PE teacher who has already been something of a mentor to you. That's great, because we recognise that all of us can benefit from having a mentor who can advise us on the basis of their experience and knowledge. In the pages of this book we want to help you to begin to analyse, deconstruct and generally reflect on the qualities of the sort of teacher you wish to become. All of us bring different qualities, talents and abilities to our teaching. But one thing is certain: in the process of becoming a 'good' PE teacher you will need to meet some challenges and be prepared to change. In fact, there is a strong relationship between professional growth and personal growth. As you learn more about yourself, you will become a better teacher.

We take as the basic assumption of this book that there is a *qualitative* dimension implicit in becoming a PE teacher. A more complete title would be 'Becoming a *good* teacher'. Of course defining what a good PE teacher is is open to debate. We will open this debate and provoke you to think about how you will define good teaching.

As you will see in the pages ahead there is a great deal about current (and past) practices in school physical education that are less than satisfactory. While some physical education teachers are inspiring, caring and competent, there are also those who give less than adequate attention to their teaching and for whom the cliche of 'rolling out the ball' was coined. The American physical educator Larry Locke once said that physical education was not so much bothered by poor teaching as it was by mindless teaching. In other words, just going through the motions, rolling out the ball, in the absence of purposeful teaching has become too common. Another term for mindless teaching would be *unreflective* teaching.

There are very real reasons why some teachers are unreflective of their work and simply roll out the ball. We do not mean to admonish these teachers but we will analyse some of these reasons and put to you certain perspectives and ways of thinking about teaching that will help you deal with some of the realities of contemporary physical education. We will encourage you to become a *reflective* teacher. We will encourage you to begin to think about your teaching by means of two orienting questions which provide a point of focus for reflection. The orienting questions are:

1. What are the implications of what I choose to teach?
2. What are the implications of how I teach?

Reflection is not 'navel gazing'

It is probably fair to say that what we come to know and accept as normal ways of doing things, of behaving (of practice) in various contexts—for example, eating, building a house, running a meeting or teaching—might appear strange to a person from another culture. One of the purposes of education is to help us to make sense of strange things and practices and so better understand the world and our place in it. However, because we live and grow up in *our* culture, there are many practices and behaviours that we take for granted as *normal,* as the only way of doing (or seeing) things. In our view, education, and teacher education, should also help us to make strange the familiar, taken-for-granted things of our culture and so question the world and our place in it.

The American social commentator and educator Neil Postman claims that what we know about a subject depends on the questions we ask about it. One of the things which this book will do is to question the things that might generally be taken as 'fact' in physical education. We want to make the familiar strange. The first part in this process is to get a sense of what counts for truth in physical education. Second, we need to ask the questions 'Whose truth is it anyway?' and 'Why do they hold it as true?'. One way or another these questions will return throughout the book.

As a result of this process you will become a teacher who develops a *reflective* orientation to your work. In this process you will learn to be careful about how things appear, the assumptions that you make, and you will understand the need to ask questions and to look beneath the surface of the common practices and ways of thinking about teaching. Accordingly, this book will not provide you with tips and tricks for teaching. Rather, it will help you ask the not so common questions, and provide the context material from which to formulate and perhaps even answer some of these questions.

Our principled position

We have a collective position with respect to good physical education teaching. It is a principled position. Good physical education teaching should make the physical education experiences for young people meaningful, purposeful, enjoyable and just. Such experiences would be underpinned by the assertion that schools should be about reproducing the best of our culture and challenging the worst aspects such that they might be improved. We believe it entails a 'moral intention to develop a certain kind of human being' (Goodlad 1984, p 109). This is consistent with the notion that schooling is about making certain types of citizen (see Section 4). It is a moral position that will determine what kind of human being or citizen we want to 'make'. Perhaps you never thought about physical education quite in those terms before, but we will talk more about this idea later.

Lest you think that this is just an attempt to impose our particular preference or bias on you, it is important to realise that *all* articulations or policies concerning teacher education and schooling are based on particular principled positions, on particular conceptions of what is good teaching and to what ends good teaching should be directed. For example, the *National Standards and Guidelines for Initial Teacher Education* (1998) and other state commissioned guidelines for teacher education (e.g. the Queensland Board of Teacher Education's *Guidelines on the Acceptability of Teacher Education Programs for Teacher Registration Purposes* 1997) all expect student teachers to develop their critical and reflective abilities. Moreover they expect that graduates should be 'practitioner–researchers' who are 'explicit and analytic' about their practice. It is these general professional attributes, among others, that we are hoping to foster in you as you engage with the ideas of this book.

The meaning of reflection

It was Grossman (1992, cited in Dodds 1993) who claimed that reflective teachers are those who 'ask worthwhile questions of teaching [and] continue to learn from their practice' (p 176). The problem with this claim is that it leaves as unexplored the possible nature of a worthwhile question. We prefer the perspective which John Dewey (1933) offered concerning the issue of reflective teaching. John Dewey led the educational theorising on the nature of reflective teaching this century (at least in the English-speaking countries). He first distinguished between *reflective action* and *routine action*. Routine action is guided by tradition and authority. It takes ends (and the traditions) for granted and focuses attention on the means to achieve particular ends. Reflective action, on the other hand, involves the consideration of the *assumptions underpinning* any belief or form of knowledge and the *consequences* which might follow from action that incorporates such beliefs or knowledge. Importantly, Dewey identified three attitudes which he claimed are prerequisite to reflective action.

- First, there must be an attitude of *openmindedness* in which there is a desire to see more than one side of an argument, in which full attention is given to alternative possibilities, and in which there is recognition of the possibility that even our dearest beliefs might be wrong.
- Second, there must be an attitude of *responsibility* which means that the consequences of our actions are considered.
- Third, there must be a *wholeheartedness* in which both openmindedness and responsibility are central components in one's life.

If you developed Dewey's three attitudes as a result of your engagement with this book then we could feel rightly proud of our achievements. Unfortunately however, as Zeichner (1981, p 5) has informed us:

> *Our tendency as educators is to perceive this everyday reality as given, objectively defined, and in need of no further verification beyond its simple presence. As a consequence, we often lose sight of the fact that the existing reality is one of many possible alternatives that could exist.*

This takes us back to the earlier point of the importance of making the familiar strange. Zeichner is arguing that the tendency of most educators is to accept the familiar everyday reality as the natural, indeed only, reality. Clearly if, as teachers, we had had Dewey's reflective action as a central component of our daily lives (and not just in our teaching lives), then such a tendency would be challenged.

Orienting questions for reflection

There are many things on which a teacher can reflect. Some can be rather trivial, others more significant. Of course we realise that who defines what is significant and what is trivial is a key issue but we have come clean with respect to our principled position on good physical education teaching.

Most often, reflection will be oriented towards the central problems that are seen to require attention in teaching (or in teacher education). Postman (1989) tells us that what we know about a subject will depend on the questions we ask of it. In this case, what we can know about reflective teaching will depend on the questions we ask of it. As Lawson (1984) has demonstrated, understanding the process of 'problem setting' (defining the problems) involves asking questions about why a particular problem is considered such in the first place, by whom is it considered a problem and the interests served by defining a problem in a particular way.

For some teacher educators (your lecturers at university or college) the *central* problem is 'How can we train student teachers to become effective teachers?' (e.g. Cruickshank 1987) and 'How can we best develop the teaching skills of student teachers?' (e.g. Siedentop 1991). For others it is 'How can we train teachers to be reflective of their work in ways which embody a critical social perspective?' (see Kirk 1986). Of course it does not have to be either/or but we are talking here about emphasis.

As we have said, we consider that we should orient our reflection by the questions: 'What are the implications of what I teach?' and 'What are the implications of how I teach?'. It is our view that when these questions are used to orient our work (either as teacher educators or physical education teachers in schools) then our reflection can keep us connected to the issue of the type of citizen we would like our education to 'make'.

It is our intention that this book will itself be oriented by the same question and that you will be engaged in not just the questions of what type of school physical education you wish to create for young people but also what kind of physical education teacher you wish to become.

Actually the notion of reflection which we consider appropriate in teacher education is best described by the term *reflective practice*. Reflective practice is a broader notion of reflection than reflective teaching. In its broadest sense, reflective practice is an intellectual disposition which functions like a set of lenses through which to view all educational and cultural practices. Reflective practice will be 'applied to' more than the act of teaching. It will have a broader function than merely what happens in specific lessons. Reflective practice will also engage issues relating to schooling and education as inherently political and ideological social structures. The development of reflective practice should foster the attitudes of openmindedness, responsibility and wholeheartedness which Dewey (1933) articulated.

The book is itself reflective

Throughout the book you will find boxed sections titled 'For Your Information', 'Let's Reflect', 'Author Reflection' and 'Over to You'. They are intended to give you some ideas/questions/scenarios to reflect on.

Physical education student teachers: Who are you?

Obviously, in writing this book for physical education student teachers we have some notion of who you are. What we think we know about you is certainly open to question. We realise that there is not really 'one you'. That is, we are on shaky ground to say there is a typical physical education student teacher. However, from our collective experiences in teacher education and from the research literature, we can make some comment about some characteristics of many physical education student teachers. In presenting the following representations we are conscious that some of you will not identify with all or part of the descriptions we use, but some of you probably will.

Like PE student teachers around the world, many of you have had reasonably positive (some very positive) experiences in sport and physical education as school students. But you probably have different motivations to teaching. Here are the voices of three local student teachers:

Sharon

I was very much into sport. I did PE as one of my (year 12) subjects and I did fairly well because we had a great teacher. I wasn't able to get the score for human movement so I went for the double degree (teaching and human movement). I don't really want to be a teacher. It's one option but it's not a huge career aspiration.

Roberta

I had a fantastic phys. ed. teacher from year 6 through to when she retired when I was in year 11. Then I got a third-year-out new teacher and she was just fantastic. Everything she did was just wonderful, she just was very encouraging. At the end of year 12 I applied for physiotherapy but missed out by three marks and phys. ed. teaching was my second choice. I'm pretty sporty like the majority of phys. ed. teachers. You would have to be otherwise there'd be no point in going into it.

James

I'm big into sport. I really enjoyed physical education in primary and secondary school. The reason I'm here is that I have always wanted to be a PE teacher from about year 7 or 8 and that was probably because the PE teacher I had, he was such a great guy and he looked cool in a track suit and I thought I could do that. Now that I've got here and been on teaching rounds I don't want to be a PE teacher any more but I'll still complete the course and get a degree.

There are a few themes running through the stories of these three student teachers: they each had a PE teacher whom they saw as a role model; they all were sports oriented and none of them saw themselves as absolutely dedicated to becoming a teacher; it was, for two of them at least, a second choice of career option.

Whether or not you are absolutely committed to being a PE teacher, like students before you most of you will enjoy doing your physical education course. Indeed, teachers tend to look back on their university/college days with considerable affection. Here is what these British physical education teachers said of their teacher training years:

'Best three years of my life' (Jane); 'Good times' (Pete); 'Brilliant, brilliant' (Diane); 'I had the time of my life' (Laura); 'It was good because we were doing sport pretty much all day every day which was really what I absolutely loved' (Grant). (Armour & Jones 1998, p 126)

Notwithstanding the fact that in most Australian university courses there is rather less practical sport in the curriculum than in Grant's course, many Australian teachers have similarly fond memories of their training years. However, not all do. And not all of you will be so positively disposed to your current experiences in university physical education. There may be some of you who, like Sandra Thomas the student in Peter Swan's (1995) short stories of life in a Physical Education Teacher Education (PETE) program (*Between the Rings and Under the Gym Mat*), feel very uncomfortable in the company of other physical educators, especially those who may be intolerant of difference. But you would be, as you well know, in the minority, and perhaps you feel marginalised because of that.

'Options generation'?

Most of you probably do not recognise anything strange or unfamiliar about the world in which we live at the beginning of the 21st century. Most Australian university students who came to university directly from school were probably born in the late 1970s or early 1980s and consequently are members of what Hugh Mackay (1997) has called the 'options generation'. Although there are numerous students who take pathways to university other than that coming directly from school, it is still the case that the majority of physical education student teachers have only recently left secondary school.

If you are in your early 20s then you were 'born into one of the most dramatic periods of social, cultural, economic and technological development in Australia's history: the age of discontinuity, the age of redefinition, the age of uncertainty—call it what you will' (Mackay 1997, p 138). Other researchers and commentators have used different labels such as 'Generation X', the 'generation on hold', and the 'post 1970 generation' (Wyn 1998). According to Mackay, the characteristics of your generation include the following:

- By the time you reached puberty the women's movement was already 'history'. You take equality of the sexes for granted.
- Most of your mothers have paid employment outside the home. You did not expect your mum to be home after school to make you cookies.
- Many of you will come from households where no-one is currently earning any wages. Unemployment is a reality for your generation. One-third of your contemporaries face bleak employment prospects.
- You know that lots of your friends (if not you) live with one parent as a result of divorce. This you regard as nothing abnormal.
- Many of you carry emotional scars as a reminder of your parents' estrangement.

- You have grown up with the idea of multiculturalism and generally assume that Australia will one day become a republic.
- You know that the global environment is a precious resource which previous generations have abused, and which needs to be protected.
- You are the most media-stimulated generation ever and also the most highly educated.
- You are utterly adapted to the idea that the technology of today will tomorrow be obsolescent. You are familiar with fax machines, mobile telephones, personal computers, email, the Internet and virtual reality.
- You recognise that everything is changing and accordingly you will strive to keep your options open.

You also are the generation who has grown up with the global commercialisation of sport and the commodification of the body—both of which are important issues relating to the field of physical education.

Joanna Wyn of the Youth Research Centre at Melbourne University claims that the post-1970 (options) generation 'are not simply producing different patterns of living: many are involved in a reshaping of what growing up means' (1998, p 45). She writes that her research findings suggest that 'pragmatism, optimism, flexibility in approach, and an ability to "juggle" competing demands on one's time are integral to the production of the complex life patterns of this group of young people' (p 45). Do you recognise yourself in there?

The thing about all this is that you probably see all these things as normal, nothing strange, just as they are. But Mackay and Wyn are telling us that such things are particular characteristics of *your* generation and we suggest that your physical education teaching will be influenced by these characteristics in ways that we probably have not even thought about yet.

A note about the authors

Like you, the four of us (Doune, Jan, Chris and Richard) studied to be physical education teachers. We became physical education teachers through the experiences of our training and other seemingly unrelated experiences. When we say that we all studied to be physical education teachers we do not mean that we all wanted to *be* physical education teachers. Like many of you, some of us were more interested in extending our involvement with and participation in sport or dance than *actually* becoming a teacher. Doing a physical education course meant that we could keep the thing we loved to do the most—namely sport—as the central activity and focus of our lives. So becoming great physical education teachers probably was not foremost in the minds of some of us, at least as we began our training. It was in the *process of becoming* a teacher that our commitment to the job of teaching developed. We recognise that it might also be the same for you.

We work at different universities across the country and we have had many different life experiences along the way, both in and out of our teaching careers. Accordingly we bring differing perspectives to the task of teacher education. These differences will find voice in this book. If you are looking for the coherent 'truth' about physical education you will not find it in these pages. What you will find are different interpretations, different understandings which are brought to bear on our understandings of physical education.

Perhaps you knew from day one that a career in teaching physical education is exactly what you wanted, and you want to be a 'good' teacher rather than the mindless (unreflective) type that Locke mentioned. Whatever your entering purposes, you will all be on a journey of becoming a physical education teacher, and this book is intended to help you along this journey and to be reflective on and of that journey.

A note on some key terms

Although we have provided a glossary of terms at the back of the book, we want to clearly define the way in which we use a few of the main key terms.

Pedagogy

This term is actually a very old word related to the function of a pedagogue. A pedagogue was, in ancient Greece, a slave who took a boy (never a girl!) to and from school. More recently it became the term to describe a teacher or schoolmaster. Pedagogy became the practice of a pedagogue and more specifically related to instruction, discipline or training.

Some contemporary educational commentators use pedagogy to refer to the art and science of teaching but in our case we prefer a broader, more dynamic use of the term. We take our lead from David Lusted (1986), who claimed that how one teaches cannot be separated from how one learns and the nature of the subject matter. In other words, instruction is connected to learning and curriculum (after Kirk et al 1997); see Figure 1.1.

Although it is sometimes useful to discuss curriculum, instruction and learning separately, and we will do this sometimes in this book, the way in which they interactively affect and depend on their interrelationship with one another is the essence of pedagogy. Sound complex? We hope all this will unfold as you read on.

Curriculum

Let us think for a moment about the health and physical education curriculum to illustrate the meaning of 'curriculum'. Firstly, curriculum means more than the terms 'activities' or 'content' which are often substituted for it. According to David Hamilton (1987), a curriculum is a cultural tool. As a tool, Hamilton argues that curriculum is shaped by its users, who include those who wield it and those whose lives are managed—or steered—according to its prescriptions. Importantly, it is the values and aspirations of the powerful social groups, rather than the powerless, that are most likely to be reflected in the curriculum:

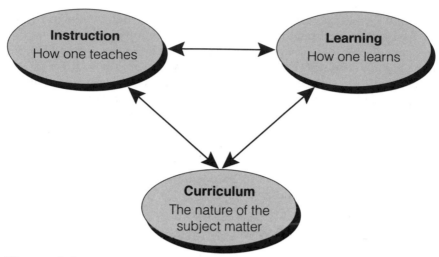

Figure 1.1   Pedagogy as process

> *In an important sense, a curriculum is a carefully selected and carefully structured storehouse of experience. The contents of the storehouse are chosen for their capacity to shape learners in particular ways.* (Author note: to make certain types of citizen.) *And the contents of the storehouse are arranged according to the sequencing that best achieves the reshaping of learners. Ultimately, however, the shaping potential of a curriculum can be realized only through teaching and learning.* (p 41)

Discourse

For the purpose of this book the notion of discourse(s) comes close to that of 'assumptions'—that is, the sets of values and beliefs which we draw on to shape our everyday practices. Such practices include the way we characterise actions, events, people and groups through language (e.g. 'effective teaching'; a 'dysfunctional family'; 'a problem student'); the images we employ (e.g. ads showing thin young women signifying particular notions of the ideal body); and other practices such as choices about the way in which classes will be organised into groups, which activities will be taught, and the means by which students will be assessed.

None of these practices is neutral or value-free—we speak, act and position ourselves in relation to others on the basis of our beliefs about how the world works and what is important. What is central for the themes taken up in this book is that discourses and the practices arising from them have consequences for all those involved. For instance, how 'effective' teaching is defined sets up particular measures of determining what this entails and thereby judges some teachers to be 'effective' or 'ineffective' on this basis. Some sets of beliefs and values (discourses) are more likely to be taken for granted as truths than others because of their association with groups which for various economic, political and cultural reasons have more power at particular times. These are often called 'dominant' or 'hegemonic' discourses. Thus we can talk about hegemonic discourses of masculinity as those which currently define what it means to be appropriately male in mainstream Australian society.

The way we think about physical education and the practices we employ in our teaching are profoundly influenced by the discourses used to describe it. The power of different groups to define what constitutes physical education has changed over time and varies depending on the context. For instance, in Western Australia 'sport education' has been influential in shaping what counts as physical education; while in New Zealand and other Australian states, concerns about health and well-being have become a major influence on what is taught. An analysis of the discourse(s) shaping physical education practice is therefore of vital significance in a consideration of becoming a physical education teacher.

A middle school focus

In Australian secondary schools and those of countries like New Zealand and the United Kingdom, the physical education curriculum for middle school students is usually very different from the curriculum for senior school students. In most cases the difference is that middle school physical education is oriented around participation in practical activities whereas senior school physical education, especially when it is an examinable subject, is more theoretical than practical.

In this book we will focus on teaching physical education at the middle school years. Thus we are focussing on physical education as a practical, activity-based curriculum which is largely conducted in the gyms, the playing fields, swimming pools and other venues where practical physical education classes are held.

Summary

- A focus of the book is the development of reflective teachers of physical education where reflection is consciously oriented by two key questions: 'What are the implications of what is taught?' and 'What are the implications for how it is taught?'.
- We believe that good physical education teaching should make the physical education experiences for young people meaningful, purposeful, enjoyable and just.
- This book assumes that most PETE students were born during or after the 1970s and hence have a particular orientation towards life in general, and towards physical activity and bodies more specifically.
- This book has a middle school focus and introduces the reader to issues of school physical education within a wider social context.

References

Armour, K. & Jones, R. (1998). *Physical Education Teachers' Lives and Careers*. London: Falmer Press.

Australian Council of Deans of Education (1998). *Preparing a Profession: Report of the National Standards and Guidelines for Initial Teacher Education Project*. Canberra.

Cruickshank, D. (1987). *Reflective Teaching: The Preparation of Student Teachers*. Reston, VA: Assocation of Teacher Educators.

Dewey, J. (1933). *How We Think: A Restatement of the Relation of Reflective Thinking to the Educative Process*. Chicago, IL: Henry Regnery Co.

Dodds, P. (1993). 'Reflective teacher education (RTF): Paradigm for professional growth or only smoke and mirrors?'. In C. Pare (ed.), *Better Teaching in Physical Education? Think About it!* (pp 65–83). Trois Riveres: Universite du Quebec a Trois Riveres.

Goodlad, J. (1984). *A Place Called School; Prospects for the Future*. New York: McGraw Hill.

Hamilton, D. (1987). *Education: An Unfinished Curriculum*. Glasgow: Department of Education, University of Glasgow.

Kirk, D. (1986). 'A critical pedagogy for teacher education: Toward an inquiry-oriented approach'. *Journal of Teaching in Physical Education*, 5(4), pp 230–246.

Kirk, D., Nauright, J., Hanrahan, S., Macdonald, D. & Jobling, I. (1996). *The Sociocultural Foundations of Human Movement Studies*. Melbourne: Macmillan Education.

Lawson, H.A. (1984). 'Problem-setting for physical education and sport'. *Quest*, 36, pp 48–60.

Lusted, D. (1986). 'Why pedagogy?'. *Screen*, 27(5), pp 2–14.

Mackay, H. (1997). *Generations: Baby Boomers, Their Parents and Their Children*. Sydney: Pan Macmillan.

Postman, N. (1989). *Conscientious Objections: Stirring up Trouble about Language, Technology and Education*. London: Heinemann.

Queensland Board of Teacher Registration (1997). *Guidelines on the acceptability of teacher education programs for teacher registration purposes*. Brisbane.

Siedentop, D. (1991). *Developing Teaching Skills in Physical Education* (3rd edn). Mountain View: Mayfield Publishing Co.

Swan, P. (1995). *Studentship and oppositional behaviour within physical education teacher education: A case study*, and *Between the rings and under the gym mat: A narrative*. Unpublished doctorate of Education, Deakin University.

Wexler, P. (1992). *Becoming Somebody: Toward a Social Psychology of School*. London: The Falmer Press.

Wyn, J. (1998). 'The post-1970 generation: Issues for researching young people in Australia today'. *Family Matters*, 49 (Autumn), pp 44–46.

Zeichner, K. (1981). 'Reflective teaching and field-based experience in teacher education'. *Interchange*, 12, pp 1–22.

chapter two

objectives

By the end of this chapter, you should be able to:
- understand something of the complex socio-cultural context in which physical education must operate;
- recognise the connection between some of the changes in society and contemporary changes in education;
- explain how physical education is influenced by changing conceptions of physical activity and the body;
- begin to construct a personal position with respect to the significance of physical education in today's schools.

The complex nature of the context for physical education

In this section we discuss some of the context in which physical education is now conducted. A basic premise which we take in this analysis is that as a cultural practice physical education is extremely complex. At one level, the surface or face value level, things appear relatively straightforward—what you see is what you get. But on closer analysis, looking 'below the surface', we find a very different scene.

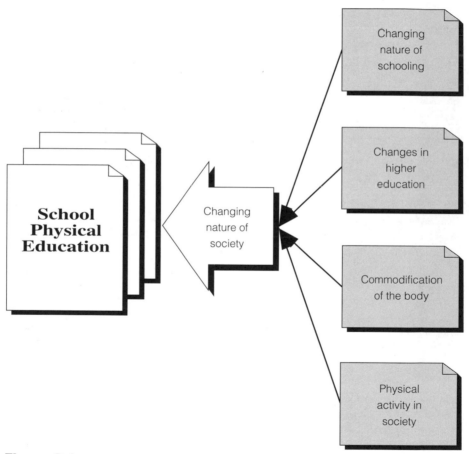

Figure 2.1   Factors influencing school physical education

In this section we try to locate physical education in the context of contemporary cultural life. As you will see later in the section on the social construction of physical education, physical education is a cultural practice which exists in connection with or in relation to other cultural practices or cultural trends. In Figure 2.1 we have represented some of the interconnections that are particularly significant for physical education. In Figure 2.2 we see that at a deeper level of analysis the picture of connectedness is considerably more complex.

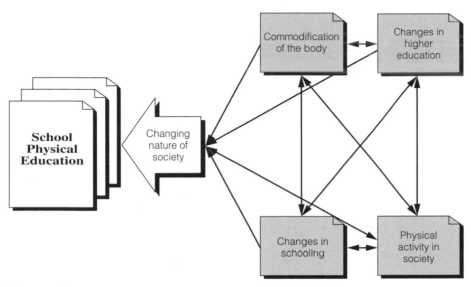

Figure 2.2 Interconnectedness of factors influencing school physical education

Before we begin that discussion, however, it is important to observe that the arrows connecting the trends or practices go both ways. In other words, these relationships are very complex indeed and descriptions of such relations will necessarily always be somewhat superficial and inadequate. Our main purpose in this section is not to produce a detailed social theory for explaining physical education but rather to help you to gain some understanding of the complexity so that you can begin to think differently about your future work.

Although to you this might be stating the obvious, we do need to be explicit about our belief that, in order to function as a teacher in the contemporary educational context, you need to understand something about the societal conditions in which schools exist and, in particular, something about the lives of young people beyond the school gate. Your success as a teacher will be related to the extent to which you can 'connect' with where the young people are 'coming from'. Possessing a few 'recipes' for teaching will not be sufficient to teach physical education successfully in the years ahead.

A slice of the real world and the importance of you

In many schools today there will be young people coming to school each day who have not eaten breakfast; who have cried themselves to sleep as their parents argued in the next room; who have slept out on the streets; who have been sexually abused; who are hungover from last night's binge drinking; who are stoned; who are depressed and so on. The multitude of experiences which young people bring to school with them each morning is mind boggling.

Some (but certainly not all) of these situations are related to or influenced by the precarious economic circumstances that many families now find themselves in. Sharon Burrow (1994) of the Australian Education Union claimed that 'we now have 1.6 million young people who are dependent on parents who are dependent on welfare in Australia. That's about a third of our school population!' (p 18). The situation is now worse.

Young people will turn up on the playground or in the gym bringing all their (good and not so good) experiences with them. Sometimes they will not be particularly receptive to what you have to offer in physical education class. Some might be plain bored and others even hostile. For some other young people it will be the highlight of their day. Our experience over the many years of involvement in physical education has taught us that physical education makes *friends and enemies* of school students. (It was Evans & Clarke (1988) in the United Kingdom who first coined this phrase.) Whether we like it or not, as teachers we must recognise that this is the current situation in schools across the country. It is an enduring issue.

What is important to understand right up front is that one of the most significant factors that will determine the experience of young people in physical education is you, the teacher. You are—by your actions, your choices, your sensitivities, your understanding, your knowledge and your attitude— responsible for what goes on in your classes. Perhaps you are unable to do much about the other circumstances of young people's lives but you can, in your classes, provide an experience of the movement culture that makes friends of young people. You can provide an experience that is meaningful, purposeful, enjoyable and just. But you have to know what to look for, what to do and, importantly, what not to do. This book will help you in this journey of understanding. It will provide you with ways of thinking about the issues and problems so that you can construct solutions that are relevant to the particular context in which you are teaching.

Changing nature of society

While recognising the interconnectedness of all the dimensions, let us briefly consider each dimension in turn. We debated whether we should start with you (as teacher) and the actual physical education lesson and gradually 'pan out' to the wider social influences—that is, begin with the small picture then widen the focus to the big picture. The other possibility was to do the reverse—that is, to progressively 'pan in' from the world view to the life in the gym. We decided to go with the latter; thus you will read of the changing nature of society, the changing context of work, the changing nature of schooling and higher education, the place of physical activity in society, the body as a commodity, and finally of the nature of physical education in schools at this period of time—the beginning of the new millennium.

'New times'

There are many social commentators who claim that we are now living in 'new times', that something is special about *these* times at the beginning of the 21st century. There are other labels used for this contemporary period; among them are: postmodernity; the information age; late-modernity; and the age of uncertainty. In defining these times it is common to read of the information explosion (i.e. how knowledge is doubling every year), globalisation (i.e. the world becoming smaller through technology), information technologies, increased reliance on expert and abstract systems (e.g. global navigation systems, electronic banking), the end of permanent structures of knowledge and meaning, and a heightened level of anxiety of people living in this risk society. According to McLeod & Yates (1998):

> The last part of the twentieth century has been an era of great change: change in the economy and in the nature and structure of jobs; change in social expectations and in family formations; and changes in education— in what schools teach and in the patterns of retention and qualifications. There has also been cultural change wrought by the influence of television and popular media, and by the wider availability of consumer goods. (p 28)

One of the terms we hear a lot of these days in relation to the changes in cultural context is globalisation. It is often cited as *the* reason behind the unprecedented changes in modern life. Globalisation is a much bandied about but misunderstood term which is not only, or even primarily, an economic phenomenon. Anthony Giddens (1994) suggests that:

> Our day-to-day activities are increasingly influenced by events happening on the other side of the world. Conversely, local lifestyle habits have become globally consequential. [A] . . . decision to buy a certain item of clothing has implications not only for the international division of labour but for the earth's ecosystem. (p 5)

Two recent examples of globalisation come to mind. In July 1998 the World Cup (for football) held in France captured the attention of the world's media. During its running, there were many thousands of Australians and New Zealanders who arrived at work each day suffering sleep deprivation caused from watching the direct television coverage which came to air at about 1 am local Australian time, 3 am New Zealand time. At another (and more serious) level, Australians and New Zealanders in the late 1990s suffered a devaluation of their currency in the wake of the so-called economic meltdown in Asia and the particular activities of a small group of wealthy Americans called 'hedgehogs' who operate in the futures market and have the power to affect currency values in countries on the other side of the world.

There is also an increasing challenge to traditional ways of doing things, organising our lives, and interacting with nature—including our own bodies. Factors which have contributed to this challenging of tradition include:

- the declining influence of traditional social agencies such as the church, the family and the school;
- the rise of other influences such as the media and popular culture;
- new scientific and technical knowledge and their applications;
- new social movements and their challenges to convention and habit; and
- the clash of values brought about by the rise of global differences and the spread of different cultures around the globe.

According to Giddens (1994) these changes and challenges have forced traditions into the open: they have been 'called to account', they have been required to justify themselves.

The loss of much of what we knew as tradition has resulted in what Giddens (1991, p 28) describes as 'a runaway world of dislocation and uncertainty'. In a world of increasing uncertainty, young people like you (i.e. those who are not 'mature age' students) choose to keep your options open. Hence Mackay's (1997) labelling of you as the 'options generation' (see Chapter 1).

In today's world we also listen to experts of differing opinions on all manner of topics and issues. We must be continually filtering information relevant to our life situations and we routinely act on the basis of choices made as a result of this filtering process. Moreover, as there are increasingly different sources of knowledge created by ever new experts with differing opinions, we now experience what some commentators have called 'radical doubt'. For some people in these 'new times' this radical doubt leads to cynicism in all forms of expertise, bureaucracy and governance in general.

At the personal level

Importantly, we all experience these 'new times' from our own particular circumstances and, reflexively, our circumstances are themselves influenced by 'new times'. But while the personal impact of these times might be challenging, threatening and anxiety-producing for some, it will be just the way life is for others. Indeed, for many of you, life in the new times is all you know. You do not have experience of a previous social context to compare today with. All you can go on is the stories of your parents, who tell you that life was different when ...

In attempting to map some of the characteristics of these new times and their impact on physical education, we always need to be able to think beyond our particular (and idiosyncratic) circumstances. We need to be able to read the trends and to try and understand something of how others (from different circumstances) are coping. Good teachers have this capacity.

Changing context of work

Let us consider for a moment the changed context of work. There is little doubt that the world of work today is significantly different from even two decades ago.

One in three jobs is now part-time or casual, as opposed to one in 20 in the 1970s. In the new work structures, the biggest winners are the employers, who can bring in labour when they need it and lose it when they don't. They don't have to worry about sick pay or holiday pay. (Nikki Barrowclough, The Age, Goodweekend, *June 6, 1998, p 19)*

Many of the jobs of the 1970s no longer exist. Secure jobs for life are a thing of the past. Unemployment levels of over 10 per cent are becoming accepted as a part of life rather than as an unacceptable factor which must be reduced. We hear of the importance of multi-skilling and working to KPIs (key performance indicators). We hear of 'downsizing', 'rightsizing' and other euphemisms for sacking workers to improve a company's (temporary) bottom line profitability. Companies no longer have the same allegiances to geographical locales, and they are prepared to move their operations (or at least parts of them) elsewhere in the world to improve profitability. More and more companies must see themselves as globally competitive. Globalisation means that decisions on GATT made in Brussells today will affect the local Australian economy tomorrow. And, as Giddens (1994) has reminded us, a decision to buy a particular brand of jeans or track shoes in Melbourne can have implications not only for the local Australian manufacturing industry but also for the lives of families in third world countries who are dependent on the small payments they receive for their work in the globalised 'sweatshop' manufacturing industry. Everything is connected.

Many of the traditions of work which the Baby Boomer generation grew up with (as normal) have been challenged and for many 50 years or older the security in what they knew as true is being undermined. Of course this is a good example of how the same circumstances are understood or experienced differently by individuals with different backgrounds. What is unsettling and troublesome for many of the Baby Boomer generation might be taken for granted as normal and untroubling for many in the options generation, or it might even be seen as an opportunity to get ahead.

Teaching has not been isolated from changes to employment conditions. Contracts (rather than permanency) are now common in government schools and the conditions for work have, in many schools, deteriorated with growing class sizes and increased performance expectations.The following comments by two teachers reflect some of these changes:

The disillusionment is compounded by the fact that it's so much harder to teach these days. You have to teach and be a social worker. The young people are more rebellious, there's more pastoral care necessary, and extra records have to be kept because everyone is worried about issues concerning the welfare of children. (Secondary teacher, New South Wales)

One thing I will say that's really changed in the 20 years that I've been teaching, is that in the first ten years, 3 or 4 lunchtimes a week teachers were involved in social activities together. Either playing table tennis or pool or cards or going for walks or playing bat tennis or basketball or whatever. But now it's very very difficult to find the time. It is really hard. And it's really easy to say look I want everyone to take two lunchtimes a week for themselves but the reality is that if you don't get your work done at school and lunchtime, you've got to do it at home. And most people prefer just to be able to leave their job and go home and relax and that's even getting really hard to do now. (Secondary teacher, Victoria)

However, these comments come from teachers who have lived through much change and are lamenting the fact that things are not what they were. Younger teachers like you whose first experiences in the profession take place under such employment conditions may well consider them as normal and they will, as a consequence, not register the same uncertainty and challenge as their more experienced colleagues.

There are also particular issues relating to work and study that might be relevant in your circumstances. Joanna Wyn (1998) argues that 'the notion of a linear progression from an education focus to an employment focus, from student to work, and from youth to adult, is likely to be at odds with reality' (p 45). We cannot assume that you have come directly from school (as would most PETE students 10 years ago), nor can we assume that your teacher education program is the only thing going on in your lives. Most likely you will have part-time employment as you do your degree and numerous other responsibilities in addition to your studies.

Changing nature of schooling

In a sense it is hard to know where to begin in discussing how the nature of schooling might have changed. On the surface of things it might be easy to walk into a school and see a great deal that is similar to what you experienced as a school student yourself. If you think of physical education classes, for example, it is true to say that they seem much the same today as they did 20 years ago. Young people are still taken to the playing field or the gym and, more often than not, organised into teams for some form of game activity. Even in the classroom many of the teaching strategies are similar at the beginning of the new century to how they were in the 1970s. However, one thing that will be evident in most classrooms is the increasing use of the computer. Like it or not, the computer is one artifact of 'new times' that is transforming schools into different places.

One advance that computer technology has produced is what is loosely termed the 'information culture'. According to some contemporary educational commentators, it is the confluence of information technology and the media (especially entertainment media) that has particular significance for education and young people. As Deakin researchers Bigum et al (1998) have commented: 'Media and information culture, broadly conceived to refer to the new articulations of broadcasting, publishing and computing and to new global circuits of entertainment and information, is now significantly instrumental in shaping what can be called postmodern identity formation, and that formation is appropriately associated with children and young people today and tommorrow—the rising generations of the postmodern age' (p 87).

There has been, it seems, a rising media-orchestrated panic over youth and schooling (Bigum et al 1998). Referring specifically to that group of young people at school between year 7 and 10, the middle schoolers, Bigum et al cite headlines like: 'The beaten generation' (*Age*, 28 May 1992); 'Disaffected youths are ganging up on society' (*Sunday Age*, 21 June 1992); 'Teen suicide rate highest in the world' (*Weekend Australian*, 18 September 1993); 'Strain on teenagers from new burdens' (*Sunday Age*, 27 October 1991); 'Young are now the long-term jobless' (*Age*, 15 July 1992). They ask:

> What are the implications of all this for education and schooling today, and for the young people who live a significant part of their lives and work and play in schools? In essence, they are twofold: one is the continuing significance of the relationship between education and (un)employment, and the other is the increasing significance of media culture in educational practice and young people's lifeworlds and indentity-work. The signs are that schooling is undergoing a legitimation crisis, increasingly and specifically from the point of view of its constituency. Many are voting not just with their feet but with their hearts and minds as well, even many of those who stay in school and at school. The traditional promise of schooling is increasingly perceived as hollow, or at least compromised.
> (Bigum et al 1998, p 90)

If schooling is undergoing a legitimation crisis from the point of view of its students, then we should recognise that this has happened within a particular structural context that requires explanation.

Much has happened in government schools in the last decade. Simon Marginson (1994) reported that some of the trends that were evident include:

- *Cuts to spending and teaching positions.* In both New Zealand and certain Australian states (especially Victoria) government spending on public education has been significantly reduced while government assistance to private schools has been increased. The number of teaching positions has been reduced, thus creating higher teacher–pupil class ratios and the elimination of certain specialist teachers.
- *School closures.* Many of the small government schools have been closed and their sites sold at public auction. The benefit of school closures is a very sensitive subject in areas where schools are lost. Basically governments believe that larger schools are more economically sustainable and that pupils benefit from wider curriculum offerings.
- *Standardised testing.* Standardised testing is increasingly being used as a way of measuring the 'output' of schools so that schools can be ranked against each other for marketing purposes.

• *Schools of the future*. This conception is most obvious in New Zealand ('Tomorrow's Schools') and in Victoria, but the principles underpinning them are to be found throughout Australia.

According to Marginson there are three significant changes evident in the 'schools of the future' concept:

(a) the relationship between school and its community has changed whereby the parents are now considered as consumers of the individual school rather than citizen members of a common system of schools in which everyone has an interest in everyone's welfare.

(b) the relationship between the school and the government has changed whereby schools have responsibility for some funding and staffing at the local level but control over educational policy is firmly centred under government control.

(c) the relationship between the school and other schools has changed. State schools are now seen to be in direct competition with each other for pupils and hence for funds. The success of one school is at the expense of another.

Whether you recognise it or not, these changes will have a profound impact on all teachers, including physical education teachers. Some of the implications of these changes will be discussed in Chapter 4, but for the moment let us just elaborate on the issue of the impact of the trend for schools to go commercial.

Kenway et al (1994) in reporting on their research into marketing education in the information age claimed that: 'Of course the broad purpose behind the commercialisation of schooling is the production of generations of young people who are active consumers. This fits in rather conveniently with the marketing of schooling which principals are now getting involved in. Consuming products, consuming education—it all becomes part of the package' (p 33). They go on to say that: 'We found that the students are intense consumers, prepared to and/or wanting to spend large amounts of money on brand names and fashionable or popular items. However, they are not critical of the consumer process, there is an unquestioning acceptance of all activities and promotions' (p 28). There are specific implications for physical education in such marketing promotions as Heinz' *Sportz for All Sortz*; Pizza Hut's *Sport It!*; and Peters' *Billabong Fun Run*.

Another change that is connected with the marketing of education is displaying of logos. Sharon Burrow (1994), former president of the Australian Education Union, claimed that: 'Ten years ago school teachers had to cut logos off any materials brought into the classroom. Even one of those National Mutual calendars was not acceptable without the logos cut off . . . Now, ten years on, the battle for the corporate dollar makes school logo heaven. There is not a lot left that is not stamped or labelled in some way' (p 13).

Burrows also provides the following account of how the line between what is morally acceptable for schools (and state education departments) and what must be done in order to survive financially is becoming blurred. According to Burrows, the following advertisement was placed in the DSE *News*, the official Victorian Department of School Education paper circulated to all schools. Extracts from the ad are as follows:

> *Your school could win $20,000 cash by finding the next Australian super model . . .*
>
> *How many computers? How much sports equipment? How many could you buy for $20,000?' . . . All you have to do is select any number of students, over the age of 14, that the school feels have potential to become a model . . . Obtain an entry coupon from* New Idea *and include two photographs, one head shot and one full body, then send your entry to . . .*

So here is a link between the nature of schools and the commodification of the body (see the section 'The body as a commodity' below). What sort of message about the (perfect) body and about the objectification of women is this advertisement sending to young people? What should physical education teachers say about it? Why does the Department of Education endorse such marketing? Where should the line be drawn with respect to what is an acceptable promotion for commercial interests?

It is our view that physical education as a profession, and each of us as physical education teachers, has a responsibility to educate young people to become *critical consumers* of the messages portrayed by the representations of physical culture in the media. Unfortunately, as Kenway et al (1994) found out, generally young people were not critical of the consumer process or of promotions. Clearly there is still much to be done.

While it is possible that many PE teachers consider that computers will not really have a significant impact on the teaching of physical education as a practical subject, most would probably agree that the issue of litigation does have serious consequences for their subject. An article in *The Age* (16 May 1998) titled 'Teachers beware: Report' claimed that schools are becoming legal minefields through court action by parents. According to Dr Nolan (co-author of the book *Schools and Litigation*): 'Because of the growing awareness by the community of its legal rights and what teachers may or may not do, schools and teachers are more liable to litigation today than was the case several years ago when the authority of the teacher over a pupil was assumed to be wholly and automatically correct' (p 12). Among the key areas of concern for schools were:

- *accidents*
- alcohol and drug abuse
- excursions
- *sporting activities*
- sending children on errands
- parental custody and access to parents
- *physical contact with a child—other than to apply first aid*

• using teachers' cars to transport students
• early release of pupils from class/school

Three of these areas (in italics) are of particular concern to the physical education teacher and will be further discussed in Chapter 19.

Changes in higher education

The university system, in fact the entire higher education system, has been undergoing immense change over the past decade. Among the factors that have affected these, Evans & Green (1995) cite:

• the development of university education as a layer of mass education;
• the push for more 'client-centred' and more 'flexible' forms of delivery;
• the increase in the use of communications and computer-based technologies;
• the requirement for universities to derive more of their funds from non-government sources; and
• the shift from collegial to corporate management approaches.

On the surface of things most of these factors might seem to be of little obvious relevance to you as student teachers. However, when we look further we find that the push for more flexible delivery methods and the increased use of computer-based technologies might mean that the traditional forms of pedagogy used in PETE programs are being challenged. As management pushes for less labour-intensive teaching (for cost reduction) some of the small group teaching and practical activities might be replaced by mass lectures and Internet communications. The implications of these trends for PETE courses are yet to be experienced.

The science of human movement

In many universities there is a distinction made between the study of physical education as education and physical education as a discipline. In most places the discipline of physical education is now called 'human movement studies'. In American universities it is called 'kinesiology'. Whatever it is called at your university, it will probably have little explicit connection with teaching physical education in schools. In fact it might even be the case that specific reference to school teaching is avoided in an attempt to cater for students whose careers will be in the field of human movement/sports science rather than teaching. In some universities human movement is taught in faculties of applied science and physical education in faculties of education.

One of the features of contemporary physical education training in universities throughout the developed Western countries is the central importance placed on the science of human movement. It is the courses in biomechanics, exercise physiology, motor control, kinesiology and sports medicine that have the greatest status in the eyes of most human movement/

physical education students and also of most university staff (Macdonald 1993; Swan 1995).

There is no doubt that the development of degrees (and postgraduate programs) in human movement/physical education has improved the status of physical education in the university. Perhaps the introduction of senior school physical education as an examinable subject has also increased the status of physical education in schools.

 author reflection

I remember years ago when I was an undergraduate student at the University of Western Australia striking up a conversation with an architecture student on the bus one day. When he asked what I was studying and I told him physical education (they still called it physical education in those days, though now the same course is called human movement) he was duly impressed. 'Gee that's a tough course, isn't it . . . you have to do anatomy in the med school, don't you?' For some silly reason I was proud at that moment because it seemed that my field had achieved some measure of respectability through its appropriation of a scientific study of the body. The extent to which all that specialised knowledge of the body was going to contribute to me being a better physical education teacher was, at that time, not even an issue.

Much of this scientific way of thinking about the body as if it were a thing can be useful for certain physical education practices; for example in determining a training program for a competitive athlete. But it does have its limitations, and much of what is required to be a good physical education teacher cannot be learned through science. Scientific knowledge of the body is simply not sufficient. Consider the following story.

 for your information

Meme

There is a wonderful book that all human movement and physical education graduates should read. It's called *Put Your Whole Self In* written by Meme McDonald (1992). The book tells the story of Meme's encounter, and subsequent involvement, with a self-help hydrotherapy and massage group in the Melbourne suburb of Northcote. The group of women (aged from 60 to 90) participated in various exercises in the water under the direction of a woman named Marj.

Marj was 79 and had no degree in human movement or physical education. She did have years of experience in swimming. The story gives a moving account of how, for these women, the hydrotherapy had transformed their lives. Their arthritic and aching bodies found relief in the support of the water. They also found support in the caring and love of one another.

The women in the Northcote self-help group didn't benefit from any of our new-found knowledge about human movement. They never had their body fat estimated, their oxygen uptake measured, their mobility tested. They didn't need cardio-funk music to work by. They didn't need any systematic recording of their progress displayed on a chart or a computer screen. But they *knew* how they had improved and they *knew* the value of the exercise classes to their total well-being. They didn't need the help of a 'modern' human movement professional. Indeed, it's doubtful whether they would have been any better off if they had been instructed by such a professional!

One way or another, the subject matter of your degree in human movement and/or teaching will be beyond your control. The trend to emphasise the sciences of human movement at the expense of the more practical teaching subjects has been slow but definite over the past 20 or so years. Many graduates of our contemporary human movement/physical education courses know a great deal about the body and the sciences of human movement but arguably less about the actual activities they will be required to teach in our secondary schools. In fact, there is growing concern among some employment-oriented bodies, such as the Standards Council of Victoria, that our current graduates, although very well prepared to teach senior physical education, are inadequately prepared to teach middle school physical education (see the Report of the ACHPER and Victorian DOE Working Party on Physical Education Teacher Training, July 1997).

It may be that the concerns of professional organisations like ACHPER and the Standards Council of Victoria will, over time, be recognised by the universities and changes made to the courses for the training of physical education teachers. In the meantime you will probably have to supplement your current course with some coaches' courses and other externally provided registrations that might benefit your job prospects on graduation.

The body as a commodity

The scene is an exercise gym cluttered with shiny weights, bikes, barbells and benches. A hazy shaft of sunlight bathes the equipment. A slender black woman walks into the gym past a few well-muscled young men and women; various bodies remove unwanted vests and tracksuit bottoms. Naked torsos ripple and glisten with rivulets of sweat. Shapely thighs and buttocks pump weights and bicycle pedals. Faces contort with exertion, exhilaration. The woman slumps elegantly against a wire screen, energy almost spent, her body gathering for a final effort. Images of male and female thighs, chests, faces, biceps, hips begin to merge as the music approaches a climax. Faces contort with exertion, pain and ecstasy. The workout is over and the woman slouches off to the shower, gracefully trailing her towel. This is an advertisement for Reebok.

The images presented in this ad, along with many other TV ads and video song clips on shows like MTV, are part of the visual world of adolescent youth. It is a stimulating world in which the body (a slim, muscular body) is a dominant icon of desirability. It is a world in which physical activity is unproblematically associated with desirable bodies and a lifestyle of consumption, fun and entertainment. They are part of a postmodern world which is argued by some to characterise Western countries in the 1990s.

The young people who watch the ad also do physical education. They change into their physical education kit, and present themselves to their physical education teacher for lessons in which their bodies are very much on display. Do they expect to engage in physical activity like the images of the Reebok ad? Do they feel that their own body does not measure up to those which make up the TV images? How do young people experience their bodies in the context of school physical education? And how might it be connected to broader cultural forces?

 author reflection

'Abs' as a commodity

Recently I was having a workout in the uni gym (they call it the cardio room now) and in came a rather thin (actually more like skinny) young male, probably a freshman. All the time while I rowed, pumped and peddled, he did sit-ups of various styles until his face was grimacing with pain. His abdominal muscles were screaming out to stop. But still he pressed on until more was impossible. He then left the gym having completed his 'workout'. In thinking about what I had witnessed I wondered why it is that so many photos of guys (meaning males) in ads show them with their shirts open? Is it to show their 'six pack' abs? Why are abs 'in' with regard to men's physique in the options generation? Why have abs become a commodity? And what are young men prepared to endure to possess them?

To answer some of these questions it is necessary to move the frame of analysis back a bit—to 'zoom out' if you like and look at the bigger picture. The following article gives something of a background sketch.

Lime green bicycle shorts

A number of years ago Jane Clifton was lamenting the closure of the old municipal swimming pools throughout Melbourne (Saturday Age, 17 April 1993). They are being closed, she argued, because they did not fit the exercise image of the 1990s. They did not have the necessary gyms, saunas, spas, aerobics room. They needed updating. And, so she claims, the local pool 'must become a centre for training, hard work . . . a miniature sports institute in every suburb'. Moreover, the 'amicable, rotund, sun-scarred pool managers of old are secretly being replaced by goose-stepping, cardio-funk androids in lime green bicycle shorts'.

As we look back at the decades of the 1980s and 1990s, the trend to which Jane Clifton was referring was developing apace. Perhaps you know of similar transformations in the gyms and pools in your locality. One of the reasons for the change in personnel (which Clifton laments) is that there are now hundreds of graduates of human movement degree courses around Australia who seek employment in the gyms and pools of the nation. Equipped with their new scientific knowledge of the body and exercise, many of them seek to take to their employment the ideas and concepts that have revolutionised the fitness and leisure industry. Of course Clifton's opinion is just that—her opinion, and there are many new physical activity, lifestyle, gyms/pools and the like that run excellent programs which cater for a wide range of individual preferences with regard to physical activity, but the fact remains that things have changed.

There is little doubt that the demand for a gym workout of one kind or another, rather than for a relaxing swim, has also been encouraged by media representations of bodies and physical activity. Let us reflect for a moment about the cleverness of some of the ads that represent the body and physical activity which are so ubiquitous in the media.

let's reflect

There was an advertisement in *Cleo* magazine a while back which pictures a young (always young) woman in a Reebok leotard. She looks to be participating in a 'Step Reebok' workout. The caption at the top of the ad asks 'What is life like on Planet Reebok?'. Down the right-hand side of the ad are some descriptors which are the 'answers' to the question: 'No limits, no biological clocks, no rules, no stretch marks, no PMT, no parking tickets, no princesses, no cellulite, no old boy networks, no silicon, no rice cakes, no pain, no means no, no fear, no quitting, no slogans'.

How clever is this ad? In their description of life on 'Planet Reebok' they have appropriated slogans which provide an image of the 'modern woman'. She is busy, she works out, she is attractive (read desirable), she is assertive (even embraces certain [selective] feminist slogans!). But she is also a representation of contradictions. She wants no biological clocks, no stretch marks, no cellulite, and no silicon, and also she wants no fear, NO to mean NO, and no old boy networks. She seems to recognise the limitations of certain patriarchal social practices yet is unaware that they are connected to the issues of youth, cellulite, silicon etc. She is a member of the 'options generation'.

Source: Cleo #259, May 1994. Reprinted with permission from Reebok.

Perhaps these tales seem less than relevant to you as a prospective physical education teacher. They are, however, intimately connected with the substance of your future work. One way or another, physical education is about bodies and physical activity. It is hard to get around that. Much of the knowledge that you will acquire in your training will be about the body in physical activity and about physical activity itself. What these tales reveal is that we in physical education are not alone in our attention to bodies and physical activity. As you well know, and the Reebok ads attest, bodies and physical activity are 'in' as subjects for media advertisements. Ads like the Reebok ad target young people like you. You are the option generation market to whom many of the ads are directed.

The important point here is that young people will be coming to school with images and understandings about the body and physical activity that have been strongly influenced by similar media ads. Have you ever noticed how happy, beautiful and full of life all the young people in the Coke ads are? Is life really like that? Can life really live up to the ads? And what if it does not? And what might all this actually mean for school physical education?

Physical activity in society

In many different forms and ways physical activity is a very significant part of our contemporary culture. In the pools, beaches, gyms, fields, halls, courts, tracks and trails of our cities and country towns, people are out swimming, surfing, working out, playing ball games, doing Yoga and Tai Chi, dancing, playing tennis and squash, riding bikes, roller-blading, jogging and countless other physical recreation activities. The list of activities that engage people on a regular or even an irregular basis is huge. Participation in many forms of recreational physical activity often requires the employment of countless people in a service industry to clean the pools, manage the gyms, umpire the matches, rent the hall, teach the classes and so on. All up, there is a lot going on and one way or another school physical education claims to prepare citizens for their participation in the forms of physical activity that constitute recreation.

Ken Alexander has said that the purpose of physical education is to 'increase a person's approach tendencies [desire] and abilities to participate in a successful, rewarding and socially responsible way, in the movement culture' (Alexander 1996, p 9). The movement culture includes all forms of physical activity that constitute our society's recreative pursuits.

One form of the movement culture that dominates is sport. We will not try to define sport here (for there are many ways of doing this) but instead focus our attention on how the cultural practice of sport (in all its forms) is so significant in modern life.

Sport as metaphor

Stanley Aronowitz, an American social commentator, has claimed that sport has become so significant in contemporary America that it is actually the metaphor for American life. On a similar line, the American academic/public intellectual Noam Chomsky laments the fact that the American citizen devotes considerable energy to engaging in sport as entertainment (a trivial pursuit) and little on engaging in issues that matter in terms of the state of local, national or world affairs. Probably the same is true for the citizens of Australia and New Zealand.

But as physical education teachers we do alright by this. It is, after all, physical activity (and sport represents the dominant form of physical activity in our culture) which is the subject matter of our field. It is *our* expertise about physical activity which we trade to the community for our wages (like the new graduates in the fitness industry). It is also through our prolonged involvement with and in physical activity that a significant dimension of our self-identity has been formed. So, any way we look at it, we have a big investment in physical activity and by and large we (as a profession) are pleased that it is such a dominant feature of our culture.

Is our subject matter trivial?

Chomsky clearly considers sport to be trivial compared with the 'things that really matter' in the world and I tend to agree with him. Big business it might be but the essence of the activity itself is trivial. It is, after all, a development of play. Sports can be considered a relatively trivial issue compared with such serious matters as: the tensions in the Middle East; the peace process in Northern Ireland; floods in Bangladesh; earthquakes in Turkey; American involvement in Latin America; the collapse of the Russian economy; the plight of the poor and homeless; racial bigotry; domestic violence; drug abuse; or the spread of AIDS. Moreover, there is little doubt that sport is a very useful vehicle for deflecting national attention away from issues of the state and political processes. However, sport, and school physical education, are sites of cultural practice which have the capacity to both reproduce and challenge the dominant ideologies which underpin the 'big issues' of violence, poverty and oppression. We believe that it should be a site for the challenging of such ideologies.

We do not wish to be misunderstood here. We are not saying that the purpose of sport or physical education is to correct the massive social and economic problems of the world. Obviously that is ridiculous. Rather, what we are saying is that as teachers and teacher educators we have a *responsibility* to recognise the way in which our profession is often implicated in broader social issues and that with such recognition comes a moral responsibility to attempt to change our practice.

There is no doubt that, for a considerable proportion of our society, physical activity is the *dominant* form of entertainment. Engagement in physical activity as entertainment can take the form of being a spectator of the participation of others (both live and on TV), or a participant in the activity itself. Certainly the physical education profession advocates the latter, and there is no doubt that catering for participation in various forms of physical activity is a major social commitment when we consider the costs of providing sporting venues, umpires, equipment, coaches etc. But the really big community dollars are spent on spectator sport. One way or another it is physical activity (certain competitive forms of sport in particular) *as entertainment* that is the most powerful dimension.

Physical education has an important role to play in helping to create citizens who value physical activity in their own lives but who are also critical consumers of the products of the physical activity industry, including media advertisements.

Physical education in today's schools

The significance of physical education

Whether you realise it or not, school physical education is a huge enterprise in Australia and New Zealand. When the salaries of teachers and university lecturers are considered, in addition to the costs of facilities and equipment, the physical education enterprise costs the state and federal governments millions of dollars annually. According to Ken Alexander, a physical educator at Edith Cowan University: 'If we assume each of Australia's approximately 12,000 schools employs the equivalent of one full-time PE teacher at a salary of $40,000, the annual cost to the nation of providing physical education is in the order of $624 million (including the 30% "on-costs" such as super-annuation, sick leave entitlements and workers' compensation)' (Personal communication, January 1999).

Similar costs are to be found in resourcing physical education in non-government schools. One way or another, our society (like most others in the Western developed countries) considers physical education to be an important school subject. But as you will soon learn, if you are not already aware, it is a qualified sense of importance.

We contend that there are complex reasons why physical education is seen to be so important. One way to think about this is to recognise that schools have an important role in helping to produce certain types of future citizen. But what sort of citizen? In whose image? Who gets to decide? These are big issues relating to the purposes of schooling in liberal democracies like those in Australia and New Zealand. The answer to these questions might well be very different in countries with totalitarian governments.

A very brief review of the historical lineage of school physical education in Australia gives a sense of the type of citizen that physical education had been marshalled to develop over the years of the 20th century. At the beginning of the 20th century there was emphasis on drilling, discipline and formal exercises designed 'with the express purpose of rendering these bodies docile and so amenable to disciplined channeling of energies and capabilities into the processes of economic production and defense of the country' (Kirk 1993, p 39). The fitness of our young men for war was a national issue in the 1930s and physical education was clearly implicated in making citizens who were more able (and willing) to fight to defend their country.

After World War II new forms of physical education developed in schools. Notions of the well-being of the individual, enthusiasm, and enjoyment rather than discipline, obedience and military bearing came to be the focus of the new school physical education. Games playing and sports rather than regimented exercise regimens became popular. The notion that sports and games were training for a competitive life beyond school and for the development of leadership and moral characteristics (such as sportsmanship) were clearly incorporated in school physical education by the late 1940s: 'The aims ... of physical education are that each individual shall be enabled to develop to his maximum potential and that each one shall acquire a sufficient degree of proficiency in at least one form of physical activity to maintain an interest in healthy activities throughout his adult life' (H.P. Kelly, Medical Inspector of Schools, *Physical Education for Victorian Schools*, Education Department of Victoria, Melbourne, 1946, cited in Kirk 1993).

So we can see that the contribution that physical education makes to the development of certain types of citizen has changed over time.

According to Alexander (1996), the purpose of physical education is to 'increase a person's approach tendencies [desire] and abilities to participate in a successful, rewarding and socially responsible way, in the movement culture' (p 9). The 'movement culture' includes all forms of physical activity that constitute our society's recreative pursuits. What does this definition tell us about the sort of citizen physical education is contributing to make? The citizen will be a participant in the movement culture, they will possess the necessary skills to do so, and they will do so in ways which are socially responsible (e.g. their participation will not hurt, injure or put down others). There is, however, no mention of physical education's role in making healthy citizens. Should this be included? What else?

Current curriculum documents advocate the development of a self-motivated (and self-disciplined), physically competent 'good sport' who values their own health and the place of participation in physical activity within it. A physically active, health-conscious self and socially responsible citizen. The former New Zealand Secretary for Education, Howard Faney, describes the purposes of the Health and Physical Education curriculum thus: 'Through learning in this curriculum, students [read future citizens] will gain knowledge, skills, attitudes, and values to enjoy a healthy lifestyle and contribute actively to the well-being of other people and the well-being of their communities. Students will take increasing responsibility for their own health and will learn movement skills in a wide range of contexts. They will develop the skills that will enable them to enhance their relationships with other people, and they will participate in creating health communities by taking responsible and critical action' (1999).

While some of these characteristics, values and attitudes can be developed through experiences in other curriculum areas, physical education claims to have a unique contribution to make; therefore it deserves a special place in the school curriculum.

According to medical sources, the health costs of lack of physical activity (hypokinetic) in the general population are enormous. Moreover, the personal and familial impact of hypokinetic disease was one of the major social problems of Western countries in the late 20th century. So if physical education helps create future citizens who know and value the significance of physical activity for their own (and their families') health and well-being then perhaps it is not so trivial after all.

We will be discussing the purposes of physical education in a later chapter so all that we want to register now is that throughout this book we will be raising issues (enduring and contemporary) that physical education teachers (like you) must deal with (or at least have an informed position on).

One size doesn't fit all

One of the things that you must understand early in your development as teachers is that school in general and PE in particular is just one small part of the lives of young people. There are other things going on in young people's lives and physical education experiences are always connected with the other 'stuff' going on beyond the school gate. Here's how physical education and sport fit into the lives of three different young people.

Sara

Sara is a 13-year-old girl in her first year year at Seaview High School. It is a relatively well-resourced school in a middle class suburb. Although she lives only four blocks from the school she is usually driven to school by her mother. Twice a week she does PE with Ms Illuka, one of the four school specialist physical education teachers. On Wednesday afternoon she has sport. The focus of the PE lessons is mostly on games playing except that at the beginning of each term a number of lessons are devoted to fitness testing. Sara is 'getting the message' both at school and at home that her looks and her fitness are supposed to be connected.

Sara and her friends are conscious of how they look. They like to wear designer label clothes. At home she sees her mother always conscious of how she looks and concerned with her own weight. Her mother always seems to be on some sort of diet and regularly attends aerobics classes to help her look and feel good. The magazines which her mother buys portray images of slender women and fine foods. The TV images are similar: all the desirable women are slim and 'attractive', and the ads bombard the living room with images of desirable women and the consumption of fast food.

Sara's father is into triathlons. He is a keen competitor and spends a considerable amount of time and money on the pursuit of his sport. He is a naturally lean guy who has always been able to eat what he likes and never put on weight. Now that he is training hard he is constantly hungry and eating. He is usually training when the food is being prepared but is very health conscious and concerned with eating the right food. Interestingly, Sara sometimes thinks that for such a health guy he is often injured because one or other of his body parts seems to break down under the stress of constant training. Sara thinks that she will be like her mother when she matures: she will always be worried about staying slim to look good.

What with his training and the long hours he puts into his own plumbing business, Sara doesn't see much of her father. Her mother's part-time job at a department store means that she is usually around when she needs her (for a ride to a friend's place). Sara's mum and dad are always happy to go to school functions and keen to attend parent/teacher nights to get an update on her scholastic progress.

Frank

Frank attends a secondary school in a different part of town from Sara. He is in his second year at Stonemeadows Secondary College situated in the western suburbs of a large capital city. Resources in the school used to be quite good under the special DSP fundings but now, with the withdrawal of the special funding, they have lost some specialist teachers and the school is in desperate need of maintenance and some new classrooms. Stonemeadows is a working class school. There is a high ethnic population (the school has young people from 16 different language backgrounds) and unemployment is around 20 per cent in the neighbourhood.

Like Sara, Frank has two timetabled PE classes each week and a sports afternoon. Frank loves sport but he does seem to get into trouble a lot in the PE classes. He reckons that Mr Mitchell picks on him. Most of his mates in class also love sport and especially sports afternoons when they can get out of class work. Mr Mitchell is always talking about the importance of fitness and, also like Sara, Frank and his mates do fitness tests at the beginning of each term. Such tests are a great opportunity for them to competitively assert their developing masculinity.

Economically, things are tough in Frank's house since his father got retrenched from the factory. Frank sees his mother and father take no exercise. His dad used to play footy but gave that up when, at 32, he 'got too old'. He thinks his mum played netball once but she doesn't talk about it like dad does his footy. Both parents smoke, consume alcohol, often to excess, and are generally unconcerned about their health unless they get sick. Frank watches a lot of TV and reckons that slim females are the most attractive and that Hungry Jack's is better than McDonald's. The pursuit of a healthy lifestyle is not part of Frank's family agenda.

To date Frank's parents haven't set foot in his school. They missed the first parent/teacher night for a reason Frank can't remember but they did say they will be at the next one.

Merisa

By the time Merisa got to Church Girl's Grammar in year 7 she already had considerable physical skills. She could play a reasonable game of tennis, she could snow ski, and she was also quite a competent ballet dancer. But all of these skills she had learned out of school. Not that her school didn't have magnificant sporting facilities and an extensive PE and sport curriculum. In fact, both tennis and skiing were on the curriculum but not until year 9, and Merisa's parents both considered that she would be advantaged if she learned both sports at an earlier age. This decision was entirely consistent with how they thought about education for their two children. It was about maximising opportunities and getting ahead. It was about learning to compete, to extend oneself and learn the discipline needed to achieve.

The school program and facilities looked more like a Club Med experience than a school curriculum. The playing fields were impressive, as were the gymnasium and the indoor swimming pool. Although Merisa was only in year 8 she had already been introduced to rowing, golf, sailing, as well as gymnastics and of course hockey and netball. In this case the school obviously valued sport in similar ways to Merisa's parents.

Most of the new activities were introduced in PE class and they were then 'taken up' as after-school sports. All girls were expected to participate in sport—no ifs, no buts. The thing about the after-school sports that Merisa didn't particularly like was the emphasis on competition and winning. There were always house competitions of some sort and the regular Saturday morning obligation to play in a school team. Although she didn't mind playing hockey through the winter she definitely didn't like having to get up so early on Saturday mornings. She knows that her dad wasn't very impressed with the 8 am Saturday start either but he always acted as the taxi on Saturdays when he was available.

What implications might there be for teaching physical education in these different contexts? One thing is certain: expecting that PE would mean the same for Frank, Sara and Merisa would be a great mistake. Clearly one size does not fit all. The schools that Sara, Frank and Merisa attend represent very different educational contexts. (These schools are discussed in more detail in Chapter 18.) To expect that you could teach the same, and have it mean the same, to these three young people in their different social worlds would be naive. We need to learn how to adapt our teaching to the specific circumstances of the school in which we teach.

Summary

- School physical education should not be seen as an isolated curriculum practice. Rather it is intimately interconnected to the changing nature of society.
- The beginning of the 21st century, while having many continuities with the past, also represents 'new times' in which many traditional social practices are increasingly challenged by advances in technology and changes in attitudes.
- There are changes to the nature of higher education (how we do things in universities and colleges); to the nature of work more generally; to the nature of schooling; and to the ways in which physical activity and the body are understood by people of all ages.
- Physical education has a significant place in contemporary schooling but its impact on young people's lives varies considerably.

References

ACHPER. (1997). *Report of the ACHPER and DOE Working Party on Physical Education Teacher Training*. Melbourne.

Alexander, K (1999). Personal communication, January.

Alexander, K. (1996). *From the great society to the great community: Enlarging the shadow of the future in physical education*. Singapore: AARE/ERA Conference.

Bigum, C., Fitzclarence, L. & Green, B. (1998). 'Teaching the lost generation?. Media culture, (un)employment and middle schooling'. In L. Fitzclarence & J. Kenway (eds), *Changing Education: New Times, New Kids* (pp 87–94). Geelong: Deakin University.

Burrow, S. (1994). 'McDonald's in the classroom'. In J. Kenway (ed.), *Schooling What Future? Balancing the Education Agenda* (pp 13–21). Geelong: Deakin Centre for Education and Change.

Evans, J. & Clarke, G. (1988). 'Changing the face of physical education'. In J. Evans (ed.), *Teachers, Teaching and Control in Physical Education*. London: Falmer Press.

Evans, T. & Green, B. (1995). *Dancing at a distance? Postgraduate studies, 'supervision', and distance education*. Australian Association for Research in Education, Hobart: Annual Conference.

Giddens, A. (1991). *Modernity and Self-Identity. Self and Society in the Late Modern Age*. Cambridge: Polity Press.

Giddens, A. (1994). *Beyond Left and Right: The Future of Radical Politics*, Cambridge, UK: Polity Press.

Griffin, P. (1981). 'One small step for personkind: Observations and suggestions for sex equity in coeducational physical education classes'. *Journal of Teaching in Physical Education* (Introductory Issue), pp 12–18.

Kenway, J., Collier, J. & Tragenza, K. (1994). 'Schools as commercial free zones?'. In J. Kenway (ed.), *Schooling What Future? Balancing the Education Agenda*. Geelong: Deakin Centre for Education and Change.

Kirk, D. (1993). *The Body, Schooling and Culture*. Geelong: Deakin University.

McDonald, M. (1992). *Put Your Whole Self In*. Melbourne: Penguin.

Macdonald, D. (1993). 'Knowledge, gender and power in physical education teacher education'. *Australian Journal of Education*, 37(3), pp 259–278.

Mackay, H. (1997). *Generations: Baby Boomers, Their Parents and Their Children*. Sydney: Pan Macmillian.

McLeod, J. & Yates, L. (1998). 'How young people think about self, work and futures'. *Family Matters*, 49 (Autumn), pp 28–33.

Marginson, S. (1994). 'Emerging patterns of education in Victoria'. In J. Kenway (ed.), *Schooling What Future? Balancing the Education Agenda*. Geelong: Deakin Centre for Education and Change.

Postman, N. (1989). *Conscientious Objections: Stirring up Trouble about Language, Technology and Education*. London: Heinemann.

Swan, P. (1995). *Studentship and Oppositional Behaviour within Physical Education Teacher Education: A Case Study*, and *Between the Rings and Under the Gym Mat: A Narrative*. Unpublished thesis, Deakin University.

Wyn, J. (1998). 'The post-1970 generation: Issues for researching young people in Australia today'. *Family Matters*, 49 (Autumn), pp 44–46.

section two

chapter
three

objectives

By the end of this chapter you should be able to:
- appreciate that who becomes a teacher and what work they do is shaped by social, cultural and economic forces;
- differentiate perspectives on the purpose of teaching;
- understand that *socialisation* and *identity* are useful theoretical tools in studying teachers and teaching.

In this section of the book we are concerned with who chooses to become teachers, and how teachers develop their expertise through both their tertiary education and their professional careers. We also address the nature of teachers' work, the impact of change on this work, and the issues surrounding careers in teaching. Much of this discussion will be approached through the frameworks of teacher socialisation and the development and maintenance of a teacher identity.

Who is a teacher?

Popular films present powerful narratives for how we see teachers and teaching. *Lean on Me, Stand and Deliver, Mr Holland's Opus* and *Dead Poets' Society* present the teacher, and usually a male teacher, as a hero figure trying to challenge poverty, inequity, ignorance, racism, oppression and violence to make the schooling system more just, safe and rewarding. In *Stand and Deliver* the mathematics teacher decides that if his pupils attending a poor, urban high school are to have equal opportunities to access university they need to learn calculus in a summer school. In doing so he faces opposition in the form of low pupil confidence and expectations, a resistant school administration and an unbelieving educational bureaucracy when the pupils eventually achieve highly on the calculus exams. In contrast, *Dead Poets' Society* is set in a wealthy private school, yet the battle of the English teacher to create social change and broaden the pupils' consciousness is equally fraught with opposition. Occasionally a health and physical education teacher appears and their portrayal is less than flattering. Think of the Aussie Rules advocate in *The Heartbreak Kid* who tries to coerce and mock students into conforming to his own ideas of 'real' sport and masculinity. Here the teacher's agenda is to reinforce the dominant, conservative, 'white' Australian sporting traditions regardless of his pupils' interests and backgrounds. What do these representations suggest about teachers and teaching? Are they accurate depictions? More importantly, how do they compare with the images and goals you may have for your own practice?

In the document *Recommendation Concerning the Status of Teachers* (UNESCO 1966), the United Nations Educational, Scientific and Cultural Organization defined teachers as 'those persons in schools who are responsible for the education of pupils' (p 3). While this definition provides us with a useful parameter, we acknowledge there are many contexts outside schools in which we may teach, such as teaching a friend how to windsurf, a parent how to program a VCR, or a niece how to skip stones. However, here we are concerned with graduates of teacher education programs who are employed in schools.

The boxed material opposite indicates the guiding principles for the status of teachers worldwide which, while composed over 30 years ago, might be considered as relevant to teachers' rights and responsibilities today.

Recommendation Concerning the Status of Teachers (1966, p 3)

Guiding principles

3 Education from the earliest school years should be directed to the all-round development of the human personality and to the spiritual, moral, social, cultural and economic progress of the community, as well as to the inculcation of deep respect for human rights and fundamental freedoms; with the framework of these values the utmost importance should be attached to the contribution to be made by education to peace and to understanding, tolerance and friendship among all nations and among racial or religious groups.

4 It should be recognized that advance in education depends largely on the qualifications and ability of the teaching staff in general and on the human, pedagogical and technical qualities of the individual teachers.

5 The status of teachers should be commensurate with the needs of education as assessed in the light of educational aims and objectives; it should be recognized that the proper status of teachers and due public regard for the profession of teaching are of major importance for the full realization of these aims and objectives.

6 Teaching should be regarded as a profession: it is a form of public service which requires of teachers expert knowledge and specialized skills, acquired and maintained through rigorous and continuing study; it calls also for a sense of personal and corporate responsibility for the education and welfare of the pupils in their charge.

7 All aspects of the preparation and employment of teachers should be free from any form of discrimination on grounds of race, colour, sex, religion, political opinion, national or social origin, or economic condition.

8 Working conditions for teachers should be such as will best promote effective learning and enable teachers to concentrate on their professional tasks.

9 Teachers' organizations should be recognized as a force which can contribute greatly to educational advance and which therefore should be associated with the determination of educational policy.

Adopted on 5 October 1966 by the Special Intergovernmental Conference on the Status of Teachers, convened by UNESCO, Paris, in cooperation with the International Labour Organization.

Source: Reproduced by permission of UNESCO.

Research on the lives and perspectives of teachers has drawn attention to who teachers are in terms of their personalities and life experiences, what teachers do, and how the sites where they work influence their activities and beliefs about teaching. More recently critical theory in education emphasises that the questions of who is a *teacher* and what is *teaching* are socially constructed and historically embedded. That is, schools, teaching and society should be examined in terms of the reciprocal relationships that hold them together across time and space. As Biklen (1995, p 5) argues, 'How a teacher under-stands the meaning of teaching and the discourses she draws upon to understand and explain her choices and actions are shaped by what it means to be a teacher in our culture'.

Cooper & Henderson (1995) bring the changing interrelationship between the teacher, teaching, schooling and culture into focus with snapshots of teachers in different historical periods. They claim that in the agricultural era, where the purpose of schools was to promote common culture and citizenship, teachers were considered as sacred professionals who were *called*—that is, they 'had a calling'. Where the church lacked appropriately educated recruits, it expanded what we now know as schools and in doing so also sought to educate those not born into the ruling elite. Thus there was a shift in the pedagogical relationships from students studying religious texts as 'disciples' to an expanded student body populated by 'discipuli'—pupils. Around the 16th century, the new merchant classes, who were reticent to send their children to 'cathedral schools' lest they be recruited into the church, established corporate-run merchant schools which used the clerical teachers. When the merchants sought to increase their control over the schools, notions of classes and curricula became important.

As societies moved towards the capitalism of the industrial era, there emerged a trend for national social regulation as rural dwellers left their land in search of paid work in the cities (Hamilton 1989). The industrial era therefore cast teachers as supervisors, administrators and managers of students who as 'raw materials' were to be standardised and controlled in order to be diligent workers. From the 1700s to the 1990s teaching methods shifted from simultaneous recitation to more individualised instruction under the influence of the Social Darwinists. If survival of the fittest was to strengthen society, then teachers needed to employ strategies which they believed fostered individual competition. Then in the 1900s there was a progressive backlash in which teachers were posited with the responsibility of meeting the needs of all students, and challenging social injustice. In this context teachers were seen as caretakers and protectors of students.

How should teachers be cast in the new times of this new century, a period which Bennett & Cooper (1991) refer to as the electronic and ecological era, when schools are expected to promote lifelong learning and be the focus of collaborative learning communities? They suggest that teachers will be facilitators, assisting students to explore, construct and consume knowledge. One thing is certain: what it means to be a teacher in the new century will be significantly affected by the place of electronic mediated communication within the context of 'new times'.

What is teaching?

What does teaching mean to you? A provocative account of teaching was offered by Postman & Weingarter back in 1969 in their book *Teaching as a*

Subversive Activity. They believed teaching should be a 'subversive activity' aimed at maximising student learning by undermining the educational bureaucracy. For teaching to be valuable, and thereby subversive, they argued for the dissolution of all subjects to free teachers to concentrate on learners, a moratorium on tests and grades to remove the teachers' 'weapons of coercion' (p 135), and for periodically requiring all teachers to take leave of absence for one year to work in a field outside education to promote their social awareness. A point Postman & Weingarter were trying to make is that conceptions of teaching are historically embedded, value-laden and driven by 'taken-for-granteds' or traditions.

In another book, Neil Postman (1986) claims that schooling should not be to produce compliant citizens but rather that education should prepare our students to '*disbelieve* or at least be sceptical of the prejudices of their elders' (p 22). In this context teaching should facilitate such dispositions.

A useful way to think about teaching is through a metaphor. Metaphors or similes about teaching are said to shed light on teachers' self-understanding and professional identity by addressing in a coherent and meaningful way what is often unspoken. Is teaching best represented as gardening (in which the intention is the cultivation of 'young plants' to maturity)? filling an empty bucket (young people know nothing or very little and their knowledge 'stores' must be topped up by teaching)? or, as suggested by Andrew below, a bus travelling on a busy and complex highway? What is your metaphor for teaching?

> *In this role as a teacher of physical education, I view myself as a bus, carrying with me the hopes and aspirations of my students. The schooling environment in which I will operate can be likened to a busy highway. There are certain twists and turns that I must safely negotiate in order to get my passengers to their desired destination, adulthood. Through this course, my passengers would learn that I am more than a service, respecting me as a friendly and helpful resource. I would take my students aboard and throughout their journey, make stops to ensure that all were on the right route and heading in the same direction. When considering teaching as commuting, it is essential that I, as the bus of learning, flow with the other influential traffic on the highway of life so as to ensure students flourish in a safe and caring atmosphere. This of course means that alternative routes may have to be taken so that each individual reaches their potential and enjoys their developmental trip through the HPE subject and life. Just like a bus, I return to where I began to commence another journey of guidance, this time with a new set of passengers. All aboard!*
>
> *Andrew Williams, Third Year Student Teacher,*
> *University of Queensland*

Educational researchers have outlined different views of teaching in line with what may be perceived as teachers' roles, knowledge and responsibilities: a craft; a fine art; an applied science; and a moral endeavour. How you view teachers and teaching shapes how you might gain and maintain your 'professional' knowledge. Some consider teaching to be a craft in which necessary knowledge of how to teach is handed down from master to student (teacher). Common sense and folk wisdom characterise much of the knowledge transmitted in the craft model. Others consider teaching to be an applied science. Thought of in this way, teaching is believed to be a composite of certain skills which can be identified by scientific means and then learned in a systematic manner. Some consider that teaching is more of an art than a science and that individuals are born to be teachers rather than 'made' through training programs.

Thinking of teaching as a craft, an art, or an applied science suggests that teachers will focus on the reproduction of dominant beliefs and practices. With their focus on tips, tools, techniques, creativity or inspiration, each view reinforces teaching *as we know it* rather than introduces teaching *as it could be*. Given the ever-changing demands being placed on teachers and teaching such as embracing technology, addressing complex socio-economic concerns of pupils, and preparing pupils for jobs which currently do not exist, these views are considered inadequate for framing contemporary and future teaching.

A fourth conception, favoured by many educators, is that teaching is a moral endeavour which is a historically located, social and political activity. It assumes that teaching is essentially more problematic than the prior views suggest. This conception recognises that the teacher should be dedicated to good judgment on behalf of the student and that there is a moral basis to the knowledge selected in the curriculum. Fullan (1993) in his book *Change Forces* argues that most importantly teachers' work should be directed towards making a difference in the lives of pupils regardless of their background, and towards helping produce citizens who can live and work productively in increasingly dynamic and complex societies. While Fullan acknowledges that this is not a new idea, he believes that what is important here is to recognise that this view of teachers' work puts teachers in the business of making improvements, of being transformative change agents. To do so in an ever-changing world is to contend with and manage the forces of change on an ongoing basis.

As Aronowitz & Giroux (1985, p 31) put it, transformative teachers 'must take active responsibility for raising serious questions about what they teach, how they are to teach it, and what are the larger goals for which they are striving. This means that they must take a responsible role in shaping the purposes and conditions of schooling'.

If you check back to our orienting reflective questions outlined in Chapter 1, you will see that they embody a similar perspective to this idea of transformative teacher.

Teaching in contemporary Australia

 for your information

The status of teaching in Australia

In August 1996 there were 203,072 full-time equivalent teachers in Australian schools with 131,408 being women and 72,564 men (75 per cent of primary teachers are female). Of the total, 143,949 were in government schools, 7,270 in Anglican, 36,902 in Catholic and 15,851 in other non-government schools (Australian Bureau of Statistics 1998). The 'typical' teacher in Australia is likely to be in their mid-forties, from English-speaking background, and increasingly on contract rather than in permanent employment. Almost half have four-year initial tertiary education, with another quarter currently upgrading their qualifications. The majority reach the top of their salary scale within ten years. In July 1997 the average weekly salary for teachers was $790.60, which represents 13.4 per cent more than average weekly earnings, compared with 36.9 per cent more in 1977. So relatively teachers' salaries have lost ground over the past 20 years. Promotion opportunities are considered somewhat limited, tend to lead out of the classroom, and tend to favour men. Overall, teachers are most likely to leave the profession within two years or after 10–15 years of service. Together these factors suggest that Australia is entering a phase of substantial change in the teaching cohort with an influx of new teachers, and must respond to various problems in teachers' working conditions (outlined in Chapter 4) if the profession is to affect positively the opportunities and well-being of young people.

As indicated in the above box, between June 1996 and March 1998 a federal Senate Inquiry was held with respect to the status of the teaching profession in Australia. Its brief was to examine the status of teachers and the development of the profession during the next five years. In particular it was asked to examine: community attitudes towards teachers and the ways in which schools operate; the expectations of teachers and factors which diminish their job satisfaction and performance; the profile of Australian teachers in terms of their tertiary education and demographics; and best practices for initial inservice and ongoing professional development. This drive for the professionalisation of teaching—the elevation of teaching to a more respected, responsible, rewarding and rewarded occupation—is common worldwide. It is linked to a fundamental premise that the standards by which teacher education and the performance of teachers should be judged must be raised and more clearly articulated.

As with previous reports such as *Teaching Counts* released in 1993 by the then Labor Federal Minister for Education, Employment and Training, Kim

Beazley, the Senate Inquiry recognised the 'need for a paradigm shift in the structure and operation of schools and school systems and to acknowledge the dramatic changes which have been wrought in teachers' experience of their profession' (p 10). High retention rates of students to the end of year 12, integration of students with a wide range of abilities (and disabilities) and social and socio-economic backgrounds, shifts in disciplinary knowledge, expansion of school-based management, and preparation of pupils for careers of the future add complexity to contemporary teaching. Also, increasingly teachers are responsible for pupils' personal, domestic, career and welfare-related matters. Such reports tend to emphasise the view of teaching in new times as moral, intellectual and strategic work.

 for your information

A Class Act: Inquiry into the Status of the Teaching Profession

Teaching in the 1990s is a highly complex and demanding activity. Despite shrinking budgets, alarmist media reports, unsupportive ministers, a crowded curriculum, and the disappearance of support services, teachers have continued to dedicate themselves to their students. The Committee has been encouraged by the evidence of the deep commitment of teachers, by their passionate concern for young people, and by the many examples of innovative and cooperative teaching practice brought to its attention.

But all is not well in the teaching profession, and it is generally agreed that there is a widespread crisis of morale amongst teachers. The status of the profession is disturbingly low. Perceptions in the community about the low tertiary entrance requirements for teacher training, and the low status accorded in this country to children, contribute to this state of affairs. As well, the feminisation of the profession—that is, the high percentage of women teachers—means that prejudiced views about the value of women's work are also a factor. Few teachers recommend a teaching career to their children or their brightest students. Some are even ashamed to admit to being teachers. While teachers themselves value their work they believe it is not understood, appreciated or supported in the general community.

The Committee considers this is an unduly pessimistic assessment of the situation. The evidence received shows that community perceptions of teachers and teaching are more varied and more positive than many teachers realise, particularly among people and families most familiar with teachers' work. This is a clear indication of the need for teachers and others, especially governments, to publicise more effectively the excellent work taking place in our schools.

The Committee believes that a tolerant, vigorous, successful society requires a quality education system, and at the heart of quality education are quality teachers.

Low morale amongst teachers works against quality teaching. As this Report shows, steps to improve morale and to address the difficulties described will go a long way to achieving quality outcomes in education. Teaching needs to be accepted as a profession. To reinforce that view, the recommendations in this Report aim to give teachers responsibility for professional standards in teaching and governments responsibility for staffing, facilities and back up support.

Senator Rosemary Crowley (1998). *A Class Act: Inquiry into the Status of the Teaching Profession*. Canberra: Senate Employment, Education and Training References Committee (pp 1–2).

The Senate Inquiry was 'in no doubt that teaching must be regarded as a profession, with all that this implies for the standards, accountability, status and autonomy that a community expects of a profession' (p 6). Such a statement reflects a number of competing discourses. On the one hand it promotes the teacher as a professional with the authority, autonomy and rewards befitting such status. The report argues that 'teachers should be intimately involved in the planning, implementation and evaluation of a school's educational program and the learning experiences of students' (p 8). On the other hand, it flags the importance of regulating aspects of the profession through the establishment and monitoring of national standards for teacher education programs, entry to employment and work practices.

The above tensions are certainly not peculiar to Australia. Commentators in North America, Britain, New Zealand and Europe explain similar contradictions. In what are labelled as 'New Right' philosophies, education is positioned as a commodity or product and therefore, like other businesses, can supposedly be made more efficient and economical through letting the competitive market forces reign. Yet, at the same time, government policies are concerned with accountability and centralised control.

Ways of understanding teachers and teaching

Much of what is known about who teachers are, why they were attracted to the profession, how they fulfil their roles as teachers and what pathways they follow for self-fulfillment has been understood through the process of *socialisation*. Socialisation is coming to participate in a social group or, more specifically, in the group we understand as physical education teachers by selectively acquiring that group's values, attitudes, interests, knowledge and skills. This trajectory of occupational socialisation has been mapped in terms of *anticipatory* socialisation (i.e. what values, beliefs, skills and expectations recruits to PETE bring with them), *professional* socialisation (i.e. the process by which recruits acquire and maintain the values, beliefs, skills and knowledge that are deemed necessary for teaching physical education), and *organisational* socialisation (i.e. in which employees 'learn the ropes' of working within particular organisational structures).

As a theoretical tool, socialisation has been criticised for often oversimplifying the process of becoming a teacher and focussing too much on the individual and not sufficiently on the interaction between the individual's own biography, their preconceptions about teaching, societal influences and the teacher education/teaching context. In other words, socialisation theories have tended to position student teachers and teachers as passive entities who willingly adapt and conform to the dominant socialisation processes. This functionalist understanding of socialisation explains neither why some teachers resist the forces of socialisation (such as those heroes in the films previously mentioned) nor how becoming and working as a teacher can be a process of transformation. More accurately, the socialisation process is interactive, contradictory and individual, although it is situated in a broader context of social, political and cultural dimensions. It is this critical perspective on socialisation that will frame much of the following discussion.

A second theoretical framework associated with the socialisation process, one more clearly focussed on the complexity of an individual's experience, is the development of *self-identity* (see Chapter 7 for further discussion of identity). As the student teacher or teacher interacts with a range of experiences they interpret these experiences through knowledge of their *self—* that is, they act and guide themselves on the basis of identification as a teacher, a daughter, a part-time bar manager, an elite sportsperson etc. This internal conversation occurs as we assume a variety of social positions or roles. One such role or set of relationships and understandings is that of a teacher.

There is differing opinion as to whether humans have a substantial (or even an essential) self, one that is inflexible, at our core, alongside variable situational selves which are manifested by a range of responses and behaviours. Do you feel there is an essential *you* in line with an unwavering set of beliefs? Do you have a set of core values which orient/shape your behaviour? Or do you feel that you constantly repackage yourself depending on the context in which you find yourself?

In the theoretical literature (e.g. Giddens 1991) relating to identity there is a general agreement that each of us has *multiple* selves that we draw on and represent as we fulfil a number of roles. The self is always being made and remade to meet the demands of different social settings and social positionings (e.g. son, mother, friend, student, pianist, triathlete). To develop and maintain a healthy self-identity we are constantly searching for ways to reduce anxiety or discontinuity as we move across contexts and roles.

Significantly for physical education, formation and maintenance of self-identity is also influenced by our bodies (Giddens 1991). People learn about their bodies in both physical and social environments, in relation to objects and to other people. It is in and through our bodies that we have a practical mode of engagement with a range of external events and situations and are therefore socially regulated. Social regulation refers to practices which sustain identities by legitimising some behaviours and outlawing others, in the case of physical education teachers focussing particularly on their bodies, physical comportment and appearance. It also refers to practices which measure an individual against more or less established, though perhaps unarticulated and certainly arbitrary, social expectations.

To meet the sedimented community expectations for a physical education teacher, a particular body shape, particular styles of dress and comportment, and particular professional and physical competencies effectively identify the teachers as 'normal'. To be 'overweight' or even 'non-athletic' would be regarded as abnormal for physical education teachers. Therefore, how the physical educator manages and presents their body is important to their identification with the profession.

Together the frameworks of socialisation and self-identity allow us to better understand how physical education teachers, as individuals and as an occupational group, learn, feel and respond.

Summary

- Teachers' work is historically embedded, value-laden and shaped by a number of traditions.
- Teaching has been viewed as a craft, a fine art, an applied science and more recently as a moral endeavour.
- There is a global drive to professionalise teaching.
- Socialisation and identity theory are ways of understanding teachers and teaching.

References

Aronowitz, S. & Giroux, H. (1985). *Education Under Seige: The Conservative, Liberal and Radical Debate Over Schooling*. Massachusetts: Bergin & Garvey Publishers.

Australian Bureau of Statistics (1998). *Education and Training in Australia*. Canberra: ABS.

Beazley, K. (1993). *Teaching Counts*. Canberra: Australian Government Publishing Service.

Biklen, S. (1995). *School Work: Gender and the Cultural Construction of Teaching*. New York: Teachers College Press.

Burrows, L. (1994). 'Physical education for all—a question of attitudes?'. *Journal of Physical Education New Zealand*, 27(2), pp 2–3.

Cooper, C. & Henderson, N. (1995). *Motivating Schools to Change*. Launceston: Global Learning Communities.

Fullan, M. (1993). *Change Forces: Probing the Depths of Educational Reform*. London: Falmer Press.

Giddens, A. (1991). *Modernity and Self-Identity: Self and Society in the Late Modern Age*. Stanford, CA: Stanford University Press.

Hamilton, D. (1989). *Towards a Theory of Schooling*. Lewes: Falmer Press.

Postman, N. (1986). *Amusing Ourselves to Death: Public Discourse in the Age of Show Business*. New York: Viking.

Postman, N. & Weingartner, C. (1969). *Teaching as a Subversive Activity*. Harmondsworth, UK: Penguin.

Senate Employment, Education and Training References Committee (1998). *A Class Act: Inquiry into the Status of the Teaching Profession*. Canberra: Senate Printing Unit.

UNESCO (1966). *Recommendation Concerning the Status of Teachers*. UNESCO: Paris.

Further reading

Armour, K. & Jones, R. (1998). *Physical Education Teachers' Lives and Careers*. London: Falmer Press.

Templin, T. & Schempp, P. (1989). *Socialisation into Physical Education: Learing to Teach*. Indianapolis, IN: Benchmark Press.

chapter four

objectives

By the end of this chapter you should be able to:

- explain why career development is not a linear process;
- consider the variety of responsibilities which might constitute health and physical education teachers' work;
- discuss why the public and private, personal and professional lives of teachers are frequently blurred;
- explain why teachers' priorities may change across their careers;
- appreciate the value of an induction program.

Teachers' careers

Teachers' ages, years of service and working conditions have been used to study teachers' engagement with the occupation of teaching over the course of a career. This section overviews these approaches to better understanding the occupational socialisation process. In doing so it should help you to anticipate your work in schools and that of your colleagues.

Approaches to teacher development

As a student teacher you are just beginning your professional development as a teacher. 'Professional' development is a career-long process which is neither gradual nor linear. Probably it will be a rather more disrupted and discontinuous subjective experience situated within the context of a school, school community and bureaucratic system. Descriptions of teachers' careers, priorities, skills and workplace conditions are frequently positioned within the discourses of occupational socialisation and often use phases or stages to outline teacher development. For example, as long ago as 1969 Fuller suggested that competence is reached in mid-career when the teachers' concerns shift from the personal to subject matter, and then is further marked in the late phase when the 'professional's' concerns become students' needs.

In the mid 1980s Sikes et al (1985) looked at the teacher's career using the teachers' age as a point of reference. They maintained that until the age of 30 teachers engage in initial experiences to establish basic pedagogical skills. The period of 30–40 years of age was found to be a 'settling down' phase when many teachers aspired to more senior positions while others were disillusioned and had wavering commitment. Between 40 and 50–55, having reached the high point of their promotional possibilities as they might regard them, some teachers may simply coast, while most have reached a plateau and are respected in their work for their competence and proficiency.

Huberman (1989, 1993) reported similar patterns in teachers' career socialisation using numbers of years teaching as a gauge but warned that the patterns should not be seen as either fixed or linear. He argued that after three years' survival and discovery, and stabilisation between four and six years, there follows a period of engagement and experimentation (seven to 18 years' teaching) or, for some, self-doubt. Between 19 and 30 years teachers might experience serenity, or position themselves as distanced and conservative. Preliminary comparative work on physical education teachers' career patterns suggested that they have a more accelerated path through these phases (Macdonald 1995) and reinforced claims that professional development interplays with the individual's biography, sex, opportunities and school contexts, among other factors.

Within the dominant models of teacher development there is reference to the change in priorities of teachers. Typically, as teachers develop expertise they shift from a concern for themselves as teachers to a concern for individual pupils and broader social agendas. Nevertheless, research addressing the identity of subject specialists suggests that underpinning this shift is an ongoing commitment to their subject area. In the case of physical education this commitment is to physical activity and the facilitation of active lifestyles.

Of course one of the issues that an aging physical education teacher must deal with is the aging of their own bodies and, as a consequence, a possible decrease in their ability to perform physical activities to the level they once did. There are issues of identity here. If you have constructed a major aspect of your identity as a physical education teacher through your own physicality, what does it mean for your sense of self as a teacher when the physicality starts to let you down? Now, of course, there are many ways of teaching physical education that do not rely on one's ability to impress the class by demonstrating physical competence. Moreover, we would advocate that you develop teaching strategies that are not based on impressing the class. However, no matter how up-front you are in terms of demonstrating your own physical competence, physical aging is something that most PE teachers eventually have to deal with.

Issues in teachers' careers

Associated with the study of career patterns and priorities which focus on the individual teacher has been a concern for supportive contexts for the professional development of teachers. Supportive contexts are frequently those which empower teachers through optimising the relationships between the teacher and their knowledge, workplace and school system. Conditions at the school/system level found to facilitate professional development and workplace satisfaction include:

- decent, safe working conditions;
- staff stability and tenure of employment;
- respect and support from the school community and administration;
- the appropriate design and management of meaningful tasks;
- reasonable demands on time;
- balance of authority and autonomy;
- space for individual histories and characteristics;
- instructional and curriculum leadership; and
- opportunities for staff development and collegial interaction.

Other more classroom-oriented and personal factors are: manageable classes; adequate resources; rewards for their work and effort; and a balance between personal and professional lives.

Several of the above-mentioned workplace conditions are particularly problematic for physical education teachers who may be disadvantaged by school priorities, traditions, status and resources. More specifically, research into the relationship between workplace conditions and physical education teacher development has suggested that satisfaction of teachers is diminished by: lack of subject status; low expectations for success; role conflict and/or overcommitment; burdensome administration tasks; poor resources and equipment; and the routine nature of the work (Evans & Williams, 1989;

AUGUSTANA UNIVERSITY COLLEGE LIBRARY

Macdonald 1995, 1999; O'Sullivan 1994; Stroot et al 1994). At a more personal level, satisfaction is further undermined by: a lack of collegial inter-action; undue surveillance and harassment; and homophobia (Macdonald & Kirk 1996; Sparkes 1993). Some of these issues will be elaborated further with respect to Australian physical educators.

As the following quotes from Macdonald (1999, p 46) show, beginning and experienced teachers alike criticise the systemic impositions which intensify their work:

> *Unnecessary things are put on. I think teachers are being asked to do more and more every year, little incidental jobs that make the job a lot harder time management-wise than 10 years ago. (Ian)*

These 'peripheral' demands create some friction with the attention teachers could direct to teaching and reflection:

> *I think it would be more rewarding if I really did have time to prepare my actual lessons properly. (James)*

> *A bit more time to reflect, time to be able to sit back and say, 'Okay, hang on, I'm going to have time out here. Let's just unpack what we did . . . What was good about it? What was bad about it. Now let's try and reconstruct it'. (Olivia)*

The proliferation of work responsibilities has been associated with the undermining of professional work in that teachers are torn between competing demands. Also, in a bid for increased efficiency, there has been a burgeoning of accountability mechanisms introduced into schools. In attending to these matters, teachers not only lose control over their own work, they risk losing sight of wider social and educational issues. In the box below, teacher Fia Adams (1994) outlines a typical day in her rural school, demonstrating the frantic and diverse nature of her work.

 for your information

A day in the life of . . . outback and isolated

I am the health and physical education teacher at Blackall State School, a country school with an enrolment of about 300 students, situated in north west Queensland. As the only HPE teacher, my responsibilities include classes in every year level from preschool to year 12, and the organisation of all sport in both primary and secondary departments.

The following account is of a typical day for me at Blackall State School.

It is 7:30 am. I enter my staffroom where a pile of papers and mail, too overwhelming to face, awaits me from the previous day. I sift through the plethora of promotional brochures in search of bargains, and to read about the latest 'hi-tech' HPE equipment. The latter may seem ridiculous with a PE budget like mine, but it is always good to stay informed (or, should I say, 'Dream about what would be reality in a large school in the city').

Being the only HPE teacher in the school, it is my job to organise all the school sporting events. I open a letter containing details of the approaching district netball carnival; an event that will require the organisation of a team, permission forms, money collection, transport arrangements and equipment organisation—all to be completed in the next few days as the carnival approaches. My morning will now include informing students about the carnival and making team arrangements.

It is now past 8 am, and time to approach the groundsman for an update on the condition of the grounds. During my first few weeks at Blackall, this was not an easy task as our groundsman believes that the oval exists to be watered, not played on. However, with much compromising and the odd well-timed compliment as the year has progressed, the groundsman and I have arrived at a satisfactory arrangement. This morning I am pleased to see that he has spared a large section of the oval from watering. Now it is back to the office to check bus bookings.

Blackall State School has one small grassed oval, which exists only because of constant flooding. Facilities for other sports are located one kilometre away from the school, therefore bus transport is essential. (No-one at university told me that I would require a bus licence to teach HPE.) Upon inquiring, I find that the bus is available for the morning and needs to be collected (yet another of my responsibilities as HPE teacher). I am relieved the discomfort of walking to the pool in 40 degree heat. This entails a five minute walk and a short return drive to school. I quickly check my pigeon hole for notices, and return to my staffroom.

My first two lessons for the day are year 11 HPE 'board' course with classes of nine students. The third lesson is a spare and I have a short time to relax before returning the bus and responding to a phone message from the local Catholic school. They will not be participating in our sports program tomorrow due to a lack of teachers. This change requires the rearrangement of the primary sports program, and ensuring the relevant teachers are informed. As our school budget cannot provide a phone in all staffrooms, making or receiving phone calls involves a walk of about 200 m to the office. This becomes annoying as I receive and make many phone calls; however, it is probably for the best, as only a door separates my staffroom from the woodwork and metalwork rooms and the constant noise makes conversation difficult.

By the fourth lesson the heat has become unbearable. The temperature has soared to the mid 40s, the pool is not available for all year levels and space beneath the covered games area is very limited. The lesson is softball skills for year 9, and although physical effort is kept to a minimum, the thought of adjourning to the shade of the buildings constantly lingers in my mind.

The bus is unavailable for the fifth lesson and 20 minutes is wasted walking to and from the pool. To compensate for this, the lesson is extended into the lunch hour. For me, lunch is a quick bite between phone calls and organising sport for tomorrow. The pool owner has just telephoned to change the pool bookings again despite the fact that it is mid-way through the term.

The joys of teaching HPE in a small country school become more apparent as I make the transition from a year 12 HPE lesson to preschool swimming in lesson seven. I have gone from demonstrating the application of a condom to coercing preschool children to put their heads in the water.

It is 3 pm and I am organising tomorrow's lessons around a visitor who is coming to conduct coaching clinics with both primary and secondary classes. The sports programs with their various training sessions are running well, leaving the remainder of the afternoon for lesson preparation, marking and unit planning for the 'board' course.

At around 5:30 pm as my day concludes, I make a list of jobs to be completed tomorrow. Many of these tasks greatly affect the running of the school. At times I wish I were not the only HPE teacher, not just because the workload could be shared but because it would be good to have someone there when I need advice.

My account of a typical day at work may give the impression that being the only HPE teacher in a small country school is not an enjoyable experience. The job is time consuming, and at times frustrating, but the task I have is a challenge. When everything runs smoothly and I can see the students are learning and enjoying physical education, I know it is all worthwhile.

Fia Adams
Blackall State School

On the other hand, the variety of responsibilities that typify physical educators' work, such as school camps, sports coaching and competitions alongside the teaching of theoretical and practical work in physical education, may also be considered rewarding and as offering a breadth of experience and opportunity.

> What's so good about teaching are the extra-curricular activities . . . like the volleyball camp, athletics afternoons, like my trip away with the State Girls' Basketball Team . . . where you spend quality time, . . . and the kids are there to learn, they want to learn . . . Most of the non-teaching things are the stuff that makes the time worthwhile because the opportunities associated directly with teaching are sometimes monotonous . . . you do the tasks over and over again. (Ben, from Macdonald 1995, p 134)

The routinisation teachers may perceive when teaching lesson after lesson may be balanced by engaging in additional extracurricular activities and the 'academic' versions of physical education. For example, some teachers successfully teaching the academic, tertiary-entrance subjects associated with the health and physical education course have found this to be particularly important to their sense of achievement and self-identity.

> Phys. ed.'s changing so much . . . There's so much reading to do, and the nature of the course is changing so much that I find it very exciting,

and I feel that I'm learning all the time . . . I think the 'Board' is what is moving forward at the greatest rate into what I'm enjoying at the moment, and I think if we lost 'Board' Physical Education the bottom would fall out of phys. ed. (Ian, from Macdonald 1999, p 47)

A gendered profession

There is evidence that historically women have been and still are more disempowered through workplace conditions than men. Women teachers' opportunities and behaviours have been hampered by the sexual division of labour in schools and the 'control myths' or norms of behaviour. These norms have dictated how women should appear, behave and procreate, together with the pressures for heterosexuality. In the words of the folk singer Ruth Alpert, 'the culture comes down'.

In 1923, a code of conduct for teachers in the United States suggested that a teacher (female) should not get married or keep company with men, be home by 8 pm, and dress in reserved colours, wearing at least two petticoats and avoiding hair dye (see Figure 4.1). Although the specific expectations for teachers' behaviours may have changed and become less prescribed, in 1995 in Queensland a teacher's photograph appeared on the front page of the state's newspaper because she wore a stud in her nose. The issue was that in wearing the stud she failed to set an appropriate example for the school's students. This interface between the private lifestyle choices and professional behaviours of teachers has been a perennial source of tension between teachers and their employing and registering authorities.

TEACHERS' CONTRACT 1923

This is an agreement between Miss _____ teacher, and the Board of Education of the _____ School, whereby Miss _____ agrees to teach for a period of eight months, beginning Sept. 1, 1923.

The Board of Education agrees to pay Miss _____ the sum of ($75) per month.

Miss _____ agrees:

1. Not to get married. This contract becomes null and void immediately if the teacher marries.
2. Not to keep company with men.
3. To be home between the hours of 8.00 pm and 6.00 am unless in attendance at a school function.
4. Not to loiter downtown in ice cream stores.
5. Not to leave town at any time without the permission of the chairman of the Board of Trustees.
6. Not to smoke cigarettes. This contract becomes null and void immediately if the teacher is found smoking.
7. Not to drink beer, wine, or whiskey. This contract becomes null and void

---

immediately if the teacher is found drinking beer, wine, or whiskey.
8. Not to ride in a carriage or automobile with any man except her brother or father.
9. Not to dress in bright colors.
10. Not to dye her hair.
11. To wear at least two petticoats.
12. Not to wear dresses more than two inches above the ankles.
13. To keep the schoolroom clean
    (a) To sweep the classroom floor at least once daily.
    (b) To scrub the classroom floor at least once weekly with hot water and soap.
    (c) To clean the blackboard at least once daily.
    (d) To start the fire at 7.00 so the room will be warm at 8.00 am when the children arrive.
    (e) Not to use face powder, mascara, or paint the lips.

Figure 4.1   Code of conduct for teachers in the United States in 1923

For women physical educators, the corporeal regulation may be particularly poignant. Experienced female physical educators talk about the image of a competent physical educator in relation to their physical appearance and skills. They clearly wrestle with internalised beliefs about an appropriate image in keeping with dominant masculine and healthist notions of appearance and skill as they age. For Lynn this was:

> Not a stress, but . . . I feel that more so than any other teacher you're a
> role model and I think that you're on show . . . I think it's self-imposed
> pressure to some extent. My perception of what a phys. ed. person
> should be is someone who is vital, not necessarily 'trim, taught, and
> terrific', but at least who appears to be an exponent of the principles and
> philosophies that they're espousing. (from Macdonald 1999, p 48)

Gail, a beginning teacher in a small town, felt awkward about having her appearance watched:

> I should not have to feel that when I get dressed up . . . they should have
> to notice me and say 'Oh, you are a lady!' That annoys me a lot. Why
> should you have to be noticed all the time? (Macdonald & Kirk 1996, p 70)

Due to the public nature of physical education teachers' work and the physicality which it embraces, those who find employment as beginning teachers in small rural towns must deal with aspects of professional and personal surveillance that their city colleagues most likely never encounter. Donald, a case in point, felt that he could not escape into a personal world in his town due to the limited venues for socialising and the constant awareness of his habits and diet being in the public eye (Macdonald & Kirk 1996).

Women who choose to have children and stay teaching often carry dual careers of paid employment in teaching and unpaid domestic commitments. Women physical educators tell of the stress caused by the multiple commitments to work (especially with the extracurricular commitments) and family life. With these structural, social and personal controls, and barriers for women, it is perhaps not surprising that when looking at teachers with more than 11 years' experience, Evans & Williams (1989) found 88 per cent of men and 38 per cent of women had achieved the top of the pay scale and that relatively few women become heads of department.

Women's careers in physical education

All teachers and Heads of Department (HOD) of Health and Physical Education (HPE) in Queensland secondary schools (state high schools, Catholic schools, non-Catholic private schools) were surveyed on career perspectives, experiences, aspirations, promotional issues and leadership styles. In total there were 556 questionnaires returned and this represents over 50% of the HPE population. Respondents comprised 43% females and 57% males. Some of the statistically significant (p < .05) findings of the questionnaire for the sample of staff who participated in the research include:

- *Women underrepresented at HOD level*
- *The top seven factors preventing teachers from becoming HODs were: lack of time for extra commitments, lack of mobility, commitment to teaching, lack of knowledge of selection process, no desire to be HOD, family responsibilities and lack of seniority*
- *Family responsibilities were more influential for females*
- *The top seven factors preventing HODs from being effective were: time required for extra-curricular activities, time taken for administrative detail, lack of uninterrupted time, insufficient space/facilities, varied ability and dedication of staff, deficient communication among administrative levels, and problem students.*
- *Although not among the highest ranking barriers to effectiveness, masculine and feminine stereotypes were ranked more highly as an issue by the females.*
- *More women taking breaks from their career to care for children and these breaks are longer than for men*
- *Fewer females applying for promotion and those who did, applied fewer times and ceased applying more quickly than males (but interestingly there was no significant difference between males and females on questions asking about the importance of a career and aspirations for leadership)*
- *There was little representation of women over 40 years of age and those with with two children or more.*

Most of the results agree with wider research on careers and educational administration in general, particularly the influence of family responsibilities

on the female career. It is interesting to note that despite women being underrepresented at HOD level, males and females both reported the same top three factors preventing promotion.
Louisa Webb (1997)

We can conclude from the above mentioned issues for teachers that power, authority or influence are very important for both beginning and experienced teachers. Here we mean that their ability to make decisions and to see these through is paramount. For beginning teachers it has been argued that a perceived lack of power over their working lives is a great source of dissatisfaction. Beginning teachers speak of the education system being 'top down to the max', their appointments to schools as 'just a numbers game', and having a school administration 'who have to do it their way' (Macdonald 1995). On the other hand it appears easier for experienced teachers to retain a more empowering sense of their own 'professional' sphere of influence (see Macdonald 1999).

Experienced teachers in one Australian study were clearly more committed to and satisfied with their professional status than has been reported for experienced and beginning teachers elsewhere (Macdonald 1999). Across government and non-government schools they shared:

(a) strong concern for the well-being of their students and the students' engagement in physical activity;
(b) the challenge of curriculum planning and implementation, particularly as it related to 'academic' physical education;
(c) dislike for intensified and routinised work practices;
(d) concern that they are perceived as competent while aging; and
(e) an appreciation of their relative [lack of] power. With respect to dominant approaches describing the phases of teacher development, the experienced teachers had retained high degrees of engagement and proactivity beyond what, for many, has been identified as a period of stability or coasting.

Support for beginning teachers

Disempowering workplace conditions have contributed to unacceptable rates of teacher attrition across most developed and less developed countries. In looking across secondary school specialists, Huberman (1993) reported that in American schools about 40 per cent were seriously considering leaving teaching while the scant statistical information on teacher attrition in physical education suggests that as many as 50 per cent or more of teachers plan to leave the profession, many early in their careers. For example, Evans & Williams (1989) projected that 40 per cent of female and 80 per cent of male physical education teachers in the United Kingdom were looking for work outside physical education. Macdonald et al (1994) reported that approximately 55 per cent of the graduates from one Australian university program had chosen to leave physical education teaching.

Given the challenges to beginning teachers, employing authorities are increasingly aware of putting programs in place which make beginning teachers feel welcome and support them in their early decision making. An induction program refers to a systematic network of strategies to support beginning teachers, ease entry into their first teaching position and lay the foundation for a strong career trajectory. An induction program may have three strands to it:

(a) *orientation*—familiarising the beginning teacher with essential information about the school, its community and the teaching tasks to be undertaken;

(b) *adaptation*—actions here might include the careful placement of teachers in schools where the environment is supportive; they teach subject matter in line with their expertise; fewer contact hours or smaller classes;

(c) *development*—either individually or alongside a *mentor*, the beginning teacher critically reflects on their practice with a view to ongoing refinement and assists them in their concerns about their ability to cope, time management, contact with parents, accessing resources, and responding to student needs. A mentor can be broadly understood as a trusted guide and counsellor in a relationship where the mentor openly, informally and willingly shares information with their proteges. Ideally, a mentor is prepared for their role in terms of leadership, role-modelling, demonstration, motivation, counselling, supervision and formative evaluation.

When you arrive at your first teaching appointment, be sure to ask about participating in an induction program.

Not only might such strategies reduce the likelihood of teachers leaving early in their careers but they can also arrest what has been called the 'wash-out' effect, said to occur when beginning teachers' progressive ideas and enthusiasm are dissipated with the pressures of beginning work in a new school. Typically this shift may entail moving from child-centred, democratic and critical approaches to teaching and learning to more autocratic, didactic and formal approaches. These shifts can be a response to the constraints of time, available resources, work conditions, school traditions and student behaviours. Veenman (1984, p 88) articulated this phenomenon as a 'reality shock'—'the collapse of missionary ideals formed during teacher training by the harsh and rude reality of classroom life'. Beginning teachers need support in order to carry over and develop their contemporary and progressive strategies.

Summary

- Teaching careers can be mapped using teachers' ages, years of service, seniority and working conditions.
- Health and physical education teachers have to balance a variety of curricular and extracurricular responsibilities.
- Health and physical education teachers' work can be routinised, gendered and disempowering.
- Induction programs into teaching can help to alleviate high levels of attrition.

References

Adams, F. (1994). 'A day in the life of . . . outback and isolated'. *Active and Healthy Quarterly*, 1(1), 6–7.

Evans, J. & Williams, T. (1989). 'Moving up and getting out: The classed, gendered career opportunities of physical education teachers'. In T. Templin & P. Schempp (eds), *Socialization in Physical Education: Learning to Teach*, pp 235–250. Indianapolis: Benchmark Press.

Fuller, F. (1969). 'Concerns of teachers: A developmental characterization'. *American Educational Research Journal*, 6, pp 207–226.

Huberman, M. (1989). 'On teachers' careers: Once over lightly with a broad brush'. *International Journal of Educational Research*, 13, pp 347–362.

Huberman, M. (1993). *The Lives of Teachers*. New York: Teachers College Press.

Macdonald, D. (1995). 'The role of proletarianization in physical education teacher attrition'. *Research Quarterly for Exercise and Sport*, 66(2), 129–141.

Macdonald, D. (1999). 'The "professional" work of experienced physical education teachers'. *Research Quarterly for Exercise and Sport*, 70, pp 41–54.

Macdonald, D. & Kirk, D. (1996). 'Private lives, public lives: Surveillance, identity and self in the work of beginning physical education teachers'. *Sport, Education and Society*, 1(1), pp 59–76.

Macdonald, D., Hutchins, C. & Madden, J. (1994). 'To leave or not to leave: Health and physical education teachers' career choices'. *Healthy Lifestyles Journal*, 41(3), pp 19–22.

O'Sullivan, M., Siedentop, D. & Tannehill, D. (1994). 'Breaking out: Codependency of high school physical education'. *Journal of Teaching in Physical Education*, 13, pp 421–428.

Sikes, P., Measor, L. & Woods, P. (1985). *Teacher careers: Crises and continuities*. London: Falmer Press.

Sparkes, A. & Templin, T. (1992). 'Life histories and physical education teachers: Exploring the meanings of marginality'. In A. Sparkes (ed.), *Research in Physical Education and Sport*, pp 118–145. London: Falmer Press.

Sparkes, A., Templin, T. & Schempp, P. (1993). 'Exploring dimensions of marginality: Reflecting on the life histories of physical education teachers'. *Journal of Teaching in Physical Education*, 12, pp 386–398.

Stroot, S., Collier, C., O'Sullivan, M. & England, K. (1994). 'Contextual hoops and hurdles: Workplace conditions in secondary physical education'. *Journal of Teaching in Physical Education*, 13, pp 342–360.

Veenman, S. (1984). 'Perceived problems of beginning teachers'. *Review of Educational Research*, 54(2), pp 143–178.

Webb, L. (1997) *Leadership in physical education—final results of a statewide survey of HPE staff in secondary schools*. Paper presented at the national conference of the Australian Association for Research in Education, Hilton Hotel, Brisbane, Queensland.

Further reading

Acker, S. (1999). *The Realities of Teachers' Work*. London: Cassell.

chapter
five

objectives

By the end of this chapter you should be
able to:
- explain how schools, as social institutions,
  are changing through a blend of
  centralised, decentralised, individual and
  collective activity;
- appreciate that change can be rewarding,
  challenging, alienating, embraced or
  resisted depending on an individual's
  perspective;
- determine what strategies can be
  employed to make the change process
  rewarding and worthwhile;
- describe how specific curricular and
  administrative changes can affect
  teachers' work.

As we have suggested throughout this text, schools and education systems, as social institutions, are changing through a blend of centralised, decentralised, individual and collective activity. The Senate Inquiry into the status of teachers was most concerned to emphasise the importance of, and need for, educational change and the centrality of teachers in this change process.

> Teachers have the capacity to change, and indeed acknowledge the imperative for change. However, teachers need to be able to bring their professional judgement to bear upon what things require changing and what things need to be preserved . . . To emphasise the role of teachers as agents of change therefore requires a simultaneous affirmation of their professional rights and their responsibilities in implementing that change. (1998, p 9)

Fullan (1993, p 4) argues that educators must constantly change because they are 'in the business of making improvements, and to make improvements in an ever changing world is to contend with and manage the forces of change on an ongoing basis'. He argues, therefore, that teachers must become experts in the dynamics of change and skilled change agents with respect to their classroom practices, through to the state level education policies and documents.

But the teacher's role as social change agent is not without its critics. There are some educators of influence who consider the role of the teacher should be confined to the preservation and transmission of knowledge and culture. They express concern over the notion that a teachers' role should also include acting as an agent for social change. An example of this conservative sentiment is found in the Education Forum's *Submission on the Draft Health & Physical Education in the New Zealand Curriculum* (1998). In their submission they report concern that the Ministry of Education has become the instrument of a set of people who are seeking, through the educational concerns of teaching children, to change the entire direction of the country!

Reactions to change

Imagine there is a staffroom debate about whether the school athletics carnival should go ahead. Some teachers argue that athletic events are irrelevant to the majority of students and that the carnival is poorly attended. Others believe that the carnival is an important tradition that develops school spirit, motivates athletic participation and assists in the identification of regional representatives. While some teachers will define the cancellation of the 'antiquated carnival' as appropriate and progressive, others will consider that this change has a high cost for themselves and their program. Much depends on the different professional and personal values and beliefs held by the teachers. Some teachers will be pushing for change while others will be resisting. Therefore, the process of curriculum change can be both rewarding and threatening. How people respond to change is a reflection of a variety of factors such as their biography, career experiences or relationships with colleagues and school administration.

Teachers' varied reactions to proposed changes remind us that curriculum change:

- can be perceived differently by different teachers.
- can, if handled poorly, produce 'winners' and 'losers'.
- may affect subject areas differently.
- may disturb or promote teachers' sense of confidence.
- has a temporal dimension in that schools or subject areas are at different points in their readiness to change.

Sparkes (1990, p 4) also emphasises that some changes are easier to digest than others and that movement towards 'level 3' (see Figure 5.1) change may be difficult.

Level 1: Surface change (relatively easy). The use of new and revised materials and activities, for instance, direct instructional resources like curriculum packs (e.g. Aussie Sport; drug education kits).

Level 2: The use of new skills, teaching approaches, styles and strategies— that is, change in teaching practices with attendant changes in the teaching role (e.g. outcomes-based education; pupil as independent learner; planning across a learning area).

Level 3: Real change (very difficult). Changes in beliefs, values, ideologies and understanding with regard to pedagogical assumptions and themes. This can involve a major reorientation of philosophy and self-image (e.g. social view of health; teaching to pupil diversity; removing competitive sport from the physical education and sports program).

Adapted from Sparkes 1990

Figure 5.1 Levels of change

In looking at conditions for teachers' readiness to implement change, research suggests that teachers need an appreciation of current or new curriculum policies and documents, and knowledge and support of their professional community which may include professional and community associations such as Australian Council for Health, Physical Education and Recreation (ACHPER). For example, the introduction of documents framed around outcomes-based education required a national program led by universities, education agencies and professional associations to inservice teachers to assist them to make sense of new syllabuses. In addition, teachers need confidence in any new subject matter associated with the proposed change. In Australia, with respect to the national Health and Physical Education Statement and Profile, and their state/territory derivatives, teachers expressed a need for information on sexuality, consumer health, and personal and cultural identity if they were to implement the documents and create change beyond the surface level. In New Zealand the conservative *Education Forum* recommended that mental health and sexuality education be removed from the Health and Physical Education Key Learning Area altogether.

Teachers find ways to cope with their ever-changing, or perhaps unsupportive or threatening jobs, and preserve their self-identity. Coping mechanisms are a way of facing problems that do not necessarily change the situation but may help to manage it. Some responses are private in that strategies are employed by individual teachers, while public strategies involve a group of teachers acting together. Lacey (1977) suggested that strategies can be thought of as:

- internalised adjustment where the teacher conforms to the status quo;
- strategic compliance where the teacher's behaviour is adjusted although they still hold private reservations; and
- strategic redefinition in which the teacher is able to influence the situation through the introduction of new knowledge, beliefs and practices.

How might these strategies be manifested by teachers with respect to the cancellation of the athletics carnival?

If we look at change as a temporal process in which aspects of practice are altered, monitored and refined, the greatest challenge is to sustain an innovation or change over time. The process of change can be assisted by:

- continually presenting the need for change to colleagues or participants in different ways and using convincing evidence;
- inviting discussion and participation from a variety of stakeholders in the process;
- linking up with people who will be your allies;
- starting small and persevering;
- sharing your success stories; and
- avoiding locking anyone out of the change process.

This indicates there is a need for teachers to have some *ownership* over the change process so that it becomes a personally and professionally rewarding experience. *Institutionalisation* is said to occur when the change is supported within an organisation or program for a couple of years, once the initial attention or support wanes.

The limits to rational change

It is important also to realise that reaction to change is not entirely (or even paramountly) rational. Individuals will accept or reject change as a result of many complicated motives, some of which they will not even recognise because they exist at the level of the subconscious, non-rational. Individuals might give a rational reason as to why a change is necessary but, at an emotional level, feel rather uneasy about the change. Such feelings will often be more powerful than the rational argument, but too often they are ignored or dismissed as unimportant. For example, Lisette Burrows (1994) suggests that the major constraints to developing inclusive practices in physical education (a positive change in practice) are not resources (although they are important), but attitudes. For instance, fear of dealing with the unknown, a concern that it may require hard work, or seeing changes as a threat to long-held values which are in turn linked to identity. We are not arguing that rationality, evidence and (even) common sense are not important in the change process. We are merely making explicit the often ignored role that the non-rational also plays in the change process. Curriculum change advocates ignore the non-rational at their peril.

Key Learning Areas and change

The widespread implementation of documents capturing a *Key Learning Area* rather than traditional, more discrete *subjects* has introduced substantial changes to the health and physical education field. As discussed in Chapter 11, the learning area embraces content from subjects such as Physical Education, Health Education, Human Relationships Education, Home Economics and Outdoor Education. These documents not only raise questions about the nature of knowledge and how it can be organised and judged, they also imply changes in the organisation and management of subject matter in schools and the work of teachers, particularly in secondary schools.

Teachers' continued identification with, and enjoyment of, particular school subjects develop from their own schooling, through their university programs, and into their teaching careers. Such a history leads to strong identification with specific subject matter (e.g. Physics, Literature, Maths, Physical Education). One's (teaching) subject becomes part of one's (multiple) identity. Most of your own secondary schooling would have been organised around discrete subjects (e.g. English, Biology, Physical Education, Home Economics),[1] further reinforced by disciplinary knowledge in your teacher education programs. It is in these subjects that teachers not only come to feel secure and successful but also are able to express themselves as experts in language, art, music or physical activity, and derive a sense of satisfaction. Curriculum changes which challenge the teachers' values and expertise are clearly going to be resisted unless there are mechanisms and supports in place to assist teachers to move outside their comfort zone.

In a national project addressing the implementation of learning areas in schools, Macdonald & Glover (1997) reported that generating involvement across secondary school subject departments was often difficult. A teacher predicted that: 'in a large school and an established school like mine, the biggest barrier is going to be having the interested parties get together to nut out who's going to do what, what approach, so we have an integrated program, we don't have repetition, and . . . (how) we can do it collegially'. However, some schools were keen to establish a genuinely collaborative project within their professional community involving a number of teachers with the aim of changing and coordinating a program's structure and subject matter. An important starting point was the teachers' willingness to become involved. This commitment was commonly seen in schools where teachers themselves chose the extent and nature of the curriculum change among a cohesive group.

The results of this project indicated that working across teaching groups or subject areas was limited by teachers' commitment to subject matter with which they were most familiar and the personal and professional costs to them as a result of moving in new directions. In some cases the subject matter boundaries and departmental cultures within the HPE area led to fairly uncomfortable interactions. For instance, a physical education teacher reported: 'I was accosted by the Home Economics Head of Department with basically the accusation that I was taking over the Health and Phys Ed area. I had to assure her that I wasn't'. He went on to say: 'There's going to be a lot of departments out there who really are going to be struggling and it'll come down to power plays and politics in schools as to what goes in learning areas'.

This example reminds us that as a profession teaching is not a homogeneous community whose members share identity, values, definition of roles and interests. Segments of the teaching profession have been established around subjects that are a basis for special and political interests, rewards and satisfaction and, in turn, division from and competition with other groups. As one example, changes to subject matter boundaries can be difficult to deal with for those teachers who closely identify with particular subject matter knowledge. This is significant for teachers who identify strongly with the occupational community of teachers through their commitment to particular subject matter knowledge at the core of their self-definition.

Decentralisation and teachers' responses to change

Decentralisation of decision making, or the shifting of decisions to school districts and schools themselves, is another educational change that has had a significant impact on teachers' work. Many decisions related to program planning and assessment, selection of executive and teaching staff, facility and equipment purchase and management, and finance now lie with schools and are supported through the strengthening of school councils and the establishment of school charters. This is nevertheless balanced by stronger centralised guidelines for teaching and learning outcomes both in Australia and New Zealand. Caldwell (1993, p ix) explains that recommendations relating to devolution are 'consistent with the lessons business has learned'. Caldwell (1993, p. xiii) looks at the decentralising tendencies as a reflection of concerns for 'efficiency in the management of public education, effects of the recession and financial crisis . . . empowerment of teachers, the need for flexibility and responsiveness, . . . interest in choice and the market forces of schooling'. He continues that there is a strong body of evidence that decentralisation enhances job satisfaction and professionalism on the part of principals and teachers. While the extent and nature of devolution varies across Australian states and territories here, we are interested in the effect that the balance of centralisation and decentralisation has on teachers and their work.

Decentralisation means a redefinition, and perhaps an extension, of teachers' professional responsibilities, a move supported by the Senate Inquiry outlined earlier. Health and physical educators may find themselves charged with seeking corporate sponsorship for their programs, designing the tender documents for new sports facilities, or justifying their performance through an annual school-based appraisal system. There are moves to introduce flexibility for teacher employment with the introduction of incentives and rewards according to location, performance and responsibilities. Prior discussions indicated that experienced teachers reported enjoying some of the fruits of the increasingly devolved education system while beginning teachers felt repressed. It is intended that decentralised management will make a significant contribution 'to the satisfaction and sense of professionalism of principals, teachers and other employees' and allow 'schools to plan for a future which differs in very important ways from the past' (Caldwell 1993, p 55).

The guiding principles for devolved decisions are those of autonomy (schools should have rights to make many of their own decisions to suit their context), accountability (schools must keep records of decisions they have made), efficiency (schools should make the optimal use of resources) and equity (schools should provide for a range of pupil and community needs) (Bullock & Thomas 1997). While decentralisation might provide more opportunities for teachers to be autonomous, we need to be aware of the accompanying accountability mechanisms. Some of these issues relating to curriculum change are further discussed in Chapter 14.

Summary

- As teaching and schooling undergo constant change, teachers must become experts in the dynamics of change.
- Some changes are easier to embrace than others. The acceptance of change depends on the individual's perspective and context.
- Coping mechanisms are employed to help manage the impact of change.
- Key Learning Areas challenge traditional subject divisions, subject matter, pedagogies and assessment practices.
- Tensions between centralised and decentralised educational policy have implications for school and teacher autonomy and accountability.

Note

1 There are states like New South Wales where KLAs have been in place for over a decade including those of Personal Development, Health and Physical Education (PDHPE).

References

Bullock, A. & Thomas, H. (1997). *Schools at the Centre?: A Study of Decentralisation*. London: Routledge.

Burrows, L. (1994). 'Gender equity in school physical education'. In *Physical Education New Zealand/ Te reo kori Aotearoa*, pp 1–12. Wellington: PENZ.

Caldwell, B. (1993). *Decentralising the Management of Australia's Schools*. Melbourne: National Industry Education Forum.

Editorial (1994). *Changing Education*, 1(2), p 1.

Education (1998). *Health and Physical Education in the New Zealand Curriculum*. Auckland: Education Forum.

Fullan, M. (1993). *Change Forces: Probing the Depths of Educational Reform*. London: Falmer Press.

Lacey, C. (1977). *The Socialization of Teachers*. London: Methuen.

Macdonald, D. & Glover, S. (1997). 'Subject matter boundaries and curriculum change in the health and physical education learning area'. *Curriculum Perspectives*, 17(1), pp 23–30.

Senate Employment, Education and Training References Committee (1998). *A Class Act: Inquiry into the Status of the Teaching Profession*. Canberra: Senate Printing Unit.

Sparkes, A. (1990). *Curriculum Change and Physical Education: Towards a Micropolitical Understanding*. Geelong: Deakin University Press.

Further reading

Fullan, M. (1999). *Change Forces: The Sequel*. London: Falmer Press.

Smyth, J. & Shacklock, G. (1998). *Re-making Teaching*. London: Routledge.

Taggart, A., Alexander, K. & Taggart, J. (1993). 'Thinking allowed: Three teachers comment on the national curriculum'. *ACHPER Healthy Lifestyles Journal*, 40(1), pp 21–25.

chapter six

objectives

By the end of this chapter you should be able to:

- express the personal, situational and societal factors that have shaped your recruitment into PETE;
- consider the relationship between who is recruited into PETE and what values, attitudes and behaviours are reproduced by PETE graduates;
- evaluate why health and physical education teachers' bodies have become symbols of professional ability, sexuality, particular personal qualities and moral worth.

This chapter will consider, and attempt to explain, the perspectives, expectations and experiences of student teachers in PETE courses. It is about their identity as physical education student teachers, shaped by their socio-economic backgrounds, sex and sexuality, body image, lifestyle, spirituality, and career aspirations. As you read this chapter, try to consider how your own biography, beliefs and experiences match those being described.

Please remember that when we use the acronym PETE (Physical Education Teacher Education) we are actually referring to the course of study for prospective teachers of the KLA of Health and Physical Education. We recognise that many Australian states and New Zealand differ in their expectations of physical education teachers to teach health education. In some instances there is no requirement at all, in others it is an equal commitment to both. In this case we have simply adopted the term used in the literature of teacher education for physical education.

As mentioned in Chapter 1, you are probably of an age where you share some of the 'characteristics' of the 'options generation' and are in a sense a product of the cultural context of 'new times'. That is not meant to be a bad thing, merely a recognition that in some ways you will confront some contemporary issues related to becoming a phys. ed. teacher which were not on the agenda a generation ago. But we also know that you will have to deal with many issues that are enduring in that they have affected phys. ed. teachers for many years.

Who is attracted to PETE?

Given that all PETE students come to teacher education with influential knowledge, skills and beliefs which affect how they receive and use new information, it is not surprising that educators are interested in who is attracted to PETE. Research into physical education teaching suggests that the biography of those recruited influences their ongoing values and practices. Yet, 'Are we attracting the type of student that we truly wish to enter our field?' (Templin et al 1982, p 131).

The process whereby a person becomes attracted to and chooses a particular occupation is termed 'recruitment'. Within this process the *subjective warrant* refers to 'perceptions of the skills and abilities necessary for entry into, and performance of work in a specific occupation' (Dewar & Lawson 1984, p 15). Listed as factors influencing an individual's subjective warrant for physical education teaching are the:

- personal (gender, ethnicity, self-concept);
- situational (socio-economic status, involvement in sport and physical education); and
- societal (perceptions of the status, conditions, rewards of the profession).

In other words, this recruitment theory suggests that, when deciding on working in physical education, prospective PETE students compare who they are, what they look like, what skills and interests they have, and their expectations for workplace rewards with what they know of physical education teaching. Some aspects of the subjective warrant can be considered attractors and other factors, facilitators. Occupational *facilitators* are social mechanisms which ease entry into physical education teaching, such as having a relative who is a physical education teacher. Economic and symbolic benefits associated with physical education teaching, which may include salary, holidays and the ongoing association with a sporting community, can be considered *attractors* (Belka et al 1991).

Dan Lortie (1975), in his book *Schoolteacher*, argued a quarter of a century ago that students' predispositions are central to becoming a teacher. Such is still the case today. In particular Lortie drew attention to the anticipatory socialisation which occurs through an 'apprenticeship of observation' during the 12 years or so that pupils spend internalising the teaching models of their own schooling. With respect to physical education, the argument suggests that your own school physical education teachers and programs have been particularly important in your subjective warrant for recruitment into physical education and have, in part, shaped your values and beliefs associated with physical education.

Recruitment into a subject specialisation is also an induction into a particular subject community. Why are you becoming a teacher of physical education and not modern history, economics or Indonesian? While we should recognise that there may be great variations within how a subject or learning area is approached as we move across contexts, affiliation with a particular subject can be central to who is attracted to teaching and how they will fulfil their teaching role. Lave & Wenger (1992) would suggest that novice or student physical educators, over time, become more closely affiliated with the physical education community. As with Lortie, they acknowledge that much is learnt about an occupational community while being peripheral to it. Gradually, through a range of meaningful social and personal experiences within and beyond PETE, students become more immersed in the language, traditions, responsibilities, knowledge bases, practices and shared values of the profession.

Lortie (1975, p 26) concluded that as occupations attracted or dispelled people engaged in occupational decision-making they 'will come to be staffed by people of particular dispositions and life circumstances'. Therefore we return to the question of who is attracted to physical education teaching in terms of their age, ethnicity, socio-economic status and educational attainment. What aspirations, values and beliefs motivate people to choose physical education? Importantly, who is not attracted to PETE and why?

Demographic profile of PETE students

PETE tends to recruit a homogeneous community of students. Look around a lecture room some time to test this theory. PETE cohorts tend to be composed of school leavers, or near to it, who look athletic and able-bodied.

Similarly, despite Australia's multicultural population, most PETE students have Anglo-Saxon origins. These patterns have been reported also in American research (e.g. Placek et al 1995). Drawing on the theory of recruitment, it appears that the subjective warrant for physical education typically proscribes young, able-bodied, athletic Caucasians.

Knowledge of the socio-economic background of Australian PETE students is scant. However, using parental occupation as a guide to socio-economic status, Macdonald et al (1998) found that, for a particular cohort of human movement studies students (many of whom would take the PETE career option), 51.2 per cent of their parents had managerial or para/professional occupations, most of which would have required university degrees. Half the students had attended non-government schools. Interestingly, non-government school pupils do not make up half the student population in secondary schools and accordingly graduates from non-government schools are overrepresented in the cohort described by Macdonald et al. This profile differs from North American reports by Hutchinson (1993) and Placek et al (1995), who found physical education students to be recruited from the lower to middle classes, many being first-generation tertiary students.

Academic ability of recruits has also attracted interest and concern. North American literature suggests that, at best, recruits into physical education could be considered above average. Ease of university entrance into physical education, 'the "bottom line" (being) . . . that those individuals admitted into teacher education tracks are, in many cases, marginal students', has led some writers to question recruitment processes and standards (Templin et al 1982, p 127). However, in Australia, PETE attracts students of high academic ability where recruitment is largely based on a single, highly competitive academic score. Some of these cross-cultural differences may lie with the strong sports scholarship programs that run in North America or perhaps the 'academic' dimension of Australian and New Zealand school physical education.

Motivations for a career in physical education

The options for students attracted to careers associated with physical activity have become more numerous and complex. The physical education teaching profession must now compete to attract students who may be similarly interested in such occupations as exercise science, health promotion, coaching, sports psychology, professional dancing or physiotherapy. Was PETE your first preference for tertiary study? Here we explore further some facilitators for recruitment into physical education.

Significant others who influence a potential recruit's career decisions include physical education teachers, coaches, family members and peers. A point of interest from a Queensland study suggests that parents who are teachers discourage their children from pursuing a career in physical education teaching (Macdonald et al 1998). However, the strongest motivation to pursue a career in physical education arises from personal interest in physical activity and the opportunity to continue an association with sport. PETE students in Canada, the United States, New Zealand, the United Kingdom and Australia typically have had extensive and positive experiences in/with sport before they get to university (e.g. Armour & Jones 1998; Dewar 1989; Hutchinson 1993; Macdonald & Tinning 1995; Placek et al 1995; Sikes 1988). Many recruits into PETE have also reported a desire to work with young people, frequently from a perspective of service to the community (e.g. see Box 6.1 below for the case of Don), and an academic interest in the body and healthy lifestyles. This attraction to a particular subject rather than to teaching more generally is not unique to physical education.

Box 6.1   *I see that I am serving God to a degree by way of staying fit. We're told that our body is the temple of the Holy Spirit, therefore I see that it would be logical for us to keep fit, not to feed all this junk into our bodies . . . If I'm being motivated (by God) to go into teaching so that I can be an example and hopefully give many people chances to hear about what I believe and why I believe it, as a way of liberating them and helping them, then I don't see any reason to go into a Christian school. I'm out there to share what's helped me. And if I'm going to do that, I need to go to people who haven't heard.*

(Don, Physical Education Student Teacher, Queensland)

Another factor which influences a potential recruit's subjective warrant for physical education is how they perceive their body and appearance in terms of their match to what they believe is appropriate for the profession. Recruits into PETE, and those perceived to *belong*, tend to have a 'look'. See Box 6.2 below.

Box 6.2   *I wasn't recognised because I was a little bit overweight and I didn't have trendy clothes and work out in the gym. That's why I didn't move into that cliquey group. To be successful here you have to socialise, you have to wear the right clothes and have gone to a recognised school. I find that hard to cope with. If you are thin and look sporty . . . Louisa came later (into the program) but she fitted straight into the group because she had that PE look and that is what counts . . . and (they) live off their image that they are a phys. ed. or . . . they run every day. Well, I run every day and do that sort of stuff.*

(Gail, Physical Education Student Teacher, Victoria)

The 'look' entails being slim/mesomorphic and dressed in designer sports clothes. To use Hargreave's (1986) terminology, the bodies which *belong* are those which are *schooled*, according to popular stereotypes, in terms of clothes and exercise and, more importantly, they are *known* to be schooled as a symbol of acceptability. A senior administrator of physical education in an Australian university endorsed that a successful PETE student would be: 'a person who was bright and outgoing—I think that's fairly important; a person who just has a certain feel—they look alive, they look vital. If you're going to convince people about the benefits of physical activity, the role model's important' (Macdonald 1993, p 265).

Observations of PETE suggest that there are strong regulating mechanisms in place which act to condone and condemn particular physical or corporeal presentations and thereby facilitate or discourage entry into the profession. We note that these corporeal presentations conform to narrow, ultimately male-defined notions of appropriate masculinities and femininities. Dewar (1990) explains that the subjective warrant for physical education is implicated in the reproduction of: 'a number of physical education programs in schools and universities that select and reward a relatively small number of individuals who tend to be privileged by, among other things, their bodies, gender, social class position, race and physical abilities' (p 77). We are concerned here with the impact that this pattern of recruitment has on the potential impact of physical education.

In some universities and colleges of Australia and New Zealand aspiring PETE students must satisfy not only the academic criteria for selection but also a series of tests of physical performance and perhaps even an interview. Such physical performance tests are usually defended by the rhetoric that 'a PE teacher needs to be able to demonstrate skills and activities' and accordingly must 'fit the physical bill'. The interviews are claimed to weed out obvious unsuitable applicants. There are those of the view that most of these tests and interviews represent a 'cloning process' whereby the PETE faculty members effectively select potential students who are most like them (or rather how they remember themselves to have been a generation earlier). The result of this process is a lack of heterogeneity among PETE students.

over to you

Look around your own institution. Is there a recognisable homogeneity of students? For example, are your classmates mainly white, Anglo-Saxon, Christian, neatly presented activity seekers? Was there an interview for your course? If there are some students who 'don't fit the mould', how did they get in? How are they treated by staff and fellow students?

There is some limited research evidence that physical education teachers who are considerably overweight are less effective in the teaching of health education concepts to secondary school students (see Box 6.3).

> ### Box 6.3
> *One interesting study by Melville & Maddalozzo (1988) is worth describing here. What Melville & Maddalozzo did was to have 850 high school students (in the United States) view one of two 20-minute videotapes. The first half of the tape focussed on the importance of flexibility to health and sports performance, while the second half focussed on body composition and its relationship to health and sports performance and on the role diet and exercise can play in controlling body composition. The difference between the videotapes was the physical appearance of the teacher. The same teacher taught the two lessons, but in one he was his normal slim, mesomorphic self, whereas in the other he wore what was called a 'fat suit' which made him look considerably fatter. After the lesson all students were given a content examination and a questionnaire to assess their knowledge and attitudes. According to the researchers, the results supported the hypothesis that the appearance of fatness in a physical education teacher does affect the teaching of exercise concepts to high school students. Also, data showed them to be very aware of the different fitness levels of the instructor in the tapes and strongly intolerant of the seemingly poorly conditioned person. They did not think he was an appropriate role model, they tended not to like him, they did not perceive him to be particularly knowledgeable, and they indicated that they would be less influenced by his message to exercise. (Melville & Maddalozzo 1988, p 351)*

Presumably the 'do as I say not as I do' does not hold well with adolescents. However, as far as we know, there is no evidence that being an able performer of physical activities is essential for a physical education teacher. Sure, it might make some intuitive sense, but we are reminded of the many coaches who themselves are not star performers. In our view, physical education would benefit from having a more heterogeneous PETE student population.

Values and beliefs about physical education

As suggested by Don (see Box 6.1), PETE students come to their course with strongly held belief structures and ideologies. In coming to understand who is recruited into physical education, an important question is what do recruits believe is the purpose of physical education? Research suggests that such beliefs are difficult to change. As one student put it: 'I think that my concept of phys. ed. was always just sport and that was cultivated through ... my experiences at school, and it takes a lot to break that down I think, and just to get the feel of phys. ed. being *education* as well as *sport*'. As the apprenticeship of observation suggests, recruits have spent many hours in primary and secondary school physical education where they have formed attitudes and preferences about the purposes and practices of physical education.

Most PETE students define the purposes of physical education as developing body awareness, coordination, fitness, and skills for lifetime sporting participation, having fun and social interaction, and getting a break from academic classes. Such conservative and limiting purposes, we would argue, reflect the PETE students' schooling and wider societal expectations associated with, for example, the discourses of competitive sport. Not surprisingly, most PETE students feel comfortable with approaches to physical education with which they are familiar, and usually want to reproduce, as teachers, the kinds of experiences they had as pupils. In looking more closely at the replicative cycles in physical education, studies have recorded PETE students' comfort with the more traditional games- and sports-based curriculum models and with custodial orientations which favour the preservation of existing policies and practices (Lawson 1988; Macdonald & Tinning 1995; Placek et al 1995).

These beliefs about, and priorities for, physical education are at odds with contemporary school syllabuses and have been criticised by those with an interest in equity. Throughout Australia and New Zealand, curriculum documents outline physical education as presenting a range of knowledge and experiences which teach pupils to be critical consumers of the physical activity culture. It has been argued by critical and feminist researchers that many of the reproductive discourses and practices of physical education have served to alienate teachers, PETE students and pupils who do not conform to the elitist, competitive, sportist, Anglo-centric and heterosexual practices in physical education (Swan 1996; Dewar 1989; Dodds 1993; Evans 1993; Fernandez-Balboa 1997; Flintoff 1993; Macdonald & Tinning 1995; Sparkes et al 1990; Wright 1995).

What happens when a student's beliefs are at variance with those espoused in their PETE program? We understand that there will be different values and beliefs expressed within a given PETE program by different faculty members in the courses they teach. Nevertheless it can be said that there is usually a dominant discourse which is represented in PETE courses and it is a discourse with which most students readily identify. We also know that in the main students resist alternatives to the dominant discourse. Therefore, if a student teacher understands physical education as sport, the sports education model of physical education will attract their interest whereas a movement education emphasis may not. A challenge for PETE programs with a commitment to a more contemporary physical education is: How can student teachers be persuaded to see broader and alternative conceptions?

Academic and life worlds of being a student teacher

The earlier comments of Gail and Don (see Boxes 6.1–2) remind us that while they are PETE students, they are also maintaining a lifestyle that is shaped by a range of discourses. A lifestyle can be thought of as a set of particular regimens, and lifestyle choices illuminate how people establish and maintain their identities. For many PETE students, due to their age, ethnicity and socio-economic status, their lifestyles are dominated by university study, part-time employment, sporting commitments and socialising. However, for others university commitments must be managed alongside long hours of paid employment or family responsibilities. The following discussion focusses on some of the ways in which the personal identity of the student interfaces with the professional world of PETE.

The body

The body has become a public symbol of personal qualities such as health, sexuality, industry, laziness, care, self-control, achievement or ability (Bellah et al 1985; Kirk & Colquhoun 1989). In postmodern times the body has become fully available to be 'worked on' by individuals through avenues such as exercise, diet and clothing. This work is particularly significant for physical educators. To be considered a good teacher in this field, one must, literally, look the part—mesomorphic, able-bodied, heterosexual, physically capable and physically fit. The discourses which drive how the body is to be managed and scrutinised are largely those from the health, science and medical industries. As suggested earlier, these discourses have come to occupy an increasingly privileged position within PETE programs and thereby serve to reinforce students' understandings of how they should know and judge their own and others' bodies. These discourses have consequences not only for those who choose to become physical educators but also for the practices or activities they should engage in.

Corporeal presentation is also an avenue through which one expresses and judges sexuality and moral worth. Writers working from feminist perspectives argue that notions of body shape, presentation and adornments are powerful in determining who is vested with popularity and authority. For women it could be argued that conformity to the specific construction of femininity for PETE students (e.g. trim, brown legs, long hair and dressed in line with the current fashion trend) is crucial to the sense of themselves as women given that the other qualities they may possess, such as athletic prowess, are potentially undermining of more dominant constructions of femininity. For male students, their bodies are symbols of masculinist notions of sporting prowess and physical fitness on the one hand, while on the other provide a vehicle for risk-taking behaviours associated with, for example, sport and alcohol.

Mellor & Shilling (1997) argue that the contemporary body, the fit, mesomorphic body, promises control, power and moral renewal. The moral dimension of the body was mentioned by Don in his Christian commitment to keep fit and not eat 'junk'. These views of the body can have a pervasive impact on how easily the student moves in and out of the PETE context and how they question, condone or reject the knowledge, traditions and beliefs embedded in the PETE culture.

Lifestyle

Lifestyle choices illuminate how individuals establish and reflexively maintain their identity. For example, Gail's sense of self related not only to how she believed she was perceived but also to the physically active lifestyle which was required in order to look appropriate as a PETE student. Just as there are pressures for the body to conform to dominant presentations, so too are there regulating mechanisms shaping a range of lifestyle decisions.

What are considered 'appropriate' physical activities for inclusion in one's lifestyle are gendered. Within our culture masculine activities preclude things artistic and by association feminine. Similarly, women's participation in activities typically played by men such as football or cricket challenges acceptable behaviours. For both sexes transgression of these expectations calls into question the students' sexuality thereby reflecting homophobic tendencies.

The lifestyle choices which are frequently held in esteem by the majority of students are those of hegemonic masculine culture and, with it, the masculine body (raucous behaviour, bodily abuse, sexual conquest and excessive alcohol consumption). An annual PETE students' ball, aptly entitled the 'Jock's Ball', makes presentations to 'the Golden Jock' who 'has helped make the Department's social life what it is'; the 'Desperate Lover' who 'tries hard but has failed to put a score on the board'; 'Animal Act'; 'Yuppie'; and 'Physical Wreck' who 'abuses their body with copious amounts of alcohol'. What do these awards tell us is being valued by the student body? These behaviours contrasted with and clearly undermined elements of the official PETE and physical education curriculum such as emphases on health, sensitivity and equity, pupil interests and enjoyment, and cooperation.

It should be noted, however, that for some young women and men, this culture is considered inappropriate, contradictory and alienating. For example, male and female Christian students in one university (see Macdonald & Kirk 1999) had lifestyles which were dominated by their commitment to their religion and church, a commitment which they felt was not sufficiently recognised by, nor consistent with, the university curriculum and culture. The Christian students lifestyle decisions included the repudiation of alcohol and pre-marital sex and valued health, sacrifice and moderation. Thus, not only were the students reflecting the embodiment of a worthy physical educator but they had internalised this alongside the tenets of a Christian lifestyle. But such students would be in the minority in most PETE programs where hegemonic masculinity dominates (see, for example, Swan 1995; Browne 1998).

Studentship

Although PETE students have generally been academically successful in school, university commitments alongside other interests and responsibilities encourage students to manage their university program in particular ways. Graber (1991) refers to the importance of studentship, interpreted as an array of strategic behaviours that student teachers may employ to move through their course with greater ease, more success and less effort. More specifically, with PETE students Graber observed behaviours such as taking short cuts, cheating, colluding, psyching-out, and image projection in which the student strategically adopts responsible behaviours. You may employ these behaviours, among others, for a variety of reasons, including pressures of meeting others' expectations, getting good grades, and completing a heavy workload.

Studentship has the potential to limit or curtail university learning. It is perhaps the responsibility of both staff and students to acknowledge this aspect of PETE in order to structure a more genuine and supportive learning environment.

 over to you

What do you consider to be the contradictions in your lifestyle and the values outlined by the course with respect to health, sexuality, equity, cooperation etc? Perhaps you could discuss your responses in a tutorial. Attention could be given to making explicit the tacit, experiential knowledge of all in the class.

Summary

- The subjective warrant is a framework through which to address recruitment into PETE.
- In Australia those attracted to PETE tend to be young, able-bodied, lean/muscular, upper/middle class, relatively high academic achieving Caucasians.
- Students are attracted to PETE with a view to maintaining their connection with physical activity and sport.
- The personal identity of PETE students interfaces with the professional world of physical education through the management of their bodies, lifestyle and student behaviours.

References

Armour, K. & Jones, R. (1998). *Physical Education Teachers' Lives and Careers*. London: Falmer Press.

Australian Council of Deans of Education (1998). *Preparing a Profession*. Canberra: Australian Council of Deans.

Belka, D., Lawson, H. & Lipnickey, S.C. (1991). 'An exploratory study of undergraduate recruitment into several major programs at one university'. *Journal of Teaching in Physical Education*, 10, pp 286–306.

Bellah, R.N., Madsen, R., Sullivan, W., Swindler, A. & Tipton, S.M. (1985). *Habits of the Heart: Individualism and Commitment in American Life*. Berkeley, CA: Harper & Row.

Brown, L. (1998). 'Boy's "training": The inner sanctum'. In C. Hickey, L. Fitzclarence & R. Matthews (eds), *Where The Boys Are: Masculinities, Sport and Education* (pp 83–97). Geelong: Deakin Centre for Education and Change.

Dewar, A. (1989). 'Recruitment in physical education teaching: Toward a critical approach'. In T. Templin & P. Schempp (eds), *Socialization into Physical Education: Learning to Teach* (pp 39–58). Indianapolis: Benchmark Press.

Dewar, A. (1990). 'Oppression and privilege in physical education: Struggles in the negotiation of gender in a university programme'. In D. Kirk & R. Tinning (eds) *Physical Education, Curriculum and Culture: Critical Issues in the Contemporary Crisis* (pp 67–100). Lewes: Falmer Press.

Dewar, A. & Lawson, H. (1984). 'The subjective warrant and recruitment into physical education'. *Quest*, 36, pp 15–25.

Dodds, P. (1993). 'Removing the ugly "isms" from your gym: Thoughts for teachers on equity'. In J. Evans (ed.), *Equality, Education and Physical Education*, pp 28–42. London: Falmer Press.

Evans, J. (1993). *Equality, Education and Physical Education*. London: Falmer Press.

Fernandez-Balboa, J-M. (1997). 'Physical education teacher preparation in the postmodern era: Toward a critical pedagogy'. In J-M. Fernandez-Balboa (ed.), *Critical Postmodernism in Human Movement, Physical Education and Sport*, pp 121–139. Albany: State University of New York.

Flintoff, A. (1993). 'Sexism and homophobia in physical education: The challenge for teacher educators'. *Physical Education Review*, 17(2), pp 97–105.

Graber, K. (1991). 'Studentship in preservice teacher education: A qualitative study of undergraduate students in physical education'. *Research Quarterly of Exercise and Sport*, 62, pp 41–51.

Hargreaves, J. (1986). 'Schooling the body'. *Sport, Power and Culture*. Cambridge: Polity Press, pp 161–181 & 241–245.

Hutchinson, G. (1993). 'Prospective teachers' perspectives on teaching physical education: An interview study on the recruitment phase of teacher socialization'. *Journal of Teaching in Physical Education*, 12, pp 344–354.

Kirk, D. & Colquhoun, D. (1989). 'Healthism and daily physical education'. *British Journal of Sociology of Education*, 10(4), pp 417–434.

Lave, J. & Wenger, E. (1992) *Situated Learning*. Cambridge: Cambridge University Press.

Lawson, H. (1988). 'Occupational socialization, cultural studies and the physical education curriculum'. *Journal of Teaching in Physical Education*, 7(4), pp 265–288.

Lortie, D. (1975). *Schoolteacher: A sociological study*. Chicago: University of Chicago Press.

Macdonald, D. (1993). 'Knowledge, gender and power in physical education teacher education'. *Australian Journal of Education*, 37(3), pp 259–278.

Macdonald, D., Abernethy, P. & Bramich, K. (1998). 'A profile of first year human movement studies students: A case study'. *Chronicle of Physical Education in Higher Education*, 9(2), pp 16–19.

Macdonald, D. & Tinning, R. (1995). 'Physical education teacher education and the trend to proletatianization: A case study'. *Journal of Teaching in Physical Education*, 15, pp 98–118.

Macdonald, D. & Kirk, D. (1999). 'Pedagogy, the body and Christian identity'. *Sport, Education and Society*, 4(2), pp 131–142.

Mellor, P. & Shilling, C. (1997). *Re-forming the Body: Religion, Community and Modernity*. London: Sage.

Melville, D. & Maddalozzo, J. (1988). 'The effects of a physical educator's appearance of body fatness on communicating exercise concepts to high school students'. *Journal of Teaching in Physical Education*, 7(4), pp 343–352.

Placek, J., Dodds, P., Doolittle, S., Portman, P., Ratcliffe, T. & Pinkman, K. (1995). 'Teaching recruits' physical education backgrounds and beliefs about purposes for their subject matter'. *Journal of Teaching in Physical Education*, 14, pp 246–261.

Sikes, P. (1988). 'Growing old gracefully? Age, identity and physical education'. In J. Evans (ed.), *Teachers, Teaching and Control in Physical Education* (pp 21–40). London: Falmer Press.

Sparkes, A., Templin, T. & Schempp, P. (1990). 'The problematic nature of a career in a marginal subject: Some implications for teacher education programmes'. *Journal of Education for Teaching*, 16(1), pp 3–28.

Swan, P. (1995). *Studentship and oppositional behaviour within physical education teacher education: A case study*, and *Between the rings and under the gym mat: A narrative*. Doctoral dissertation, Deakin University.

Templin, T., Woodford, R. & Mulling, C. (1982). 'On becoming a physical educator: Occupational choice and the anticipatory socialization process'. *Quest*, 34, pp 119–133.

Wright, J. (1995). 'A feminist poststructuralist methodology for the study of gender construction in physical education: Description of a study'. *Journal of Teaching in Physical Education*, 15, pp 1–24.

Further reading

Benn, T. (1996). 'Muslim women and physical education in initial teacher training'. *Sport, Education and Society*, 1(1), pp 5–21.

Clarke, G. (1996). 'Conforming and contesting with a difference: How lesbian students and teachers manage their idenity'. *International Studies in Sociology of Education*, 6(2), pp 191–209.

Skelton, A. (1993). 'On becoming a male physical education teacher: The informal culture of students and the construction of hegemonic masculinity'. *Gender and Edcuation*, 5(3), pp 289–303.

Squires, S. & Sparkes, A. (1996). 'Circles of silence: Sexual identity in physical education and sport'. *Sport, Education and Society*, 1(1), pp 77–101.

section
three

chapter seven

objectives

By the end of this chapter you should be able to:

- discuss the notion of identity and how this relates to the experiences of young people in contemporary society;
- understand the diversity of backgrounds and experiences which secondary school students bring to physical education lessons;
- recognise the relationship between students' identities and their knowledge, skills, and attitudes in relation to physical activity and physical education;
- begin to reflect on ways in which physical education might be responsive to the diverse interests, experiences and needs of students.

The purpose of this section is to provide some insight that will help us better understand the students who come to our physical education classes: who are they? where do they come from? what do they like? how do they think of themselves? what can be said about the world in which they live and the way they engage with it? what sets of values and beliefs do they bring about physical activity, physical education and schools, and what implications will this have for teaching physical education?

An important starting point is to recognise that we cannot talk about or respond to students as though they are all the same. Up until recently the literature on young people has tended to talk about adolescents as though they are a homogeneous group with characteristics shared by all members of the group—no matter what their social class or cultural heritage, no matter whether they are female or male, able-bodied or disabled, and with no regard to their sexual preference. While it is still useful to talk generally about concerns that are shared by many young people in contemporary Australian and New Zealand society, we also need to acknowledge that there are as many differences within this age group as there are differences between this age group and other age groups.

For the purposes of this book we need to be talking about children and young people between about 10 and 18. The statistics do not always neatly cover this age range but the box below provides some figures which help to describe some of the characteristics of students participating in secondary schooling in Australia. They paint a picture of the diverse backgrounds of young Australians and some of the key issues with which young people have to deal.

 for your information

A profile of young people in Australia (ABS 1996)

- Young people between 15 and 24 make up 14% of the total population.
- Indigenous youth make up 2.7% of the youth population of Australia.
- 15% of young people are born overseas.
- More young people are staying on at school (71%).
- Young people are at higher risk of unemployment than older people (16% compared with 8% for all in 1997).
- Young women are at greater risk of violence than older women (figures for 1996; McLennan 1997).

How we describe young people and their behaviour usually depends on where we are speaking from and the context in which young people are being talked about. How young people see the world may be very different from the way in which the adults in their lives see it. However, how these adults, parents, teachers, police, health workers and politicians see young people and define their behaviour will determine how they will be treated in families, in the streets, in schools and in legislation. Much of the sociology literature on youth, for instance, points to the ways in which adolescence is often defined as a 'social problem'. The same writers argue for a 'more compassionate and reasonable understanding of what it means to be young in a rapidly changing world'. In particular, they ask that we make the effort to see the world from the point of view of young people.

Recent legislation designed to specifically control the behaviour of young people in public spaces can be seen as an example of the ways in which adults and young people might define the same behaviour differently. Whereas young people may describe gathering in groups to talk in malls as a way of meeting up with friends and chatting away from the supervision of adults, adults may define this behaviour as threatening and likely to lead to violent situations. It is the adult definitions, however, which have power and in this case have led to laws to control their actions. As another example in the context of schools, failure to wear the physical education uniform may be construed by teachers as lack of respect for them and the subject and evidence of a poor attitude to participation in physical activity. From the students' point of view, however, it may be more about embarrassment—wearing clothing that makes them feel physically exposed and uncomfortable and hating the process of changing in front of peers, as well as wearing clothing which bears little resemblance to the kinds of clothing they would wear in any other contexts in their lives.

It seems important to begin to understand where students are coming from to be able to program and plan physical education experiences which are likely to engage their interest and meet their needs.

Young people—who are they?

One powerful source of definitions about adolescence comes from developmental psychology. Within this field the developmental notion of adolescence is used to explain young people's behaviour. A developmental approach to adolescence describes it as a transitional stage between childhood and adulthood, characterised by specific tasks which need to be completed before successfully achieving the maturity of adulthood. While it is useful to be able to talk about a period in individuals' lives which seems to mark the transition from childhood to adulthood, one of the main criticisms of the developmental approach is that it takes the characteristics and tasks of adolescence to be the same for all people across cultures and socio-economic groups and for all young women as compared with all young men. Even a few examples serve to show that this does not fit with the realities of young people's lives. For example, the experience of a young man recently arrived in Australia from rural Cambodia will be vastly different from that of an affluent young woman at an elite school in a large Australian city; the experience of a young mother trying to complete her final year at school will be different from that of a young male Aborigine living with his traditional community in the Northern Territory.

Joanna Wyn & Rob White (1997) suggest that a more useful way to think about 'youth' is to understand it as a *relational* concept whereby how we understand particular ages changes over time, from one cultural context to another and in relation to different social institutions. For instance, young people may be expected to be very different people in the context of their homes as compared with their schools or even their work lives. Young people's everyday experience, the way they make sense of the many different social worlds they inhabit, is a product of their own histories and the social institutions with which they interact—these institutions include the electronic and print media, the family, schools—and so on. This means that the changes in behaviours that developmentalists like to see as biological or psychological are often largely produced by the contexts in which young people live.

In addition, the kinds of challenges that young people are likely to experience are those which continue throughout life rather than being limited to a particular life stage. For instance, bodies continue to change, and sometimes dramatically; in contemporary society a job is no longer something achieved in young adulthood (marking the end of adolescence) which one holds onto throughout life; young people are remaining at home longer, returning home for brief periods of their lives; and people are partnering, marrying, separating sometimes frequently throughout their lives. These can no longer be regarded as tasks to be completed once and for all to achieve adulthood.

Even those physical changes which seem to be universal will differ in their meaning for different individuals and different groups of people. In some cultures, in some families and in some peer groups pubertal changes will have a far greater significance than in others. For instance, for one girl menstruation may mean little more than the inconvenience of wearing a pad, for another it may be seen as a significant move to adulthood and preparation for motherhood, while for yet another it may be a traumatic experience marked by pain and embarrassment. In traditional indigenous cultures, the transition from child to adult may be clearly marked and celebrated, in other cultures there are more ambiguities about a young female or male person's developing sexuality.

Most of the young people in secondary schools will, however, have common challenges which are to do with expanding social, financial and academic demands and with increasing tensions between their own desires and their parents' expectations around independence, responsibility and security (see Glover et al 1998, p 12). As it is for most of our lives such challenges can be sources of enjoyment and pleasure but also of unhappiness, anxiety and anger. During this time there are also likely to be changes in relationships with parents and peers, with more time being spent with peers. Not surprisingly peers are going to become important influences, often more so than parents, on what young people think and do.

These personal challenges also need to be understood in the context of contemporary Western society—what some have called the postmodern world. This is a world characterised by rapid social, economic and cultural change and where the media and other forms of information technology such as the Internet have become important sources of education, perhaps even more important than the print media and schools. It has been suggested that in the postmodern consumer society the body has become increasingly important as an indicator of an individual's worth. The body provides evidence of personal values such as self-discipline through evidence of work on the body and of status and wealth through clothing, cosmetic use, comportment and grooming. Physical education becomes important in this because of the centrality of the body to its practice. Later in Section 3 questions will be raised about the kinds of values that are promoted or contested in physical education in relation to the postmodern disciplined (worked-on) body.

Identity

The concept of identity has been used to describe the ways in which individuals deal with the complex and multiple contexts in which they live. Identity has now become understood not so much as a fixed set of personality traits but as a much more dynamic set of meanings about how we see ourselves and how others see us (and let us know this). It has to do with how we locate ourselves in relation to social groups, whom we see as being like us and whom we classify as different from us/'other than us'. These classifications are closely linked to relations of power. Some cultural meanings have a particular value in some contexts and not others. And some contexts are more important when it comes to access to cultural and social 'goods' (social and economic power, for instance). While being an excellent skateboard rider, for instance, may have a great deal of kudos among a male adolescent peer group, being clearly identified as a 'skatie' by carrying a skateboard on public transport may incur a disproportionate amount of unwanted attention from security or police officers.

Rather than being fixed we are working with an understanding of an individual's identity as fluid and dynamic, constantly negotiated and performed in relation to changing contexts and circumstances. Thus one of the authors' sons, Tim, negotiates a different set of relationships (enacts a different identity) with his skateboarder friends than he does as a son in her family, and this again is likely to be different from that negotiated with teachers at school. A more pertinent example perhaps is that of young people from homes where cultural values are very different from those of their peer group or the school more generally. These students recognise the different expectations of these different contexts and are often very adept at enacting the different identities and different relationships necessary to each of these contexts. This is not, however, without a cost. Having to enact an identity at school that repudiates your cultural or sexual identity, because it is the only way you can be accepted or even safe, is very distressing for many young people. On the other hand, teachers may find the identities constructed by young people puzzling or incomprehensible, and even threatening to what they believe to be their identity as a teacher.

The resources that we use to shape our identities are developed over time through interactions with other people, including what others say and do, but also through interacting with what is written, photographed, filmed, created as art and so on. In this process, language is clearly important; but also other sources of meaning making such as dress, gestures and television images provide the resources from which we construct identity. For instance, young people come to adopt a range of gestures, forms of speech ('cool'), dress (baggy clothes and trousers that have to hang off your hips, hats backwards, forwards, no hats) which distinguish one group from another and which identify each teenager as belonging (or not belonging) to a particular group (home boys, skaties, jocks etc.). At the time of writing these were all current terms. They may no longer be so, but this indicates how among some cultural or sub-cultural groups the means of identification change rapidly.

One of the questions that arises in relation to identity is why individual young people choose to construct their identities in certain ways rather than others. The following quote, while talking specifically about the construction of masculinity, describes how Rob & Pam Gilbert (1998) explain the process by which the social practices and meanings associated with every aspect of boys' lives—schools, families, sport and so on—work to shape boys' identities.

> No one of these practices is all-powerful in itself. Boys will respond to them in active, selective and even oppositional ways . . . However if these practices are structured by a dominant view of what it is to be masculine, their combined effect will narrow the possibilities for boys rather than expand them. To construct and maintain a sense of who they are, boys must draw on the available terms, categories and ways of thinking, acting and interacting which these various contexts provide, including the specific forms of masculinity associated with them. (p 51)

In all of this the body is becoming increasingly important as a source of identity, both in terms of how bodies look and how we feel in and about our bodies. Chris Shilling (1993) argues that the more people attach value to how we look and what we do with our bodies, the greater the likelihood that our self-identities will be tied to them. Our bodies can be important in the sense of power (or lack of it) we have in relation to others. Bob Connell (1995) points to the ways in which boys learn through sport particular masculine embodiments of force and skill. Those boys whose bodies do not measure up—that is, are small, show no signs of muscularity—may be subject to ridicule. Sport thus becomes one of the contexts for reinforcing dominant forms of masculinity and marginalising others.

Gender and sexual identity

One of the main criticisms of the developmental approach to adolescence is that it is based on masculine experience. For instance, one of its central assumptions is that of a progression from dependence to independence. Carol Gilligan (1982) has argued that women are more likely to seek connectedness—that is, to develop interdependence rather than independence. Either way, the implication is that if you do not achieve one or the other, depending on the schema, you are not normal. Developmental psychology also assumes that a normal sexual identity is heterosexual.

Another way of thinking is to regard gender and sexuality as socially constructed and see masculinity and femininity as constructed in relation to each other. As evidence of this, cross-cultural and historical studies demonstrate how the meanings associated with what it is to be female or male have changed over time and differ from one culture to another. For instance, what it meant to be feminine for a middle class woman in 19th century England was to be fragile, incapable of exertion, dependent on men (fathers, brothers, husbands) and yet capable of having many healthy children. On the other hand, young middle class men were expected to be physically daring, courageous, independent and capable of developing careers to support a family. Contemporary young women in Australia may no longer regard it as necessary to be physically fragile but dominant notions of femininity are still constructed around heterosexuality, shaping the body to attract the attention of men and being nurturing and supportive; while in most social contexts young men are still expected to be strong, independent and capable of earning enough money to support a family.

These ideas about femininity and masculinity are clearly changing and are more powerful for some groups than for others. However, power relations between men and women and between different groups of men and different groups of women are still important in understanding the behaviours and experience of female and male students in schools. Connell (1995) uses the concept of 'hegemonic masculinity' to describe how some forms of masculinity are prescribed as normal and highly valued and others— subordinated masculinities—are in contrast devalued, indeed stigmatised. Hegemonic masculinities may vary with age, location and culture but a good sense of what is valued can be found by looking at media images of prominent men. Wealth, power and, for some specific groups of men, physical prowess in sport are important in providing status in Western society. Increasingly a particular kind of physical appearance is also becoming important, especially for young men.

Subordinated masculinities vary from one context to another but among boys and young men are generally associated with those who do not demonstrate physical prowess in sport, may indicate a liking for and ability in traditionally female occupations, are interested in intellectual or academic work. A range of derogatory terms such as 'nerd' or 'poofter' serve to indicate attitudes and to marginalise those males who do not 'fit' with hegemonic notions of masculinity. At the same time terms such as these, together with harassment and violence, serve to demonstrate for all boys the dangers of being different. As pointed out in the discussion on identity, the social practices associated with sport can be very important in Western society in reinforcing hegemonic notions of masculinity and in perpetuating homophobic attitudes. Sport, as a part of physical education, can also be implicated in this process.

Where wealth, power and sporting prowess are markers of hegemonic forms of masculinity, ideal notions of what it means to be female are also constructed in relation to these. Women's magazines provide constant instruction on how to be attractive to such men. This advice usually suggests ways of becoming more physically attractive—through advice on diet, exercise, dress and behaviour in and out of bed. It might also provide information about how to cook exciting food and to support a male partner in other ways. These magazines and other media texts such as film and television produce messages about femininity which assume a heterosexual women who is slim and fits a particular and arguably narrow understanding of physical attractiveness. These provide a set of confusing discourses from which girls draw to think about and evaluate their bodies. Some examples of the consequences of this are evident in Figure 7.1, a quote from Maria Pallotta-Chiarolli's collection of *Girls' Talk.*

dear diary

It's the fourth day of the holidays and I am bored **BEYOND BELIEF.** Mum says I'm not fat. She says I'm constipated. I bought this really dumb workout tape and I can't even do half the things on it. I think I should get my stomach stapled. I feel really spaced out.

My body is really weird. Everyone else gets fat on their thighs and their bum and I've got no bum and skinny legs and I just get fat on my stomach and abdomen (like some of the Koori girls at schools). Mum says some Irish women are like that, broad shoulders and busty with not much waist and skinny legs.

Emily's mum says it's all about racism and who won what war when and made out that their culture's woman was the best shape. So now the Coke bottle is the best shape and that's a war too. Emily's mum is a feminist but she did have a nose job so my mum reckons she mustn't be a fanatic. (I just think she must have had a really big nose.)

Figure 7.1 Excerpt from *Girls' Talk: Young woman speak their hearts and minds,* edited by Maria Pallotta-Chiarolli (1998, Sydney: Finch Publishing, pp 23–24).

The ideal body promoted on television, film and in magazines is not an image or even a set of behaviours that most women can live up to, although many young and old women spend their lives trying. While these images may suggest that girls and women need to exercise and often do specific exercises to shape different parts of their bodies, they are rarely images associating physical activity with power. The message for young women is most often that physical activity is to improve the way you look rather than to improve your strength or power. Images of female athletes are important because they do demonstrate women who use their bodies powerfully. On the other hand, the commentary and forms of coverage often minimises this effect and emphasises the more feminine aspects such as how they look, their relationships and their emotionality (e.g. Hargreaves 1994; Lenskyj 1998). In the following quotes (see Boxes 7.1 and 7.2) the words used to describe the male tennis players and their actions draw on metaphors of battle and dramatic action. While to a lesser degree this is the case for the description of Steffi Graf's win over Monica Seles, the language used to describe Seles' achievements draws on stereotypical notions of femininity which trivialise her behaviour, 'squeaking and giggling', and make reference to her body shape and weight.

Box 7.1 **Terminator Sampras blows Agassi away**

Knuckles bleeding, aces knifing through the whipping wind, Pete Sampras outlasted Andre Agassi to capture a third US Open tennis title here yesterday and again the world No.1 ranking in the esteem of his greatest rival, if not the rankings themselves. Sampras spilled blood diving for a volley, rocked Agassi with 24 aces, and when they engaged in the most crucial base line rallies beat the defending champion at his own game to win . . . two months after taking his third straight Wimbledon. (The Australian, 12 September 1995, p 22)

Box 7.2 **Graf wins lead role in theatre of dreams**

Steffi Graf proved a lot of things for herself and for women's tennis here yesterday when she recovered from a second-set thrashing to beat Monica Seles . . . in a dramatic US Open final that earned the German her fourth grand slam title in New York and her third of the year.

. . .

It was obvious from the moment she (Seles) appeared in that exhibition against Navratilova in July that the talent had been preserved even if the waistline had expanded, and both were much in evidence as Seles pounded her way, squeaking and giggling, through the Canadian Open, losing fewer games than any champion in the history of the tournament. (The Australian, 11 September 1995, p 28)

School playgrounds and classrooms are also important sites for the construction and valuing of specific forms of masculinities and femininities rather than others. Bullying, sexual harassment, interactions between students and teachers and the curriculum itself can all contribute to maintaining narrow forms of gender. For instance, boys who do not demonstrate physical toughness when injured in a physical education class may be ridiculed by other students. Even comments like 'C'mon, get on with it, you're not hurt that badly', 'Boys don't cry', 'You're acting like a girl' or 'You've got to be tough' from the teacher reinforce ideas that boys must be tough, must endure pain stoically and that conversely girls are weak.

Ethnicity

All of us have an ethnic background in terms of our belonging to or identifying with a particular cultural group with a specific set of values, behaviours and customs. The term 'ethnic' or 'ethnic background' is often used to indicate non-English-speaking background, a person who is not seen as or does not identify with the majority ethnic group whose first language is English. Here we will use the term 'ethnic minority' to refer to those young people whose background is different from the majority Anglo-Australian population. Indigenous Australians are usually categorised separately in recognition of their status as first peoples. As a cultural minority group with different linguistic and cultural traditions from the majority of Australians, indigenous Australians share a number of issues with ethnic minority groups including discrimination and racism. Being in a minority means that the interests, needs and experiences of that minority are often disregarded in schools.

Australia has been described as having one of the world's most diverse populations in terms of ethnicity, culture and national origin. Fifteen per cent of young people are born overseas and around 3 per cent of young people identify as Aboriginal (ABS 1997). Young people who were born overseas are now more likely to come from Asian countries (43 per cent) than European countries (25 per cent).

Australia's policies have moved from a position encouraging the assimilation of migrant groups into an Anglo-Australian culture to one which now recognises and values a diversity of ethnic groups and cultural values. Policies, however, do not ensure shifts in attitudes and in the relationships between white Australians and migrants and white Australians and Aboriginal Australians. Schools have a major part to play in creating safe and supportive environments where difference is acknowledged and valued. As Guerra & White (1995) suggest, this implies in education that 'equal weight needs to be given to encouraging the things we have in common, the preservation and sharing of our differences and the benefits attained from them, and openness to cultural change and development' (p 4). Each state in Australia has a plan for implementing multiculturalism in their education systems. In general terms multicultural education is expected to assist people to understand, appreciate, accept and tolerate other cultures in the environment which they share with other people of other ethnic, racial and cultural backgrounds.

The *NSW Multicultural Education Strategic Plan 1993–1997* provides a typical example of the approaches that state education systems have adopted to implementing multiculturalism in education. Its main objectives are as follows:

- *all students understand the role that cultural and linguistic diversity plays in the lives of individuals, their families and the nation; and*
- *students from language background other than English (LBOTE) have equal access to educational opportunity. (*Multicultural Education Strategic Plan *1992, p 3)*

In order to get both results, the New South Wales public school system and its component schools require strategies that could deliver the following results:

- *student learning is enriched by teachers and staff who are cross-culturally aware and able confidently and competently to impart multicultural values;*
- *student learning is assisted by curriculum and resources which reflect and promote diverse cultural and linguistic traditions;*
- *student learning is enhanced by research that identifies good practice and ensures quality of multicultural education;*
- *student learning is supported by the participation of parents and community in the life of their local school;*
- *student learning is enriched by schools and regions where excellence in multicultural education is recognised and acclaimed;*
- *student learning is supported by the provision of programs and teachers that meet the special teaching and learning needs of students from language background other than English (LBOTE).* (Multicultural Education Strategic Plan *1992, pp 4–14*)

Implementing a multicultural education approach is not always an easy task. It requires in the first instance that we recognise that traditional forms of schooling including physical education are imbued with cultural values and social practices derived from our British heritage. These values and practices may no longer be appropriate to the diverse values, experiences and needs of the students in physical education classes today.

oty over to you

How might the organisation, programming and teaching of physical education take account of the diverse cultural backgrounds of the students in a school?

Young people and schools

Most school/systems want to create safe and supportive environments for all their students. This is not a simple or easy task. As several commentators point out, schools are places which are very alienating for some students and, for others, places where they are harassed or where they simply do not feel recognised and respected. One Australia-wide project, the National Middle Schooling Project, was set up to enable teachers to work in collaboration with university academics to investigate how schooling can better meet the needs of young people in what have come to be called the 'middle years' of schooling—that is, those years which include upper primary and junior secondary education. The project worked on the assumption that 'conventional approaches to curriculum, pedagogy and organisation in these years are not always in the best interests of all young adolescents and their communities' (p 5).

One of the outcomes of the project was a recognition by some that the school could draw on students as resources to enhance the learning community of the school. Students were identified as 'active resources for learning—rather than passive recipients of knowledge'. In consultation with students and often parents, schools explored and reflected on ways of working with students that improved their learning outcomes. For instance, one significant issue to emerge was the need to provide students with support or to 'scaffold' their learning:

> project teachers quickly became aware that students need considerable support to be able to successfully engage in these processes (e.g. complex thinking and problem solving). They found that they needed to be as explicit as possible in outlining what was required in tasks and that various kinds of scaffolding needed to be provided to help students to successfully engage in complex processes. (Cormack et al 1998, quoted in Cumming 1998, p 8)

In relation to assessment, Cormack again wrote that:

> this project . . . revealed that assessment processes are a 'minefield' of cultural assumptions. Terms such as 'presenting professionally', 'thoughtfulness', 'cooperation' are typical assessment criteria that appear in the examples provided in this report. We came to see that being 'thoughtful', for example, might mean different things to different people in ways strongly influenced by factors such as cultural background, poverty, race and gender. It is all too easy for educators to interpret such criteria according to their own backgrounds and experience with negative consequences for some groups of students. (Cormack et al 1998, quoted in Cumming 1998, p 9)

In trying to understand why some students become 'troublemakers', Connell et al (1995) challenge the assumption that it is necessarily a problem with the family or with the student. They suggest that rather than thinking about troublemakers as particular kinds of persons with problems, it is more useful to think of troublemaking as 'a particular relationship, a form of *resistance* to conventional schooling' (p 84). Their interviews with students from a range of schools suggest that their resistance is developed in response to teachers which are strong on control (heavy-handed discipline), unfair in the allocation of rewards and punishment, rarely demonstrate respect for students, are boring and rarely listen to students.

Further insight into young people's experience of schooling is provided by the more recent Gatehouse Project (Glover et al 1998) conducted with schools in Victoria. While the project is specifically interested in adolescent depression and youth suicide, one of its main activities is to work with schools to create school environments which enhance young people's emotional well-being. As a starting point the research team asked students (13–14 years old) at 26 secondary schools to respond to a survey measuring a range of health outcomes including depression, deliberate self-harm, substance use and abuse, and smoking. Students were also asked to respond to a survey measuring their perception of the quality of their social environment. This survey specifically measured perceptions of victimisation, students' feelings about the quality of the relationships in their lives including family and friends, and feelings of being recognised and valued for their contributions to school activities.

The following graphs (Figures 7.2a–c) show results of a survey of students' experiences of security and victimisation and their perceptions of social connectedness. It is interesting to note the different forms that bullying and victimisation can take and disturbing to note the numbers of students involved.

The main messages for schools and teachers from this project are the importance of creating school environments and experiences of schooling which provide a sense of security, of social connectedness and of being recognised and valued.

The Commonwealth project on gender and school education conducted by Cherry Collins and her colleagues (1996) supports this. They found that sex-based harassment—that is, behaviours which are designed to embarass, frighten or hurt a student—were part of school life for 90 per cent of the students (approx. 10,000) who responded to their survey. Both sexes were equally likely to be the subject of harassment. Other major issues were about privacy and safety associated with using the toilets and, for girls, around

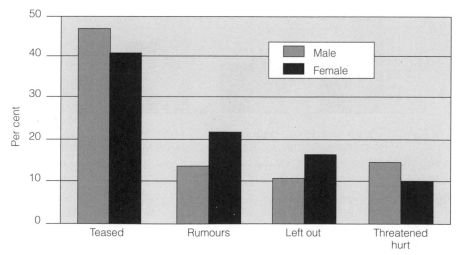

Source: Gatehouse Project, Centre for Adolescent Health, Victoria and Australian Institute of Family Studies.

Figure 7.2a   Security and victimisation

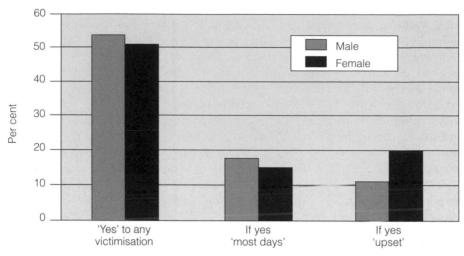

Source: Gatehouse Project, Centre for Adolescent Health, Victoria and Australian Institute of Family Studies.

Figure 7.2b   Students reporting 'yes' to: any victimisation; victimisation occurring most days; and finding victimisation upsetting

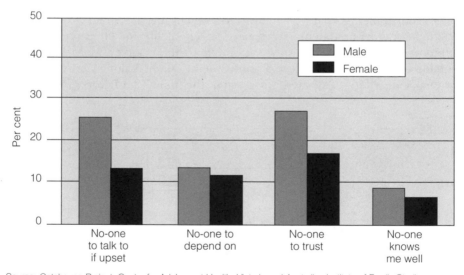

Source: Gatehouse Project, Centre for Adolescent Health, Victoria and Australian Institute of Family Studies.

Figure 7.2c   Social connectedness: perceptions of young people

menstruation. For instance, 77 per cent of the girls claimed that they could not access sanitary pads or tampons at school. They also found that boys' disruption of coeducational classes and their domination of resources were serious issues.

Physical education classes through their emphasis on physical performance, their opportunities for body contact and for public display have considerable potential for undermining students' emotional well-being and physical security. For instance, boys who do not fit with hegemonic notions of masculinity, including boys from Asian backgrounds, report fears of intimidation and physical abuse in physical education classes—particularly those which include only boys. Girls in mixed classes have reported avoiding physical education because of the ridicule they receive from male teachers and from the boys in the class when the lesson involves traditional male activities. In addition, Hargreaves (1984) suggests that girls and boys whose bodies do not conform to the mesomorphic ideal valued and often embodied by physical education teachers may feel marginalised. If early experiences of physical activity are influential on students' long-term participation, as has been suggested in the research, then it would seem important to take into account the diversity of students' experiences and needs to recognise and avoid both subtle and less than subtle practices which are likely to alienate some students. For instance, teachers need to recognise how their comments might affect students. Casual comments, perhaps intended as a joke, can be taken quite differently by a student who already feels uncertain about their skill, their body, and their place in the class.

On the other hand physical education classes have the potential to enhance students' emotional well-being if teachers and students construct an environment in which all students feel safe, and their efforts and contributions are valued. Moreover, some of the strategies the Gatehouse Project team suggests to provide students with opportunities for interaction with other members of class, such as small group work with different combinations of students, are already fundamental to teaching in physical education.

oty over to you

- Who gets constantly recognised within the class, at school assemblies etc.? Who does not?
- Whose performance is drawn attention to and in what ways?
- What consequences does this have for other members of the class?
- What activities are chosen for lessons and whose skills and abilities does this privilege?
- What room is there for recognising improvement?
- How is improvement recognised?
- Who gets most of the attention in class and why?
- What are the consequences of this for other students in terms of how they feel about themselves and how and what they learn?
- How are groups organised and what is the consequence of this for all members of the class?

> • To what extent are students consulted as decisions are made about content, teaching approaches and class organisation?

Summary

- How we see and engage with young people in physical education classes is very much predicated on our understanding of the ways in which they see themselves and their relationships with others, especially teachers and the meanings they associate with physical activity.
- Young people are not a homogeneous group but construct their identities in relation to key social categories such as gender, sexuality, ethnicity and race as well as their ability or perceived lack of it in physical activity, their body shape and so on.
- Particular identity constructions are not equally valued in Australian society, and this profoundly influences the experiences of young people in schools, including interactions with teachers and with other students.

References

Australian Bureau of Statistics (1997). *Participation in Sport and Physical Activities, Australia, 1995–96*. Canberra, Commonwealth of Australia.

Collins, C., Batten, M., Ainley, J. & Getty, C. (1996). *Gender and School Education*, Melbourne: Australian Council for Educational Research.

Connell, R.W. (1995). *Masculinities*. Sydney: Allen & Unwin.

Cumming, J. (1998). 'Challenges and responses'. In J. Cumming (ed.), *Extending Reform in the Middle Years of Schooling* (pp 5–13). Canberra: Australian Curriculum Studies Association.

Gilbert, R. & Gilbert, P. (1998). *Masculinity Goes to School*. Sydney: Allen & Unwin.

Gilligan, C. (1982). *In a Different Voice: Psychological Theory and Women's Development*. Cambridge, MA: Harvard University Press.

Glover, S., Burns, J., Butler, H. & Patton, G. (1998). 'Social environments and the emotional wellbeing of young people'. *Family Matters*, 49, pp 11–16.

Guerra, C. & White, R. (eds) (1995). *Ethnic Minority Youth in Australia: Challenges and Myths*. Hobart: National Clearinghouse for Youth Studies.

Hargreaves, J. (1984). *Sport, Power and Culture*. Cambridge: Polity Press.

Kirk, D., Burke, P., Carlson, T., Davis, K., Glover, S. & O'Connor, A. (1996). *The Social and Economic Impact on Family Life of Children's Participation in Junior Sport*, Canberra: Applied Sports Research Program.

Lenskyj, H.J. (1998). ' "Inside Sport" or "On the Margins"?: Australian women and the sport media'. *International Review for the Sociology of Sport*, 33(1), pp 19–32.

McLennan, W. (1997). *Youth Australia: A Social Report*. Canberra: Australian Bureau of Statistics.

NSW Multicultural Education Strategic Plan 1993–1997, Department of School Education, Sydney.

Pallotta-Chiarolli, M. (ed.) (1998). *Girls' Talk: Young women speak their hearts and minds*. Sydney: Finch Publishing.

Shilling, C. (1993). 'The body, class and social inequities'. In J. Evans (ed.), *Equality, Education and Physical Education*. London: Falmer Press.

Wyn, J. & White, R. (1997). *Rethinking Youth*. Sydney: Allen & Unwin.

Further reading

Thorne, B. (1993). *Gender Play: Girls and Boys in School*. Buckingham: Open University Press.

Wexler, P. (1992). *Becoming Somebody: Toward a Social Psychology of School*. London: Falmer Press.

Withers, G. (1998). *Schools and the Social Development of Young Australians*. Melbourne: Australian Council for Educational Research.

chapter eight

objectives

By the end of this chapter you should be able to:

- discuss the relationship between students' social and cultural locations and their participation in physical activity;
- understand how different groups of young people construct their own meanings about physical activity and physical culture;
- recognise the problematic place of young people's bodies in the context of a consumer culture and discourses of fitness and healthism.

There are two main approaches which have been taken in investigating young people's participation in physical activity. The first approach includes those studies which are primarily concerned with documenting rates of participation in sport and physical activity and the factors which work against or enhance participation. Some of the most important examples of these in Australia are *Sport for Young Australians* (Measurement & Consulting 1991) and the *NSW Schools Fitness and Physical Activity Survey* (Booth et al 1997). These studies have often been motivated by a concern that the fitness levels, skill and participation of children and young people are declining. Many of these have focussed primarily on organised forms of physical activity, usually competitive sport. One of the limitations of these studies which the researchers themselves point out is the overrepresentation of Australian-born, English-speaking middle class families in the surveys and interviews. While there is some statistical information about the skill levels and participation of young people from cultural minority groups and the poor working classes in physical activity (Booth et al 1997), there is very little research quantitative or otherwise which documents their experiences, perceptions or attitudes in relation to physical activity.

Most participation research has relied on self-reporting, either through asking young people to recall how often they participated in physical activity over specific periods in the past or, less often, through the keeping of a diary of activity. While each of these methods have problems—for instance, differences in definitions of physical activity, estimating amount of time, the intensity and type of involvement, and most of all the accuracy of memory—certain patterns do emerge. Different groups of students engage in different forms of activity and to different degrees. The Australian Bureau of Statistics regularly publishes statistics on participation in sport and physical activities by Australians. Tables 8.1–8.3 provide its main findings from information collected between 1995 and 1996. The ABS distinguishes between 'organised activity'—that is, physical activity defined in the report as 'organised . . . by a club, association or school (outside school hours)'; and 'social sport and physical activities'—that is, 'those sport and physical activities not organised by a club, association or school' (ABS 1997, pp 31–32). Like most of the participation surveys, the statistics do not pick up on all those activities such as walking, jogging, swimming, skateboarding, surfing, rollerblading or dancing for fun that are not carried out in connection with formal organisations.

The ABS figures concur with most other studies in reporting that, in general, males are more likely to be involved in organised sports than females. Participation in organised sports and physical activities peaks between the ages of 9 and 14 and declines substantially after 20.

One of the largest surveys of young people has been that commissioned by the Australian Sports Commission to provide it with information to support the introduction of the *Youth Sport Program* (Measurement & Consulting Services 1991). The study sought to understand the meaning of sport to Australians between the ages of 13 and 18 years by surveying and interviewing

Table 8.1 Participation organised sport and physical activities—grouped by age and sex

	Club		School		
Age	Females	Males	Females	Males	Persons
12–14	64.3	53.6	31.6	27.5	68.8
15–19	50.7	58.3			54.6
20–24	35.2	39.1			37.2
25–34	31.1	35.0			33.1
35–44	24.0	32.2			28.0
45–54	16.6	26.0			21.4
55–64	18.5	21.1			19.8
65 and over	14.0	19.8			16.6

a representative sample of this population. It also surveyed parents. The researchers concluded that young people's experience in and of sport varies enormously. For a large number it was very positive, 'a chance to be exuberant, to feel warmth and companionship and to be pleased with themselves' (p 5). For others it was about 'waiting for a go, being rejected for the team they aspired to, being subjected to unfair coaching, being belittled when they made a mistake'. A large majority of parents in this study were very supportive of their children's involvement in sport and thought that 'playing sport is a good thing for children' (p 10).

The researchers argue that, from their results, there seems to be a large market for fun sport, based on 'personal challenge and personal relevance' rather than 'overt competition', and that custodians of 'official sport' may be turning young people away because of their insistence on purity. They see the best role of the school in sport 'as an environment in which to introduce

Table 8.2 Participation in selected organised sport and physical activities—grouped by sex 15 years and over

Females	%	Males	%
aerobics	6.9	golf	5.1
netball	4.1	cricket	2.6
tennis	3.0	lawn bowls	2.5
swimming	2.2	tennis	2.4
basketball	1.4	basketball	2.2
golf	1.4	AFL	2.1
lawn bowls	1.4	soccer	1.9
tenpin bowling	1.2	swimming	1.5
martial arts	1.1	fishing	1.4
dancing	1.0	touch football	1.4

Table 8.3 participation of children aged 5–14 years in selected organised sport and physical activities

Females	%	Males	%
netball	17.4	soccer	15.7
swimming	14.0	AFL	13.8
dancing	10.5	cricket (outdoor)	12.4
tennis	7.8	swimming	11.6
basketball	6.5	basketball	11.5
gymnastics	4.5	tennis	7.8
athletics	4.1	rugby league	6.3
softball	3.1	martial arts	4.6
aerobics	2.8	athletics	4.5
hockey	2.6	T-ball	2.4
martial arts	1.9	rugby union	2.1

children to a breadth of sporting experiences. This giving each child the basic skills and confidence needed to explore community based sport options' (p 14). They suggest that, for some children, where there is a larger cultural gap between a child's family and the broader community, the school seems to be the only access the child has to organised sport.

In another study funded by the Australian Sports Commission, Kirk and his colleagues (1997) investigated the social and economic impact of children's sport participation on family lives. The sports included in their study were cricket, football, gymnastics, hockey, netball and tennis. They demonstrated how parents made a substantial contribution to their child's participation in sports through time, money and emotional support. Of particular importance is the researchers' suggestion that, given the requirements of many of the most popular sports in Australian society, it is the structural characteristics of families rather than sporting background (although it is likely that the two are related) that promote children's participation. In other words, 'club and representative sport is realistically available only to the children of parents who are in reasonably well paid employment' (p 44).

Young people growing up in rural and isolated areas often have very limited access to the kinds of facilities that young people in cities may take for granted. They are also often limited in the kinds of activities they can pursue simply because there are not enough people around to play with. The opportunities for children from poor families in both rural and urban areas are likely to be restricted through poor access to facilities and because of the economic cost of participation in any physical activities.

These studies have been motivated primarily by a generalised assumption that participation in organised sport is 'good' both for the social development of the individual and for 'the nation' insofar as it provides a base for the identification of elite athletes. Other research, such as the New South Wales Fitness and Physical Activity Survey (Booth et al 1997), has been prompted by

a concern for the perceived decline in the fitness of primary and secondary students. This project tested and surveyed a large sample of students in New South Wales to develop benchmark measurements for cardiovascular and other components of fitness and to measure specific fundamental motor skills such as throwing, catching and kicking. The study found differences in the skills and fitness levels of girls and boys and between girls of different social and cultural backgrounds.

One of the limitations of this study was the lack of suitable standardised tests for the measurement of those skills associated with dance and gymnastics—activities in which girls might have been expected to perform well. As a result we need to be careful about interpreting the results. Inevitably girls and young people of cultural minority groups fare less well in comparison with the skill and participation rates of young white boys in sport and exercise. This may be attributed in part to how 'activity' and 'skill' are being defined. One of the consequences of such comparisons is that girls, particularly those from cultures in which physical activity such as organised sports and exercise for fitness is less likely to be valued, become identified as 'problems'. While we as physical educators want to provide opportunities for increased participation and the enjoyment of physical activity for all, we need also to be sensitive to social and cultural experiences which may produce different ways of seeing and valuing physical activity.

In a study (Wright et al 1999) which took a slightly different approach, parents and teachers from a range of schools were surveyed and interviewed about their perceptions of their children's or their students' engagement in physical activity. The study found that while there were few discernible differences in the meanings parents and teachers associated with physical activity and health, the opportunities for children to be active differed considerably depending particularly on available income, geographic location and the resources available to their schools. It concluded that the issue seemed to be not so much about convincing teachers or parents that physical activity is valuable in young people's lives, but rather to provide opportunities and programs that meet the needs of all children, understanding that those needs are diverse and may vary for different groups of children and for different children within those groups.

Research from social geography shows socio-economic factors working in a variety of subtle ways that may not be immediately obvious. In a study which asked young people to map their routes in and around their local neighborhood, Malone & Hasluck (1998) showed how young people's participation in recreational activities was severely limited by the restrictions on their use of public space. Many of the young people in their study, and particularly the girls, rarely travelled further than two blocks from their homes because of fears about personal safety and strategies to keep them out of public spaces. A council-run community sporting complex, for instance, equipped with three indoor basketball courts, a gym, a canteen and meeting rooms which attracted young people from all over the region was rarely frequented by the 'locals'. The locals, who were less well off, were prevented from participating by the entrance fee that needed to be paid before they even got into the complex, the need to be a member of a team before they could participate, and absence of facilities for sitting and chatting. The manager of the complex explained to the researchers that the entrance fee was indeed intended to keep out those without 'legitimate' user status and the lack of chairs and tables was to discourage young people from hanging around and causing trouble. It follows that the reasons that certain groups of young people appear in the statistics may go beyond the absence of a desire to participate and may be connected with limited opportunities which they have experienced for most of their lives.

Physical culture: meanings and identities

A different way of thinking about young people and physical activity is proposed by David Kirk (1997). He suggests that, rather than limit ourselves to 'participation' in physical activity, we should develop an understanding of young people's 'engagements' with 'physical culture' where 'physical culture' is taken to mean all of the social practices which are involved with maintaining the body (e.g. the work done on bodies through exercise/bodybuilding), representing the body (such as media images and language) and regulating the body (determining how the body should move, be shaped etc.). He argues that young people do not merely participate in physical activities, they are also consumers of the commercialised and commodified products of physical culture, ranging from foodstuffs to membership of exercise clubs and sports clubs to sportswear. Young people construct their identities in relation to the meanings associated with these social practices. For instance, for some young men bodybuilding is both a way of feeling more masculine and of demonstrating their masculinity to others. For physical education students, wearing brand name sportswear may be a way of identifying themselves as PE students and/or as athletes.

On the other hand, the cultural meanings that young people associate with physical activity and sport are likely to influence the choices they make about participation. They are likely to choose physical activities and sports which they see as consistent with their identities as constructed in other contexts. People take up different meanings and associate different values with participation in physical activity depending on their own experiences, investments, and social and cultural location. Bourdieu (1984), for instance, writing about the French population, found that the working classes were more likely to take up an instrumental relation to their bodies and to pursue sports which demand 'a high investment of energy, effort or even pain ... and which sometimes even endanger the body itself' (p 213). The middle classes and particularly middle class women, on the other hand, were more likely to be concerned with the cultivation of the healthy body.

Different generations are also likely to take up different orientations and different practices in relation to physical activity, partly because meanings associated with physical activity change over time but also because people's investments in physical activity change at different times in their lives. For instance, in the study described above (Wright et al 1998) parents and teachers seemed to have very instrumental orientations to physical activity—they valued physical activity for what it was 'good for' whether this was health, fitness or the socialisation of their children. Research with children and young people suggests that 'fun' plays a much larger part in their motivation to participate. It is also likely that what is 'cool' and 'uncool' or activities which are associated with particular subcultures are likely to be taken up or avoided depending on young people's orientations to those groups. What might have been acceptable at 12—for instance, participating and winning events in the athletics carnival— for a 14-year-old girl might mean being stigmatised as 'athletic', a 'try hard', not like other members of her friendship group. In Figure 8.1, a young woman has to negotiate her identity in the context of stereotypical notions of femininity and the homophobic attitudes that often shadow women who participate in sports that are traditionally associated with men.

Some of the meanings associated with physical activity and sport go beyond specific individuals and groups. They are recognisable as widespread beliefs that are promoted through social institutions such as the media, government policies, and education and families. These sets of beliefs or ideologies are often taken for granted. However, if we examine them historically it becomes evident that they change over time and are not universally accepted. On the other hand, they are highly influential in determining what happens in schools in terms of physical activity and sport.

Historically, for instance, sport has been valued in the British and then Australian and New Zealand school curriculum because of its association with values such as loyalty, courage, manliness and the development of leadership, and patriotism. In today's schools, sport and team games continue to take up

WEIGHTLIFTER?
You must be GAY!

SAREE WILLIAMS 19

In the past few years I've been involved in a sport which many people call a non-traditional sport for girls and women. I've gained the respect of my peers, won numerous titles, and I also hold many records. I am a female weightlifter who has entered the male weight-lifter's domain.

I'm not the first female to do so. There are many female weightlifters today but we still have to fight for our right to compete in the prestigious compet-itions such as the Commonwealth and Olympic Games. It was only in 1997 that females gained the right to compete in the year 2000 Olympic Games.

There were many things to overcome when I first took up weightlifting. One of those things was to learn not to listen to people who said things like 'Weightlifter? You must be gay'. What has my sexual orientation got to do with me competing in a sport or not? Another common comment was 'You're a weightlifter, you must be on drugs'. That kind of remark

is one of the hardest things to just sit back and listen to.

Another obstacle is that some coaches still don't like females competitively involved in their sport. We have a right just as males do to take part in any sporting activity if we want to. Some other obstacles which can make it hard and can even deter women from taking part in one of these so-called non-traditional sports are facilities which don't cater for females and the attitude of the people in charge of such facilities.

We are fortunate these days to have women who have already been there and done that, so we can go to them for some advice and support. For example, some people say, 'You can't be a good mother and compete at the same time'. They're proven very wrong.

So what is a weightlifter?
We are all different shapes and sizes.
We come from all different countries.
We are different sexualities.
We can be female.

> **So what is a weightlifter?**
> **We are all different shapes and sizes.**
> **We come from all different countries.**
> **We are different sexualities.**
> **We can be female.**

Source: Maria Pallotta-Chiarolli (1998). *Girls' Talk*: Young women speak their hearts and minds. Sydney: Finch Publishing

Figure 8.1 Negotiating identity in sport

most of the space and time in the physical education curriculum and continue to be associated with social values such as cooperation, fair play, the ability to win and lose and work hard towards a collective goal. The rationale for the inclusion of physical education in the school curriculum, however, has shifted to include its contribution to fitness and health.

While competitive sport and games continue to dominate secondary school physical education, a shifting social and economic context has produced a greater emphasis on health and the benefits of producing citizens who are at less risk of cardiovascular disease. As a consequence, more emphasis has been placed on links between health and exercise and the development of cardio-respiratory fitness. Within this set of beliefs obesity and being overweight have come to be seen as evidence of moral weakness, laziness and an inability to exercise self-discipline. It follows that the slim body has become highly valued and taken as evidence not only of health but of self-discipline.

In contrast to sets of values associated with sport as described above where the emphasis is on the individual as a member of team, the emphasis on fitness, or 'healthism', defines health problems as essentially individual problems. 'Healthism' has been defined by Sparkes (1989) as 'a belief that the attainment and maintenance of health is a self-evident good which accepts unquestionably the link between exercise, fitness and health' (p 9).

There have been shifts in recent years in the ways in which fitness and physical activity are linked at least partly in response to the resistance of many people to a model which seems to expect a considerable amount of hard work in leisure time. Medical and exercise scientists now argue that accumulated moderate activity over the total day has health benefits (Pangrazi et al 1996). This challenges the early 'exercise prescription' model with its emphasis on fitness as a measurable outcome and the necessity of vigorous exercise for 20 minutes a day before any health benefits could be claimed. Essential to both of these models, however, is the notion of the individual's responsibility for living a healthy lifestyle. They take very little account of the structural constraints that not only influence priorities but which also limit the opportunities people have to engage in a variety of physical activities. The exercise–fitness–health model is widespread and influential in Western society because it fits with those other values around the slim body as an attractive body.

The issue here is not whether physical activity has health benefits but rather how particular sets of beliefs influence what happens in physical education in terms of choices of activities and expectations of students. Equally important is the way in which the ideologies of healthism and individual responsibility affect how teachers and students relate to those who do not measure up, whose not so slim bodies may be interpreted as evidence of negative attitudes to physical activity, to physical education and even to themselves. The fashion and fitness industries, health promotion and physical education are all at times implicated in furthering this set of beliefs. It follows that physical education should not only be concerned with assisting students to develop skills and attitudes to enhance their participation in physical activity but should also be developing those skills required to become critical consumers of the 'physical culture' in which they engage.

Teachers need to be aware that the values they associate with certain activities may not be shared by all or even most of their class. Such a situation also provides the basis for conflict and resistance by some students. Part of the problem may be that teachers do not ask students about what they think is important and why. This does not necessarily mean accepting the students' position but it does provide a position from which to plan so that students' meanings and interests are taken into account when programming and planning lessons.

Summary

- There is now a considerable literature documenting young people's patterns of participation in organised and, to a lesser extent, recreational physical activities.
- The opportunities young people have to participate in sport seem to depend very much on where they live and the socio-economic status of their parents.
- In contemporary Australia more young people are choosing to participate in non-organised forms of physical activity such as skateboarding, dancing and surfing.
- Young peoples' participation in physical activity extends to their consumption of the commodities and cultural values associated with sport, recreation and exercise.
- Participation and the ways young people engage in physical activity and physical culture are still profoundly gendered.

References

Australian Bureau of Statistics (1997). *Participation in Sport and Physical Activities, Australia, 1995–96*. Canberra: Commonwealth of Australia.

Booth, M., Macaskill, P., McClean, L., Phongsavan, P., Okely, T., Patterson, J., Wright, J., Bauman, A. & Bauer, L. (1997). *NSW Schools Fitness and Physical Activity Survey*. Sydney: New South Wales Department of Education and Training.

Bourdieu, P. (1984). *Distinction: A Social Critique of the Judgement of Taste* (R. Nice, trans.). Cambridge, MA: Harvard Univesity Press.

Kirk, D. (1997). 'Schooling bodies in new times: The reform of school physical education in high modernity'. In J.-M. Fernandez-Balboa (ed.), *Critical Postmodernism in Human Movement, Physical Education and Sport*. Albany: SUNY Press.

Kirk, D., Carlson, T., O'Connor, A., Burke, P., Davis, K. & Glover, S. (1997). 'The economic impact on families of children's participation in junior sport'. *Australian Journal of Science and Medicine in Sport*, 29(2), pp 27–33.

Malone, K. & Hasluck, L. (1998) 'Geographies of exclusion: Young people's perceptions and use of public space'. *Family Matters*, 49, pp 12–15.

Martinek, T.J. & Hellison, D.R. (1997). 'Fostering resiliency in underserved youth through physical activity'. *Quest*, 49(1), pp 33–49.

Measurement and Consulting Service (1991). *Sport for Young Australians*. Canberra: Australian Sports Commission.

Miller, S.C., Bredemeier, B. & Shields, D.L.L. (1997). 'Sociomoral education through physical education with at-risk children'. *Quest*, 49(1), pp 114–129.

Pallotta-Chiavolli, M. (1998). *Girls' Talk: Young Women Speak their Hearts and Minds*. Sydney: Finch Publishing.

Pangrazi, R.P., Corbin, C.B. & Welk, G.J. (1996). 'Physical activity for children and youth'. *Journal of Physical Education, Recreation and Dance*, 67(4), pp 38–43.

Sparkes, A.C. (1989). 'Culture and ideology in physical education'. In T. Templin & P. Schempp (eds), *Socialization into Physical Education: Learning to Teach* (pp 315–338). Indianapolis: Benchmark Press.

Wright, J. et al (1999). Parents' perceptions of their children's participation in physical activity. *ACHPER Healthy Lifestyles Journal*, 46(1), pp 11–17.

Further reading

Hall, M.A. (1996). *Feminism and Sporting Bodies: Essays on Theory and Practice*. Champaign, IL: Human Kinetics.

Hargreaves, J. (1994). *Sporting Females: Critical Issues in the History and Sociology of Women's Sports*. London and New York: Routledge.

Jarvie, G. (1991). *Sport, Racism and Ethnicity*. London: Falmer Press.

Messner, M. & Sabo, D. (eds) (1990). *Sport, Men and the Gender Order*. Champaign, IL: Human Kinetics.

Penney, D., Carlson, T., Kirk, D. & Braiuka, S. (1999). 'Junior sport policy, provision and participation'. *ACHPER Healthy Lifestyles Journal*, 46(1), pp 5–10.

chapter nine

objectives

By the end of this chapter you should be able to:

- understand the experience of physical education from the point of view of young people;
- see how students' social and cultural locations influence their engagement in physical education;
- recognise how traditional physical education practices often take little account of the diverse social and cultural backgrounds of students in the class;
- reflect on what a culturally inclusive and gender-sensitive physical education practice might look like.

What do we know about the physical education experiences of young people in secondary schools? When students are asked for their views of physical education their responses, not surprisingly, are very much linked to both the local (i.e. the school context) and the social and cultural context. In Williams & Woodhouse's (1996) study of secondary school students in the United Kingdom, physical education was liked by most of the 2,993 students surveyed, more so by the boys (84 per cent) than by the girls (63 per cent). Only 5 per cent of boys and 15 per cent of the girls who responded to the survey said that they disliked PE, the rest indicating that they 'didn't mind' it. There were marked differences, however, in what activities students liked in physical education with the disparity most obvious in the responses of female and male students to winter team games and to dance. Whereas 11 per cent of boys said they disliked winter team games as compared with 29 per cent of girls, 68 per cent of boys responded that they disliked dance in comparison with 22 per cent of the girls. The schools that students attended seemed to make a difference.

Significant differences were found between students' liking of physical education and particular aspects of physical education at some schools as compared with others. This could be attributed to content, teaching and teachers but also to the availability of facilities—gymnastics and dance, for instance, are likely to be much more enjoyable if there are good indoor facilitates. Williams & Woodhouse also pointed to the greater disparity between the activities that girls participated in outside school—individual activities such as Keep Fit—and the team games which dominated the PE curriculum.

In other studies students have not always been as positive. In their study of 21 physical education teachers and their students in urban America, Ennis and her colleagues (1997) discovered that students found some tasks embarrassing, boring and irrelevant. Some students preferred to receive a failing grade rather than participate: 'Students in many of the observed physical education classes reflected negative feelings about the content and the class environment' (Ennis et al 1997, p 60).

Now it is true that the context in the American urban schools in which Ennis' research was conducted is rather different from that found even in most urban schools in Australia and New Zealand. Nevertheless, similar patterns of response to physical education classes can be found in many of our secondary schools which do not have the same severe problems. For instance, many of the Australian students that we talked to in our research (see Tinning & Fitzclarence 1992) found school physical education to be irrelevant and/or just plain boring.

Some people who have not enjoyed their physical activity at school come to be much more active and to enjoy activity in their later years. Perhaps there is something to be learned from what they look for in physical activity when they are able to make choices about their participation which is worth considering when planning for school-based physical education. One of the authors, Jan Wright, interviewed women over 35 years of age about their past and present experiences of physical activity and physical education (Wright & Dewar 1997). In the following quote, Jan talks to a woman who had been relatively active in sports such as surfing outside school but who earlier in the interview talked about how she avoided physical education classes and school sport whenever possible. She describes herself as doing this because of the emphasis on the skilled students and the unrealistic expectations, as she saw them, of her physical education teacher. On the other hand she has now, as a middle-aged woman, begun tap dancing. Her talk about her tap dancing has some important messages for those who would teach physical education. She provides insight into why people choose to be active which go beyond health and fitness to pleasure and feelings of empowerment.

Interviewer (I): How did you get into tap dancing?

Subject (S): At the time there was a very active women's social circle from the Women's Network where women would perform on various nights in all sorts of ways, mediums, and I heard about the tap dancing group and decided that I liked the whole concept of what they were trying to do and that was basically a group of political women who were learning to tap dance for fun and who were tap dancing to political songs. So there was no 'singing in the rain' type music. It was all good strong women's songs and the women . . . ranged in age (in fact I might have been the youngest and I can't think how old I would have been but I'd say about 36 or something like that and I think the eldest would have been about 54 or so). Nobody had a very good body. We were all either very thin or very overweight, there was sort of no in-betweens. None of us was startlingly beautiful and we all tap danced in t-shirts and long pants and we decided that our uniform would be t-shirts and long pants and that we would do sequins and things on the t-shirts as the mood took us and it was a real hoot. It was really, really funny and nobody . . . like when you made mistakes people just thought that was even better in some ways and then we performed about three times I think at some of these women's nights and people just loved us because we were such a delight and it was so obvious that everybody was having a wonderful time doing it.

So the fact that we weren't very good didn't seem to matter to people and I always thought that was the most important part of my enjoyment of it. It was like not having to be wonderful, to be able to say to people, 'Look, I do this'.

Not long after that we were going to organise the next show and the teacher stopped; she said she couldn't come for that period, and so we thought we would use another young woman who was a tap dancer and she came along and within two lessons, a week's span, everybody had stopped going because she was just 'Oh, no you can't do that, it would be embarrassing' and it was just awful and I couldn't bear to be in the same room with her after that.

She got another woman to dance with her and they danced at the next one themselves and they were very good, they were excellent but nobody enjoyed it in the same way that they had enjoyed the others . . . It was because they were perfectionists, the same ethos, you know, you do it to show people how good you are. A waste of time.

I: Yours was much more of a sharing, they could see how much you enjoyed it.

S: Yes, and people did see how much we enjoyed it . . .

I: What's enjoyable about it?

S: I think the rhythm; I think all of us related to the music that we were dancing to quite well; they were political statements that we all felt strongly connected to . . .

We were there for the social and the political and the enjoyment type aspect and they completely missed the point I think.

I: That is an important thing. I think school is incredibly guilty of missing the point.

S: I think they completely missed the point in terms of trying to connect people with their bodies and their bodies with their lives. It's 'Okay now get into this, this is all physical', with no concept that the physical is also connected to a whole lot of other social stuff as well. I think sometimes that's why rap dancing and stuff like that has been really successful because it's integrated those two really well.

I: In many ways kids do it themselves, like skateboard riding becomes a rebellion partly because society helps to position it in that kind of way.

S: So that was part of the tap dancing. I guess the other part of it in terms of the rhythm was I really enjoy music and I like to dance but it was music that I had chosen to listen to and to be with . . . so it was easy to get that enjoyment. I guess for the first time in a long time I started to relate to my body again, learning coordination again and things like that, even at a very minuscule level we still had to do that. That was nice too because it was like a rediscovery of some things that had been buried for quite a while . . .

Physical education and ethnicity

Traditionally physical education has not been very sensitive to social and cultural differences. While there has been more talk about catering for 'individual differences' in the literature, this has primarily focussed on difference in physical ability and skill level. While these are clearly important, physical education teachers also need to be aware of the different needs and interests, indeed requirements, of different cultural groups in the communities in which they teach. This is not only a matter of making token adjustments to the specific needs of certain groups but of recognising that physical education programs need to be structured to recognise the diversity of students in our schools. For instance, as pointed out in Chapter 11, the physical education syllabuses in Australia and New Zealand developed from a British and later North American tradition which favoured specific competitive team games which are clearly divided for gender. In other cultures different activities have prominence and different meanings are associated with physical activity. For example, in Asian countries dual games such as badminton and table tennis might be more popular and team contact games rarely practised. A general touchstone, however, seems to be a valuing of physical activity as it contributes to the health of individuals.

There are only now beginning to be studies which ask students from different cultural minority groups about their experiences in school physical education and sport. Most of these have been with Asian boys (boys whose parents come from Indian and Pakistan) and young Muslim women in Britain. In Australia researchers are also beginning to explore the meaning of physical activity and physical education with young Muslim women.

These studies often challenge the stereotypes and assumptions teachers bring to their teaching of students from other cultures. In this section, the focus will primarily be on Muslim students and their experiences of physical education. This focus has been chosen for a number of reasons: there are increasing numbers of Muslim students in Australian schools; Muslim students (particularly Muslim girls) are often identified by teachers as 'a problem' because of their apparent resistance to physical activity and physical education; and there is more research on these young people in relation to physical education in the English language literature than most other specific ethnic groups.

One of the main issues seems to be teachers' anticipations that students from Asian (in the United Kingdom) and Muslim backgrounds are not interested in physical activity. Generalisations are made which construct these students as lazy, as uninterested and as problems in physical education. Research suggests that these assumptions are inaccurate—perhaps what they do is to provide a way of avoiding addressing the specific needs of these students. In Scott Fleming's (1991) research of Asian boys, for instance, the religious requirements for regular prayer constrained some of the boys' participation in sport, rather than their lack of interest: (Rashid) 'It's quite difficult for me. I have to pray five times a day. If I have to pray at 12 o'clock and there's a match, I can't play . . . If it's a matter of "life and death", you can pray afterwards. But sport doesn't count as a matter of "life and death"' (p 37).

From the research on Muslim girls, it is clear that, for them, participation in physical activity is something to value, particularly as it relates to health, and that most would enjoy being able to participate. The critical theme, however, seems to be the constraints that are put on their participation by a culture which takes little account of their religious and cultural needs. For Muslim girls to participate in physical activity there are specific religious (and sometimes additional) prescriptions which need to be accommodated. These are primarily to do with modesty and with religious practices. Devout Muslims, for example, will feel guilt and shame at being put into situations where their bodies and legs are exposed to the gaze of non-Muslims and to all males. It follows that any insistence on the usual physical education uniform of shorts or a skirt produces a major barrier to participation in PE. If students, however, are permitted to wear loose light clothing worn with the proper head covering this may go far to solve the problem.

There are other constraints to which teachers need to be sensitive. Muslim girls may need to be taught swimming separate from boys and to be supervised by a female teacher. There are also specific constraints on participation during the period of Ramadan for both female and male Muslim students. During Ramadan, Muslim students will not be able to eat or drink between sunrise and sunset. It follows that they should not be expected to engage in vigorous physical activity. It may also mean that swimming should be avoided in case water enters the mouth.

Arrangements which best meet the needs of all students need to be negotiated with the students themselves and their parents. Muslim students may stand out in classes because of their dress and because of specific religious prohibitions on contexts in which they can participate, but it must also be remembered that male and female students from other cultural heritages bring to physical education different experiences and different interests. It should not be assumed that they will share the same enthusiasm as their Anglo teachers for competitive team sports and other activities we may take for granted as essential.

Gender and physical education

One of the key questions which comes up in talking about gender and physical education to teachers and student teachers is the issue of single-sex or coeducational physical education classes. This is a useful question to explore because in doing so some fundamental assumptions about gender and physical activity and physical education need to be examined. Let us say at this point—probably unhelpfully—that there is no one or simple answer to this question. Like so many of the decisions that need to be made in choosing content, ways of presenting learning opportunities and so on, it depends on the context and on the consequences for the students that flow from the decision. Like any decision, the consequences need to be monitored and the practices changed if they are not working to the benefit of students. In this case the question is: What do you look for?

Prior to the Equal Opportunities Acts in the 1980s separate girls' and boys' physical education classes were the general rule except for social dance. This arrangement was predicated on an understanding that girls and boys had very different interests, needs and capacities. These differences tended to be explained as innate biological differences or differences that were so ingrained through learning that they were unlikely to change. Boys were assumed to possess attributes such as strength, toughness, competitiveness and an inherent liking for the rough-and-tumble of contact games. Girls, on the other hand, were assumed to have a greater potential and enjoyment for the graceful and flexible movement in activities such as dance and gymnastics and to enjoy games as they provided opportunities to socialise with their friends.

One of the main consequences of this separation of classes and the curriculum for girls and boys was that it helped to maintain the narrow stereotypes of what was appropriate female and male behaviour. These assumptions ignored the differences within groups of boys and within groups of girls. These who did not fit these stereotypes were likely to be named as strange or different—'tomboys' for the girls and 'sissies' or 'gay' for the boys. The opportunities for boys and girls to learn skills and to act in ways other than those associated with traditional masculinity and femininity were extremely limited—perhaps more so for the boys than for the girls. Moreover, it helped to maintain the belief that girls and boys were so different from one another that they could not play games or enjoy physical education together. Thinking about this, it is helpful to reflect on the following scenario.

 let's reflect

Tom was a boy who loved dance and drama and was beginning to discover that he was very good at these through the classes he attended outside school. The government school that he attended was a big rugby school and rugby was a major component of the physical education program. Although most PE classes were mixed for several units the class was split, with the girls doing jazz dance and the boys some kind of football.

After the boys in his class found out about his dancing, they took every opportunity to threaten him verbally or physically. He came to dread PE, especially when they played football or the rough and tough rumbles that the male PE teacher used frequently as 'fun' warm-ups. The other boys in the class used these contact activities to threaten and physically harm him. This had been going on for several years now and although it was often obvious that he was being singled out for shaming and physical harassment, no teacher seemed to feel that it was necessary to intervene.

Meanwhile Kate and Soraya looked out of the window of the dance room with envy at the boys playing rugby. They played rugby league on the weekend in a girls' team and would have liked some opportunities in PE to develop their skills and to play against the boys. Every time they suggested that they might join the boys' group the teacher had said that the girls were required to complete the dance unit and that it was too rough out there for them.

In the 1970s and 1980s differences in the forms of educational provisions for girls and boys were challenged by arguments for 'equal opportunities'. Unfortunately this was generally interpreted as the 'same' opportunities for girls and boys. One of the ways in which many schools responded was to introduce coeducational physical education, on the assumption that if the teacher and the content were the same for all the students in the class it would follow that their outcomes and experiences would also be equal. As we have pointed out this was, of course, not the case. The experiences of students in these classes differed depending on their level of skill, their confidence, their prior experience with the activities and the ways in which other students interacted with them.

For instance, imagine a coeducational soccer lesson in, say, the second year of high school, taught by a male teacher. Most of the boys are likely to have had some experience of soccer or at least of kicking the ball around with friends. If coeducational classes have not been the norm for them before, they expect and are used to a lesson that consists mainly of a brief but vigorous practice and then a full game with the teacher taking a refereeing role. The teacher has a considerable challenge ahead of him. How well prepared is he to meet this challenge? If he has taught only boys before, it is likely that he is used to (and probably prefers) their expectations of a lesson. The girls seem reluctant to get in and give it a go. They take longer to get dressed and he has to take more time working through the skills while the boys in the class get impatient. From most of the girls' point of view, the agenda being set here is not one they share. It is not that they would not like to learn how to play soccer but they have already experienced the boys' ridicule of their kicking skills and from their point of view playing the game is just a waste of time and an opportunity for further humiliation. The boys rarely pass them the ball and when it does come their way they often do it incorrectly, confirming their own, the teacher's and the boys' expectations that they are hopeless. Even those girls that do have a reasonable level of skill in this sport still have trouble gaining access to the ball as the boys monopolise the play, their main concern being to beat the other team.

While this is not the only possible scenario in coeducational physical education classes, the research suggests that it is certainly not a rare example. As with many other areas of the school curriculum, decisions about what will be taught and how it will be taught are often designed to suit the boys—who tend to be louder and make more fuss if their needs are not catered for. In physical education this means that the content is often dominated by traditional competitive team games and other competitive activities. Other possibilities such as jazz and creative dance, gymnastics and aerobics are allocated proportionally much smaller amounts of program space. One of the consequences of this is that girls become constructed as the 'problems' because of their greater reluctance to participate in the areas of the program that count through their apparent lack of enthusiasm and lack of skill.

At this point is seems that there is no right way to go and to a certain extent that is true: there is no *one* way to go. Some schools have tackled this problem with a great deal of thoughtfulness: they have consulted students through surveys and conversations and they have considered the consequences of their decisions. They have not all come up with the same solutions, nor do most see the decision arrived at as permanent. Most have required a well-considered argument to put to the executive of their schools because of the timetabling changes required for more flexible organisation of classes. For instance, several schools in South Australia who participated in the Girls and Physical Activity Project (GAPA)[1] decided, where possible, to request that whole year groups be timetabled for physical education at the same time. They then chose to organise the year on ability and to group the most highly skilled female and male students together in coed groups, the middle group single-sex and the lowest ability coed as well.

Their argument, based on the surveys with the students, was that many of the highly skilled girls welcomed the challenge of playing with the boys; the disparities in skill and confidence were most marked in the middle group and the least skilled group all needed similar attention to skill development and knowledge of activities. Another school in New South Wales, unconnected to the GAPA, also persuaded the executive of the school to prioritise physical education on the timetable and, on the basis of a student survey and teachers' concerns, organised all years, except the first year of high school, into single-sex classes. While they hope to work towards mixed classes again in the long term, this has been a decision made on the basis of teachers' concerns about the kinds of opportunities available to girls in coeducation classes.

To a certain extent most of these decisions are made in a context where the model of PE that predominates is that of the traditional transmission model, where the emphasis is on the teaching and learning of skill in the contexts of games, dance and gymnastics. Other models of teaching and learning, as described in this chapter and the next, provide different possibilities for approaching the single-sex/coeducation question. If the emphasis is less on physical performance and more on problem solving (constructivist approaches to learning, 'games for understanding', 'games sense') or approaches that provide for more student involvement in all stages of teaching and learning (approaches modelled, for instance, on the Sport Education in Physical Education Project (SEPEP)) or where the timetabling allows for more choice in activities and tasks for students, then creative ways of approaching this and other issues of difference are possible. The challenge is to find ways of organising and teaching PE which provide all students with opportunities to participate in activities which are relevant and culturally appropriate. A checklist for reflection is shown in the following box.

 let's reflect

Programming: choices of content
- On what basis are choices made?
- Who do they benefit?
- How do they challenge or reinforce narrow constructions of masculinity and femininity?
- Do they recognise and provide opportunities to meet the interests of different groups of girls and boys?
- Do they acknowledge the range of capabilities and interests girls and boys bring to school?

Organisation: single-sex or mixed physical education classes
- What are the consequences for all students? What are the consequences for teachers?
- Does it challenge the relationships between girls and boys?
- Does it challenge narrow constructions of femininity and masculinity or reinforce them?
- Does it bring about change?

Assessment: equitable assessment procedures
- Whom do they benefit?
- How do they challenge or reinforce narrow constructions of masculinity and femininity?
- Do they recognise and provide opportunities to meet the interests of different groups of girls and boys?
- Do they acknowledge the range of capabilities and interests girls and boys bring to and acquire at school?

Personal practices
- choices of language
- interactions with students
- dress and expectations about dress
- management strategies
- choices of activities

Disability and physical education

Schools in Australia and New Zealand are increasingly moving towards a policy whereby all students with disabilities or with learning or adjustment problems should be enrolled in regular schools unless there are compelling reasons for doing otherwise. The challenge here is to design educational opportunities in physical education which do not merely provide token accommodation for students with disabilities but which enable them to participate in activities with the same outcomes of fun, value and learning that are possible for other children in the class. As has been the case for most of this section 'good practice' in this area may require fundamental rethinking of traditional methods of teaching, assessment, and the purpose/objectives/outcomes of physical education. This can be a considerable challenge for teachers but also an incentive for reflection and for change which benefits all students.

Clarke & Nutt (1997) suggest some guidelines:

- Do not make assumptions about ability. A young person's needs and abilities are more important than any category of disability.
- Tasks can be simplified by reducing demands in one aspect of the task.
- Open-ended tasks can encourage young people with special needs to explore the full potential of their abilities. Possibilities of problem solving.
- Importance of verbal and visual clarity of communication—using different ways of communicating the same message.
- Importance of sensitive and supportive encouragement. This might involve negotiating with the student the exact nature and extent of their involvement in PE lessons.

In Australia a project called *Willing and Able: PE and Sport for Young People with Disabilities* has been designed to provide support for 'teachers, coaches and community leaders to assist them in redressing barriers to participation facing young people with disabilities in physical activity' (Downs 1995, p 2). The core resource of the project *An Introduction to Inclusive Practices* (1995) provides 'teachers with planning tools and ideas to successfully implement inclusive physical education and sport programs' (p 2). In 1998 this resource was evaluated by talking to teachers who had used it. The teachers' stories, collected by means of personal journals, provide some insight into the experiences and practices of teachers who are addressing the needs of children with disabilities.

Teachers described how at first they were fearful about working with students with disabilities, often because of their own preconceptions. These feelings changed as they came to know the children by 'their *ability* rather than their *disability*'. They also learnt that inclusive practices did not necessarily mean radical changes and sometimes did not require changes in content or teaching strategies at all. Figure 9.1 gives one example of how a teacher planned to include David, a student with Vater syndrome—a condition where a child may be born with a range of defects including blockages which may affect the oesophagus, kidneys, cardiovascular system and so on—in her PE classes.

VATER SYNDROME – DAVID	
Impairment	**Considerations for PE**
one hand and arm malformed one leg shorter anal abnormality involving soiling problems heart murmur hole in the heart only one kidney	unable to run walks with a limp balance affected fitness level low

Kicking skills *(a Sport It unit)*	**Adaptations/considerations**
holding football to kick	could not hold in two hands or freely swing his leg
kick into the river	soccer ball, kick along ground, land in the river, partner retrieve
kick long ball	when kicking – used soccer ball (class used football) – runner for David
wall pass game	partner moved while David remained stationary
phantom kick	allowed David experimental time against a wall – seeing if he could get toe under ball – where best to place non-kicking foot for balance, whether a side kick was better
punt kick into hoop	soccer kick as close to hoop as possible

Source: *Willing and Able* (1998).

Figure 9.1   Teacher's plan to include student with a disability

Postmodern age and physical education: student alienation

Perhaps one of the greatest general challenges to physical education is what Tinning & Fitzclarence (1992) describe as the 'apparent disjunction' between school physical education and the lives of young people. While acknowledging that there have always been students who have not enjoyed physical activity, they suggest that we are seeing increasing numbers who value physical activity in their out of school lives but who find little appealing in school physical education. Sophie, for instance, is only one of the many students in their study who likes sport and physical activity but who describes physical education as boring and repetitive: 'I love sport and everything, netball or anything like that. But at this school it's so boring. I've being doing basketball since year 7 and soccer since year 7 and netball all since year 7. It just gets so boring I'm sick of it' (p 288).

Tinning & Fitzclarence go on to describe how the teacher of one class is surprised to see those students whom they perceive to be apathetic in classes enthusiastically participating in aerobics, working out with weights and swimming at her local gym. They suggest that explanations lie in what they describe as postmodern youth culture. They point to the multiplicity and appeal of images on television, film, video song clips and magazines, a world of images in which the body (a slim, muscular body) has become one of the most desirable symbols of youthful attractiveness (see Chapter 2). They compare these images of physicality, of bodies and physical activity, with students' experiences of physical education where their own bodies are on display. They raise the question: What meaning and relevance does school physical education have in their daily lives in this context?

Perhaps another place to look is the kinds of physical activity which students do engage in voluntarily outside school hours and to ask what relationship school physical education has to these interests and preoccupations. It might also be useful to look at what young and older people do after they leave school. What kinds of physical activity do they choose? As pointed out previously, the statistics rarely pick up on informal non-club sport. But some of this research plus qualitative research with parents and teachers suggests that young people walk, swim, skateboard, surf, dance and do aerobics. Up until their senior years of high school, they also play a great deal of sport, but this is replaced by more informal forms of physical activity as they get older. For instance, aerobics has more participants in the 18 and above age groups, according to the ABS statistics, than any other specific category (ABS 1997).

One of the issues here is what Brettschneider points out as the difficulty many adults have in understanding the world of young people. Their view of the world is restricted by what they/we have always done 'while the developments outside the school, the social changes in youth culture go unnoticed' (1990, p 2) or even resisted as problems to be countered. Perhaps one starting premise would be to listen to students in an attempt to understand the world from their point of view. This might mean working with students to provide PE programs which are relevant and sensitive to their needs, acknowledging that these needs will differ for different groups of students on the basis of gender, ethnicity, disability and their personal biographies.

Physical education for changing times and for diverse contexts

What is needed is a curriculum that is responsive to difference, a curriculum which seeks to meet the needs of:

- both female and male students;
- students from different social and cultural backgrounds and with differing capabilities with regard to learning and to physical skills;
- students in a changing environment and in an environment marked by fragmented and shifting values, in an environment in which the

media is one of, if not the major, source of meanings about society and cultural values and in which identities are framed within both a local and global context (students who identify as Australian and Muslim). What a challenge!

In practice this means:

- being responsive to difference;
- considering the consequences of all PDHPE programs and practices for all students;
- avoiding practices which marginalise or exclude students from minority cultures or groups;
- avoiding stereotyping students—being consultative; listening to the students and their parents;
- challenging the centrality of organised team games through promoting games like handball, modified games, touch;
- challenging the centrality of the teacher-directed command-style approach through challenging the notion that girls, students from cultural minority groups, students with disabilities, students without specific skills etc. are 'the problem'.

Summary

- As a practice which draws largely on team games, traditional forms of physical education have not always been responsive to the diverse needs and experiences of female students, students from cultural minority groups, students with disabilities and those students whose inclinations do not necessarily lie with competitive forms of activities.
- A culturally inclusive and gender-sensitive curriculum takes into account the diversity of the school population, provides opportunities for students to participate in decision making about the curriculum and, where necessary, negotiates appropriate forms of practice with the community of the school.
- While there is generally no one 'best practice', critical reflection on the consequences of physical education practices for students is a key component in making decisions about the organisation of classes, choices of content and teaching approach.

Note

1 The Girls and Physical Activity Project was a school-based project funded by the Commonwealth Schools Commission and conducted by the South Australian Education Department 1986–87.

References

Australian Bureau of Statistics (1997). *Participation in Sport and Physical Activities, Australia, 1995–96*. Canberra: Commonwealth of Australia.

Brettschneider, W.-D. (1990). 'Adolescents, leisure, sport and lifestyle'. In W.T.A. Almond & A. Sparkes (eds), *Sport and Physical Activity: Moving Towards Excellence* (pp 1–14). London: E&FN Spon.

Clarke, G. & Nutt, G. (1997). 'Physical education'. In M. Cole & D. Hill (eds), *Promoting Equality in Secondary Schools*. London: Cassell.

Downs, P. (1995) *An Introduction to Inclusive Practices*. Australian Sports Commission, Canberra.

Ennis, C., Cothram, D., Davidsons, K., Loftus, S., Owens, L., Swanson, L. & Hopsicker, P. (1997). 'Implementing curriculum within a contest of fear and disengagement'. *Quest*, 17(1), pp 52–72.

Fleming, S. (1991). 'Sport, schooling and Asian male youth culture'. In G. Jarvie (ed.), *Sport, Racism and Ethnicity*. London: Falmer Press.

Tinning, R. & Fitzclarence, L. (1992). 'Postmodern youth culture and the crisis in Australian secondary school physical education'. *Quest*, 44(3), pp 287–304.

Williams, A. & Woodhouse, J. (1996). 'Delivering the discourse—urban adolescents' perceptions of physical education'. *Sport, Education and Society*, 1(2), pp 210–213.

Wright, J. & Dewar, A. (1997). 'On pleasure and pain: women speak out about physical activity'. In G. Clarke & B. Humberstone (eds), *Researching Women, Sport and Physical Education*, London: Macmillan, pp 80–95.

Further reading

Burns, R. (1993). 'Health fitness and female subjectivity: what is happening to school health and physical education?'. In L. Yates (ed.), *Feminism and Education*. Melbourne: La Trobe University Press.

Ennis, C.D. (1999). 'Creating a culturally relevant curriculum for disengaged girls'. *Sport, Education and Society*, 4(1), pp 31–50.

Evans, J. (ed.) (1993). *Equality and Physical Education*. London: The Falmer Press.

Griffin, P. & Genasci, J. (1992). 'Addressing homophobia in physical education: Responsibilities for teachers and researchers'. In M. Messner & D. Sabo (eds), *Sport, Men and the Gender Order*. Champaign, IL: Human Kinetics.

Hutchinson, G.E. (1995). 'Gender-fair teaching in physical education'. *Journal of Physical Education, Recreation and Dance*, 66(1), pp 42–47.

Scraton, S. (1992). *Shaping up to Womanhood: Gender and Girls' Physical Education*. Buckingham: Open University Press.

chapter
ten

objectives

By the end of this chapter you should be able to:
- identify the different approaches to teaching physical education and assumptions underpinning these;
- understand the relationship between teaching outcomes and learning outcomes for students;
- critically reflect on the connection between different teaching approaches and their consequences for student learning and teacher–student relationships.

Jan's son Tim is a 'skatie' or skateboard rider. She asked him how he learnt to perform tricks on his skateboard. He said, 'I asked other people (where to put my feet and what to do with them), worked out how it felt best for me and then just practised'. Jan's observations of him riding with his friends and by himself in the backyard suggest that it was a combination of close observation of those more expert than himself including skating videos, trying things out and talking with his friends about how certain tricks were performed, and the repeated practice of a trick over and over again, with many partial successes (and several near disasters), until he could perform it with some flow. What she also noticed was that Tim was not easily deterred by lack of success, he persisted at his practice, and practised every moment he had available until a skill was mastered. This was not a part of his character that had been obvious before. She noticed that there was a wide range of ages and skills among his skateboard-riding friends, with some of the youngest being the most skilled. She also noticed that all of his skateboarding friends were male and that she rarely saw a girl skating at the skate park or in the public spaces the boys frequented.

As physical educators it struck us that there was something to be learned from Tim's experience. In Chapter 9 we talked about young people's disaffection with physical education. Here was a teenager who had tried and was reasonably successful at many competitive team and individual sports but who rarely lasted in any of these for more than a year. Skateboarding has persisted for at least three years without any sign of his enthusiasm decreasing. He practices in every spare moment (if that is an appropriate way of describing his riding) without encouragement from adults.

The same could be said of many young people who have learned to ride surfboards, to dance the latest dances, to perform tricks on their BMX bikes, to rollerblade and so on. They do these most often without adult intervention (except for the financial support). What messages can we take from this for teaching physical education? How can it help us understand how young people learn to move and what motivates them to do so? The premise that underpins this chapter is as follows: what it means to be a teacher rests with how we understand students as learners.

Where you look to answer the question of how young people learn, in part, depends on the assumptions about what students should or need to learn in physical education and why. Some of the fundamental premises that seem to be agreed on across different approaches to physical education teaching is that students learn at different rates and in different ways and that they learn best if they are engaged in activities that are meaningful and relevant to them. It would seem, then, that teaching/learning opportunities in physical education need to be varied in order to be responsive to the different learning styles, experiences and interests that students bring to classes. Recent writing by Kirk & Macdonald (1998) suggests that learning is also related to the social contexts in which students learn (schooling contexts) and the social contexts in which physical activity occurs in the wider society—that is, in contexts associated with sport, exercise and physical recreation.

To go further than this we must start to examine our assumptions about what kinds of learning physical education is designed to produce. The way in which different assumptions about the purposes of physical education were arrived at and their implications for curriculum will be discussed in more detail in Chapter 11. Teaching in physical education has usually emphasised one of two main purposes: teaching physical skills and strategies ('*in* or *of* the physical'); and teaching for the development of social, psychological and cognitive attributes (teaching '*through* the physical'). More recently teaching *about* the scientific and socio-cultural knowledge associated with physical activity has also become important to some physical educators. Each of these depends to some extent on slightly different aspects of learning theory. Learning physical skills requires, among other things, an understanding of the principles of motor learning; learning through the physical requires an understanding of how social, cognitive and emotional learning occurs; learning about the physical and physical culture also involves theories about cognitive learning, as well an understanding of the ways in which people use cultural resources to make choices about what they think and do. Teachers of physical education need to be able to draw on all these approaches to learning to fully attend to the complexity of the subject and to meet the various needs and learning styles of students in their classes. These approaches are not exclusive from one another and may all be included in any one lesson or across a unit of work to achieve curriculum outcomes.

Another dimension to teaching/learning is added by Mosston's (1966) spectrum of teaching styles, which has been widely drawn on as a form of classification of teaching methods. His categories range from the most teacher-centred, the *command style*, to the most student-centred *guided discovery*, where the teacher guides the learner through a series of learning tasks. In between these extremes is *task-based learning*, where the teacher allows the student some control over their learning, as in the use of task cards in circuit training or gymnastics, and *reciporocal learning* where students work together in peer teaching situations providing each other with feedback.

These categories are based on teacher and student decisions across three aspects of a lesson: pre-class decisions about subject matter, teacher role and pupil role; execution decisions about organisational matters such as when to start activities, how long to spend practising, how the class will be arranged

oty over to you

Using Mosston's three groups of decision making, analyse how you arrange your teaching. Who makes the decisions, in what circumstances and why? Use the following checklist to assist you in your analysis.

	Decision maker	
	Teacher	Pupil
Pre-class		
During class		
Evaluation		

(in groups, pairs etc.) and the mode of communication; and evaluation decisions such as the use of testing devices, the use of norms, the communication of the results. Traditional physical education lessons where the teacher directs the students' learning through making all the decisions about content, organisation, time and so on would be typical of the command style of teaching. See the box on the previous page to assess your own teaching style.

Learning *in* the physical

Traditionally much of the interest in learning in physical education has been in the area of motor skill acquisition. Questions which are central to this area include the following:

- Is whole or part teaching of a skill the more effective for student learning?
- Is extrinsic or intrinsic motivation more likely to enhance students' learning and their desire to continue participating in physical activity?
- What forms of feedback are most useful in assisting students to improve their performance of a skill?
- What forms of practice are most effective for the learning of a motor skill?
- Under what conditions are skills best practised?

Teaching skills also assume some capacity on the teacher's part to analyse students' performance—that is, to recognise the sequence of movement patterns so that they can give useful feedback which will assist the student to improve with further practice. The assumption here is that what students do follows from the teachers' behaviour. Little account is taken of the sense or meaning that students make of tasks. Their involvement in the tasks and accurate performance of a skill is taken as evidence of their learning. Students' 'time on task' and the appropriateness of instructional strategies—that is, ways of describing, demonstrating and providing feedback about tasks—are taken to be indicators of 'effective teaching'. Most of the ways in which student teachers are evaluated by their supervising teachers and lecturers are informed by this approach.

Much of the research which evaluates the technical effectiveness of physical education lessons uses measurements of Academic Learning Time (ALT), defined as 'time spent on tasks where pupils experienced a high success rate' (Underwood 1988, p 13). Tools for measuring ALT-PE were devised by Siedentop et al (cited in Underwood 1988, p 124) and have been used widely in research in North America from that time. The calculation of ALT-PE is carried out by measuring the amount of time spent in a lesson on categories of activities under three major subdivisions: general content; PE content knowledge; and PE motor content. What becomes interesting to the observer is how much class time is spent on each of the categories and how this fits with the purposes of the lesson. Amounts of positive and negative feedback and feedback with information are also often calculated (see Chapter 16 for details).

If we refer back to Mosston's classifications, the 'of the physical' approach tends to be characterised by maximum teacher control over the decisions which affect what will be taught, how it will be taught and how it is to be evaluated. Teaching from this approach usually involves an explanation of a skill and a demonstration by the teacher or a competent student, followed by organised practice with the teacher providing feedback. Traditionally this is the approach most of us have been exposed to in our own secondary schooling and is the one often recommended for beginning teachers by their lecturers and supervising teachers because it provides for maximum control.

Although the traditional method is easily criticised for its 'pouring-in' rather than 'bringing-out' qualities, for not being sensitive to the concerns of the learners, and for establishing (or rather maintaining) a teacher/learner hierarchy, it is nonetheless an important teaching method for teaching certain types of physical skills. Consider, for example, the task of learning to do a back dive from a one-metre diving board. To advocate pupil experimentation would be somewhat irresponsible given the considerable aversive consequences associated with an incorrect performance. Too much rotation and the child would land on their stomach. Too little rotation and the child would land on their back. In both cases the result would be painful and hardly consistent with trying to build up confidence in diving. In this case, teacher direction through the structured sequencing of progressive activities would help to reduce the negative results from uninitiated trial-and-error learning. Moreover, in the end it comes back to what you are trying to achieve in a lesson and how this sits with the syllabus outcomes guiding your teaching.

Other ways of thinking about learning to move

Remember the *Karate Kid*? For the teacher, Mr Miyaki, learning karate was a matter of body/mind practice rather than breaking down the skills and teaching particular parts in isolation. Just as it was for Mr Miyaki, at times it is difficult to find words in the English language to describe the body/mind relationship which underpins traditional Eastern movement forms such as karate, Tai Chi, Tae Kwon Do and so on. Traditional Western ways of thinking about the body in physical education seem to ignore the connections between the physical and the mental except insofar as what can be observed—that is, improved performance is taken to be evidence of cognitive functioning. Body and brain are regarded as separate entities connected in ways which are difficult to define.

In other ways of thinking about the body, particularly those deriving from Eastern philosophies, a more holistic approach is taken which sees the mind and body as inseparable. This quote from the Japanese philosopher, Yasuo Yasua, provides an insight into the differences between traditional Western and Eastern ways of working with the body:

> *We can gradually approach the inseparability of the body–mind only by long accumulative training. According to the view held in modern sports, however, the training and enhancement of the body's capacity has nothing to do with the enhancement of one's moral personality, that is, the training of one's mind. In contrast in the East, physical training that is not accompanied by the training of the mind as well is regarded as an aberration, for the mind and body cannot be essentially separated.*
> *(Yuasa 1987)*

There are also those in the West who have developed ways of working with the body which take greater account of the inseparable relationship between mind and body. For instance, Moshe Feldenkrais and Mathias Alexander, among many others, have developed ways of re-educating the body, through systematically changing habitual movement patterns. Both these approaches are now used by elite athletes and with people whose habitual movements have reduced their range of movement.

It seems worth considering alternative ways of thinking about the body and teaching skills if the needs of all students are to be considered. This also provides an opportunity to extend what counts as physical education and to work in areas that may be novel for both female and male students, providing a neutral ground where neither group has more experience than the other with a teaching approach and content.

Learning *through* the physical

Physical educators often make claims about the capacity of physical education to influence students' social, cognitive and emotional, as well as physical development. Often our rhetoric assumes that this will happen automatically as students engage in physical activity and particularly team games. However, this is not the case. Students are just as likely to learn the values of competition, winning at the expense of others through cheating, aggressive play, valuing individual stardom rather than collaboration and so on. They may also learn that team games are a place where other students can take the opportunity to visit violence upon them, that they are useless at physical education in comparison with others in the class, or that they hate physical activity because from their experiences in physical education it is a source of humiliation, of physical discomfort or simply boring. If we believe that emotional, social and cognitive development is an important outcome of physical education then classes, programs and assessment tasks need to be planned and taught with these outcomes in mind; they do not happen just because students are actively involved and seem to be spending appropriate amounts of time on the task.

If we return to Mosston, clearly one of the ways in which students will have more opportunity to engage in 'thinking' in physical education is if they are involved in decision making and problem solving. At the other end of the Mosston continuum is a method characterised by maximum pupil control over the decisions which are made about the subject matter, the class organisation and the means of evaluation. The 'indirect method' as it sometimes called is rarely used in its pure form.

In situations where the teacher believes that pupil choice is important but so also is teacher direction, the teaching method which represents a possibility for such interactive decision making is to be found in the middle of the methods continuum. The labels for the midground method include the *limitation method* (Bilborough & Jones 1966) and the *problem solving style* (Mosston 1966). Essentially the decisions made in this method are shared between the teacher and the pupils, although not necessarily in equal proportions. Typically the teacher would impose some limitation on the possible activity (most likely by suggesting a particular movement problem) and the pupil would experiment within the limitations to determine their best response. Obviously there would be multiple responses to the same problem and class discussion might follow focussing on the similarities and differences in the class responses. For example, in gymnastics the teacher might pose the problem of finding different ways of getting on and off pieces of apparatus while taking weight on different parts of the body. While the teacher sets the problem, the pupils are free to find a range of ways of moving, with no specific response being the correct or more accurate one.

The limitation method seems rarely to be taken up in secondary physical education except with classes in the early years of secondary school. You are likely to be most familiar with it as movement education, educational gymnastics and/or creative dance/movement. More recently, however, constructivist theories of learning have provided a stronger theoretical foundation for student-centred approaches and for understanding how students might learn *through* physical activity.

Towards a social constructivist approach to learning

In a different way, pupils' learning can be supported by the process of *scaffolding* whereby the degree and kind of assistance that teachers provide change as pupils become more competent at a particular task. Scaffolding can be provided by teachers or more skilled or knowledgeable peers and must be suited to a student's current level of proficiency. As discussed above, physical education has traditionally relied heavily on a transmission model of teaching where the teacher is assumed to be the authority who transmits information and skill to those who are less expert. In education generally there has been a shift in thinking, if not always in practice, away from the transmission model to one which places more emphasis on collaborative learning as students interact with one another to solve problems. This is based on the work of two important theorists, Jean Piaget and Lev Vygotsky. The following accounts are very selective but point to aspects of these writers' work which are relevant to the teaching of physical education. The work of Vygotsky, in particular, has been extended by Lave & Wenger (1991) to take more account of the social contexts in which students themselves are situated and the social contexts in which their learning is embedded.

Piaget is probably best known for his argument that there are specific stages of cognitive and motor development, each of which must be completed successfully before progressing to the next. This position has now been challenged, as have many developmentalist arguments which claim universal stages for all individuals irrespective of culture, experience, sex and so on. What is important for our purposes is that Piaget was one of the first theorists to suggest that learning occurred *through interaction with the environment*. He argued that pupils are active seekers of knowledge; that they are self-motivated and form ideas and test them against the world without outside pressure.

Vygotsky also thought that pupils were active seekers of knowledge but that rather than being an individual process, learning happened *through interactions with others* and this happened mostly through language. One of the most important features of Vygotskian theory is that it is based on an understanding of learnings as cultural so that, as a pupil/person interacts with other members of a specific culture, so they come to master activities and think in ways which have meaning in their culture. Learning for Vygotsky is something that also builds on the learner's existing knowledge and understanding.

Vygotsky's concept of the *zone of proximal development* refers to a range of tasks that a pupil cannot do alone but can accomplish with the assistance of more skilled or knowledgeable peers. In a similar way he uses the notion of *intersubjectivity* to describe how two participants in an interaction—for instance, in a problem solving activity—who bring different understandings of the problem can through dialogue come to a shared understanding. In a different way, pupils' learning can be supported by the process of *scaffolding* whereby the degree and kind of assistance that teachers provide change as pupils become more competent at a particular task. For instance, with the sport education model, teachers provide assistance in the learning of skills through direct teaching in the initial stages of a sports unit but gradually withdraw their involvement as students become more expert.

In emphasising the importance of social interaction and particular peer interaction in learning Vygotsky's ideas have promoted new ways of thinking about teaching and learning which point to the importance of setting up situations to promote teacher–pupil and pupil–pupil interaction. Although there are debates as to whether the social construction of meaning occurs best between teacher and pupil or pupil and pupil it is likely that both approaches have something to offer. What seems to be important here is the collaborative construction of meaning rather than the transmission of knowledge from teacher to pupil. This requires carefully planned tasks, activities and the interactions designed to extend students' understandings. For instance, researchers who have investigated the possibilities of peer collaboration suggest that cooperative learning does not happen automatically by simply organising students into groups. Groups are more likely to foster learning if they are structured so that students are working together towards a common goal, when guidelines for working together are made explicit and when the group consists of students of various ages and abilities.

Constructivist learning and physical education

Prain & Hickey (1995) provide examples of interactions in physical education which have been designed to scaffold student problem solving and to challenge dominant transmission modes of teaching. Through the close analysis of the language of lessons taught by a group of student teachers they demonstrate how different forms of questioning either work against or assist student understanding of the principles underpinning the performance of specific activities. They point out how the most common form of questioning in physical education, where the teacher initiates (I) a question (to which they already know the answer), the pupil responds (R) and the teacher evaluates (E) the pupil's answer, assumes that skill acquisition and close control of the class is of prime importance. The following is an example of an IRE sequence taken from the introduction to a warm-up activity.

Barry:	Fiona, what do I do if I call 'hare'?
Student 1:	Knees up high.
Barry:	Knees up high, good. And what do I do if I call 'hound'?
Student 2:	Kick our legs behind.
Barry:	Great.

(Prain & Hickey 1995, p 80. Reprinted by permission.)

In contrast, the approach taken by several students was designed to engage pupils in learning through problem solving and scaffolded interaction with the teacher. Through their analysis of the interactions between student teacher and pupils, Prain & Hickey were able to demonstrate how the teacher's questions and interactions encouraged the generation of new meanings and individual interpretations. Pupils were encouraged to discuss their own understandings and experiences through the teacher's invitations to elaborate on their answers and through questions that did not assume one right answer.

One student teacher, Sarah, set up three groups of hurdles. One group was set up at 8-metre intervals, another at 6 metres and the third at 4 metres. The pupils were asked to form groups and decide which set of hurdles they preferred and to identify the reasons for their preference. The following is a transcript of the some of the discussion after students had attempted all hurdles. It is useful in reflecting on this example to look at who does the most talking; who provides the information; how Sarah's questions assist students to arrive at solutions to the problem; and how this sequence of interactions is different from the IRE sequence described above.

Sarah:	*Who wants to start us off?*
Student 1:	*I reckon the first ones are best because you've got more time to pick up speed whereas the second ones are too close.*
Student 2:	*Yeah, I reckon the first ones as well, because you've got more time to run up and think about how you're going to jump them.*
Student 3:	*I think the first set were the second most difficult because you get too much time to run and you get puffed out of breath.*
Student 4:	*The first ones are good because you get to jump on the same foot every time whereas the second ones I didn't get time to change my feet and jumped right foot, left foot and right foot again (referring to the three-hurdle sequence).*
Sarah:	*And what's that got to do with it?*
Student 4:	*It's just harder.*
Student 5:	*Because it depends on what foot you like to jump with, and you need to get the right (meaning preferred) foot up, the one you jump with.*
Sarah:	*But how do you know which one you jump with?*
Student 5:	*It just feels right.*
Student 4:	*And sometimes, if you've got your feet wrong, the one that you're supposed to jump with hits the hurdle.*
Student 6:	*If you have enough space, you've got time to get the foot you want to jump with in front.*
Student 5:	*Yes*
Student 7:	*I like to jump with my right foot because it feels better, and I just do. I liked the second hurdles best because they're just exactly right.*
Sarah:	*What do you mean by exactly right?*
Student 7:	*They're just the right distance apart for me and it feels comfortable jumping them.*

(Prain & Hickey 1995, p 82. Reprinted by permission.)

Whereas the constructivist approaches discussed so far look to the immediate social context as important to a student's ability to take up (internalise) new concepts and ideas, Lave & Wenger (1991) take a different approach with their theory of situated learning. Like the constructivists described above, Lave & Wenger argue that learning occurs through the 'active involvement of individuals in the construction of knowledge through meaningful social activity' (Kirk & Macdonald 1998). However, rather than taking learning to be purely a cognitive process, they see it as a social practice, evidenced by and happening through increasing participation in communities of practice. In some ways this can be compared to an apprenticeship, where a person shapes their identity and their relationships with others and their society through learning the ways of behaving, values, knowledge—that is, the social practices—of their occupation (their community of practice).

Kirk & Macdonald (1998) suggest that the theory of situated learning provides important ways of rethinking school physical education to be responsive to contemporary contexts of physical activity and physical culture. Like Tinning & Fitzclarence (1992) they point to the discrepancies between school physical education and the cultures of physical activity outside the school. Specifically they contrast the transmission mode of physical education with the communities of practice associated with sport, exercise and recreation. While physical education may make claims to prepare students for participation in physical activity outside school, they argue that school physical education rarely does this. They do suggest that there are forms of physical education currently available that have begun to address this issue. For instance, sport education (as described in more detail in Chapter 12) as a form of physical education modelled on community sport provides opportunities for students to learn not only how to become players but also how to become managers, coaches, officials, publicists and so on. They also recognise, however, that the contemporary practice of sport is associated with cheating, drug taking and violence and that students need to develop the skills to be critical consumers of sport as well as enthusiastic participators.

Teaching moral and social responsibility through physical education

In ways not dissimilar from that of situated learning, other writers in the area of physical education (such as Martinek & Hellison 1997 and Miller et al 1997) have looked to providing young people with opportunities to participate in the community as socially responsible and self-regulating individuals. Although the work of Martinek & Hellison and Miller and his colleagues has been with young people at risk, their approaches provide directions for physical education more generally for students to be involved directly in activities which develop social and moral attributes. They are concerned with the ways in which learning contexts can be explicitly designed to promote these attributes. Miller et al (1997), for instance, describe four sets of intervention strategies to achieve the goals of developing empathy, moral reasoning capacity, task-oriented motivation and self-responsibility skills. These are cooperative learning, promoting moral community, creating a mastery climate and shifting power to students as they develop the skills to assume greater responsibility. They emphasise a process where students come to recognise and identify with communal norms through peer discussion of critical issues as they arise. For example, instances of cheating or aggression might generate a peer discussion about the appropriateness of these behaviours in the particular group or class in which they have occurred.

They also suggest that there are two main ways in which people are motivated to demonstrate competence: through 'task orientation' where skill mastery and self-improvement are of central importance; and 'ego orientation' where beating others is of most importance. They argue that the latter is more likely to foster cheating and aggression given the importance of winning. Situations which emphasise the importance of competition against others, where the feedback is based on comparison with peers or a standard and where an audience is important, foster ego orientation. Situations which are cooperative, where there is no audience and where feedback is based on personal mastery and improvement, are more likely to foster task orientation and intrinsic motivation for tasks.

Which of these orientations does the teaching environment in physical education foster? Physical education environments are often characterised by competitive situations such as relays, competition to see who can finish a drill first or who can perform most successfully often with all or part of the class as an audience. Our assessment procedures compare one student with another rather than measure their progress given their capabilities.

In their program Miller et al (1997) 'de-emphasised zero-sum competition and emphasised individual improvement, learning and having fun'. For instance, students might negotiate contracts individually or collectively with the teacher as to the ways in which they might best improve their fitness on the basis of what they can do in and outside class. Rather than comparing each student against a standard or other members of the class, students can then maintain a record of progress for the various fitness components throughout the term or a year. In this way teachers can work with individual students to set appropriate goals, provide feedback on individual per-formance, personal effort and progress rather than comparisons with other students. Students can be assessed on their progress, their documentation of their own fitness plan and its appropriateness to their lifestyle and needs, and their ability to reflect on what has made it easy or difficult to maintain.

The work of Thomas Martinek and Don Hellison (1997) and Nicholas Cutforth (1997) provides further examples of ways of working with young people. Although the programs they describe and the principles they have developed are primarily designed to provide guidelines for working through physical activity with young people at risk, there are more general messages for working with the diversity of students we are likely to find in physical education classes. The principles and approaches these writers espouse are designed to promote participants' sense of personal and social responsibility. For instance, they emphasise the importance of being sensitive to the ways in which students are different from one another—including acknowledging the different ways young people may take up identification associated with race, ethnicity and gender (and disability for that matter). Such injunctions are about avoiding stereotyping and about reflecting on the assumptions we have about cultural groups, about boys as compared with girls and so on. As Martinek & Hellison point out, 'It is therefore crucial to be sensitive to each (person's) individuality as well as the more generic cultural differences' (1997, p 42). They also suggest that it is important to treat young people as resources to be developed rather than problems to be managed; to work from their strengths rather than their weaknesses and to emphasise their competence and mastery, thereby building their self confidence, self worth and ability to contribute.

What can be learned from these programs with at-risk youth is that pupils can be active agents in their own development, that they can learn at different rates, and that physical education classes can be settings in which students and teachers share decision making, explore and practise values, teamwork, goal setting, peer teaching, conflict resolution and other practices associated with developing social and moral responsibility.

Learning about the physical: becoming critical consumers of physical activity and physical culture

Learning about the physical extends to both scientific and socio-cultural fields of human movement. However, the purpose here is to focus on socio-cultural knowledge about physical activity as this assists young people to develop the understandings and the skills to become more critical consumers of physical culture. Although learning about the physical can (and should) begin in primary school, most senior syllabuses in physical education now refer explicitly to 'critical inquiry' or 'critical thinking' in relation to learning *about* physical education.

'Critical' from our point of view requires an understanding of the ways meanings about health and physical activity are socially constructed—that is, how these meanings change over time and differ for different groups of people. Such a notion of 'critical' assumes, however, that some meanings are more likely to be taken for granted—that is, they are dominant or hegemonic—and others are likely to be marginalised. The important point here is that the meanings we might sometimes take for granted are not necessarily shared by other cultures or by those who have had a different set of experiences from our own. It is possible, for instance, to generate a series of commonly held beliefs or myths which are often used to support particular policies and practices in relation to sport and physical education.

One such myth is that all Australians are obsessed by sport. Although many Australians watch and participate in sport—and this statement usually refers to competitive team and a few individual sports such as tennis and golf—this does not take into account the considerable percentage of the population who do not watch, who do not participate, or who participate in recreational and leisure activities unrelated to sport. It fails to take into account the many people from cultures where sport is not central to their lives and who would nevertheless still judge themselves to be 'Australians'.

One of the key features of contemporary physical culture is the promotion of messages about the body, physical activity and sport through the media. It would seem important, then, to assist students to develop skills which will enable them to become critical 'readers' and 'watchers' of the print and electronic media. Being a critical reader means being able to recognise how language use and choices of visual images help to create particular sets of meanings which connect with values and beliefs that are important to the consumer. While the most obvious examples are advertisements (see for example the Reebok ad on page 33) because their express purpose is to persuade, cultural messages are promoted in all media coverage, print and electronic, including coverage of sport, stories about athletes and editorials that cover issues around physical activity and the body.

A starting point is to ask questions (to interrogate) media coverage. For instance, using any newspapers or magazines such as *Inside Sport* (women's sports magazine) or specialist magazines for surfing, rollerblading, soccer, AFL, aerobics and so on, carry out the following analysis of the print media.

 over to you

Media text analysis

Looking at any newspaper as a whole,

1 What proportion of it is devoted to what broad topics—that is, local news, international news, sport and so on?

Looking specifically at the sporting sections of the magazine or newspaper:

2 What proportion of the coverage is given to which sports? What proportion is given to men's sports as compared with women's sports; the sports played by cultural minorities in the community; the sports played by different social class groups? Whose sports are absent? Whose present? Are there differences in the ways the various sports are presented? For what readership does it seem intended? Who is excluded?

Choose one or two texts and look at these more closely.

3 (a) If there is a photograph, what images are portrayed? How has it been taken? (What camera angles have been used? Is it live or staged? How does it relate to the text? What kind of relationship does it construct between the reader and the people in the photograph?)

(b) How does the headline fit with the text (and/or accompanying photographs)? What metaphors or other language devices are employed to catch your eye? What does it promise?

(c) In the article(s), who or what are the main protagonists (participants)—for example, particular athletes, coaches, teams, locations? How are they described—that is, what attributes (adjectives) are associated with them? What actions are they associated with (what processes—verbs—are used with the participants)? How are these processes qualified (what adverbs are used with them)?

(d) How is the article written? What is assumed about the reader (in terms of prior knowledge, values, interests, understanding of technical language)?

Relate what you have found from your analysis of the text(s) to:
4 (a) what you understand as the dominant discourses or sets of values and beliefs that describe social class, race, ethnicity, age, sexuality and gender in Western culture.
(b) How are these (re)produced or challenged by these texts?

Similar questions can be asked about television coverage of sport and physical activity. Which sports receive the most coverage? Why is this the case? How do the camera shots and the commentary reproduce or challenge dominant sets of values and beliefs such as those about nationalism, law and order, gender, sexuality, social class, ethnicity, race? How do they work to construct one particular view of the world rather than others?

Summary

- What happens in classrooms in terms of teaching practices are based on particular assumptions about how students learn. These assumptions, however, are rarely examined and teaching occurs on the basis of what has been done before.
- In physical education, the traditional approaches tend to be teacher-centred and focussed on the acquisition of physical skills.
- Constructivist learning theory suggests alternative forms of practice which are more student-centred and engage students in problem solving and a more complex engagement with physical activity.

References

Bilborough, A. & Jones, P. (1966). *Physical Education in the Primary School*. London: University of London Press.

Cutforth, N.J. (1997). 'What's worth doing?: Reflections on an after-school program in a Denver elementary school'. *Quest* 49(1), pp 130–139.

Kirk, D. & Macdonald, D. (1998). 'Situated learning in physical education'. *Journal of Teaching in Physical Education*, 17(3), pp 376–387.

Lave, J. & Wenger, E. (1991). *Situated Learning: Legitimate Peripheral Participation*. Cambridge: Cambridge University Press.

Martinek, T.J. & Hellison, D.R. (1997). 'Fostering resiliency in underserved youth through physical activity'. *Quest*, 49(1), pp 33–49.

Miller, S.C., Bredemeier, B. & Shields, D.L.L. (1997). 'Sociomoral education through physical education with at-risk children'. *Quest*, 49(1), pp 114–129.

Mosston, M. (1966). *Teaching Physical Education: From Command to Discovery*. Columbus, OH: Charles Merrill.

Prain, V. & Hickey, C. (1995). 'Using discourse analysis to change physical education'. *Quest*, 47(1), pp 76–90.

Tinning, R. & Fitzclarence, L. (1992). 'Postmodern youth culture and the crisis in Australian secondary school physical education'. *Quest*, 44(3), pp 287–304.

Underwood, G. (1988) *Teaching and Learning in Physical Education: A Social Psychological Perspective*. London: Falmer Press.

Yuasa, Y. (1987). *The Body: Toward an Eastern Mind-Body Theory*. Albany: State University of New York Press.

Further reading

Kirk, D., Macdonald, D., Jobling, I. & Nauright, J. (1996). *The Sociocultural Foundations of Human Movement*. Melbourne: Macmillan.

Hickey, C. & Fitzclarence, L. (1999). 'Educating boys in sport and physical education: Using narrative methods to develop pedagogies of responsibility'. *Sport, Education and Society*, 4(1), pp 51–62.

curriculum

issues

section
four

chapter
eleven

objectives

By the end of this chapter you should be able to:

- recognise how particular discourses have shaped the physical education curriculum over time;
- understand that competing discourses represent vested power relations at play in the process of curriculum development;
- appreciate how physical education has contributed to the making of certain types of citizen;
- appreciate the significance of the discourses of health and sport in the development of the physical education curriculum;
- recognise the centrality of discourses of the body, and in particular of the science of the body, in the development of physical education curriculum;
- appreciate how the privileged discourses of PETE affect how teachers think about physical education in school.

Introduction

The shore of physical education is strewn with the wrecks of systems and movements, many of them good in themselves, but left to drift when the personal support and enthusiasm of the founder was removed from the helm. (Fred Eugene Leonard 1923, p vii)

If you were suddenly transported back to the mid 1960s and enrolled in a typical PETE program of the time, you would notice some familiar and some unfamiliar aspects of the course. In the PETE curriculum you would recognise some subjects but not others. For example, you would not find units on biomechanics, exercise physiology or sports psychology. But you would find units on the anatomical bases for physical education, the principles of PE, practical activities, and perhaps body mechanics and teaching methods. The PETE curriculum, like the school curriculum, changes over time. Some of the changes are cosmetic, some substantial. The similarities are reflections of the enduring issues of the field, the differences are reflections of the way in which all curricula include manifestations of contemporary issues of the field. As the quote above suggests, some of the ideas and curricula cease to be popular when their initiator ceases to provide the advocacy necessary to sustain them. In this chapter we will look at some of the enduring issues which have oriented much of the thinking of the field and its school curricula manifestations.

One of the subjects that sometimes finds a place in a PETE course is the *History and Philosophy of PE* in which the major events, people and ideas of the field are studied. For many PETE students, however, this subject has seldom been highly regarded. Indeed it is sometimes referred to by the pejorative name of Hiss & Piss! Most students would see the relevance of learning about the muscular system of the body but few see the relevance of learning the history of the field. Topics such as 'The place of physical education in ancient Greece and Rome', 'Friedrich Ludwig Jahn and popular gymnastics in Germany', 'Per Henrick Ling, the father of Swedish gymnastics', which are often recognised content in a history of physical education (see Leonard 1923), would probably not enthuse a contemporary PETE student like you.

These topics of history are not 'essential' knowledge for physical education given that it is possible to teach PE without ever having heard of the likes of Swedish gymnastics or Per Henrick Ling. But they are examples of major ideas, key people and ways of thinking which have influenced physical education, and accordingly physical education curricula. As you will learn in this chapter, all school curricula include ideas and ways of thinking which are considered to be important or significant. But who makes the judgments as to the significance or otherwise of an idea or a particular piece of content? Physical education as a field is itself made up of individuals with differing and competing opinions with respect to what (and whose) knowledge is most important. Indeed, this is at the very heart of the contestation inherent in curriculum development.

A history of the present

History is not mechanical, not passively suffered: history is made. If we hope to play a worthwhile part in it, we must begin by thinking carefully about what material we have to work with, the historical moment we are in. (Connell 1987, p 1)

Through the work of curriculum theorists such as Ivor Goodson we have come to better understand the relationship between history and the present. Goodson (1992) argues that in order to understand, and change, contemporary curriculum practice we need to examine how those practices have come to be constituted or made up as they are. For example, when we pick up a curriculum document such as the *Health and Physical Education KLA* what we see is something constructed by *certain people for certain purposes*. In one sense it represents how the particular investments of one group have become privileged over another group.

Viewing curriculum this way demands that we recognise that 'meaning' is not stable or universal, but rather that it is contested and negotiated. Curriculum is not like some inscribed tablet handed down from a higher being on the mountain. Curriculum is a human-made thing. It involves struggles for ascendancy between competing groups, with competing views of what should be foregrounded in the practice and purpose of a particular discipline. For those that win the day, their prize is to set the agenda for what will be recognised as legitimate curriculum practice.

Physical education curriculum practice, like any other area of the curriculum, is the product of struggles and contestations between particular groups (or ideas), some of which have had more power to have their version of what is important heard at any one time. Two examples of such contestation or struggle are:

(a) the gendered nature of physical education. Whereas feminist scholars argue (and have demonstrated) that physical education harbours many sexist beliefs and practices, many physical education advocates assume that physical education is essentially gender-neutral and that when boys and girls participate in the same experiences, they take away the same meanings and outcomes.

(b) the assumptions underpinning curriculum orientation. Historically, those espousing the importance of measurement and the scientific bases of human movement have been challenged by those emphasising a more student-centred and problem solving approach to physical education (and of course vice versa).

In keeping with our use of the term 'discourse' to refer to the knowledge values and ways of seeing that serve to regulate and control social relations and practices, these positions can be understood as constituting some of the major discourses which have influenced the development of physical education. In this chapter we explore some of the discourses which we, and others, have identified as those which have been, or are currently, dominant

discourse

in physical education curricula and those which their dominance marginalises. Two groups of enduring discourses are those around health and sport. These, in different ways, intersect with discourses that have to do with gender, ethnicity, social class, dis(ability) and the commodified body.

The discourses that constitute the values and beliefs of physical education are not simply abstract concepts; they affect our everyday practices as physical education teachers (and PETE educators). Moreover, our everyday practices— the way we organise classes, our choices of activities, the way we interact with students—contribute to the reproduction of these discourses or make change possible, no matter how small. To this end, in our view it is an important process to 'unpack' the 'taken-for-grantedness' of the contemporary curriculum. By this we mean to actively reflect on the enduring and contemporary discourses, issues and themes that make up our curriculum. In one sense this is part of the 'duty' of a reflective teacher.

Physical education and the making of citizens

One way to think about where our current physical education curriculum 'comes from' is to consider the ends to which physical education has been put since its inception. If we consider physical education as a 'vehicle' used for particular purposes then we can see how these purposes might have changed over the years and also how they might have remained the same. Certain discourses or ways of thinking about physical education will have prominence as they accord with the ways in which governments, scientists, the military, parents and educators have conceived of the purpose of physical education.

Like all curricula, physical education has always found its place in the schooling of young people because of the specific contributions it has claimed to make to the development of certain types of citizens. All states (governments) have a vested interest in having schooling produce certain types of citizen. For example, what state would want its young people not to acquire the skills of literacy and numeracy? Literate and numerate citizens are essential for developing and 'mature' states. Think of the rhetoric that surrounded the development of Australia as a 'clever country' (see Jones 1983) and the place of the school curriculum in that development. The education of young people in information technologies (IT) is now considered essential to the development of a 'clever country'. The 'clever country' will also have citizens who understand languages other than English (LOTE) to be productive in the global market. Contemporary school curricula will include both IT and LOTE because these contribute to the making of a certain (clever) type of future citizen.

Over the years physical education has been used in the schooling of young people to produce healthy, disciplined, docile, fit, nationalistic, courageous, active citizens. At different times in the past century some of these attributes or characteristics have had more prominence than others and have been used in relation to different groups of people.

In what follows we will look more specifically at the development of the physical education curriculum over the past 100 years or so with the purpose of making explicit the discourses that have influenced particular versions of the curriculum. As we do this, it is important to realise that the actual writing of text takes on a linear form which actually belies the relatively non-linear development of curriculum ideas. While it is true that certain events occurred before or after certain other events, major ideas tend to circulate and mix with one another rather as water colours might run together on a painting. Trying to pull them apart is therefore always problematic. While there are limitations with two-dimensional drawings, Figure 11.1 attempts to represent some of the connections that underpin our discussion.

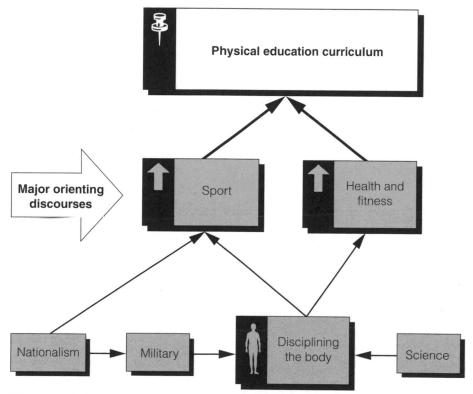

Figure 11.1 Influential discourses in the physical education curriculum

Health and fitness

When you ask teachers why PE is important in the school curriculum, many will argue in terms of the health benefits it fosters. The prominence of health in the physical education curriculum is not something that is new. Since its inception in the late 19th century, the role of physical education as a vehicle through which young people could be developed into healthy adults has been at the forefront of its educational mission.

One of the long-standing argued contributions of school physical education has been to help ameliorate some of the problems of the increasingly sedentary lifestyle of young people. In Victoria, as early as 1866, Gustav Techow, an immigrant who was a former Prussian army officer and physical culturist, published a *Manual of Gymnastics Exercises* in which he claimed that his ' "systematic culture of the muscle" ... had a counterbalancing effect on the "pernicious influences of civilized life, from the lengthened and arduous labours of the office and the workshop, the keen strife of ambition and the lust of enjoyment"' (Kirk 1993, p 41). Physical educators of the late 19th century (although they were not called that then) believed that 'ordinary people were inherently weak and feeble, needing to be protected from their own folly and rashness'. Lawson (1993) claimed that these early human movement professionals were worried (and rightly so) about the ill-health caused by industrialisation and they advocated, with evangelistic zeal, 'exercise programs aimed at restoring and maintaining the bodily health of the masses' (Lawson 1993, p 3). According to Lawson, professionals at that time, believed that 'without compulsion and regulation, persons needing these [exercises] the most would not experience them'. Moreover, 'Without professional regulation, the health, lifestyles, and lives of ordinary people will be adversely affected' (p 4). Does this all sound somewhat familiar? It should, for this is a very similar discourse to that which is championed by many human movement professionals today.

In the early 20th century, with the introduction of compulsory primary education, the purpose of PT (the forerunner to modern physical education) and variations of Swedish gymnastics (a system of exercises developed by Per Henrick Ling) were decidedly therapeutic in terms of their designed benefits to the health of the individual. Such a curriculum for physical activity was set in the context of widespread concern over the increasingly 'unhealthy' environment of life in the growing cities. In mid to late 1930s when the 1933 *Syllabus of Physical Training for Schools* was published: 'The conditions of modern civilization with its crowded localities, confined spaces, and sedentary occupations; the increasing need for study and mental application; and the many social circumstances and difficulties which restrict opportunities for natural physical growth, all require that children and young people should receive physical training by well-considered methods devised in a broad and Catholic spirit to promote and encourage the health and development of the mind and body' (Board of Education; p 9). Importantly, this British syllabus became the curriculum document for Australian physical education for schools from the mid 1930s to mid 40s. In 1946, the curriculum *Physical Education for Victorian Schools* (known as the Grey Book) became the first Australian written physical education textbook for teachers and it, too, foregrounded the role of physical education in ameliorating the increasingly harsh and sedentary conditions of modern city life.

The influence of these conditions and habits must be anticipated and counteracted by physical education, and young people and old must be provided with healthful means of spending the leisure that is available to them.

Healthy young children display an irresistible desire for movement . . . The inability to satisfy this urge, or the deliberate suppression of it, will invariably have a harmful effect on the physique, the bodily and mental health, and the personality of the individual. (Education Department of Victoria 1946, p vi)

Although the contribution of physical activity to children's health has long been one of the main legitimations for the inclusion of physical education in the curriculum, the meanings attributed to health and the movement activities themselves varied considerably for male as compared with female students and whether one attended a private or government school (Wright 1996).

In the 19th and early 20th century, games and calisthenics (derived from Swedish gymnastics) were the favoured forms of physical activity for the physical education of the daughters of the wealthy middle class. Such activities were thought to ensure that they developed bodies capable of producing healthy children, as is indicated in a quote from the headmistress of a private girls' school: 'Important as are bodily vigour and active strength . . . in the men of a country who may have to endure the supreme test of physical fitness in war, the vitality and passive strength—potential energy—of its women are even more important, since Nature has ordained women to be mothers of the race' (Burstall, quoted in Atkinson 1978, p 126).

For the education of working class girls and boys attending government schools health meant something very different. For them health was conceived in terms of order, cleanliness and neatness (Wright 1996). Indeed, the regimentation of marching and drill in addition to exercises based on the Swedish system of calisthenics was seen to provide a means 'to mould behaviour of undisciplined boys, to inculcate habits of sharp obedience, smartness, order and cleanliness' (Crawford 1980, p 38).

For middle and upper class males in private schools, however, health outcomes were considered less important. In the private boys' schools physical education consisted primarily of competitive team games and sport intended to develop the masculine virtues of courage and loyalty seen to be essential to their future roles in leadership (see 'Sporting discourses', below).

Fit to fight

Throughout the 20th century the occurrence of wars has influenced the physical education curriculum. The military influence in schools began during the late 1800s in response to the widespread concerns over discipline. At the turn of the century physical education in Victorian state elementary schools consisted mainly of class drill, which typically employed a mixture of military manoeuvres such as marching and squad drill and physical exercises associated with Swedish gymnastics (sometimes known as calisthenics) (Kirk 1993, p 39).

The threat of war (whether real or perceived) has clearly been a source of stimulation and invigoration for physical education. The threat of war has often been accompanied by a heightened focus on marching and military drill. In the 19th and through to the mid 20th century, drill, which was frequently taken by service officers, was seen as a means of inculcating obedience and the ability to work in unison and respond to commands. For young men and women this regimen was seen as the ideal way to inculcate habits associated with compliance, obedience, neatness and respect (Kirk 1992). Activities such as rifle drill were also introduced into the physical education curriculum as a means of directly training young men for a future participation in armed combat.

In more recent years the threat of the cold war in the 1950s, 60s and 70s motivated a concern for the fitness of young population that might have to go to war. When the youth of the United States recorded poorer outcomes on tests for physical fitness than their European counterparts, President Kennedy mobilised a major fitness campaign in and outside schools. As was common practice at that time in history, Australia followed suit with national fitness testing (ACHPER fitness tests) and an increased emphasis on physical education for fitness encouraged in Australian schools.

Fitness for health

Although sport, games and motor skills have been the dominant focus of physical education since the 1960s (see Gray 1985), the health promoting benefits of exercise have been a regular and significant inclusion in the objectives of physical education. For example, in the Victorian education department's *Suggested Course of Study for Primary Schools: Physical Education* published in 1970, among the list of the aims of physical education the first was: 'To establish a sound basis for healthy living' (p 3). Similarly in the South Australian *Daily Physical Education Program* published in 1982, the first listed benefit of physical education is to 'become fitter and healthier' (p 3).

It is, however, the 1970s and 1980s which can be identified as the period of increased health consciousness for Australian and New Zealand and other Western cultures and which provided the strongest contextual influence on physical education's contribution to the development of the healthy citizen. The 'new' health consciousness was manifest in such cultural practices as the purchase of unleaded petrol, the increase of fibre in the diet, the banning of smoking in many workplaces, the mandatory wearing of seatbelts, and the jogging and aerobics boom.

The new health consciousness began in the late 1960s and early 1970s when there was a developing awareness of the increase of diseases associated with affluence. Some medical researchers of the time labelled the group of diseases, which included stroke and coronary heart disease (CHD) in its various forms, the 'hypokinetic diseases'. Hypokinetic diseases, as the name suggests, are associated with a modern lifestyle which is increasingly sedentary. Associated with decreased physical activity, modern Australian lifestyles were also claimed to be characterised by abundance of food, an increase in stress and an increase in cigarette smoking. Accordingly, it was during the 1970s that 'lifestyle' became a key concept in the discourses of physical education and health. It is no accident that the flagship journal of the professional association for health and physical education in Australia (ACHPER) is called the *ACHPER Healthy Lifestyles Journal.*

Within this context some Australian states mandated that physical education be conducted on a daily basis in all primary schools. In this health-oriented physical education (HOPE, as Tinning 1991 called it) the assumed relationship between health and exercise was essentially that exercise equated to fitness which in turn equated to health. This unproblematic triplex was part of a set of assumptions and beliefs described by Crawford (1980) as 'healthism'. According to Kirk & Colquhoun (1989), healthism has a number of main assumptions:

- that health is a self-evident good;
- that individuals are responsible for their own health;
- that the body can be considered analogous to a machine; and
- that exercise equates with fitness which, in turn, equates with health.

For some physical educators, these four assumptions actually represent the core beliefs that underpin the way in which they think about and conduct their professional (and private) lives.

One explicit response to the concerns associated with hypokinetic disease was the development of a physical education curriculum that foregrounded fitness and health. The *Daily Physical Education Program* (1982) was a response to concerns over health. As the then Director-General of the South Australian education department stated, 'the growing community concern for the health and well being of children has been an important consideration in the development of daily physical education' (1982, p v). Further, the opening sentence in the section on the benefits of the Program states unequivocally that 'the Daily Physical Education Program lays great stress on the fact that regular, vigorous physical activity makes a positive contribution to children's health' (1982, p 4).

The Program was very much a health-based physical education curriculum and as it was purchased by thousands of primary schools throughout Australia it actually became something of a de-facto 'national curriculum' (Tinning 1987). It consisted of seven volumes (one for each year level of primary school), and each volume contained complete details of the organisational guidelines for physical education and 40–50 complete lesson plans in each of the program areas of fitness, dance, movement exploration, games skills and water activities. Apart from the fitness lessons, the emphasis of the other program areas was skill development.

Importantly, it was the Daily Physical Education Program that first identified fitness as a *separate* area of physical education. No longer was it seen to be acceptable to assume that adequate fitness (and by association health) would be developed merely by participation in the conventionally defined activities of physical education. Fitness was seen to be too important to a healthy lifestyle to leave to chance and, accordingly, it was defined as a separate area of the Program. The organisation of the Program suggested that fitness was so central to the purposes of physical education that it warranted a special session on the school timetable in addition to regular skill development lessons. What we see in this example is that the Program was a representation of a particular view with respect to the contribution of physical activity to health. It was a narrowly defined conception of health, but it was the one that gained the privileged position in the curriculum.

In New South Wales, however, following the growing importance of health education in North America, moves were afoot to introduce a separate health studies syllabus (New South Wales' 1965 syllabus was already a Health and Physical Education Syllabus). In 1983/84 a Health Education Syllabus was released and health education was incorporated into the training of preservice physical education teachers. By 1991 health, personal development and physical education had been combined in the PDHPE KLA, which was most often taught by physical education teachers. The integration of health and physical education in New South Wales foreshadowed curriculum developments in Australia more generally.

It is important to recognise that while all this curriculum development was happening for primary school physical education there was little attention given to curriculum development for secondary schools. The most significant curriculum development for secondary school physical education from the mid to late 1980s was the introduction of senior school physical education as an examinable subject. Kirk (1993) goes as far as saying that: 'Apart from the Year 11 and 12 examinable courses in Physical Education that appeared in schools in the mid ninteen seventies [sic], programs in primary and secondary schools consist of the same elements as those mapped out in the Victorian Grey Book of 1946' (p 50). We say more about this curriculum innovation later but for the moment we will stay focussed on health in physical education for the middle school years.

Towards a broader view of health

During the 1990s there have been some big changes regarding the physical education curriculum in both Australia and New Zealand. In both countries the introduction of new Health and Physical Education frameworks that incorporate the traditional school subjects of health, physical education, home economics and outdoor education has had major implications for physical education. This new relationship between subjects has been possible partly because of an expanded concept of health which included physical, mental, social and sometimes spiritual well-being. This is particularly evident in the *Health and Physical Education in the New Zealand Curriculum* (1999), where the

Maori concept of Hauora is used to locate well-being as a central concept underpinning the framework.

However, as was the case in the early versions of the Australian 'national' curriculum, such a notion of health may threaten the independence of physical education which may be subsumed (and perhaps marginalised) under the 'health' umbrella. Indeed, in Australia, when the various state ministers of education agreed in 1989 on the principle of a 'national curriculum' which developed skills and competencies in eight Key Learning Areas, physical education was *not* designated as one of areas but was to be subsumed under the Health KLA. Only a hasty name change in April 1993 from 'Health' to 'Health and Physical Education', brought about through concerted lobbying of CURASS (the Australian Education Council's Curriculum and Assessment Committee) by a number of peak interest groups such as CAS (Confederation for Australian Sport) and ACHPER, in addition to the recommendations of the Senate Inquiry, saved the term 'physical education' from disappearing without trace under a 'Health' umbrella.

The key problem for many physical educators and school sports advocates seemed to be that physical education was in grave danger of somehow losing its *identity*, on the one hand to sport, and on the other to fitness and health. How could such a crisis of identity and meaning come about? How could a subject that was well established in most schools, and which has widespread support from a range of interest groups, be so vulnerable to redefinition or submergence in another field?

The reason can be found in the fact that the practices constituting physical education, like any other school subject, are neither fixed nor stable. We have learned from the work of curriculum historians that bodies of knowledge (areas of study), their naming and organisational forms in educational institutions, are constantly in process. Moreover, it is the rule, rather than the exception, that groups within professions and other interested parties regularly contest dominant definitions of a field.

Sporting discourses

Just as health discourses have been an enduring feature of physical education practice, so have those associated with sport. As sport has been incorporated into physical practice, so have the meanings and values about sport which are circulating in the wider culture. Again, while these values have changed over time in many ways some beliefs about the values of sport—for instance, as character building, as training for productive citizenship, as a source of national identity—have been enduring.

oty | over to you

Think back to your own experience of physical education.

- What activities dominated what you did in the PE program? What did you do most of? What did you do little or none of?

We would be surprised if your answer to this question was not 'team games and sports'.

- Given that most syllabuses suggest an even selection between gymnastics, dance, games, aquatics etc., why do you think that the one activity was more dominant?
- What were some of the consequences for students in your classes whose interests might lie elsewhere?
- What were some of the consequences for students from cultural minority backgrounds whose culture did not value team games in the way they are valued in Australia and whose experience did not include extended practise at team games outside the school?

Although sport as an institutionalised form of competitive physical activity with rules and regulations and officials to oversee these is a relatively new creation, its beginnings have integral links to the development of physical education. As Goldlust (1987) points out, modern sport was created by the administrators in British private boys' schools in the late 18th century to introduce discipline to the riotous sons of the affluent middle classes. Games which resembled modern football and cricket, played by local villagers and used by the boys as a pastime, were formalised as activities with written rules.

As pointed out above, these sports then became central to the education of a gentleman and very soon spread throughout Europe and most importantly to the colonies of Australia and New Zealand. When sports were taken up and recreated by the working classes—for instance, rugby league and Australian Rules football—they were valued for their potential to entertain and to provide an income (although somewhat smaller than today) and generally remained outside the school day and, for most of the early 20th century, outside the physical education curriculum. Physical education lessons at that time actually looked different from sports.

As with their private school counterparts, the introduction of sport in the curriculum in the emerging secondary school system was almost exclusively focussed on young males. At this stage sport was not considered appropriate for girls or younger children, who were viewed as too susceptible to injury. Nor was it considered even remotely important, if considered at all, to cater for ethnic, indigenous and/or other marginal groups. Girls were soon invited to be part of the culture of school sport, although their role was to be

Source: Her Majesty's Stationery Office. Crown copyright is reproduced with the permission of the Controller of Her Majesty's Stationery Office.

somewhat less exciting. Concerned about the general lack of support for the boys' sporting endeavours, George Dean, then Secretary of the Melbourne State Schools Association, argued the obligation of women to be more directly involved: 'Now that the rounder rules are printed, it is hoped that more women will take an interest in the games. In some schools, women teachers take a keen interest in the game, and at these places the games are always followed by afternoon tea for the players, thus making the games social functions' (Report to the Minister of Public Instruction, 1908–9, p 70).

Sport now holds a prominent place in the physical education curriculum. Sport is taught in physical education because it is seen to be important to transmit culturally valued activities to the next generation. In some schools it might be difficult to distinguish between a physical education class and a sports period. Sometimes the terms 'sport' and 'physical education' are used synonymously in the context of school curriculum. What is also important to recognise is that sport does not come as a neutral site into physical education practice. It brings with it values and beliefs which are often limiting and oppressive to specific groups of people. This process has been documented fairly thoroughly in the sociological literature on sport and particularly the media coverage of sport as it reproduces cultural messages about gender, race, ethnicity and sexuality. Some of the ways in which this happens are discussed Chapter 7.

In particular one of the consequences of the prominence of sport in the curriculum, particularly with coeducational physical education, had been the marginalisation of dance and gymnastics, areas of physical activity which provide for interests and capabilities which can be quite different from those associated with sport. A consequence of the domination of the physical education curriculum by sport and games has been the construction of female students as 'problems' because they appear less enthusiastic and less skilled than the male students. What is rarely taken into account is that if dance and gymnastics were the dominant forms of physical activity in the curriculum it would be the boys who would be perceived in this way.

The tendency to interchange the terms 'physical education' and 'sport' is considerably more problematic than is often given merit. Whenever physical education has become explicitly focussed on the promotion and development of sport-specific skills, there has been an implicit and explicit privileging of masculine over feminine. Given that a heavy emphasis on competitive team games is so central to the practice of sport (in Western cultures), it is not surprising that the traditional masculine values of courage, strength, loyalty and aggression emerge as the dominant virtues of sporting participation. Indeed, it is widely recognised that sport is a site for the legitimisation of patriarchal understandings of maleness and femaleness.

Also of considerable concern is the extent to which traditional constructions of sport as a social and cultural practice are being increasingly corrupted and/ or distorted. Arguments that participation in sport contributes to the formation of fully rounded individuals are more fragile than ever before. Claims that sport 'fosters social cohesiveness and group unity [. . .] helps to reinforce a sense of solidarity of the communities from which opposing players are drawn [. . .] acts as an avenue to social mobility; sport has often provided realistic opportunities for the common people to acquire prestige and success' (Nettleton 1985, pp 88–89) are increasingly problematic at the beginning of the 21st century. The contemporary context is one in which the heightened exposure of media images of racial vilification, violence, thuggery, exclusion and sexual harassment throws considerable doubt onto the espoused social value of sport. Institutional forms of violence, sexism, elitism, racism and individualism now cast a shadow across the dominant claims of sport's inherent worth.

Further, the work of Fitzclarence & Hickey (2000) and Messner & Sabo (1994) provides powerful insight into the way in which sport can be used as a medium through which to marginalise, alienate, victimise and terrorise the uninitiated or unauthorised. In many ways sport can be seen to legitimise a coercive set of practices that institutionalise pernicious forms of male behaviour. Where the discourses of winning and commodification supplant traditional notions of the 'spirit of contest' there is a clear need to redefine the knowledge and values that comprise the contemporary practice of sport in the school curriculum.

Notwithstanding such challenges to sport as an institution, there is still a popularist conception of school sport as something of a universal good. Olympic swimming star Ian Thorpe captures this opinion in the following statement quoted recently in the *Australian* newspaper (1 September, 1999): ' "School sports are very beneficial", Thorpe says. "They build self-confidence and ideals of team spirit. Being in team environments is vital for learning aspects of life which you have to adopt in going into the workforce. It's not just about fitness but about getting the best out of yourself. If you go into sport and enjoy it and you do your best, you have captured the ideals of sport and will benefit for the rest of your life" '. Many sports practices might be highly problematic but the fact remains that the school physical education curriculum is still significantly influenced by contemporary sporting discourses.

Performance and participation discourses

It is useful to think of contemporary sporting discourses as privileging either performance or participation in sport. Whitson & Macintosh (1990) claimed that the field of physical education was dominated by what they called the 'discourses of performance'. The main consideration with performance-oriented discourses is how performance can be improved or enhanced. Questions of means are dominant. In our universities these discourses are represented in courses on biomechanics, exercise physiology, sports psychology, test and measurements, sports medicine, fitness training and so on. The language of performance discourses is about selection, training, exclusion, survival of the fittest, competition, peaking, no pain no gain, threshold workloads, progressive overload etc.

On the other hand, the 'participation discourses' (Tinning 1997) refer to the discourses which underpin the focus or orientation towards physical activity that is about inclusion, equity, involvement, enjoyment, social justice, caring, cooperation, movement etc. The knowledge which the participation discourses utilise most is derived from the social sciences (sociology, psychology, social psychology, anthropology etc.) and education (teaching and learning).

Of course, the notions of participation and performance are obviously linked, but there are those who regard participation-oriented ideas such as 'sport for all', and even school physical education itself, as of major importance because they provide a broad base for subsequent selection of the best performers for competitive sport (Pyke, 1983). Overall, we contend that it is the performance discourses that are privileged in much of what stands for school sport and, more recently, sport education.

One of the ways in which physical education has responded to some of the rising tide of criticisms of sport has been the incorporation of the term 'sport education' to give a sort of quasi-educational credibility to sport in schools. Sport education is not a neutral term. It has meaning(s) in the context of particular political environments. We are not referring here to political in the sense of party politics but rather to the power plays, lobbying and vested interests involved in personal interactions, and to the discourses which comprise educational policy and other documents pertaining to physical education.

A brief consideration of the recent history of physical education reveals that the term 'sport education' was almost unknown in the 1980s. In 1986 in the forward to the *Aussie Sports Manual*, the general manager of the Australian Sports Commission referred to 'Aussie Sport' as a 'sport education'. The Victorian Education Ministry published a document in 1987 titled *Sport Education* in which it claimed that 'Sport education is part of ... a comprehensive physical education program. Sport education involves education *about* sport, *through* sport and *for* participation in sport' (p 7, original emphasis). Considered in this way, sport (as participation) can be defended in the school curriculum as a means of achieving physical education (as an end).

In the early 1990s a Senate Inquiry investigated and reported on the state of physical education and sport in Australian schools. The inquiry found almost unanimous support for physical education but, at the same time and somewhat paradoxically, noted a disturbing and steady decline in resources and time allocation in schools across Australia. A major problem which the Senate Inquiry acknowledged was that it was not at all obvious exactly what the supporters of physical education meant by the term. Importantly, and rather ironically, the Senate Inquiry itself contributed to the confusion, as it was the first official review of the state of affairs in school physical education *and* sport yet it chose to call its inquiry *Physical and Sport Education*. This subtle name change represents a significant slippage which is itself part of the conceptual problem surrounding the meaning of physical education. Unfortunately, in the Senate Inquiry (and its Victorian counterpart, the *Moneghetti Report*) there is little, if any, serious discussion about what is *educational* about sport education.

Sport education is, however, used in an explicitly educational way in the curriculum model known as SEPEP (Sport Education in Physical Education Program). A discussion of this form of sport education can be found in Chapter 12. Notwithstanding the success of SEPEP in many Australian and New Zealand schools (see Alexander et al 1995), a question our field needs to engage is whether developments in sport education in general are going to contribute further to the identity problems faced within physical education (see Tinning 1995).

Body discourses

Schooling is a central institution that society employs to discipline the bodies of its future citizens. By 'discipline' we mean the process of training young people as compliant, healthy, docile participants in contemporary and future communities. Think for a moment about the way in which young children are placed at desks within classrooms. They must learn to sit at their desk unless directed by the teacher to do otherwise. The active body of the young child is disciplined to 'sit and stay'. One of the first things that the kindergarten children learn is that they must discipline themselves with respect to their toilet demands.

While recognising that the cultural construction of the body has shifted across time, Kirk (1993) acknowledges that physical education is a 'key site' for the passing on of 'dominant social and cultural values and norms' (p 29). In the context of educating young people, physical education has continuously been viewed as the curriculum site where young bodies learn the virtues of discipline and dexterity. Here, the channelling of (excess) energy through physical activity is seen as a vital way of promoting productive citizenship. The cathartic and instrumental value of physical education has a long tradition.

As a curriculum site in which young people acquire understandings through and about their bodies, physical education is thought to play a prominent role in the production and reproduction of dominant understandings about what it is to be healthy, disciplined, male or female, and purposeful.

Science

In very fundamental ways, how we think about health and physical education is integrally related to the ways in which we think about our bodies. Jan Broekhoff, an influential American physical educator, argued that rationalised movements (such as physical education) 'can only emerge in a society when man [sic] has gained the capability of looking at his own body as if it were a thing'(1972, p 88). Broekhoff made important links between ways of thinking about the body and the forms of physical education that dominated European culture in the late 19th and early 20th centuries, in particular the Ling system of Swedish gymnastics. In other words, when it was possible to think about the body in an objective, rationalised way, it was then possible to construct curriculum activities that were designed specifically to develop particular parts of the body.

 over to you

Activity

Look at the extract overleaf from the *Syllabus of Physical Training for Schools*, 1933.

Notice the way in which the exercises are designed to work a particular part of the body, namely the trunk.

Notice also that the pedagogy recommended is one of command and response in which the teacher/instructor makes specific predetermined commands to facilitate certain movement exercises.

Trunk turning

The body turns as far as possible to the left or right. Both knees are quite straight and both feet kept firmly on the ground. The body and head are well stretched throughout the movement. These main points of trunk rotation must be observed in all forms of the exercise. With young children the head should also turn, as this ensures a fuller range of movement. (Fig. 48.)

COMMANDS:

Trunk and head to the left—turn!
As far as possible to the right—turn! etc.
Trunk forward—turn!

When the children are familiar with the movement it should be performed continuously, finishing in the turn position to give opportunity for testing the position and correcting if necessary.

Trunk to the left (right)—turn! Trunk and head turning from side to side—begin!—Stop! Trunk to the front—turn!

The body and head are turned as far as possible to each side.

FIG. 48.

Trunk turning.

NOTE: From the introduction of the exercise the turns are taken from side to side without pause in the forward position. The arms are relaxed and swing with the body. As momentum is gained the arms help to pull the body further round.

There are various forms of this exercise, many of which are described in the tables as they occur. Kneeling and sitting positions (Fig. 49) are particularly suitable in the early stages as they prevent a hollow backed position of the body and so aid in correct performance.

FIG. 49.

(Cross-legged sitting.)
Touch knee with ear.

(Feet close, arms forward, fists touching.)
Trunk turning with single elbow bending.
('Drawing the bow.') (Fig. 50.)

To aid the turn, the right (left) arm with elbow bent and kept at shoulder level is drawn strongly back. The head and left (right) arm do not move.

COMMANDS:

Feet—close! With fists touching, arms forward—raise!
With the right arm, draw the bow—pull! Let go!
Later continuously, **Pull**, and **Pull**, and **1**, and **2**, etc.

FIG. 50.

Trunk turning with single elbow bending. (''Drawing the bow.'')

Source: *Syllabus of Physical Training for Schools*, 1933, London.

So the way in which the body was thought about *underpinned* the conception of physical education. In other words, as the discourses for thinking about the human body changed, so did the possible ways of thinking about physical education. Importantly, the same is still true today. Contemporary physical education curriculum in schools, colleges and universities are also underpinned by certain understandings of the body. And almost universally those understandings are generated through scientific discourses.

Scientific ways of thinking about the body are represented in the metaphor of the *body as machine* which is so universal in physical education curriculum. There are two specific orientations that this metaphor has in physical education. The first is the body as machine in a *biological* sense. When we talk about energy systems, metabolic rate and weight loss, improving aerobic fitness or developing strength through progressive overload, we most often apply the body as machine metaphor as a way of thinking. The second is a *biomechanical* sense. This is most often applied to how we think about motor skill performance. When we talk of the lever systems of the forearm, the summation of forces in a discus throw, the push and pull action of the hand in the front crawl stroke, or the positioning of the centre of gravity in a balance activity, we are thinking of the body as a biomechanical machine. In both senses we are applying scientific logic and thought to understand how the body works.

All of this serves to consolidate the view that physical education is about the function of the body or the body as a machine that moves, runs, jumps, throws, catches, strikes and so on. It is worth pondering the extent to which this form of knowledge actually equips physical education teachers to deal with the complex practices and relations associated with teaching and learning in schools. We can ask how such scientific knowledge actually helps teachers to understand and reconcile the bodily experiences of pleasure, of rejection, of pain (in the absence of injury), of nurture, of empathy, of gender and of alienation that are so deeply embedded in the movement cultures associated with sport and physical education. Remember the story of Meme and the women in the hydrotherapy class related in Chapter 2? Would the technical knowledge of the exercise sciences really have helped these women?

Research by Macdonald (1993) and Swan (1995), in particular, has shown clearly that most Australian PETE courses privilege scientific knowledge of the body in their curriculum. Your course is probably similar. The prospective PE teacher will learn about the body as if it were a machine. They will come to understand the scientific body as a 'natural body' and probably not even contemplate the idea of the body as a 'social body' (also).

Kirk (1993) proposes a different way of thinking about bodies—an alternative discourse—which understands the body not merely as a machine but as one which is socially constructed. What become important here are the *meanings* that people have about their bodies, the way they think about and evaluate their and other people's bodies and how this affects what they choose to do and not to do. In addition, the reasons why people 'take up' certain meanings rather than others need to be considered. Why, for instance, do young women (including physical education students), who may be very well aware of the ways in which the media sets up impossible ideals of body shape, still exercise and diet excessively in an attempt to achieve such a shape? Clearly, understanding that some meanings gain prominence is not enough: we need to understand the pay-offs or investments that young people have in taking up some meanings and not others. In this sense we need to understand the ways in which the body is socially constructed.

In our view, there is much that is worthwhile in studying the science of human movement, but it is not enough. It is, after all, a particular (and limited) way of viewing the body and physical activity. There is also a need to consider the body from the perspective of other discourses from those of science. Kirk's idea of understanding the body in nature and in culture is a nice way of thinking about this issue.

In the history of physical education there have been other discourses that have attempted to take a more 'holistic' view or which focussed on the body as an expressive 'instrument' or as the 'site' through which mental, social and even spiritual health might be developed. However, these have mostly been marginalised—not least because they have often been linked to a female practice of physical education and/or been unsupported by scientific theory. Movement education, dance and gymnastics for these and other reasons have often been marginalised in physical education.

New exercise programs and regimens have been generated, many of which were adapted and implemented in schools. The role and function of physical education in the school curriculum quickly evolved from a therapeutic one to a scientific one. Health optimisation (by way of scientifically ordered exercise) featured heavily in this shift. It must be stressed that shift from therapeutic to scientific did not happen instantaneously. As Kirk (1992) reveals, many schools and teachers remained persuasively committed, even if not in practice, to the 'holistic' notions of health that had become widespread after World War II. In particular, many all-girl schools, and many female teachers, continued to practise physical education as a place for the healthy development of mind and body. This scientisation of physical education had a very masculinising effect on curriculum programming and implementation. With heavy emphasis being placed on endurance and strength in emerging definitions of health, (mesomorphic) male bodies were once more privileged in the physical education curriculum.

Some of these concerns have been considered in various curriculum developments in physical education. For example, Fitzclarence & Tinning (1990) claimed that the early 1980s versions of physical education as a senior examinable subject in Victoria 'were considered to be heavily scientised, masculine and overly theoretical. We were concerned with the trend in physical education to define the subject in increasingly narrow and fragmented ways with knowledge drawn primarily from the biological/physical sciences'. Commenting on their role as curriculum writers for the then (1987) new Victorian Certificate of Education (VCE) senior physical education, Fitzclarence & Tinning said that: 'Our response was to place such biological/ physical science understandings alongside knowledge drawn from sociocultural understandings' (p 181). By introducing alternative discourses (to those of science) into the curriculum, they were challenging what they called hegemonic physical education. In this sense hegemonic meant the version (or way of thinking) of senior physical education that was overly theoretical and overly scientised.

Notwithstanding the attempts to include socio-cultural perspectives along with scientific perspectives in more recent conceptions of senior physical education in both Australia and New Zealand, the privileging of scientific discourses remains an issue for the file of physical education.

Military

Strong historical connections with the military also illuminate the role of physical education in the process of disciplining young bodies. It is assumed that heavy regimens of exercise and activity render the body more docile. A nice example of this belief is represented in the following comments by advocates of the use of drill in physical training: 'with a compulsory system of drill, incipient larrikinism would receive a severe check, and the military spirit . . . of the colony would be greatly fostered' (Victorian Minister of Public Instruction Reports 1890, p 264). As mentioned earlier, throughout the 20th century the occurrence of wars has affected the physical education curriculum. The threat of war (whether real or perceived) has clearly been a source of stimulation and invigoration for physical education. The heavy emphasis on marching and drill that accompanied the threat of war was widespread and widely supported practices in physical education. In this context, drill, which was frequently taken by service officers, was seen as a means of inculcating obedience and the ability to work in unison and respond to commands. For young men this regimen was seen as the ideal way to inculcate habits associated with compliance, obedience, neatness and respect (Kirk 1992). Activities such as rifle drill were also introduced into the physical education curriculum as a means of directly training young men for a future participation in armed combat.

The military practices were not, however, universally popular, especially for girls. Indeed, individuals such as Rosalie Virtue, the physical training organiser employed by the Victorian Education Department during the 1930s, argued that: 'Drill has no place in the daily physical training lesson for school girls' (*Education Gazette and Teachers' Aid*, May 1933). Over time those who argued against the military discourses gradually won the day. In the 1946 curriculum *Physical Education for Victorian Schools*, which drew heavily on the 1933 *British Syllabus of Physical Training*, the incorporation of exercise and games, swimming and dance, as well as aspects of health education, in effect legitimised a new conception of physical education.

The disciplined look

It is not enough to work hard on one's body, to discipline it one must also shape it in such a way that it represents clear messages of discipline and control. In this context, certain physical attributes and deportments are seen as visual testimonies of a person's self-commitment and control. Slender and/ or mesomorphic bodies are unproblematically equated with 'health', and health is unproblematically correlated with 'quality of life' (see Colquhoun 1990). Fat bodies are positioned as undisciplined bodies and equated with failure and inadequate self-control. Broken or flawed bodies are marginalised and viewed as non-productive and/or low-achieving bodies (Sparkes 1999).

It is also not enough to know that the disciplined 'look' has significant meanings for young people—we need physical education to actively problematise the social construction of the body and to work towards empowering students to reconcile their particular body in both nature and culture.

Summary

- The 'search for meaning' in different physical education curricula does not culminate in the 'truth'. But it does reveal a fluid or changing physical education. Central to this is the recognition that physical education has been influenced by a range of different factors in the past, and is likely to continue to be in the future.
- Through its strong historical links to sport, the military and health, school physical education has been understood and practised differently across different times and spaces.
- The general purpose and form of physical education at different points in history can be broadly mapped by considering the discourses that are privileged in the representations of the subject.

References

Alexander, K., Taggart, A. & Thorpe, S. (1995). 'Government and school contexts for the development of sport education in Australian schools'. *ACHPER Healthy Lifestyles Journal*, 42(4), pp 4–6.

Atkinson, P. (1978). 'Fitness, feminity and schooling'. In S. Delamont & L. Duffin (eds), *The Nineteenth Century Woman* (pp 92–133). London: Croom Helm.

Australian Sports Commission (1986). *Aussie Sports Manual*. Canberra: ASC.

Board of Education (1933). *Syllabus of Physical Training for Schools*. London: His Majesty's Printing Office.

Broekhoff, J. (1972). 'Physical education and the reification of the human body'. *Gymnasion*, ix, pp 4–11.

Colquhoun, D. (1990). 'Images of healthism in health-based physical education'. In D. Kirk & R. Tinning (eds), *Physical Education Curriculum and Culture* (pp 225–251). London: Falmer Press.

Connell, B. (1987). *Gender and Power*. Sydney: Allen & Unwin.

Crawford, R. (1980). 'Healthism and the medicalisation of everyday life'. *International Journal of Health Services*, 19(3), pp 365–389.

Curriculum Branch (1987). *Sport Education*. Melbourne, Ministry of Education (Schools Division).

Education Department of South Australia (1982). *Daily Physical Education Program Levels 1–7*. Adelaide: Australian Council for Health, Physical Education & Recreation.

Education Department of South Australia (1982). *Daily Physical Education Program Levels 1–7*. Adelaide: Australian Council for Health, Physical Education & Recreation.

Education Department of Victoria (1946). *Physical Education for Victorian Schools*. Melbourne: Government Printer.

Education Department of Victoria (1970). *Suggested Course of Study for Primary Schools: Physical Education*. Melbourne: Government Printer.

Fitzclarence, L. & Hickey, C. (2000). 'Learning to rationalise abuse through football'. In C. Hickey, L. Fitzclarence & R. Matthews (eds). *Where the Boys Are: Gender, Sport and Education*. Geelong: Deakin University Press, pp 67–82.

Fitzclarence, L. & Tinning, R. (1990). 'Challenging hegomonic physical education: Contexualising physical education as an examinable subject'. In D. Kirk & R. Tinning (eds), *Physical Education, Curriculum and Culture: Critical Issues in the Contemporary Crisis* (pp 169–193). London: The Falmer Press.

Goldlust, J. (1987). *Playing for Keeps: Sport, The Media and Society*. Melbourne: Longman Cheshire.

Goodson, I. (1992). 'Studying school subjects'. *Curriculum Perspectives*, 12(1), pp 23–26.

Gray, R. (1985). 'From drills to skills: Movement education'. *ACHPER National Journal, 109* (September), pp 70–73.

Health and Physical Education in the New Zealand Curriculum (1999). Wellington: Ministry of Education.

Jones, B. (1983). *Sleepers, Wake! Technology and the Future of Work*. Melbourne: OUP.

Kirk, D. (1992). *Defining Physical Education: The Social Construction of a School Subject in Postwar Britain*. London: Falmer Press.

Kirk, D. (1993). *The Body, Schooling and Culture*. Geelong: Deakin University.

Kirk, D. & Colquhoun, D. (1989). 'Healthism and daily physical education'. *British Journal of Sociology of Education*, 10(4), pp 417–434.

Lawson, H. (1993). 'After the regulated life'. *Quest*, 45, pp 523–545.

Leonard, F.E. (1923). *History of Physical Education*. New York: Lea & Febiger.

Macdonald, D. (1993). 'Knowledge, gender and power in physical education teacher education'. *Australian Journal of Education*, 37(3), pp 259–278.

Messner, M.A. & Sabo, D.A. (1994). *Sex, Violence & Power in Sports: Rethinking Masculinity*, Freedom, CA: Crossing Press.

Nettleton, B. (1985). 'Education'. In *Australian Sport: A Profile*. Canberra: Australian Government Publishers, pp 88–89.

Pyke, F. (1983). 'No base, no pinnacle'. *ACHPER Victoria Newsletter*, June, 8.

Report to the Minister of Public Instruction (1908–09). Victoria, p 70.

Sparkes, A. (1999). 'The fragile Body-Self'. In A. Sparkes & M. Silvernnoinen (eds), *Talking Bodies: Men's Narrative of the Body and Sport* (pp 51–75). SoPhi, University of Jyväskylä, Finland.

Swan, P. (1995). *Studentship and Oppositional Behaviour Within Physical Education Teacher Education: A Case Study and a Narrative*. Unpublished Doctorate of Education, Deakin University.

Syllabus of Physical Training for Schools (1933). Board of Education. London: His Majesty's Stationery Office.

Tinning, R. (1987). *Improving Teaching in Physical Education*. Geelong: Deakin University Press.

Tinning, R. (1991). 'Health oriented physical education (HOPE): The case of physical education and the promotion of healthy lifestyles'. *ACHPER National Journal*, 134, pp 4–11.

Tinning, R. (1995). 'The sport education movement: Phoenix, bandwagon or hearse?'. *ACHPER Healthy Lifestyles Journal*, 42(2), pp 19–22.

Tinning, R. (1997). 'Performance and participation orienting discourses in the field of human movement: Implications for a socially critical physical education'. In J.-M. Fernandez-Balboa (ed.), *Critical Aspects in Human Movement: Rethinking the Profession in the Postmodern Era*. New York: SUNY Press.

Whitson, D. & Macintosh, D. (1990). 'The scientization of physical education: Discourses of performance'. *Quest*, 42(1), pp 40–65.

Wright, J. (1996). 'Mapping the discourses of physical education'. *Journal of Curriculum Studies*, 28(3), pp 331–351.

chapter twelve

objectives

By the end of this chapter you should be able to:

- understand the positioning of health and physical education in the one 'learning area' within the 'national curriculum';
- recognise the assumptions underpinning the rise of an 'outcomes-based' curriculum model where the focus of educational success is measured in terms of the acquisition (or otherwise) of certain 'agreed' learning outcomes;
- appreciate the nature and scope of sport education, its key assumptions and its ambiguous relationship with physical education;
- understand that 'game sense' is a games-based approach to physical education that is based on the belief that students learn best by doing;
- explain the problematic nature of the 'fundamental motor skills';
- appreciate the emergence of a bicultural dimension to curriculum in physical education in New Zealand. By contrast, recognise the absence of a bicultural approach in Australian PE curriculum;
- appreciate the influence of vocationalism within the curriculum and how physical education might become increasingly involved in directly preparing students for the world of work.

Introduction

It was the best of times, it was the worst of times, it was the age of wisdom, it was the age of foolishness, it was the epoch of belief, it was the epoch of incredulity . . . it was the spring of hope, it was the winter of despair, we had everything before us, we had nothing before us.

Charles Dickens, A Tale of Two Cities

Dickens' description of life in two cities provides an interesting metaphor from which to contemplate the current state of physical education in the school curriculum. Juxtaposing a period of great possibility amid considerable contrition, Dickens portrays a simultaneous picture of vulnerability and opportunity. The same could be said for physical education at the turn of the second millennium. Indeed, the recent introduction of a 'national curriculum' in both Australia and New Zealand has considerable significance for physical educators.

Although the concept of 'national' is somewhat different in Australia (with its states and territories) from New Zealand, we will use the term to mean 'across the whole country'. At one level physical education has been able to garner the necessary political support to secure a place in the Key (Essential) Learning Areas that comprise the nationalisation of the school curriculum. At another level, physical education, at least in the context of Australia, has been the focus of numerous crisis meetings, state reviews and a senate inquiry. At the centre of these inquiries and reviews are concerns that as a curriculum practice in schools, physical education is run-down, undervalued and under-achieving. The decline in physical education is attributed to numerous factors, including its depreciating status, lack of resource allocation (physical and personnel) and an increasingly 'crowded curriculum'. While physical education's identification as part of a Key (Essential) Learning Area in the 'national curriculum' appears to shore up its position in the short term, physical educators still have to resolve substantive issues related to curriculum form and practice.

For many physical educators, evidence purporting children's poor and declining physical skill levels, lack of fitness and increased obesity levels is seen as overwhelming ground for the inclusion of physical education in the school curriculum. From this perspective, the regular involvement of students in physical education classes sits as the most practical curriculum response to such issues. Unfortunately, claims about physical education's capacity to offset these concerns cannot really be substantiated.

As it is currently practised in schools, physical education is unlikely to be able to substantially alter students' physical condition and/or skill level. To this end, such claims are often made in relation to physical education's role in 'laying the foundations' and/or 'providing a positive entry' on which such attributes can be built. However, positive attitudes and healthy practices are not inevitable byproducts of participation in physical education. Commentators such as Tinning et al (1993) and Dodds (1993) have revealed considerable concern about what actually happens in physical education classes. They argue that physical education, in many cases, not only fails to achieve many of the outcomes it espouses under the rhetoric of enhanced health, fitness, skill and self-esteem, but often exacerbates the very problems it seeks to overcome. They argue that where physical education is poorly or insensitively taught, it is more likely to have a negative influence on learners than a positive one.

In this chapter we will explore a number of curriculum models that have currency in the contemporary context of physical education. While this is not an exhaustive account of current curriculum models and/or programs, it does represent some of the major influences that are shaping and informing contemporary practice(s).

Health and Physical Education as a Key Learning Area

In April 1991, the Australian Education Council launched the national collaborative curriculum projects for the development of eight Key Learning Areas (KLAs). These comprise Mathematics, English, Health and Physical Education, Studies of Society and Environment (SOSE), the Arts, Languages other than English (LOTE), Technology, and Science. This process has been similarly undertaken in New Zealand with the formation of seven Essential Learning Areas (ELAs). These learning areas form the template of knowledge, skills and processes to be taught and learnt in Australian and New Zealand schools. In Australia, the national collaboration produced a 'Statement' and 'Profile' for each of the KLAs. The Statements outline the major elements of content to be taught in schools and the Profiles describe 'student learning outcomes' at eight levels of achievement, including a framework to chart the progress of students and report on student learning.

Importantly, the Statements and Profiles generated for each of the KLAs as part of Australia's construction of a 'national curriculum' were not meant to be syllabuses or programs. Curriculum syllabuses and programs are oriented more directly to determining what will be taught and how it will be taught. In this case, the Statement sets out to describe what is unique about Health and Physical Education as a KLA, while the Profile provides a direct focus on what students should learn and how such learnings should be assessed and reported. However, while the Statement and Profile are supposed to provide the scaffold for the development of school-based work programs, these documents are unapologetically anchored in a socially critical framework. Guiding the development of work within the KLA are three organising principles, namely social diversity, social justice and supportive environments. While there is no direct effort on behalf of the writers to provide specific content or assessment strategies, their preferred definition of the field is prominently marked out.

The conflation of Health and Physical Education into one KLA has clearly marked the emergence of a formal alliance between these traditionally discrete subject areas. Also included in this new alliance is the traditional subject Home Economics. The integration of physical education into health-based curriculum offerings in the Australian and New Zealand 'national curricula' is underpinned by concern about economic productivity, swelling health budgets, job creation, and technological developments which demand increasing time and recognition in the curriculum. In the early development of the Australian 'national curriculum' physical education was in danger of disappearing altogether under the nomenclature of 'Health'. Such an arrangement would almost certainly have resulted in physical education programs that could only be defended for their contribution to health benefits. Under the current arrangement, however, physical education has overwhelmingly maintained its status but been forced to question and redefine its purpose and function to accommodate broader educational outcomes.

The Australian national Profile in Health and Physical Education is divided into seven key concepts known as strands, each comprising specific sub-strands. The focus of these strands and their core sub-strands is illustrated in Table 12.1 below.

Table 12.1 Australian national Profile in Health and Physical Education

Strands	Sub-strands
Human Movement	– movement patterns
	– manipulative (sporting) skills
Physical Activity and the Community	– fitness
	– leisure and recreation
Human Development	– growth and development
	– sexuality
Human Relations	– interaction, relationships and groups
	– ethics and values
	– personal and cultural identity
Safety	
Health of Individual and Populations	– health promotion
	– consumer health
	– environmental health
People and Food	– influence on food choice
	– selecting, planning and evaluating food

Clearly not all of the strands in the Health and Physical Education learning area are directly achievable in the context of physical education. Rather, learning within this area draws from a range of traditional school subjects, including physical education, health education, home economics and outdoor education. Studies in this KLA focus on the significance of personal decisions, behaviours, community structures and practices in promoting health and physical activity. It is noteworthy that the *National Statement on Health and Physical Education* (1994) at no point offers any definitions of traditional content knowledge-oriented 'subjects'. Rather the Statement locates the area of Health and Physical Education as being concerned with: growth and development; fundamental movement patterns and coordinated actions of the body; fitness; physical activity; effective relationships; identity; safety; challenge and risk; the role of food; and the multidimensional nature of health, home and school.

The similarity of curriculum orientation that informs the new Health and Physical Education learning area in the New Zealand curriculum is shown in Table 12.2.

Table 12.2 Health and Physical Education in the New Zealand curriculum

Strand A	Personal health and physical development
Strand B	Relationships with other people
Strand C	Movement concepts and motor skills
Strand D	Healthy communities and environments

One of the most critical transformations associated with the curriculum merger of health and physical education is that physical education teachers can no longer live independent lives in the gym or out on the oval. They are now expected to recognise their contribution to learning outcomes as part of a broader learning framework. Within the framework of the national curriculum it becomes the collective responsibility of teachers in the Health and Physical Education KLA to provide learning opportunities for all the outcomes of the curriculum area. Teachers of health education, home economics and physical education will need to work in new collaborative ways while still concentrating on the achievement of particular outcomes.

While physical education teachers can reasonably be expected to place more importance on physical activity, they are now encouraged to consider the social aspects of student involvement. In the New Zealand context Ian Culpan, one of the writers of their new national curriculum in health and physical education, claims that the new curriculum (introduced in 1999 and due to be fully implemented in all schools by 2001) will 'give PE teaches the power to develop far more creative and relevant programs for students. There is now the ability for teachers to provide something for everyone' (cited in Worrall 1999). The uptake of this challenge clearly depends on the amount of inservice and preservice support available to facilitate this shift. Australia is further down the track of implementing its 'national curriculum', with the federal government having spent over $300,000 on inservicing health, PE and home economics teachers through the National Professional Development Program. In New Zealand the government has allocated some NZ$6 million to the inservicing of teachers for implementing the new curriculum. Governments, at least, are taking this very seriously.

Drawing once more on Dickens' metaphor of 'good times and bad times', the emergence of Health and Physical Education as a Key Learning Area in the national curricula in Australia and New Zealand has the potential to be both generative and destructive. The successful integration of these two subjects can help consolidate the position and status of physical education in the school curriculum. Conversely, the failure of physical and health educators to make the merger a successful one is likely to place increased pressure on each of these subdisciplines. Recognising that curriculum change will inevitably take time, the acceptance and ultimate success of the national curriculum depends on the capacity of physical and health educators to reconcile their differences and consolidate their strengths. From this platform they will be able to deliver on the sorts of learning outcomes that are currently viewed as integral to establishing a central role in the school curriculum.

Outcomes-based curriculum

A central part of the national curriculum agendas in both Australia and New Zealand has been a commitment to outcomes-based education. Broadly speaking these can be understood as the skills and knowledge that a student acquires as a result of their participation in a particular subject area (or Key Learning Area). The outcomes associated with KLAs are expectations of the sequential learning experiences that students will develop across time. The outcomes-based approach to curriculum, in its purist form, is relatively new to both Australia and New Zealand. To this end, there is not a strong empirical basis on which to judge its effectiveness at this stage. On the other hand, a broader interpretation of outcomes in education reveals that they have been with us for a long time, whether planned or unplanned. Whatever students learned at school were for all intents and purposes 'learning outcomes'. What we do know is that common curricula do not necessarily result in common learning (or outcomes).

> Outcome-Based Education (OBE) means organizing results: basing what we do instructionally on the outcomes we want to achieve . . . Outcome-based practitioners start by determining the knowledge, competencies, and qualities they want students to be able to demonstrate when they finish school and face the challenges and opportunities of the adult world . . . OBE, therefore, is not a 'program' but a way of designing, delivering, and documenting instruction in terms of its intended goals and outcomes. (Spady 1988, p 5)

Despite the fact that outcomes have always been present in education, the shift to an outcomes-based curriculum model signals a number of fundamental shifts. Foremost in these shifts is the emergence of a set of common, agreed, learning outcomes that are thought to represent the sort of experiences students will have. Important in this context is the realisation that not all children will achieve specific outcomes at the same time, therefore as a Profile of student learning outcomes Statements *will inform* teachers' decisions about curriculum, *not form* teachers' curriculum. Given that we know that students learn and progress at different rates (see Chapter 10), it is inevitable, and indeed expected, that common outcomes will form uncommon curricula. To this end, outcome should be understood as what students are expected to know or do by the end of the teaching process (a unit, a term, a year etc.). For example, it is espoused in the national Profile for Health and Physical Education that students at level four should be able to 'evaluate beliefs about fitness and undertake activities to develop personal fitness' (1995, p 84). A curriculum must be designed to facilitate this outcome. Thus, outcomes provide the framework for the development of curricula.

Outcomes also need to be seen to function at different levels. The outcomes we have been discussing in the context of the KLA are *learning area outcomes* and relate specifically to the learning in Health and Physical Education. There are also more *overarching outcomes* that tend to be espoused in a school charter. These outcomes will generally reflect the longer-term aspirations of the school and its community. They will include the sort of qualities and characteristics the school is seeking to nurture in its student population at large. At the other end of the spectrum are the shorter-term outcomes, often referred to as *progressive outcomes*. These represent short-term goals and targets that provide students with feedback about their development along the way. Recognising that individuals need progressive feedback in their pursuit of mastery, these outcomes can provide important short-term focus in the overall pursuit of leaning area outcomes and overarching outcomes.

 over to you

Given a particular topic (such as gymnastics, swimming, hockey, dance), grade level and teaching context, select a learning outcome statement and work it through each of the questions below.

Learning outcome:	
Example: Examine different stereotypes of people which arise from their culture, gender, race, age and religion (Level 3, p 47, CSF)	
What activities might contribute to the achievement of the learning outcome?	Give some examples of what a student might actually 'do' in a class situation in relation to these activities.
What will you look for in determining whether students are achieving the learning outcomes? (Consider whether these are process or product.)	When and how will you record the information?
How will you involve the students in this assessment?	How can this information be communicated in the reporting process?

Source: *Board of Studies, 1995.*

Of course, the rise of Outcomes-Based Education (OBE) is not a politically neutral phenomenon. Due to concern in the 1980s that American students were not learning enough at school, OBE was deployed widely as a means of providing, at least notionally, a 'success for all' philosophy. In this context outcomes were seen as a way of homing teachers' attention in on what 'really counts' and providing readily identifiable learning criteria from which teachers (and schools) could assess their work. Such an approach also enables schools and teachers to be held *accountable* for the educational attainment of a broadly identified set of goals. The effectiveness of a particular school and/ or teacher can now be judged according to the extent to which they are able to achieve agreed outcomes. Where such outcomes are not achieved, it is frequently seen to be the school, teacher or curriculum that is at fault or flawed, not the outcome!

A further issue that arises along this line of discussion is the extent to which it is realistic that common outcomes be espoused for all learners. The view that all learners can achieve the same outcomes, albeit at different rates, is inherently equitable. Such an objective implies that all learners will be given the same opportunities to succeed in all areas of the curriculum, even if it means varying the learning conditions and duration of the curriculum. What is not tolerable is a situation where less is expected of a particular group on the basis of class, gender or physical ability. Were this to become a reason for altering the distribution of resources, the whole notion of common learning outcomes would enter a tiered system, where different outcomes were offered to different groups.

Sport education

The relationship between physical education and sport has always been somewhat contentious. As an umbrella term 'physical education' has typically been used to describe a wide range of activity-based experiences, one of which is sport (see Figure 12.1). While the positioning of sport as simply a subset of experiences within a comprehensive physical education is common in curriculum documents, this arrangement tends to understate their relationship in practice. When the practice of sport was constructed as a separate aspect of the school curriculum, characterised by distinct nodes of time given to inter- and intra-school competitions, its relationship to physical education was quite straightforward. In more recent times, however, the 'educational' potential of sport has been better recognised within the context of physical education, to the point where it now has the momentum to dominate such programs.

Sport education as a legitimate curriculum practice gained momentum through the 1980s. The Australian Sports Commission's development of the Aussie Sport Campaign was prominent here. The Aussie Sport program that emanated from this was a comprehensive sport education program designed to assist teachers to make sport more accessible and enjoyable for students in the upper primary and lower secondary years. It provided a series of activity

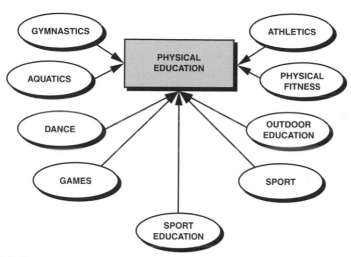

Figure 12.1 The physical education model

manuals that could be used by teachers to develop students' basic skills and assist them in the delivery of a wide range of sports. As a multi-sport approach to the delivery of physical education it bought the practices of the primary and secondary school into closer alignment.

Most secondary schools had been using the multi-sport approach to physical education for some time. Under this curriculum arrangement sports such as basketball, volleyball, netball, tennis, hockey, gymnastics, badminton, soccer, athletics, swimming, football (in its various cultural forms) were programmed on a cyclical basis. According to climate and the availability of resources, students would experience short exposure (around four weeks) to each of these sports on a cyclical basis through their middle school years. As the dominant form of curriculum practice, it was expected that competent physical education teachers would have a degree of expertise in the development of a wide range of these sports. Given that the secondary school system was well endowed with physical education specialist teachers, the Aussie Sport Program made its greatest impression in the primary sector. Regardless of this, the concept of sport education as a curriculum practice was given life.

The appellation 'Physical and Sport Education' that has now become so widely used had a notable insurgence following the 1992 *Senate Inquiry* into the status of physical education and sport in Australian schools. While this report did not actually clarify or consolidate the relationship between physical education and sport (some would argue that its use of these two terms was, in fact, confusing), its application of these terms repeatedly inferred a degree of co-dependence. What was resounding in the pages of the Senate report was a clear aggregation of sport and physical education in both practice and nomenclature. Reports around the country, such as Victoria's *Moneghetti Report*, took their lead from the Senate Inquiry and proffered curriculum reforms that drew heavily on the increased provision of sport in schools. Through the many deliberations that took place, a clearer understanding of sport education began to emerge: 'Sport education includes the development of sport skills, an understanding of rules of various sports and an appreciation of codes of behaviour' (Moneghetti Report 1993).

Arguably the most widely recongnised version of sport education in the Australian curriculum context is the Sport Education in Physical Education Program (SEPEP) that has been developed out of the Sport, Physical Activity Research Centre (SPARC) at Edith Cowan University. This work has been built on previous work out of Ohio State University, under the auspices of Daryl Siedentop. Importantly, SEPEP does not claim to be a de-facto physical education curriculum. Rather it presents itself as a program for teaching sport in the school curriculum. Underpinning its structure is a belief that sport is a powerful medium through which to involve students in a wide range of developmental experiences. Designed around a commitment to 'participation', the SEPEP model offers students an array of tasks associated with the planning, implementation and involvement in a sporting competition.

SEPEP is designed to nurture a range of healthy skills and attitudes in relation to being good players and team members. Aimed overwhelmingly at the middle school years, SEPEP is structured around the conduct of a competitive season. Within normal physical education sessions the SEPEP approach to curriculum delivery places emphasis on the organisation, implementation and celebration of sporting seasons. Incorporating around 20 sessions, a successful season is not meant to be judged in terms of where teams finish on the ladder, but on the manner in which teams and team members have conducted themselves during the season. While there is anecdotal evidence that an emphasis on participation rather than competition can be successfully developed in the context of SEPEP, it has to do so against the dominant social discourse of 'winning'. The problem for some, such as Tinning (1995), is that, whether it is Sport Education, Aussie Sport, Sports Fun, Sport for All or SEPEP, it is still 'sports'-focussed, and sport is not the most reinforcing form of physical activity for many individuals.

One of the key features of the SEPEP model is its pedagogic emphasis on student-centred learning. The idea that teachers do not have to be centre stage all the time has been welcomed by many physical education teachers tired of the demands traditionally associated with being a good teacher. Whereas traditional curriculum approaches have placed a great deal of emphasis on teachers' need to instruct students, SEPEP proffers the reverse. With students sharing the roles of coaches, captains, team managers, umpires, publicity officers and serving on a sports management board, teachers are invited to adopt a much more facilitatory role. Once these responsibilities have been established, it is the intention of the program that the students conduct the sessions, plan future sessions and arbitrate over conflicts that may arise. Of course, the success with which they fulfil these tasks and subsequently participate in a series of positive and developmental experiences is what will ultimately make or break a program.

Among the catch-cries of the sport education fraternity is one that sport education should be simultaneously challenging and enjoyable. It is challenging in that it aims to develop skills and fitness with the intention of maximising team performance. However, probably its most challenging aspect emanates from the demand for participants to work effectively together in the management, organisation and decision-making processes that will underpin the cultivation of a supportive learning environment. Its emphasis on enjoyment is seen as a spin-off of constructive competition. In the context of student learning in the middle school years and beyond, enjoyment is not seen as having infantile status signified through laughter and frivolity. In the context of sport education, enjoyment is seen as the provision of interesting and challenging activities.

Games sense

In physical education games have typically been presented as isolated or discrete entities. Games such as cricket, soccer, volleyball, netball, football and tennis are all thought to have specific qualities that are self-contained within the game. Interestingly, those students who are good performers in one game are often good performers in other games. While this generalisation does not apply universally, it is remarkably common to have the students that dominate one sport go on to dominate the next. In particular, people who are good at racquet sports tend to be able to apply a deft hand to games like tennis, squash or badminton.

Advocates of a games approach to curriculum development in physical education claim that there is considerable similarity between games. They favour a classification system that places games into categories, based on notable similarities. This classification usually differentiates between 'Invasion Games' (such as football, soccer and basketball), 'Striking/Fielding Games' (such as baseball and cricket) and 'Net/Racquet Games' (such as tennis, badminton and volleyball). Each of these classifications is thought to represent fundamentally different tactical considerations. Conversely, within each of these categories the games are thought to employ remarkably similar strategy and skill patterns. This way of thinking invites teachers to see the development of 'games sense' as something that involves the development of a range of fundamental principles that potentially feed into more than one game or situation.

Like SEPEP, and other sport education models, games sense is an approach to physical education that attempts to break the shackles of 'skill and drill' as the way to develop students' capacity to successfully participate in sporting life. It has long been the belief that it is only when the basic skills have been mastered that students should progress to game situations. As a curriculum model games sense reverses this approach. To this end, games sense is built on the belief that students will learn to play games best by playing them.

Concerned that an overemphasis on skills and drills tends to sanitise the students' learning experiences, games sense puts participation in games (albeit modified) as the foundation from which teaching and skill refinement should proceed. As a games-based curriculum it is espoused that student learning will be more enjoyable, more meaningful and more individualised. It is argued that 'the primary purpose of teaching any game should be to improve students' game performance and to improve their enjoyment and participation in games, which might lead to a more healthy lifestyle' (Werner et al 1996, p 30).

Advocates of the games sense approach to curriculum delivery in physical education argue that it has a number of fundamental advantages. Foremost here is that it is thought to tap into the overwhelming desire of students to be involved in games. 'Can we play a game now?' would have to be one of the most frequently asked questions of physical educators. Rather than cajoling or lampooning students into lines and other formations to practise skills, games sense is predicated on the benefit of letting them do what they will invariably want to do, play a game! However, the playing of a game in the context of the games sense approach requires more than simply picking teams and umpiring. It requires a fundamental shift in the way teachers approach skill development and organise sequential learning activities.

The teacher's role in the context of games-based curriculum models is to organise the conditions and experiences that will facilitate learning. The fact that games sense proffers a view that students will learn by doing does not relieve teachers of their professional responsibility to develop the necessary culture and environment in which the program objectives can be achieved. To some extent at least this requires students to play a more active role in their own learning.

Successful implementation of this model would see students engaged in concepts related to decision making, risk taking, problem solving, perceiving self and others (across time and space), and strategies and tactics. Indeed, part of developing genuine games sense involves knowing where to be, when to be there and what to do when you get there. These are extremely difficult concepts to teach and yet can be applied at the most sophisticated levels by even the least academic people.

One of the biggest hurdles facing curriculum models like games sense is the extent to which teachers can be trained to effectively implement such programs. It is one thing to put students into game situations to accommodate their interest. Most teachers would agree that such a shift would be popular among students. It is another thing to be able to use the game situation to analyse, teach and remediate. The specific pedagogic knowledges, skills and attitudes required to successfully implement such a program are somewhat understated in existing support material. Further to this, short of being wholly embraced as dominant curricula, such models have to be capable of being integrated with other (more dominant) curriculum models.

Back to fundamentals

Running in almost the opposite direction to the contextual models of SEPEP and games sense is the 'back-to-basics' movement, popularly referred to as Fundamental Motor Skills (FMS). Central to this movement is the belief that motor skill acquisition is the primary task of physical education programs.

Educationally this approach to physical education curriculum design and implementation is built on the belief that there are certain skills that need to be mastered if individuals are to successfully engage with the sport and movement skills most common to a (our) culture. To this end, it is reasonable to assume that fundamental motor skills are culturally dependent. Put another way, the specific movement sequences associated with the development of a football punt kick would have considerably less relevance in soccer-mad Spain than they do in football-mad Melbourne. Notwithstanding this, there are fundamental movement skills that appear to traverse cultures. For instance, it is argued by supporters of the FMS movement that running, leaping, catching and throwing are foundational skills on which other more specific skills are built.

The FMS approach to curriculum design and implementation in physical education represents a practical shift away from contextual learning in favour of a more developmentally measured (read scientific) approach. Advocates of FMS are concerned that good fundamental motor skill development is not a necessary outcome of games and/or sports participation. Drawing largely on the sub-disciplines of biomechanics and skill acquisition, FMS advocates proffer the benefits of a scientifically 'informed' approach to teaching and learning in physical education. By breaking down the ingredients of a 'successful' participation in sporting culture, advocates of FMS argue that specialised teaching needs to be provided in specific areas of skill development. These are understood to include the ability to catch, dodge, perform a vertical jump, run, throw, catch, punt, bounce, kick and strike. FMS advocates are concerned that if such skills are not mastered, individuals are destined for an unhappy and unsuccessful participation in sport. Under-pinning this is their general belief that 'failure breeds failure', and is ultimately expressed in participant avoidance and rejection.

While the FMS movement currently has more purchase in the primary school curriculum, its heavy emphasis on the need for specialised instruction is likely to increasingly implicate the middle school years. In practical terms the FMS approach to physical education curriculum delivery is built on the belief that skills need to be broken down and developed sequentially. For example, mastery of the overhand throw is thought to be revealed when a performer completes this skill:

- with their eyes fixed on the target throughout the throw;
- standing side-on to the target;
- drawing the throwing arm back (to almost straight) behind the body during preparation;
- stepping towards the target with their opposite foot during the throw;
- sequentially rotating their body in a proximo-distal form during the throw; and
- following-through (across the body) with the throwing arm.

(Education Department of Victoria 1996, p 24)

The great challenge to anyone engaged in the delivery of a physical education curriculum involves knowing precisely how to teach, diagnose and remediate such sequences in a manner that is meaningful, motivating and enjoyable to participants.

Increasing pressure on schools to document the effectiveness, or otherwise, of their practices and programs has been accompanied by an intensification of teacher accountability. The push to fundamentals is certainly not exclusive to physical education. Rather, it is symptomatic of a broader political thrust towards measurable outcomes as a basis for 'benchmarking'. This approach, it is argued, ushers in a form of 'bottom up' curriculum modelling, built on the identification of essential content to be taught and mastered by students. Compounded by a national push for the unification of learning outcomes, the identification of readily measurable learning objectives has considerable political currency. In this context the identification of FMS within physical education is both practically and politically strategic.

Prominent in the push for the adoption of an FMS approach to curriculum design and implementation in physical education is its status of being 'research-based'. Without wanting to go back through the core studies that are trumpeted as validating the merit of this approach (Kelly et al 1989 and Ulrich 1985), it is useful to revisit their collective insight. These studies, together with numerous others, make four important assertions about the delivery and development of fundamental motor skills:

1. that it is reasonable to expect all able-bodied people to achieve mastery of these skills;
2. that the earlier fundamental motor skills are taught the more effectively intervention and correction strategies can be introduced;
3. that the better (more expert) the quality of instruction the more effectively (read efficiently and correctly) these skills are learned; and
4. that mastery of these skills is foundational to a long and positive association with an active or sporting lifestyle.

While such research applies considerable weight to the FMS approach, its implementation is not seen as unproblematic. Criticism of the FMS approach is couched in the belief that it is inherently reductive, gendered and narrowly focussed.

Fundamental Motor Skills is believed to be reductive in the sense that it breaks movements down into small components that are thought to comprise the whole. Such a heavy focus on 'correctness' of technique is thought to over-sanitise the development of movement competencies and reduce the provision for individual flare. Indeed, the history of sport is littered with performers who achieved great success with unconventional, or what could be considered 'incorrect', styles or techniques. Janet Evans, Michael Klim (swimming), John McEnroe (tennis) and Alan Thompson and Paul Adams (cricket) are but a few who would appear to defy the logic of biomechanical purity.

Of further concern is the gendered nature of FMS on the grounds that it privileges competitive sporting activities as a basis for deciding what is 'fundamental' in the area of motor skill proficiency. Obvious by its absence is any direct account of the physical skills associated with activities like gymnastics and dance: namely, rhythm, timing, grace and flow of movement, and general aesthetics. Rather, research into the FMS focusses attention on girls as being specifically deficient in the area of motor skill development (Wright 1997). And finally, at a time when the national curriculum seeks to broaden the learning outcomes associated with health and physical education, FMS works to narrow ways in which individual participation is monitored.

Bicultural awareness

Bicultural approaches to curriculum development are rare, if they exist at all, in the context of Australia. Historically, Australian physical education curriculum documents have made no explicit reference to the Aboriginal movement culture, however rich it has been and continues to be. Despite broad recognition of Aboriginal peoples' physical prowess, the Aboriginal culture has received little more than token recognition in mainstream curriculum theory or practice in physical education. The national Statement and Profiles in Health and Physical Education, although written with input from an Aboriginal and Torres Strait Islander adviser, continue the neglect of Australia's Aboriginal heritage. While it might be argued that the emphasis on diversity, tolerance and supportive environments in the national curriculum in Health and Physical Education pave the way for a broader recognition of Aboriginal culture, this connection is in no way explicit.

Source: David Moore.

New Zealand, on the other hand, has made a much more serious effort to recognise cultural diversity within the construction and implementation of Health and Physical Education. Back in 1987 the curriculum document called *Physical education syllabus for junior to form 7* and its companion document *Physical education: A guide for success* both recognised Maori movement culture as one of the eight content themes which make up the physical education experience of young people. The Maori dimension of movement, understood as *Te Reo Kori*, occupied (at least in policy) a place in the curriculum alongside swimming, gymnastics, ball activities, fitness, athletics, sport, dance and outdoor education.

Te Reo Kori seeks to celebrate aspects of the Maori language and movement. Its dual function is to introduce non-Maori students to the culture and knowledges specific to its indigenous population, while providing Maori students access to their traditional cultural practices and values within the mainstream curriculum. Combining aspects of dance, language and movement Te Reo Kori encourages students to develop their skills, appreciation and knowledge of the Maori culture. Salter (1999) explains: 'Te Reo Kori is movement, involving learning experiences derived from traditional Maori culture practices. While their origin is specific to Maori and the activities affirm Maori students, their application is also intended to be inclusive of and appropriate to all. Te Reo Kori is about mastery of basic Maori movement, not rigid duplication of traditional cultural performance' (p 19). In this light, Te Reo Kori is not meant to be seen as a medium through which to apply a rigid transmission of traditional forms of Maori movement and performance. Rather, it is positioned as the foundation for the development of physical, social, emotional and spiritual well-being. While the practical translation of Te Reo Kori in schools was problematic, it represented a genuine attempt to enhance biculturalism in curriculum practice.

The development of the new national curriculum framework for Health and Physical Education has, however, failed to include Te Reo Kori as one of the Key Areas of Learning (not to be confused with the Australian term Key Learning Area) within the HPE Essential Learning Area. The politics behind this 'repositioning' are complex, but Salter (1999) certainly sees this as a trivialisation of Maori knowledge. While the new curriculum uses the concept of Hauora[1] as the Maori philosophy of health that is unique to New Zealand, the removal of Te Reo Kori is considered a backward step for bicultural education in health and physical education.

While there are contextual reasons that distinguish the curriculum histories of physical education in New Zealand and Australia, it is worth contemplating how serious recognition of the indigenous movement culture might be addressed within the Australian KLA in Health and Physical Education. In pursuit of this, Australian physical educators would do well to reflect on New Zealand's efforts to connect its indigenous culture with that of its English/European descendants. Learning from the New Zealand experience would encourage Australian physical educators to consider their previous neglect of Aboriginal movement culture, dance and language. This might not only foster a greater understanding by non-Aboriginal students of indigenous culture and heritage, but also provide Aboriginal students opportunities to access aspects of their traditional culture and values and to enhance their identity and self-worth.

Vocationalism in schools

Vocational education has emerged as a core educational issue in the new millennium. It has been simmering away in numerous forms since the 1970s and seems to have steadily gained momentum. Underpinning the rise of vocational education in schools has been the seemingly intractable rise in youth unemployment rates. This has been coupled with profound technological and organisational changes in the workplace and an explosion in retention rates in post-compulsory schooling. The big issue here has been the capacity for schooling, as an institutionalised practice, to respond to these changes.

What we do know is that mainstream schooling has typically targeted its curriculum to be almost exclusively dedicated to the role of preparing school leavers for higher education. Interestingly, while secondary education has primarily focussed on serving the needs of those intending university entry, only around 15 per cent of those that complete their secondary education make this progression (McGraw 1996). Policy makers and curriculum designers have been faced with the problem of reorganising the process of schooling to play a much more direct role in laying the foundations for employment opportunities.

It is against this backdrop that vocational education and training (VET) has gathered momentum. However, despite the obvious demand for degree of curriculum change in mainstream education, the VET movement has encountered considerable resistance. The widespread perception that vocational instruction is less prestigious than its academic counterpart has been the foremost concern. Positioned as the 'non-academic' dimension of the school curriculum, parents and students alike have shown a clear reluctance to get involved in the programs on offer. What this has done is set up a sort of divide between the vocational and the academic, in which the latter is seen to be infinitely superior. A study carried out by the Curriculum Corporation (1994) revealed that vocational education was typically identified with lower-achieving students. Interestingly, research on students at risk of school drop-out clearly identified dissatisfaction with subject content and school culture as the key reasons for premature departure (Holden & Dwyer 1992). Despite this, VET programs have ongoing problems trying to position themselves as viable educational alternatives.

One of the major factors for the lack of integration between the vocational and academic aspects of the school curriculum appears to lie at the feet of teachers. As discussed elsewhere in this book, a teacher's work is already complex and demanding enough without new expectations being placed on them. Indeed, there is a long history of good ideas never achieving their potential on the basis of teachers not supporting them (in practical ways). The introduction of VET programs into school settings clearly requires considerable time and expertise. Many teachers would feel inadequately trained to undertake the roles associated with establishing meaningful relationships with industry and determining and evaluating the inputs and outcomes of the experience. A notable difference here is that VET programs tend to talk in competencies, as opposed to learning outcomes—the fundamental difference being that competencies are *context-specific* skills. As such, competencies are not externally defined or pre-specified goals, but are specific skills required by an organisation for a particular function. Where the organisation of work changes, so too do the competencies required.

The general lack of teacher training in the area of VET programs has meant that they tend to remain under the charter of a (select) few and be poorly integrated into mainstream curriculum practice in schools. Physical education has already been identified as a medium through which to build pathways to particular careers (apprenticeships and traineeships). The Victorian document *VET in Schools: Certificates in Sport and Recreation* recognises sport and recreation as multi-million dollar industries and identifies a range of careers that exist within them. Among these is 'athletic career education'. The athletic career education stream specifically targets elite junior athletes with a view to providing them with the 'knowledge and skills necessary to successfully manage their sport/career at this level' (Board of Studies 1998, p 1; see Table 12.3).

Additional to this are VET streams in fitness instruction, sales and marketing (for the sport and recreation industry), sport and recreation administration, and sports training and conditioning. Students opting to undertake any of these streams must first successfully complete the core modules associated with the VET program. Students are given academic credit, within their secondary school programs, for the successful completion of many of the VET modules.

Summary

- The positioning of health and physical education in the one 'learning area' within the 'national curriculum' in both Australia and New Zealand represents a significant challenge to and opportunity for physical education.
- The new national curriculum adopts an outcomes-based approach where achievment is measured in terms of the acquisition (or otherwise) of certain explicit learning outcomes.
- 'Sport education' is now an accepted term in many Australian schools. One manifestation of sport education is the curriculum model SEPEP which is currently popular in many secondary schools in both Australia and New Zealand.
- 'Games sense' is a games-based approach to physical education that challenges conventional games teaching approaches by learning what is needed about games play by actually playing the game. Skills and tactics are learned in the game context rather than as isolated activities.

Table 12.3 Athlete Career Education Stream Core

Module core	Module title	Hours	Prerequisites	Credit transfer	VET unit
SRT501	Self-Awareness for Sports People	5			*
SRT502	Assertiveness for Sports People	5			*
SRT503	Leadership for Sports People	5			*
SRT504	Dealing with Conflict	5			*
SRT505	Effective Time Management for Sports People	5			*
SRT506	Stress Management	5		*	*
SRT507	Effective Personal Presentation and Public Interaction	5			*
SRT509	Managing Personal Income and Budgeting	5			*
SRT510	Personal Financial Planning	5	SRT509		*
SRT511	Personal Health and Fitness	5		*	*
SRT512	Basic Sports Psychology	5			*
SRT515	Nutrition for Sports People	5		*	*

Source: Board of Studies 1998, p 4.

- A back-to-basics 'push' exists in Australian physical education under the title 'Fundamental Motor Skills'. Fanned by the sports lobby's fear that young people were becoming less competent in terms of so-called fundamental movement skills, considerable resources have been channelled into attempts to improve the situation. There are some serious challenges to the assumptions on which this FMS focus rests.
- In New Zealand a bicultural dimension to curriculum in physical education has been taken seriously. By contrast, in the Australian PE curriculum there is no real consideration of the movement cultural heritage of our Aboriginal people.
- Vocalionalism has emerged as a core educational issue at the beginning of the 21st century. The VET movement has also had an impact on physical education with the introduction of certificates in sport and recreation occupying a place in the curriculum beside physical education. How physical education might become increasingly involved in directly preparing students for the world of work is a challenge for our learning area.

Note

1 Hauora, the unique Maori philosophy of health, while compatible with the World Health Organization orientations, moves away from a medical model and embraces the spiritual, intellectual, emotional, physical and mental dimensions of health.

References

Board of Studies (1995). *Curriculum and Standards Framework: Health and Physical Education*, Melbourne: Board of Studies.

Board of Studies (1998). *VET in Schools: Certificates in Sport and Recreation*. Melbourne: Board of Studies.

Curriculum Corporation (1994). *A Statement on Health and Physical Education for Australian Schools*. Melbourne: Curriculum Corporation.

Curriculum Corporation (1994). *Vocational Education in Australian Schools*. Melbourne.

Curriculum Corporation (1995). *National Profile for Health and Physical Education*. Melbourne: Curriculum Corporation.

Health and Physical Education in the New Zealand Curriculum (1999). Wellington: Ministry of Education.

Dickens, C. (1906). *A Tale of Two Cities*, London: Dent.

Directorate of School Education (1993). *Report of the Committee for the Review of Physical and Sport Education in Victorian Schools* (Moneghetti Report). Directorate of School Education, Victoria.

Dodds, P. (1993). 'Removing the ugly "-isms" in your gym: Thoughts for teachers on equity'. In J. Evans (ed.), *Equality, Education and Physical Education* (pp 28–39). London: Falmer Press.

Education Department of Victoria (1996). *Fundamental Motor Skills: A Manual for Classroom Teachers*. Melbourne: Department of Education.

Holden, E. & Dwyer, P. (1992). *Making the Break: Leaving School Early*. Institute of Education, Melbourne: University of Melbourne.

Kelly, L., Reuschein, P. & Hauebstricker, J. (1989). 'Qualitative analysis of bouncing, kicking and striking motor skills: Implications for assessing and teaching'. *Journal of the International Council for Health, Physical Education and Recreation*, 26(2), pp 28–32.

McGraw, B. (1996). *Their Future: Options for Reform of the High School Certificate*. Sydney: Department of Training and Education Coordination.

Salter, G. (1999). '*Me ako ki tikango Maori i roto i te reo kori*': Culture and learning through Te Reo Kori'. *Journal of Physical Education New Zealand*, 31(2), pp 18–21.

Spady, W. (1988). *Outcome-Based Education*, ACT: Australian Curriculum Studies Association.

Tinning, R., Kirk, D. & Evans, J. (1993). *Learning to Teach Physical Education*. Sydney: Prentice Hall.

Tinning, R. (1995) 'The sport education movement: Phoenix, bandwagon or hearse?'. *ACHPER Healthy Lifestyles Journal*, 42(2), 19–22.

Ulrich, D. (1985). *Test of Gross Motor Development*. Austin, TX: PRO-ED.

Werner, J., Thorpe R. & Bunker, D. (1996). 'Teaching games for understanding: Evolution of a model'. *JOPERD*, 67(1), pp 28–33.

Worrall, R. (1999). 'New curriculum heralds fundamental change'. *New Zealand Physical Educator*, 1(1), pp 5–7.

Wright, J. (1997). 'The construction of gendered contexts in single sex and co-educational physical education lessons'. *Sport, Education and Society*, 2(1), pp 55–92.

Further reading

Games Sense: Developing Thinking Players—A Presenter's Guide and Workbook, den Duyan, N. (1997). Canberra: Australian Sports Commission.

Department of Education (1996). *Fundamental Motor Skills: A Classroom Manual and Video for Teachers*. Melbourne: Victoria.

chapter thirteen

objectives

By the end of this chapter you should be able to:
- recognise that the control of the curriculum exists at different levels from national, state and school;
- appreciate the importance of planning in the curriculum-making process;
- understand some of the various considerations necessary in the conduct of appropriate curriculum planning;
- comprehend the essential differences between various models of planning;
- appreciate the necessity of lesson planning as a student teacher and understand what needs to be considered for successful planning;
- list the purposes of evaluation and assessment in the curriculum process.

Control of the physical education curriculum

Until recently in Australia, decisions regarding physical education lay in the hands of the school and the states and territories, together with support from national professional associations. During the 1990s the federal government also got in on the act by seeking to coordinate school curricula nationally in line with socio-economic and educational agendas. Therefore, as we saw in Chapter 11, the school curriculum is shaped (or made) by many people across a range of sites and organisations and for a range of purposes.

In important ways, a physical education curriculum (like all curricula) is a response to a particular identified problem. If, for example, a certain group or agency, such as a state government, considers that we should teach our young folk how to play the valued sports of our culture, then the problem of how to do so becomes the starting point for making a curriculum. The problem is set or defined by a particular interest group and a curriculum is developed as a response to the problem. A nice example of this was the *Daily Physical Education Program* developed in the early 1980s. It was a curriculum designed as a response to the new health consciousness which identified inactivity in young children as a major problem in the development of coronary heart disease in later life (see Tinning 1991).

over to you

Make a list of who or which groups appear to control schooling. A comprehensive list should include people and organisations both within and beyond the school.

Consider how this list might change for different types of schools if you focussed more on who controls health and physical education.

Perhaps it is useful to represent the control of the curriculum on a continuum from tightly managed central control through to more localised control at the school and classroom level. See Figure 13.1.

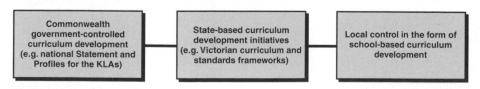

Figure 13.1 Levels of control on curriculum

Nationalisation of programs

During the 1980s and 1990s under the Australian federal Labor government there were shifts to nationalise and centralise many governmental functions. Education, constitutionally under state government jurisdiction, has been subject to these trends. In 1989 state and federal education ministers met in Hobart to draft some goals and principles for coordinating Australia's education system. An outcome of the Hobart Conference (as the meeting became known) was the agreement that the curriculum for Australian schools should be structured around eight Key Learning Areas:

- Arts
- English
- Health and Physical Education
- Language Other Than English (LOTE)
- Mathematics
- Science
- Studies of Society and Environment
- Technology.

Curriculum documents to be used in each state and territory in eight Key Learning Areas were then written—one of them being in the KLA of *Health and Physical Education.*

Studies in the Health and Physical Education KLA focus on the significance of personal decisions and behaviours and community structures and practices in promoting health and physical activity.

It is noteworthy that the national Statement on Health and Physical Education (1994) which provides the basis for curriculum development by the states did not offer any definitions of traditional content knowledge-oriented 'subjects'. Rather the Statement locates the area of Health and Physical Education as being concerned with: growth and development; fundamental movement patterns and coordinated actions of the body; fitness; physical

 over to you

The positioning of physical education within a Key Learning Area was highly contentious, as discussed in Chapter 12. Arguments for and against this positioning have centred around the status of physical education and the readiness of teachers to work across the learning area.

Make a list of the advantages and disadvantages of physical education being part of the health and physical education learning area from the perspectives of pupils, teachers and the community.

Discuss your responses in a tutorial class.

activity; effective relationships; identity; safety; challenge and risk; the role of food; and the multidimensional nature of health, home and school.

The approach of these documents reflects a shift to outcomes-based education (see discussion in Chapter 12). In outcomes-based education levels of attainment of pupils or standards pupils have reached in relation to various strands of subject matter become a focus for reporting to parents and the government. Curriculum planning and teachers' actions (input) become secondary to demonstrable pupil learning (output). The output represents what pupils *know* and can *do*.

Concerns with respect to outcomes-based education include the problems of aligning learning to the discrete, unitised outcomes and the potential for the monitoring of outcomes to override other educational concerns.

State-based decisions

In Australia, the funding (and hence the control) of schooling rests primarily with the state and territory governments. Non-government schools tend to draw selectively on governmental procedures, initiatives and documents as befitting their aims and philosophies. The philosophy underpinning state control is that there are benefits to centralised coordination, such as efficiency, consistency and accountability.

Many of our curriculum documents such as the syllabuses and framework documents, together with policies pertaining to issues such as safety and equity, are written by educators employed in state government departments. Where school-based assessment occurs, it is important for reasons of comparability across schools that there are state-wide mechanisms for moderating the judgments made at the school level. These state- and territory-level decisions in many ways control the breadth and nature of judgments which teachers make.

School-based curriculum development

The philosophy of school-based curriculum development (SBCD) is that of all institutions and agencies: the school and the teacher should have the *primary responsibility* for determining curriculum subject matter, teaching methods, pupil learning and evaluation procedures. In short, the curriculum is best designed where students and teachers meet. Here it is the teacher who is considered to have a wealth of information on which they can draw to shape a program to suit the particular group of pupils. They are also in a position to form partnerships in the planning and implementation processes with others such as colleagues, parents, therapists and local businesses. Such a model clearly gives considerable professional autonomy to schools and teachers.

Principles underpinning SBCD are outlined below (after Skilbeck 1982):

- Curricula are best designed where teachers and students meet as a response to students' needs and interests.

- Freedom is essential for teachers and students to enjoy a full educational experience.
- As a complex social institution, the school must be free to respond to the environment.
- Curriculum development is a skilful and onerous task and teachers need support to do it.
- SBCD does not preclude a range of voices in curriculum design and development.

As with most educational ideas there are pros and cons, depending on your perspective. Those who argue for school-based curriculum development claim that it:

- allows for the development of educative experiences and relationships—that is, flexibility and diversity in teacher/student interactions;
- means that schools can escape the pressure from external authorities—for example, universities;
- overcomes the demonstrated failure of centre-periphery models of change; and
- promotes teacher satisfaction, collegiality, enthusiasm, professional practices etc.

Those who argue against it claim that it:

- makes heavy demands on teachers for curriculum making;
- positions teachers as very influential;
- requires extensive infrastructure support;
- creates discontinuity across the system/s.

The issue of responsibility for curriculum development and implementation is further discussed in Chapter 14.

Planning for teaching

Outcomes-based education, while shifting the teachers' focus from how to proceed with curriculum making to concerns about what pupils achieve, nevertheless requires teachers to have a systematic, thoughtful and well-documented approach to planning. Good quality teaching is usually underpinned by careful planning because planning:

- is the point at which teachers translate a state-level document into a workable plan suited to the needs of the pupils and their context;
- assures that there is a progression both within and between lessons;
- helps the teacher to stay on task;
- reduces the teacher's anxiety and helps to maintain their confidence during teaching;
- is required by the institution's policies and professional codes of practice. (after Siedentop 1991)

Teachers' approaches to the planning task and the nature of their plans vary according to a range of factors, such as the context in which they are working (e.g. primary or secondary schooling), and their experience and priorities (e.g. experienced teachers may be responsible for the school-level planning while beginning teachers focus on planning for lessons and units). It is stressed that while plans for teaching are important in focussing and maximising learning, plans frequently form a guide only, and should be modified appropriately according to the needs and interests of the learners and instructors and the changing demands of the learning environment.

Situational analysis

For decades educators have recognised the importance of understanding the socio-cultural and physical situation in which learning is to take place before embarking on a detailed plan for teaching and learning. As an initial part of the planning process, the teacher should undertake a *situational or context analysis* in order to understand the uniqueness of the configuration of factors which bear on the learning context and the learners.

A situational analysis assists teachers to account for internal and external factors which shape and influence the particular learning situation. Critical examination of the factors comprising a situation helps to fulfill the potential of the situation and allows the teacher to justify their actions in terms of the learning context. Although no list of factors is necessarily exhaustive, attention at your practicum school site should be paid to the following:

External factors
- directives of curriculum documents;
- communities' needs, issues, interests and traditions;
- cultural, social and policy expectations which could affect physical education;
- community structures and organisations as resources; and
- flow of resources to the schools.

Internal factors
- the school's physical education programs;
- aptitudes, needs, interests and abilities of the pupils;
- organisational structures and ethos;
- available resources; and
- perceived weaknesses or problems with existing practices.

(after Brady 1995, pp 38–49)

oty **over to you**

Consider the following pupils. How will you gain information about them and their context? What questions might you ask? What might the information gathered mean to your curriculum making?

Scenarios

1 Jane attends a state school in a low socio-economic area where opportunities to develop her physical skills have been limited. While she has an artificial left leg, she is a keen participant in physical education.

2 Yu is Indonesian with relatively little English. He is keen to participate in physical education both inside and outside the classroom but you notice resistance from the other students to his inclusion.

3 Andrew is a devotee of football. He attends Saturday morning coaching and appears highly skilled. However, he is impatient with less skilled peers and with the pace of 'practical' physical education classes. Consequently, he often seems to go 'off task'.

4 While Alicia 'appears' to be part of the physical education lesson, she acts as a 'competent bystander'. She has little interest or skill in physical activities involving balls.

Levels of planning

The word 'planning' carries with it several connotations determined by its purpose, such as a school or year level program, or by units of time, such as lesson, unit, semester, or yearly. For the purposes of this discussion, we will focus on the shared elements which underpin the conventional hierarchy of planning which occurs in most schools (see Figure 13.2).

PROGRAM
e.g. year 8 physical education

UNIT
e.g. basketball

LESSON
e.g. lay-up and set shots

Figure 13.2   Levels of planning

The same language and approaches may shape the planning process regardless of whether planning for a single lesson, a unit or a program.

Models for curriculum planning

Given the variety of sites and purposes for physical education, we would argue that there is no one best way to approach planning. Different models may better suit different contexts. The models we outline below range from inflexible to flexible in terms of the sequence, beginning point, and relationships among elements of the planning process.

Objectives model/rational curriculum planning

Conceived back in 1949 by Ralph Tyler, the objectives model was a response to increasing concerns for accountability and measurement of outcomes in education (in case you had not noticed, such concerns have been put back on centre stage as we begin the 21st century). It has since gone under names such as the 'rational' or 'scientific' model. Tyler's rationale for the model was oriented on four questions:

1. What educational purposes should be attained?
2. What educational experiences are likely to attain these purposes?
3. How can these experiences be effectively organised?
4. How can we determine whether these purposes are being attained?

The linear model is represented as a series of steps moving from the selection of aims and objectives, to content or subject matter, to methods, and finally assessment and evaluation. The steps are then followed sequentially and logically. The success or otherwise of teaching or instruction is determined in the evaluative phase in which a judgment is made regarding the extent to which the means (the selection and organisation of subject matter) has fulfilled the ends (objectives). Arnold (1988) refined this model and argued that it could be most useful if it were understood to be cyclical, in that the stage of assessment and evaluation should inform and refine the future selection of objectives. See Figure 13.3.

The educational literature varies in its interpretation of the terms aims and objectives, but the following understandings are widely shared:

- *Aims* tend to be wide, broad-brush and long-term statements of intent.
- *Objectives* are derived from aims and have a short-term focus for what the pupil should achieve in the course of the lesson.

Some qualities of worthwhile objectives include relevance to the learners, comprehensiveness of a range of learning, and specific wording.

Objectives are often categorised according to the cognitive, psychomotor and affective domains, although it should be noted that these categories are socially constructed categories and are not discrete. Cognitive objectives focus on the learning of ideas, principles and concepts. The acquisition of simple physical reflexes through to skilled and aesthetic movement is the focus of psychomotor objectives and the affective domain attends to the development

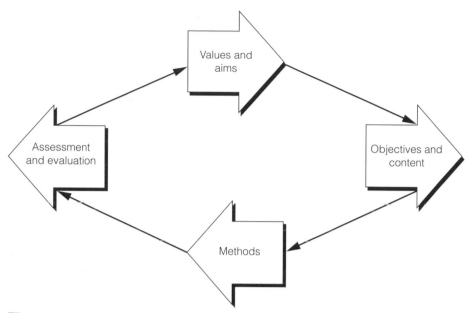

Figure 13.3 The cyclic nature of planning (after Arnold 1988)

of personally and socially responsible behaviours and values. In planning with objectives, teachers will typically use certain key words in their objectives statements (see Table 13.1).

Table 13.1 Key terms (after Kirk et al 1996)

Cognitive (thinking)	Psychomotor (doing)	Affective (feeling)
Define, recall, explain, compare, use, apply, solve, analyse, contrast, create, propose, assess, justify	Run, jump, catch, balance, stop, change, react, dive, shoot, strike, express, create	Listen, attend, answer, obey, share, decide, value, organise, judge, act, perform

Those who advocate this planning model argue that it provides the teacher with a clear direction, purpose and sequence. However, the values and ways of proceeding in rational curriculum planning are consistent with the hegemonic view of the world termed *technocratic rationality* (see Tinning 1990). This way of looking at the world/operating prioritises:

- efficiency;
- refining what is rather than taking new directions;
- profit/outcome; and
- accountability.

In education this is manifested in:

- tight and sequential procedures for planning, teaching and evaluating;
- concern for maximising the use of centralised materials and resources;
- less concern with asking 'why' and more concern with 'how to' (procedures); and
- preoccupation with assessing the measureable product/outcome rather than considering individual pupil growth.

The objectives model provides little scope for the idiosyncracies of the pupil, unexpected changes at the learning site, or responsiveness to unintended learning. Furthermore, the model needs to be reviewed in light of outcomes-based education in terms of its language and substance. It could be argued that outcomes can be viewed as aims within this model. In other words, following a situational analysis, your planning process would begin with the identification of outcomes to which the pupils should work, and then proceed with outlining the relevant subject matter, teaching methods and assessment.

The objectives model is presented as the dominant model of curriculum development and of curriculum practice, and has been taught in our teacher training courses for the past 30 years. But the model does not necessarily describe what happens in practice (see 'Real-life planning', p 212).

Interaction planning model

The interaction model uses the same elements as the objectives model—namely objectives, selection of subject matter, selection of methods and assessment and evaluation—but in different relationships. The planning process is more flexible in that any element can be the starting point and the sequence is not prescribed. Moreover, because the elements are seen as interdependent, a change in one element affects other elements. Thus the benefits of the interaction model are thought to be that it is more realistic for both teachers and pupils and that its flexibility allows for creativity and responsiveness. Critics would argue that it is this flexibility which may give rise to disjointed experiences.

Process planning approach

The process approach to planning rejects the elements and principles of the objectives and interaction models. For example, the process approach does not employ objectives (or indeed outcomes) but rather prioritises the method or process of instruction and learning. Using the process approach, the planner is acknowledging that learning is complex and dynamic, that the pupil is an active participant in shaping the learning process, and that the outcomes of learning can be unanticipated and varied. Accordingly evaluation can be considered more broadly than the 'mere' achievement of pre-specified objectives/outcomes.

Selection of what to teach

What is chosen to be taught is referred to as 'content' or 'subject matter'. It includes the knowledge, concepts, skills, ideas and attitudes related to the area of learning. The selection of content or subject matter should be guided by the contextual information, such as the learner's needs, interests and abilities, together with an account of the time and resources, and in relation to the relevant curriculum documents. Typically teachers draw content from a variety of sources such as textbooks, manuals, journals, videotapes and pamphlets, together with their own ideas and experiences and the pupils' input. Some guidelines for the selection and scope (i.e. breadth) of subject matter follow:

- the knowledge, attitudes and skills that the pupils possess;
- the social world of and demands on the pupil;
- that which is motivating, challenging and enjoyable for pupils;
- the time and resources available;
- the program's goals;
- balance between new subject matter, mastery of subject matter and learning skills;
- accuracy and significance; and
- in the early stages, that with which the instructor is familiar.

Issues of *scope* and *sequence* are useful ways to consider the selection and organisation of subject matter for teaching and learning. 'Scope' refers to the extent of subject matter which is to be included, while 'sequence' refers to the organisation of the subject matter over a period of time.

In earlier years, for example in the 1970s, the scope of secondary school physical education pertained to the range of physical activities that would be taught, such as swimming, softball, rugby, netball, gymnastics, golf and tennis. The introduction of the Health and Physical Education KLA in the 1990s has, however, radically changed the nature of the scope of traditional physical education. While similar physical activities might be chosen, the outcomes expected from participation in such activities reach far beyond the development of competence in a physical skill.

The scope of the Health and Physical Education learning area is far broader than the performance of physical activities. Now health and physical activity are approached as social and cultural commodities. The learner is now meant to be challenged to understand how social, cultural, economic and biological factors shape our actions, values and attitudes with respect to health and physical activity. Subject matter should explore conflicting and different views, responses, morals and ethics with respect to health and physical activity, and how personal decisions can be made in order to develop active and informed citizens.

The content which is most likely to be taught in 'physical education' is meant to promote the integration of cognitive and physical dimensions of being physically educated (mind/body dualism is to be challenged). While specific physical activity experiences are important, conceptual under-standings which can be transferred across time and content are central. Programs should address the social construction of 'healthy' bodies and the impact this has on identity, eating patterns, exercise regimens, friendship patterns and body image, and how physical activity plays a central role in contemporary popular culture, entertainment and business. As such, Glover (1994) claims the challenges to physical education in 'new times' include the selection of subject matter which:

- progresses across the years of schooling;
- provides all pupils with a sense of relevance, success and reward;
- is consistent with environments in which pupils work independently and creatively; and
- develops technical competencies in pupils as well as developing their ability to be critical consumers of physical activity.

Sequencing what is taught

Sequencing suggests organising the subject matter into manageable steps to facilitate learning both within and across units. At the lesson level, the sequence or flow should ensure that the pupil is engaged throughout the time available. Marsh (1992) outlines some traditional ways of establishing sequences:

- going from simple to more complex tasks (e.g. handstand to handstand forward roll);
- moving from whole to part (e.g. attempting the triple jump before dissecting its constituent actions);
- chronological ordering of events (e.g. dates and numbers of women participating in the Olympic Games);
- spiralling of subject matter which is revisited over time in more detail or from new approaches (e.g. in the games sense approach, progressively more complex movement problems can be posed); and
- moving from concrete tasks to concepts (e.g. exploring different body positions to understand the concept of centre of gravity).

Learning tasks should be sequenced in progressions that maximise learning and move the pupils towards the desired goals. Opportunities should be given for the pupils to gain confidence through modifications of the tasks, to refine and extend the tasks, and to have tasks arranged so that there might be transfer or links between them.

 over to you

Think back to your own physical education experiences at secondary school.
On what basis were the activities you did in PE chosen and sequenced?
What activities did you experience each year?
Did you experience the same activities each year?
Were there any major events in the school calendar that tended to influence the PE content?
Did they help you to refine and extend your knowledge and skills?
Were you ever involved with the teacher in choosing what activities you would do as a class?

Real-life planning

When you go on teaching rounds (the practicum), have you noticed how the teachers plan their lessons? Certainly they are not required to write plans of the detail expected of most student teachers, however a brief perusal of a typical work program for a physical education teacher will reveal that lessons are not generally driven by stated objectives. The research of Clark & Yinger (1979) and McCutcheon (1980), for example, established that for practising primary classroom teachers in the United States planning begins with a number of activities which they consider to have educational worth and then the objectives are written mainly as a means to justify the activities. Perhaps you could take note when next on teaching rounds to see if this observation is also true of Australian teachers. Judy Placek (1984) found similar results when she studied the planning behaviour of American secondary school physical education teachers. According to Placek, 'teachers focused upon what students would do in the gymnasium rather than on objectives or what the students could learn' (p 47).

 over to you

When on teaching rounds ask teachers how they plan. Is their response consistent with what the research tells us? Ask them why it is that they plan as they do.

Of course, just because most teachers plan their teaching in this way does not necessarily mean that they should. More importantly, the practice of experienced teachers is not *necessarily* the practice which we should advocate for student teachers. We return to this issue in Chapter 15.

Planning lessons as a student teacher

One way of considering what lesson planning should address is to use the distinctions that Shulman (1986) made between the different content knowledge(s) which are part of all teaching. Lesson planning, if it is adequate, will engage each of the forms of content knowledge. In your planning you will require knowledge of the activity (concept or whatever) you intend to teach. You will need to give consideration to issues of how you will arrange the human, spatial and temporal conditions such that the class can be purposefully involved in the chosen activities, and you will need to consider where you will obtain such knowledge. Considered in this way it is obvious that lesson planning is a good deal more than simply listing the activities and the equipment needed.

From our perspective, some form of lesson planning is necessary in teaching physical education. It is necessary on a number of counts. First, it is not good enough to simply work it out as you go. There is an old saying that 'If you don't know where you are headed then it doesn't matter much which direction you take to get there'. In the case of physical education teaching, it *does* matter where you end up with respect to what the class learns from the lesson(s) and, accordingly, it is necessary to first know where the lesson is heading—what skills, attitudes, behaviours etc. it is intended to facilitate. Planning is necessary to provide this direction.

Second, thinking beforehand about the forms of class organisation, ways of distributing and collecting equipment etc. can enable possible management problem areas to be identified and perhaps overcome by alternative pedagogical strategies.

Third, if you are attempting to teach a particular skill, or set of related skills, then thinking about and planning the sort of feedback which might be useful to learners can help make teacher input into improved child performance more productive. If, for example, a lesson is supposed to develop skill in dribbling a soccer or hockey ball, then pre-planning which included consideration of the main teaching points that are most often applicable to this skill might enhance the teacher's ability to offer useful feedback to each learner. The greater your lack of subject content knowledge (in this case how to dribble a ball), the greater the need for pre-planning likely teaching points. For this very reason alone, lesson planning is of value to the student teacher. Of course, merely planning appropriate teaching points does not mean that you will be any better able to recognise the instances when such feedback might be applicable. Such discrimination skill cannot be learned by pre-planning.

In the dribbling the ball example, pre-planning is a form of learning about the subject matter of physical education. It may necessitate going to books or other instructional media in order to learn more about how to execute the dribble.

The place of objectives in planning

One of the things which is often unrealistic about most textbook-advocated rules for lesson planning is that they suggest that objectives should be stated for what it is that the children are supposed to learn in that particular lesson. The use of lesson behavioural objectives is an example of this advocacy. Although it is useful to expect that an individual lesson will contribute to certain learnings, it is often unrealistic to expect clearcut, definable learnings from each and every lesson. Some things simply take more time than that. In the case of our own student teachers, most of their lessons would be classed as abject failures if the criterion for the worth of the lesson was whether they had achieved particular learning objectives in that given lesson. They usually attempt to slip by this problem by defining their objectives as a restatement of the lesson procedures. For example, 'By the end of the lesson the children will have practised dribbling skills with hockey and soccer balls'. Said in this manner they try to avoid the issue of defining what it is that the students are *supposed* to learn, or of considering what they *might* learn from the activities.

We are not suggesting that you should not have as clear a vision as possible of what it is that you would like the students to learn by participating in certain movement experiences—indeed, you should. But we are saying that in most situations worthwhile learnings are not attainable in a single 45-minute session.

Worthy considerations in lesson planning

In essence a lesson plan should be a representation of what it is that you intend to do in a lesson. For the moment we are not concerned as to whether or not the activities of the lesson are chosen first (that is, before the statements of objectives) or afterwards. What we are concerned about is the advance thinking which should be done in order to facilitate the conduct of the lesson activities.

Accordingly, it will be important to think about the order in which you wish to conduct the activities. Consideration of such things as the equipment to be used, the class formations and the spacing will all be essential in this regard. It is usually a good idea to minimise the number of changes of equipment and class formations if at all possible. For example, if the class is to use balls for some activities and hoops for others, it is sensible to conduct all the ball activities then all the hoop activities rather than swap and change from one to another. Such considerations are mainly concerned with efficiency and minimising the amount of time spent on management.

You might find it strange to think this way but if you were a student teacher in the 1960s, for example, then a major consideration in your lesson plan would have been to ensure that different parts of the body were exercised in turn. For example, a lesson which contained two successive leg exercises was unwise due to fatigue, so the idea was to rotate activities between arm, trunk, legs etc. This concept is seldom considered in today's physical education curriculum because activities are typically not focussed on a particular body part of group of muscles. However, the concept is still appropriate and should be considered where applicable. This idea is embedded in circuit training methods and even in modern aerobic lessons.

Although there is no absolutely right way to plan and conceptualise a lesson for physical education, there is a broad framework which is relevant to most lessons. This framework allows us to think of the lesson in two main parts. The first part of the lesson, which is often preceded by a brief, introductory warm-up activity, is devoted to the revision of previously learned skills and activities and the introduction of new skills. The second part is devoted to the use of those skills in a game or some other applied context.

 over to you

Look through a number (say four) of basic physical education curriculum books in the library and jot down what they suggest should be the framework for lesson planning. Draw out the common threads or ideas of organisation. What are some of the differences? Which planning model makes the most sense for you and why?

The amount of detail that you should put into a lesson plan is very much an individual decision. In general terms, however, the more attention to detail you address in your plan, the better placed you will be to anticipate any potential problems which might occur in the lesson. Some of the things that you should consider or take into account in your planning are listed below.

- What has the class done before in physical education?
- What facilities and equipment are available to you?
- What do you hope the class will learn from the lesson?
- Where does this lesson fit in terms of progressions with other lessons?
- What activities are to be taught and practised?
- How do you intend beginning the lesson? Do you intend to revise previously learned activities?
- Are there any specific safety concerns which need to be considered?
- How do you intend to organise the class for the activities?
- Are demonstrations to be used? Who will demonstrate?
- Are there any teaching points that need to be given to the class specific to each activity?
- Are there any pre-class arrangements, such as ground markings, which need to be made?
- What is the approximate time you intend to spend on various sections of the lesson?

- How will you arrange for maximum participation from the class?
- How will you evaluate the lesson?

The difficult thing for all planning is to balance the time you have to spend on planning with the competence and confidence you have in the area you are teaching. If you are less than confident in teaching a particular aspect of physical education then spending more time planning your lessons will be of considerable value to you and your class.

Evaluation

Evaluation may be defined as a judgment about the worth of something, whether it be a program, a teaching practice or a pupil's response. As we see in Chapter 15, judgments will always be made about your teaching. In a teaching–learning process evaluation occurs at several levels, is ongoing and forms an important feedback mechanism for change.

When evaluating, procedures should reflect:

1. continuity—to provide feedback and modification;
2. breadth—to address the range of issues;
3. compatibility—with the learning processes and outcomes;
4. participation—by a variety of stakeholders associated with the learning process.

Consider a junior secondary school physical education program as an example. Important issues to evaluate might include:

- resources embracing staffing, specialist support external to the school, equipment, facilities and library materials;
- subject matter in terms of whether it was relevant, challenging and enjoyable, and its appropriate sequencing;
- the timetable, which should be considered in terms of whether the time available was adequate;
- quality of teaching considered in terms of appropriate methods and expectations for the students, and the extent to which the environment is supportive of pupils and teachers;
- pupils' learning addressed through gathering data on what the students learned (both intended and unintended), who was achieving and why, or why not;
- ongoing mechanisms for communication and change.

Apart from scrutinising various relevant documents (e.g. programs, schedules, budgets), the methods for collecting information can be many and varied. They include rating scales, inventories, checklists, tests, interviews, observations and diaries.

Assessment

Assessment falls under the umbrella of evaluation. It refers to obtaining and interpreting information about the knowledge, skills, characteristics and attitudes of pupils both formally and informally. Assessment is said to serve educational, social and political purposes. Educational ends are served in that assessment can help the teacher and pupil to determine the learner's progress and make changes in the program to maximise learning. Social ends are met where assessment may reveal groups of learners with special needs such as those of a particular sex, ethnicity or disability. Political purposes of assessment relate to, for example, the sifting and sorting process associated with competitive and institutionalised recording of learning outcomes or 'scores' and thereby affording further opportunities and life chances to particular pupils.

In schools, teachers instigate a variety of assessment tasks in order to gather information about the progress of the pupil in relation to the subjects being undertaken. Frequently, a label or grade is awarded for the learner's achievement and therefore it can be considered as a *summative* assessment. *Formative* assessment is undertaken to inform the learner and teacher during the program or unit. *Diagnostic* assessment occurs when a teacher takes a series of measures based on knowledge, skills and attitudes that can inform the nature of the program to follow.

What follows are some examples of the purposes of assessment:

- to determine whether learning is occurring;
- to diagnose;
- to provide feedback to improve performance;
- to motivate, award;
- to certify;
- to select and screen; and
- to hold learners accountable.

Both the teacher and the pupils should be informed/need to know:

- why the assessment is being conducted;
- who is to be assessed;
- what specifically will be its focus (i.e. criteria for performance);
- how the assessment is to be conducted;
- when the assessment is to be conducted; and
- how the assessments might be used.

These approaches suggest that the teacher shifts from being the 'test giver', where the assessment is important insofar as it provides a measure, to a diagnostician, who uses assessment in a collaborative way to encourage learning.

In implementing assessment tasks, a teacher should be aware of:

- using a range of tasks covering a range of learning styles;
- pupils' ages and developmental levels;

- the key foci/principles/content of the unit;
- fully briefing the pupils with respect to the nature of the task;
- where appropriate, guiding the pupils in their application to the task;
- using a balance of techniques suited to a range of students;
- providing clear criteria;
- selecting tasks which are manageable within the lesson/unit organisation; and
- giving meaningful feedback to the pupil and others.

And with outcomes:

- using tasks which inform the teacher about a range of learning outcomes;
- using tasks which inform judgments about the outcome statements.

These considerations are consistent with 'authentic' assessment. They suggest that the teacher shifts from being the test giver to a diagnostician.

 for your information

Some ideas for assessment tasks/instruments include:
- checklists (physical, social skills)
- objective skills observations (e.g. throw for distance)
- subjective skills observations (e.g. perform a sequence, game play)
- questioning (verbal, handraising, written)
- pen and paper tests (e.g. short answer questions, essays)
- research reports
- drawings, artwork
- student journals, notebooks
- ticking/drawing smiley faces
- participation records
- role plays, debates
- videotape analysis

Reporting

Increasingly, schools are being required to report extensively on pupil learning and achievement. An effective reporting process is built on assessment and recording. Figure 13.4 represents the sequence of assessment, grading and reporting in relation to chosen learning outcomes.

Commonly, teachers record (systematically note) pupils' progress and achievement in line with a grading system. Grading systems may be:

- numerical (e.g. 7–1, a percentage)
- yes/no; tick/cross
- letters (e.g. A, B, C, D, E)
- words (e.g un/satisfactory; very high achievement).

These are frequently supplemented with anecdotal record and comments, folios of pupils' work and statements outlining the pupils' extra curricula activities. In selecting a system of recording teachers need to consider that they may have large amounts of pupil information to deal with and that such data need to inform the pupils' progress towards particular learning outcomes. As outcomes provide a framework for curriculum planning, pupil learning and assessment, they are now central to the reporting process in terms of indicating the pupils' progression across the learning area outcomes and over time.

Teachers and education authorities use the above records in various combinations, together with other strategies, to report to various stakeholders in education. While parents are the major audience, other stakeholders in the reporting process include governments, education authorities, school administrators, employers, tertiary institutions, teachers and the pupils themselves. As reporting should be meaningful to *all* these groups, reporting takes a variety of different forms, from results of formal testing to informal teacher–parent discussions. Common reporting strategies are:

- school reports;
- educational authority certificates;
- parent/student-teacher interviews;
- speech nights and school assemblies;

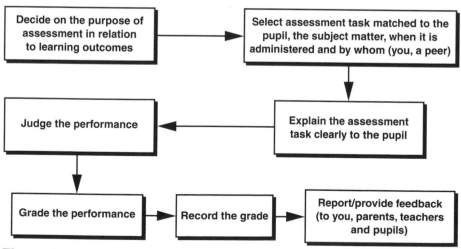

Figure 13.4 The sequence of assessment, grading and reporting

- school newsletters, development plans and policies;
- school curriculum and program documents;
- open days and classroom visits;
- formal school meetings; and
- out-of-school displays and performances. (After Brady & Kennedy 1999, p 157)

Brady and Kennedy (1999) suggest that effective communication is central to the reporting process so that the intended meaning is both conveyed and interpreted. To aid this communication teachers need to be active listeners, avoid jargon which may distort the message, and select appropriate forms of communication and reporting strategies. In summary, 'good' recording and reporting:

- are organisationally possible;
- provide valid representations of the pupils' achievements;
- are meaningful to the various audiences; and
- where appropriate, ensure confidentiality and/or include pupils' input.

Summary

- Control of the physical education curriculum exists on three levels: at the national level with the setting of the national designation of the Health and Physical Education Key Learning Area; at the state level with the various state curriculum documents oriented by the KLA; and at the school level by the school policy and teacher implementation.
- Planning for teaching should occur on a number of levels: the school program level; the unit level; and the lesson level.
- Various models are used in curriculum planning: the objectives model, the interaction model; and the process model. Each has its own pros and cons.
- Selection of subject matter should consider both scope and sequence.
- Planning lessons is a necessary part of student teaching. Detailed and thoughtful planning will make a major contribution to the implementation of successful teaching experiences.
- Evaluation, assessment and reporting are increasingly important features of curriculum implementation. There is greater expectation and accountability on teachers to deliver justifiable assessments based on actual evidence.

References

Arnold, P. (1988). *Education, Movement and the Curriculum*. London: Falmer Press.

A Statement on Health and Physical Education for Australian Schools. (1994). Melbourne: Curriculum Corporation.

Brady, L. (1995). *Curriculum Development* (5th edn). Sydney: Prentice Hall.

Brady, L. & Kennedy, K. (1999). *Curriculum Construction*. Sydney: Prentice Hall.

Clark, C. & Yinger, R. (1979). *Three Studies of Teacher Planning* (Research report # 55). East Lansing: Michigan State University, Institute for Research on Teaching.

Curriculum Corporation (1994). *A Statement on Health and Physical Education for Australian Schools*. Melbourne: Curriculum Corporation.

Glover, S. (1994). 'The national statement and profile in health and physical education: Reflections from one of the writers'. *Changing Education*, 1(2), pp 6–7.

Kirk, D., Nauright, J., Hanrahan, S., Macdonald, D. & Jobling, I. (1996). *The Sociocultuural Foundations of Human Movement Studies*. Melbourne: Macmillan Education.

McCutcheon, G. (1980). 'How do elementary school teachers plan? The nature of planning and the influences on it'. *Elementary School Journal*, 81(1), pp 4–23.

Marsh, C. (1992). *Key Concepts for Understanding Curriculum*. London: Falmer Press.

Fenny, D. (1998). 'School subjects and structures: Reinforcing traditional voices in contemporary "reforms" in education'. *Discourse*, 19(1), pp 5–17.

Placek, J. (1984). 'A multi-case study of teacher planning in physical education'. *Journal of Teaching in Physical Education*, 4(1), pp 39–50.

Siedentop, D. (1991). *Developing Teaching Skills in Physical Education* (3rd edn). Mountain View: Mayfield Publishing.

Shulman, L.S. (1986). 'Those who understand: Knowledge growth in teaching'. *Educational Researcher* (February), pp 4–14.

Tinning, R. (1991). 'Physical education as health education: Problem-setting as a response to the new health consciousness'. *ACHPER National Journal*, 134 (Summer), pp 4–10.

Tyler, R. (1949). *Basic Principles of Curriculum and Instruction*. Champagne-Urbana, IL: University of Chicago Press.

Further reading

Brady, L. & Kennedy, K. (1999). *Curriculum Construction*. Sydney: Prentice Hall.

chapter fourteen

objectives

By the end of this chapter you should be able to:

- recognise the stakeholders in the curriculum change process and the relative different degree of power they have in that process;
- appreciate the underpinning educational issues and the level of change required to implement the following alternative curriculum models:
  - the social responsibility model
  - the integrated model
  - the communitarian model;
- understand something of the complexities of changing curriculum but also the necessity of being active players in the deliberations regarding such change.

Introduction

Discussions about mainstream and alternative curriculum models can be relatively tricky to engage. The distinction between what is mainstream and what is alternative is, of course, quite fluid. One thing we can be sure of is that curriculum does change and that what is mainstream today may (will) not be mainstream in the future. This realisation compels physical educators to recognise that curricular offerings come and go and that they should be willing and able to participate in the processes of change. As such, PETE course developers like us must deal with a tension between how much emphasis they place on preparing student teachers to operate effectively in the contemporary settings they will experience in the immediate future and preparing their students for the changes that will inevitably come.

As we argue in Chapter 5, change is a constant in the professional world of the teacher. How future teachers are prepared for professional practice in a changing world is a key challenge for teacher education. For example, if PETE students are not properly prepared to work with contemporary curricula (such as the KLAs) they are likely to confront a degree of professional criticism. That is, they would be ill-prepared for teaching in the (curriculum) world as it currently exists in schools. On the other hand, if they are ill-prepared to participate in and adapt to change then they are likely to experience a high degree of professional anxiety at some time in the future when change inevitably occurs. The challenge for all PETE courses is to provide sufficient grounding in both of these areas so that their students can successfully negotiate the present and the future. Importantly they do not have to be either/or choices.

Another tension that bedevils such a discussion relates to questions about when a curriculum becomes mainstream and when it is alternative. At a very simple level it could be expressed that everything that is not mainstream is alternative. While this is useful at a macro level it tends to present different curriculum modes as pure and/or coherent. That is, that the understandings we all have of each curriculum are coherent and will be similarly reflected in our implementation of it. Of course, we know that this is not the case! Imagine how easy it would be if each of the schools you worked in embraced precisely the same goals and implemented them in precisely the same ways. Your task, and indeed our task, would be a lot simpler; once we established a formula that worked you could apply it in all settings and be assured of success. As appealing as this may sound superficially, the fact that we work with people (students, other teachers, parents and administrators) who have individual needs, investments and histories means that such unity will never be achieved.

The purpose of this chapter is to present some alternative ways of thinking about the practice of physical education in schools. Our main purpose for doing this is to expose you to different ways of thinking about your subject and to put some alternative perspectives on the record. After all, how would we have got to where we are today if it was not for people reflecting on what they were doing and trying to do it *better*? In this chapter we are going to explore the potential and need for curriculum change through looking at a number of emerging discourses. For this purpose we have selected the following themes:

- the need for schools (including physical education) to play a greater role in the preparation of good citizens;
- the need for physical education to be better integrated with a wide range of broader educational objectives; and
- the need for schools to build closer links with their communities and other educational and health service providers.

These themes are not meant to be representative of all possible emerging discourses that could potentially affect the practice of physical education in schools. Rather, our treatment of these four themes is merely as the content model through which you might undertake a similar analysis on different themes, now or in the future. The model we use here invites you to contemplate the practical and theoretical grounds on which alternative discourses might develop or dwindle around a number of core questions:

- What is the educational issue?
- How can this be viewed as a curriculum model?
- What sort of change is required?

Before proceeding with our speculations about the prospect of change within the themes we have chosen, it is important to recognise that there are a range of *stakeholders*[1] who will necessarily participate in any such undertaking, albeit reluctantly. We will thus begin by discussing the process of curriculum change and how the different stakeholders interact and negotiate this process. What we want to make clear is that the different stakeholders hold different levels of power in this process.

Changing curriculum

Given that the ultimate goal of any curriculum offering should be to improve the educational experience of teachers and learners, it would reasonable to assume that these groups would be at the forefront in any deliberations about changing curriculum. In practice, however, teachers and learners are a fair way down the curriculum decision-making power chain. Indeed, the process of curriculum change typically starts with governments and is passed down to teachers and students via a raft of curriculum committees. While the notion of 'school-based curriculum development' (see Chapter 13) has fairly broad application, the parameters under which curriculum decisions are made at the school level are usually tightly defined and controlled.

Of course, this is not meant to depict student teachers as powerless, but rather to present your potential role in process of curriculum change as one that requires thoughtful and strategic action. Further, failure to recognise the complexity of the change process can invite unwarranted 'victim-blaming', based on a superficial reading of a person (or group) standing in the way of a perceived 'greater good'.

over to you

When next on a practicum placement, ask your supervising teacher(s) the following questions:

- What role do they play in determining their current curriculum?
- If they had total control, how they might do things differently?

Share your insights in a class discussion and draw your own conclusions about what level of control teachers have, how strict are the parameters under which teachers can make decisions, and what are the sorts of changes that practising teachers would like to see.

Government and policy

Governments, and the educational bureaux (departments, boards and committees) they establish to support them, play a considerable role in the construction of curriculum. This is no more evident than in the contemporary development of national curricula in Australia, New Zealand and Britain. Each of these countries has embarked on new curricula under the direction of their respective national governments. Although education is often presented as a state or community concern, national governments retain legal and constitutional authority to directly influence its trajectory. Commentators such as Kirk (1997) and Penny (1998) point out that the national curriculum directive in Australia appeared at a time when schools did not appear to be calling out for change. Rather, a more realistic picture would have depicted teachers as already tired of the constant flow of change that swept through education during the late 1970s and 1980s. On top of this there was a growing scepticism (and considerable research evidence to support the concern) about the capacity for change 'made from above' to deliver on its visions and promises.

Whether we want to view governments as proactive or reactive in the process of curriculum setting, their role in defining the process and its parameters cannot be overstated. Even if the changes they preside over are merely a response to broader social and economic pressures, they have enormous clout in the distribution of funds and resources.

One of the core reasons why 'top-down' approaches to curriculum reform dominate this terrain is funding and resource allocation. It is not that teachers and their students do not (or cannot) think about and/or engage with change. Rather, it is more typically a case of their not having the time or structures to consolidate and propagate their ideas. Governments, on the other hand, have a clear and comprehensive structure of support that enables them to do what teachers and students cannot—that is, mobilise change. In practical ways, governments can change/alter the conditions under which finances and resources are allocated and put in place a wide range of structures to encourage compliance. For example, when employment conditions and promotional opportunities are connected to teacher compliance, it is a determined, or foolish, person who decides they will not 'play ball'. This is what makes government-sponsored approaches to curriculum change the most powerful and influential.

 for your information

In Australia the National Professional Development Program (NPDP) was funded by the national government to facilitate the new (in 1994) 'national curriculum'. Across the country various inservice professional development projects were conducted in all the Key Learning Areas. The NPDP-funded project in Health and Physical Education (HPE) brought teachers, teacher educators and education department curriculum developers together to produce resources to enable teachers to implement the HPE KLA.

Community values

Until recently the community has not been viewed as a direct stakeholder in the processes of curriculum design and delivery. While schools were recognised as important components of community, the community itself held very little sway over what happened in the classroom or gym. It was not that the local community did not care about the manner in which its young were being educated, but rather there was not really a strong culture of interaction between the two institutions (i.e. schools and communities). Generally speaking, schools reported student progress a couple of times a year and parents were only really summoned to the school as a direct response to their sibling's actions, or inaction. Of course much has changed with regard to the ways schools interact with their immediate community. As teachers in the contemporary context not only do you stand accountable to your employer and your students, but you are also likely to be increasingly scrutinised by the broader community in which you teach.

over to you

Map the nodes of connection that you recognise between the school and its immediate community during your next practicum placement. Look carefully at physical education and other subject areas to see whether the links or connections are similar or different. Consider how we might improve our current levels of interaction with the school community, with a view to enhancing our educational image and/or profile.

Early in the 21st century the landscape of compulsory education is much more one that seeks to connect schools with their community. This process of devolution, understood as the shifting of authority from governments to school communities, has already had considerable impact on schools and teachers. Prominent in this shift has been the provision in some states of school communities, represented in local school boards or councils, to hire and fire teaching staff. Where this provision was previously administered centrally, with Departments of Education, its allocation in local contexts provides a much more direct chain of command between teachers and the immediate community they serve. It is now much more incumbent on teachers to embrace and uphold the values of their immediate community. A large part of this involves teachers delivering curriculum in the form and manner prescribed by the school community.

let's reflect

What might this mean for physical education? Does it mean any more than, for example, providing soccer in the curriculum at a school in a largely European ethnic community?

The extent to which the devolution model is any more empowering for teachers is hotly contested. While on the surface it appears that school communities will band together to make collective decisions about what is best for their students, the extent to which this model will support (or even tolerate) opposition or difference is clearly limited. Assuming the school community stakeholders (namely, school executive, teachers and students) are in agreement on issues of curriculum design and delivery, this process is likely to be harmonious. However, where particular groups or individuals feel that their needs and commitments are not being adequately catered for, this is likely to produce conflicts that must be dealt with at the local level. Once again, this time under the guise of 'school-based curriculum development', we are bound to have a situation where the dominant group controls the curriculum agenda while marginal groups and/or individuals are forced to follow suit. The major difference here is that such conflicts now reside within the local community. Unless resolved in a satisfactory way, such a situation can readily regress to where individuals are in conflict with their 'neighbours'.

 over to you

In a tutorial session set up a role-play situation to explore the debate over the introduction of a 'hot' topic in the HPE KLA during a local school council (or board of trustees) meeting. The topic might be inclusion of a certain sexuality education topic, or even a proposal to include standardised testing of all children in certain motor skills. Experience the diversity of opinions and the process of trying to arrive at a collective decision that avoids alienating certain people/groups in the school community.

Discuss the process in the context of school-based curriculum development.

Of course, governments are not absent in the processes of school-based curriculum development. Although, as self-managing structures, school communities are presented as being in control of their own curriculum reform, there exists a wide range of checks and balances that, albeit less directly, encourage conformity. As such, 'successful' schools continue to be defined and rewarded according to government definitions. School principals often have the unenviable task of having to mediate between the school community and the government bureaux. Though they are notionally there to serve the school community, governments have an array of levers to pull to ensure that principals fall in behind the dominant agenda. To this end, the role of the school community in making the substantive decisions about the nature and form of curriculum is fairly well regulated.

 over to you

A Victorian primary school which had chosen to be a 'School of the Future' was awarded the distinction of being designated a 'sporting excellence school'. Under this designation the school was given increased resources for the physical and sport education curriculum and was expected to achieve certain learning outcomes from the HPE KLA. Attached to the performance-based outcomes, the principal received an attractive salary 'package' that included the opportunity to buy a new car under the 'salary sacrifice option'. In other words his salary package was contingent on 'his' teachers delivering (achieving) the learning outcomes.

In your tutorial class, discuss the extent to which the principal might be compromised were he to consider that certain of the performance outcomes were inappropriate. Is it a good idea to link the achievement of certain student learning outcomes to rewards for principals or teachers?

Teachers

Interestingly, it is ultimately up to teachers as to whether curriculum change or reform will live or die. Despite their apparent lack of authority in the processes of curriculum construction, it is teachers who are ultimately charged with the responsibility of implementing such curricula. No matter how colourful, glossy or thoughtful a particular curriculum document is its impact is ultimately determined by the extent to which teachers embrace it and can work with it. Big factors in this equation involve the ease and continuity with which curriculum reform can be undertaken within their day-to-day demands and routines. In the hustle and bustle world of being a teacher it is not surprising that the prospect of curriculum change is typically met with scepticism and/or resistance. For many this presents itself as a taste of considerable negotiation and contestation; both of which consume time in an already busy schedule. Indeed, where such change is being developed and controlled external to themselves, teachers are likely to have little investment in its success. In the absence of any genuine commitment to a new curriculum teachers, like all other people, will readily opt for the security of what is familiar and known to them (Sparkes 1990).

There have been numerous attempts to introduce new curriculum models, many of which have been either entirely unsuccessful or only partially successful. The *Daily Physical Education Program* (1982) introduced into Australian primary schools in the 1980s is an example of curriculum renewal that met with mixed results (see Tinning & Kirk 1990). Another good example was seen in Britain in the late 1980s where the two curriculum innovations—namely, Health Related Fitness (HRF) and Teaching Games for Understanding (TGFU)—were developed as a means of presenting physical education for 'everyone'. Central to these curricula designs was an educational belief that too much emphasis was being placed on skilled performance and competition in physical education, resulting in an array of non-inclusive and elitist practices. Underpinning the introduction of HRF and TGFU was a genuine commitment to broadening the place and purpose of physical education in the school curriculum. Seeking to challenge existing patterns of authority and power, both of these models invited students to play a more active role in the decision-making processes with a view to encouraging responsibility and self-esteem.

Regretfully, Evans & Clarke (1988) reported that initial enthusiasm for the

HRF and TGFU models quickly abated and was replaced by conventional wisdom and practices. Not able to make the sort of shifts that were deemed necessary to implement these new curricula models, physical education teachers returned to the known and familiar. Largely unsupported in their attempts to bring about curriculum reform, most teachers found their attempts to bring about change cumbersome and unsatisfying. Among the insights that can be gleaned from this example were the following points about the importance of teachers in the process of successful curriculum change:

- Attempts to facilitate curriculum change need to be supported by extensive inservice opportunities for teachers.
- For curriculum reform to be embraced by teachers they need to have some genuine commitment to its success.
- Curriculum reform cannot simply be dropped on teachers without adequate provision for them to digest, interpret and plan its implementation.
- The closer the curriculum reform can be connected to teachers' existing understandings and practices, the more likely it is to succeed.

Student teachers (and PETE)

Student teachers also have a role to play in the process of curriculum change or reform. It is no secret that it is during their undergraduate training that most teachers experience the most intensive training phase of their professional lives. It stands to reason that the preservice phase presents itself as an ideal forum through which new curriculum models can be efficiently and effectively introduced. This has been highlighted in recent years where student teachers are often more familiar, and at ease, with the new KLAs than their supervising teachers. Perhaps you have already experienced this. Unlike the costly and time inefficient procedures associated with providing widespread inservice to practising teachers, preservice programs accommodate large numbers of emerging teachers in 'one place'. This is part of the reason why curriculum change often takes a long time to affect practice in a substantive way. Sometimes there is resistance from experienced teachers to the 'new' ideas being championed by an enthusiastic student teacher or newly graduated teachers. Accordingly, reliance on curriculum change advancing through 'young' teachers coming out of teacher training institutions makes for a long and slow transition.

Anecdotally, we know that one of the reasons that many teachers get involved in supervising student teachers is to be exposed to fresh ideas and practices. For some supervising teachers this represents an opportunity to access the most contemporary thought and practice in the field 'delivered' by student teachers like you. Indeed, it not uncommon for students like you to feel that you know a lot more about new initiatives in curriculum and teaching when in school settings. In taking on a role in student teacher supervision, practising teachers get to discuss and observe various aspects of student teaching. When student teacher(s) take with them new ideas and practices into practicum setting, they have the potential to influence their supervising teachers.

As we will see in Chapter 15, in most situations the practicum is not a good place for the student teacher to experiment with new approaches and ideas. Working with a group of undergraduate student teachers, Hickey (1997) reported a number of restrictions that needed to be overcome before students would even begin to 'experiment' with their teaching. Although many of his students had revealed a strong interest in 'alternative' approaches to their practice, Hickey reported that none of them was willing or able to explore such approaches in the context of their practicum. Foremost in their explanation of this was the fact that their performance was constantly being monitored and evaluated. They felt that it was much easier and, indeed, safer to teach in a manner that they understood to be expected of them.

In light of this and numerous other insights it seems that a number of changes will need to be made if student teachers are to seriously consider and engage alternative curriculum offerings. There needs to be:

- a continuity of support within their PETE courses. It is incumbent on the lecturers involved in PETE courses to develop a coherent and consistent approach to different curriculum models.
- support from outside of their courses. Supervising teachers, and any others invited to participate in the preparation of student teachers, need to be fully aware of the messages and approaches being delivered in PETE courses.
- opportunity to experiment (in a thoughtful manner) with different ways of organising and delivering curricula without fear of failure or reprisal. Without this support students will either reject such offerings or be at risk of negative assessment.

School students

Of course, the final and most important link in the 'curriculum chain' is the students. After all, when all is said and done, curriculum is developed to optimise the educational experience of students. Despite the lofty claims made about what particular curriculum offerings will do for students and how much better off they will be as a result of particular initiatives, students play a relatively minor role in the process of curriculum change. Quite simply, students are not thought to be good judges of such issues. It is generally assumed that if it were up to students to determine curriculum they would choose to engage in activities that were frivolous and based mainly on having fun. Even what has become known as the 'learner-centred curriculum' is overwhelmingly steered by teachers (presumably acting on behalf of students). By the time it gets to the level of students, the parameters for curriculum decisions are extremely tightly defined and controlled. It is a bit like inviting someone to choose, but only from the options you are willing to provide.

Alternative approaches to PE curriculum

What follows is an outline of some of the emerging discourses and an analysis of their potential to generate alternative curriculum approaches to PE in schools. Although some of these themes currently exist, to a lesser and lesser extent in some contemporary curricula, we believe that such existence is largely peripheral to 'core curricular practice'. In our discussion of each of these curriculum orientations we will outline the underpinning basis on which such initiatives are based and what implications their application would have for teachers and learners in physical education. A further part of our discussion involves our attempts to 'crystal ball' the sorts of *change(s)* that might be required if these curricular approaches were to gain momentum and what implications their evolution might have for physical education teachers.

While you read through each of these curriculum orientations, we invite you to think about the ways you (could) incorporate aspects of their respective ideals into your practice. To a greater or lesser extent each of these orientations has some recognition in the contemporary national curricula and therefore they are not fictional or radical. However, to be 'true' to what they espouse, respectively, would require a considerable shift in, or consolidation of, what is currently being done. In the implications section of each of the following descriptions we will present you with an outcome statement that is pertinent to the promotion of an aspect of the particular orientation. We ask you to consider how you might design a program to accommodate such goals.

Social responsibility

The idea that schools need to play a more deliberate role in the promotion of good citizens is not new. As revealed in our earlier description of the historical construction of physical education, the development of a certain sort of citizen (such as disciplined, ordered and productive) has long been thought to be one of the functions of schooling. Movies such as *To Sir with Love* and *Blackboard Jungle* dramatised this dimension of schooling extremely well. In both of these cinematic dramatisations of schooling (set in the 1950s and 60s) a teacher is forced to 'throw away' the formal curriculum and develop alternative ways of finding 'connection' with his students. Of course this theme did not begin with these movies and it certainly did not end with them. Recent cinematic productions such as *Lean on Me* and *187* are more contemporary versions of this theme. Indeed, the idea that the school curriculum needs to play a greater, more explicit, role in the preparation of 'good citizens' has considerable momentum within the contemporary social context.

What is the educational issue here?

At the core of the 'social responsibility' orientation are growing community and government anxieties about a breakdown in social cohesion. This anxiety is based on the social increase in substance abuse, unemployment, homelessness, antisocial and risk-taking behaviours (particularly among young males), juvenile crime and suicide. From these emerge ongoing debates about the types of schooling and curriculum appropriate to the interests of the nation and of young people, their families and their communities. In particular, there are growing concerns about what might be the educational consequences of a so-called decline in family values or an apparent breakdown of the family or the emergence of new family forms (step families, single-parent and same-sex parent families). Anxiety about the nature of families also finds expression in public concern about young people's health, diet and fitness which are, of course, traditionally viewed as 'core' business in the practice of PE in the school curriculum.

In the context of physical education there continues to be some debate about what sort of curriculum would be most effective in pursuit of developing social responsibility. It must be said that traditional 'sport-skills' models are not oblivious to this orientation and frequently proffer a view that physical education, as it is currently practised in schools, does contribute to the development of good citizens. This relationship is housed in a belief that the development of sports-related skills nurtures positive feelings towards an active lifestyle and group participation and affiliation, both thought to be central to the production of socially responsible citizens. However, there are a number of commentators who share a concern that despite such claims, traditional PE programs are overwhelmingly benign in confronting the contemporary problems experienced by many young people (Tinning & Fitzclarence 1992). One such commentator is Don Hellison (1985; 1995), who has long argued that traditional assumptions about the relationship between PE and social responsibility are intensely problematic and frequently overstated. Hellison argues that PE needs to be less focussed on the development of sports-related skills and to pay much greater attention to preparing young people to deal with the personal and social instabilities in society.

> *Our students also need to learn how to take responsibility for their own learning, for making wise choices, and for developing meaningful and personally satisfying lifestyle if they are going to make any sense of the world in which they are growing up. They also need to learn how to cooperate and to support and help one another if they want to achieve any social stability in this rapidly changing world. (Hellison 1985, pp 4–5)*

Social responsibility as a curriculum model

The most coherent example of a social responsibility model in the context of physical education is probably found in the work of Don Hellison. Hellison's model for *Teaching Responsibility Through Physical Activity* (1995) is an excellent example of a 'social responsibility' approach to PE. Working with young people labelled 'delinquent' or 'at risk', Hellison has spent some 20 years developing and refining a model that puts social responsibility at the forefront of curriculum goals. We would encourage you to have a look at Hellison's work and consider how it might be useful in the context of your educational goals and practices. By outlining its basic practical and theoretical application here, we invite you to consider how the practice of physical education in schools might be adapted to play a more direct role in the promotion of social responsibility. In particular, we want to point out the recognition that Hellison gives to the need to foster such attributes in thoughtful and sequential ways.

Hellison's model for teaching responsibility comprises four interacting levels. The first level focuses on the issue of *respect*. During this level, Hellison emphasises the need for teachers to adopt programmatic practices that encourage students to play an active role in the maintenance of control and order (both as individuals and as members of a group). Rather than relying on the external control of authority figures, Hellison employs a range of strategies through which individuals are called on to monitor their own participation. Included in these strategies are negotiated approaches to deciding and enforcing appropriate behaviour.

Level two of Hellison's model takes up the theme of *participation*. Within this level of the model emphasis is placed on increasing the meaningfulness of individual participation. Hellison believes that teachers need to offer students the opportunity to negotiate their level of involvement in classes. Further to this, there is a need to broaden the criterion for successful participation in physical education to include attributes such as patience, persistence, honesty, cooperation, participation and improvement.

The third level emphasises the need for students to accept greater *self-direction*. Central to this level is the shift towards students being able to work and play independently without the need for direct authority and supervision. The primary means for nurturing this developmental stage is putting students in direct contact with the consequences of their decisions and actions. By accepting responsibility for their actions and decisions students enter an important phase of their personal and social development in which they become more self-responsible and self-monitoring. This is by no means a simple process but one that Hellison believes to be core to the development of responsible and productive citizens.

In the final level of his model Hellison discusses the need for students to engage in processes associated with *caring* for others. Prominent here is a developmental shift from concentrating on personal choices and behaviours to becoming a responsible member of a group. Here, students are invited to consider not only the effects of particular decisions on themselves, but also how these impinge on the needs and desires of others. To do this, Hellison argues that students need a sense of themselves as part of something bigger. As a member of a group, class or team, students need to recognise and accommodate the mutual costs and benefits of individual actions and decisions.

What level of change is required?

The sorts of curriculum development and/or change that would need to be undertaken to facilitate the foregrounding of social responsibility within mainstream physical education are not insignificant. Indeed, Hellison would be the first to acknowledge the complexity of a more widespread distribution of his model. The primary ingredient for the success of such a process would be a level of commitment of teachers in charge of its implementation. Such a program could not easily be presented as a recipe or formula on account of the complex and context-dependent nature of its uptake. Indeed, it is most likely, at least in the short term, that curriculum innovations required to foster a social responsibility are destined to happen at the grass roots level. To this end, such change is likely to be bottom-up, beginning with individuals, such as Hellison, and seeping outwards.

The current 'national' curriculum documents for Health and Physical Education in both Australia and New Zealand provide a fertile and supportive framework for the pursuit of learning outcomes that are sympathetic to Hellison's responsibility model. It would be possible for a teacher to so structure the learning experiences for HPE as to develop responsibility in students (see for example the outcome for level 5 below). However, it would also be possible to achieve many of the learning area outcomes without an explicit focus on developing responsibility.

> ### LEVEL 5 Outcome Statement
> *Explain the personal and community factors involved in defining beliefs about what is right or wrong, good or bad behaviour.*
> *Evident when students, for example:*
> *– discuss various understandings of the role of personal conscience, community practices, peer pressure, family tradition and religious beliefs in shaping personal values and standards of behaviour. (Health and Physical Education—A Curriculum Profile for Australian Schools 1994, p 88)*

Despite the limitations associated with changing curriculum from the bottom up, the prospect of success is much greater when such innovations can be readily integrated into the mainstream curriculum. For example, the outcome statement described above is clearly compatible with a curriculum aspiration to nurture and reinforce a sense of individual and group responsibility. This statement has been taken directly from the national Profile for Health and Physical Education in Australia. Such curriculum objectives clearly pave the way for teachers such as you to legitimately consider ways to incorporate any educational aspirations you have for development of social responsibility through PE. In the interest of achieving such goals in your practice we would encourage you to think in new and innovative ways about the sort of curriculum practices (from planning to evaluating and reporting) that are most likely to best serve you and your students.

Integrated approaches to physical education

It is widely recognised that the division of school curricula into separate subjects has restrictive effects on teacher knowledge and practice as well as on student learning. Foremost here, the break-up of curricular content into discrete subject areas leads to the formation of rigid boundaries in teacher knowledge and identity. In many situations the separation of the school curriculum into narrow fields of discipline hampers the development of cross-disciplinary interaction and insight (Macdonald & Glover 1997). The call for more integrated approaches to curriculum development and implementation are forwarded in the belief that student learning would be much more coherent and developmental if it were approached in a less fragmented way. Aspects of this theme have also been represented in cinema, in movies such as *Rock 'n' Roll High School Forever* and *Dead Poets Society*. In both of these movies young people's development is nurtured through a broadening of learning beyond traditional subject boundaries.

What is the educational issue?

One of the main contemporary forces behind the push for more integrated approaches to curriculum development is based on concern about the need for schools to play an increased role in the area of pastoral care. Current secondary school curriculum structures are viewed as particularly unsupportive of such a development. Within this context teachers and/or students are forced to regularly move around the school in the delivery and receipt of particular curriculum content. These nodes of teaching and learning are routinely broken down to around 50-minute time slots at the end of which participants will pack up and move on to their next session. At stake here is a strong likelihood that teachers and their students will not get to establish anything more than a superficial working relationship.

Social analysts of the 1999 shooting of 46 students (25 fatally) at Columbine High School in the United States frequently asked questions about why the warning signals associated with such an event were not detected and what was the input or lack of input that enabled the perpetrators to conceive of and plan such a devastating act. Both of these questions raise issues about the extent to which teachers in a subject-divided curriculum are currently able to influence and mentor the young people they work with.

While not without its own limitations, the primary school model of one teacher being allocated a group of students for a complete year of their schooling clearly lends itself to a greater integration of personal and curriculum goals. Although the primary school curriculum is still, to a large extent, represented in separate discipline blocks, the fact that one teacher is responsible for development across (almost) all discipline areas[2] lends itself to greater continuity between student, teacher and curriculum. Further, this arrangement has the potential to reduce the level of competition that often exists between separate subject areas (notably in the secondary school system) in pursuit of curriculum time and resource.

A further shortcoming of the current separation of curriculum areas in the secondary school relates to the lack of interaction and exchange between staff in each subject domain. Taking up this issue in the context of English and physical education, Prain & Hickey (1998) argue the potential benefits that might come from greater interaction between the two curriculum areas. These two disciplines are thought to be unlikely 'bed-partners', on the grounds that they are underpinned by starkly different assumptions about the nature of learning. English is understood as being intensely cognitive while PE is avowedly practical. However, Prain & Hickey believe that there would be much to gain from each of these areas interacting with the other. Specifically, they argue that PE would benefit from focussing more on students' capacity to understand and express their learning. They believe that greater cooperation between these two subject areas would better integrate (rather than separate) the way students understand and experience themselves as physical, emotional and cognitive beings.

Integration as a curriculum model

The merging of Health and Physical Education in the 'national' curriculum documents of Australia and New Zealand are contemporary examples of the integration of subjects that were previously constructed as discrete curriculum areas. While none of these curricula represent extensive models of subject integration they do offer the potential for such developments. Not only is the integration of these two disciplines thought to bring their respective discipline content into closer alignment, but the sum of their parts is thought to be the basis for new and richer student learning. Specifically, the integration of Health and PE has the potential to better unite student welfare and health with student knowledge and behaviours.

Greater coherence between PE and Health has the potential to enhance the learning and reputation of these important curriculum areas. As separate offerings they were often marginalised in the school curriculum and frequently forced to compete for time and resources. The vocational emphasis that currently dominates the educational agenda, expressed in an increasing focus on technology, numeracy and literacy, stood to further compound the problems associated with maintaining PE and Health as separate subjects in the curriculum. Although not conceived as such, to some extent the integration of PE and Health has been a strategic initiative within the current educational climate. More importantly, the integration of PE and Health can also be seen as a window of opportunity for educators committed to the promotion of a healthy, knowledgeable, caring and thoughtful existence to band together within a common framework.

There are, of course, likely to be difficulties with the integration of traditionally separate subject areas. Despite there being obvious commonalities between PE and Health, learning in one subject typically takes place in a classroom while the other takes place mainly in a gymnasium or on a sporting field. Compounding this is the desire of some people to defend their traditions. It is reasonable that those teachers who have their identity in either of these merged areas will experience some sense of loss and/or confusion. When any of us are happy doing things a particular way, we are likely to resent someone insisting that we change. No matter how persuasive the rhetoric, the success of such curriculum integration rests squarely on the shoulders of those who must implement it—namely the teachers. Without their consent and support, the integration of Physical Education and Health will result in little more than the manipulation of some surface variables, such as names and titles. Despite the considerable resources directed at supporting this integration model (e.g. in NPDP projects), there continues to be much uncertainty about how it will be practically lived out in schools.

What level of change is required?

When curriculum integration has the support, in terms of finance and resource allocation, of government and policy makers, it will rapidly develop momentum. As has been the case with the development of the 'national curriculum', resourcing and legislative clout has meant that these initiatives have had an immediate impact on schools. Regardless of teacher and student consent, all Australian schools are now compelled to recognise and accommodate the goals of this curriculum. With the documentation and legislative structure in place it is extremely difficult for, and indeed unwise of, schools and teachers not to attend to its implementation.

All that said, it is still at the teacher–student interface where the real value of any curriculum initiative will be experienced. If we are to learn anything from the past we must understand that such initiatives need the support of teachers to be truly successful. To this end it is important that teachers are encouraged to cooperate in such initiatives within cultures that support and encourage their participation. The presence of a supportive educational environment is integral to the successful implementation of any curriculum.

 over to you

On your next practicum visit, try to ascertain the level of teacher, PE department and school support for the new health & physical education Key Learning Area. Perhaps ask some of the following questions:
- How is implementing the KLA working for you?
- If you had a choice would you do things (in relation to the KLA) differently from the current practice in your school?
- What are the greatest impediments to implementing the KLA?
- What would you need to make it work better?

Communitarian approaches to physical education

If we do not pay close attention to our children's developing sustaining connections, connections of all sorts, then they will always be at risk of not finding satisfaction and meaning in life, no matter how competent they may become. (Hallowell 1993, p 196)

In this section we will describe how the principles of 'community' might provide a foundation for the reorganisation of the contemporary school curriculum. An important aspect of any such development is based on the perceived need for greater communication between schools and other members of a community. This is something that schools have been relatively poor at in the past.

There was a time not so long ago when many schools were locked up at 4:30 pm and community access to its resources deemed 'off-limits'. Within their institutional frameworks, schools have often presented themselves as separate and distinctive in the process of educating young people. While schooling has always been seen as an important site for inducting young people into the adult community of work, its curriculum and practice have not really been open to community input. The communitarian thrust is built on the belief that schools can no longer be expected, or encouraged, to accommodate all aspects of a young person's education. Advocates of this model of curriculum believe that schools need to be positioned alongside families, clubs, community workers, external educational providers and electronic forms of communication in considering and planning young people's education.

Another factor supporting the push for schools to adopt more communitarian approaches to curriculum delivery is in part a response to some of the perceived consequences of globalisation (see Chapter 2). The rise of globalisation is thought to create increased feelings of social disconnection for many individuals. Where it was once taken for granted that people would interact and identify with their local community, the onset of globalisation has made presumptions about such a relationship much more problematic.

Consider, for example, the way in which many young people wear the logos of teams—the Chicago Bulls, LA Lakers and Dallas Cowboys emblazoned on their baseball caps, windcheaters and other apparel. If you did not know better you might think the logos were for local teams, or at least teams within our own country. No! What is happening here is that these young people are indentifying with (connecting their identity to) sporting teams who tread the boards or play on the fields of countries literally on the other side of the world. In a postmodern way, they are signifying that they are members of a community. But the community is global, not local.

While new (broader) forms of community are now on offer in a globalised context, communicating and interacting with the people with whom you physically share your day-to-day lives offers a local form of community which we would argue is essential to a fulfilling and productive citizenry. Whereas the challenge for schools was once to get young people to understand the world beyond their immediate community, the new challenge seems to be to (re)connect young people with their local community.

What is the educational issue here?

In modern times, the school is one of the three most important institutions for our young. The second is the family, and the third is our health care system. When these three institutions are efficient and effective, our children and youth are healthy, stay in school and achieve their potentials. (Lawson 1995, p 291)

For too long schools have functioned as discrete sectors in the development of young people, under a narrowly defined understanding of education. While schools have undertaken to report student progress at regular intervals during the schooling year, they have been much less proactive in seeking understanding about a student's home life. What has tended to emerge is a one-way flow of information, from school to home. Only in instances of crisis have most schools genuinely sought connection to the home lives of the young people they educate. Even then, the school usually adopts the position of authority and positions parents as attendants. A communitarian approach to curriculum proffers a different view of this relationship based on some notion of 'collective obligation'. Within this notion families are seen as a *central* part of a young person's life and education and are integrated into the educative process. In the interest of developing a more coherent set of strategies for overseeing the development of young people, schools and families would work together.

Another key group with a considerable investment in having closer affiliations with schools is healthcare workers. Included in this are the vast community networks that work in youth welfare and counselling, suicide prevention, drug education, youth employment, family counselling and community development. While there have been some attempts to include aspects of these in the school curriculum, instances of genuine connection between these community agencies and schools are still relatively rare and underdeveloped. The integration of healthcare professionals and schools could be better developed in the form of a 'social trust network' (Lawson 1995). Under this arrangement schools and healthcare professionals would interact around the recognised needs of the school and its individuals. The referral of individuals in crisis, or at risk, should be seen as only one dimension of the sorts of communication that could exist between these groups. Other forms of interaction could include the general education of young people about the support structures and community programs that are available to support them.

Extending the community approach to physical education, Hal Lawson (1993) argues the need to integrate the resources of schools with those of the broader community. Central to this approach is a belief that potentially important community resources (namely, families and clubs) are currently underexploited in the vast majority of physical education programs. As sites where young people congregate in numbers, community sporting and recreational clubs could play a more prominent role in the delivery of a comprehensive PE program. Lawson argues that a process of integrating schools and community is already underway in some cities in the United States. He believes that physical educators need to be proactive in such developments to maximise this opportunity. 'The question is not whether school physical education will be impacted, but how' (Lawson 1995, p 290).

Communitarianism as a curriculum model

National curriculum developments recognise the value of schools making greater use of their local community as a means of providing students with clearer pathways to active and healthy lifestyles. Within these developments, closer school/community links are seen as a means of providing PE with a valuable opportunity to play a more direct role in community development by encouraging 'participation'. The Victorian Curriculum and Standards Framework (CSF) speaks directly to the potential benefit of school–community links through the articulation of the 'Physical Education and Community Strand'. Within this strand a range of outcomes are proposed in which learners benefit through their connection with their local community. Of course, schools are not the only beneficiaries of the linking process. Clubs and associations can use their connections as a vehicle to recruit players, and other members of the school community, such as parents and teachers, to bolster the expertise of the club. The strand also encourages students to engage with a range of community issues such as those associated with the provision of sport and recreation at the 'local' level.

LEVEL 6 Outcome Statement

Examine the factors that influence community decisions to support and promote sporting, recreation, leisure and outdoor facilities and activities.
This will be evident, for example, when the student:
– gathers and shares data on requirements for participation in activities in the community (cost, time commitments, skill level, equipment, eligibility, location). (Health and Physical Education–Curriculum and Standards Framework, p 36)

The development of closer links between school physical education and community sporting and recreation programs needs to begin with the recognition of 'shared interest'. Just as the school has much to offer the community, so too has the community much to offer the school. In developing links the school, on account of its personnel and infrastructure, has the potential to play a leading role. Strategies for promoting this might involve opening up school facilities to accommodate the recreational needs of families. While this has been happening for years in some communities, in others the school is still largely closed at 4:30 pm. A range of community activities could take place on weekends, after school and/or during times of school recess (holidays, lunchtimes etc.). Community workers could also use the school as a vehicle for recruiting and training young people to participate in community programs and events. Here, a club and its administration become part of the school to provide mentoring opportunities for students to observe and experience the management and organisation of a club. As well as gaining valuable experience, students participating in community programs could have their activities acknowledged as part of their PE program.

 over to you

Have a close look around the school you are next in and identify examples of community involvement. You might have to look quite closely, as some interactions are probably not very visible.

Consider the impact of any examples you find, and how physical education measures up against other curriculum areas.

The Health Promoting Schools model (see the *ACHPER Healthy Lifestyles Journal* special edition, 1996) is another example of a model that has the potential to unite student welfare, health and physical education. A Health Promoting School is one where members of the school community work collaboratively to provide students with an environment that will have the best possible impact on students' health and well-being. Health within this concept is seen as encompassing physical, social and emotional well-being. A Health Promoting School focusses not only on the formal (explicit) curriculum but also on the informal (covert, null) curriculum, and incorporates school management structures and teacher–teacher, teacher–student and student–student relationships as well as interactions with the broader school community. In this sense a Health Promoting School recognises that 'a broad range of interconnected factors affect our health and that the physical and social environments combine to create a broader school environment or ethos' (VicHealth Health Promoting Schools Project Kit, undated, p 2).

What level of change is required?

Fundamental to a communitarian model of curriculum is the need for teachers to play a direct role in developing connections between schools and families and community workers. Unfortunately, traditional notions of good teaching practice give little or no attention to the potential for teachers to play an intermediary role between school and community. Rather, the work of physical education teachers in the middle school years focuses almost exclusively on their role in the processes of skill development. If physical education curricula are to develop in ways that embrace community connections and values, there is a need for a reconsideration of which goals are foregrounded and how the goals are best achieved. In the educational pursuit of developing physically educated citizens, learning opportunities should extend far beyond the boundaries of the formal (timetabled) curriculum.

Interestingly, the development of school–community links is not something that seems ever to have been discouraged from outside the school. In some ways this seems to lend itself to a bottom-up (beginning with teachers and community members) form of curriculum development that has the in-principle support of the 'upper' layers of curriculum developers (namely, school administration and the government bureaux). The issue therefore becomes not so much of working to give the development of school–community links legitimacy but rather to give them life. In the interest of promoting a more communitarian approach to curriculum, physical education teachers need to be able to think differently (more laterally) about their programs. This need not require a radical rethinking of current curriculum practice but rather a more gradual seeking out of opportunities to connect with and engage the resources and knowledge that exist within the immediate environment. Unfortunately, very few schools or teacher training courses have sought to engage their students in an exploration of the sort of practices that might support and develop this sort of curriculum initiative.

Summary

- The curriculum change process involves numerous stakeholders. The stakeholder groups have their own vested interest in introducing a new curriculum model but they also have different degrees of power in the process.
- It is usually the case that school students, as one of the stakeholder groups, have little if any say in the curriculum change process.
- Governments have the resources and power to introduce curriculum change, however, the ultimate success of the change will require acceptance from teachers.
- Among the many possible alternative curriculum models within physical education, in this chapter we have analysed three models—the social responsibility model, the integrated model and the communitarian model—with a view to understanding their implicit educational purposes and the levels of change required to implement them.
- The complexities of changing curriculum are significant. It is imperative that teachers see themselves as active players in the deliberations regarding such change.

Notes

1 The term 'stakeholders' is relatively new to the educational context and, although it comes from the discourses of management and economic rationalism, it is now common parlance and it does convey the message that different individuals do have different stakes in the educational process.

2 We recognise that there is increasing use of specialist teachers (e.g. for LOTE, for IT) in many primary schools and that this trend may undermine the continuity of relationships currently enjoyed by students and teachers

References

ACHPER Healthy Lifestyles Journal (1996). Special edition: Promoting Health in Schools, 43(2).

ACHPER (1982). *Daily Physical Education Program Levels 1–7*. Adelaide, SA: Australian Council for Health, Physical Education & Recreation.

Evans, J. & Clarke, G. (1988). 'Changing the face of physical education'. In J. Evans (ed.), *Teachers, Teaching and Control in Physical Education*. London: Falmer Press.

Hallowell, E. (1993). 'Connectedness'. In E. Hallowell & M. Thompson (eds), *Finding the Heart of the Child* (pp 193–209), Braintree, MA: Association of Independent Schools in New England.

Hellison, D. (1985). *Goals and Strategies for Teaching Physical Education*. Champaign, IL: Human Kinetics.

Hellison, D. (1995). 'Teaching responsibility through physical activity'. Champaign, IL: *Human Kinetics*.

Hickey, C. (1997). Critical pedagogies, student teachers and mine canaries: The limits to rational change. *Paper presented at Australian Association for Research in Education (AARE)*, University of Queensland, Brisbane, November.

Kirk, D. (1997). 'Physical education in the Health and Physical Education Statement and Profile'. *ACHPER Healthy Lifestyles Journal*, 44(1), pp 5–7.

Lawson, H. (1995). 'International changes and challenges: Their import for new models for practice'. *Quest*, 47, pp 411–426.

Lawson, H. (1998). *Globalisation and the Social Responsibilities of Citizen-Professionals*. Paper presented at the Education for Life, Garden City, New York.

Macdonald, D. & Glover, S. (1997). 'Subject matter boundaries and curriculum change in the health and physical education key learning area'. *Curriculum Perspectives, 17*(1), pp 23–30.

Penny, D. (1998). 'School subjects and structures: Reinforcing traditional voices in contemporary "reforms" in education'. *Discourse*, 19(1), pp 5–17.

Prain V. & Hickey, C. (1998). 'Embodied learning in English and physical education', *Curriculum Perspectives*, 18(3), pp 15–22.

Sparkes, A. (1990). *Curriculum Change and Physical Education: Toward a Micropolitical Understanding*. Geelong: Deakin University.

Tinning, R. & Fitzclarence, L. (1992). 'Postmodern youth culture and the crisis in Australian secondary school physical education'. *Quest*, 44(3), pp 287–304.

Tinning, R. & Kirk, D. (1991). *Daily Physical Education in Australia: Collected papers on health based physical education in Australia*. Geelong: Deakin University Press.

VicHealth Health Promoting Schools Project Kit (undated). VicHealth, Melbourne.

section five

chapter fifteen

objectives

By the end of this chapter you should be able to:

- recognise the potential conflict situations in the practicum;
- describe something of the power relations that exist within the practicum;
- understand some of the issues involved in working collaboratively with your supervising teacher;
- appreciate the significance and problematic nature of evaluation of practicum performance;
- describe your own development of expertise across practicum experiences.

The practicum and the student teacher

This section will look at how and why you will undertake practica within your teacher education and how you can maximise your practicum experiences while recognising the institutional and cultural constraints of these experiences. We suggest that there are ways in which you can be *active* in shaping your own progress although we recognise that there will also be limitations given the interplay between the university's expectations, supervising teachers, school culture, and your own biography and socialisation trajectory.

How the practicum is shaped also depends largely on the kinds of knowing and doing that are considered essential to professional competence. If we see the essential knowledge for teaching only in terms of rules, facts, established procedures or recipes applied non-problematically, we could see the practicum as a form of technical training. However, in our view this would be an inadequate approach to the practicum, just as it would be to teacher education. As previously suggested, we support a reflective process whereby student teachers are encouraged to make sense of the unexpected, uncertain and routine situations which arise by asking new questions, and revising strategies for action based on the principles of social justice, diversity and supportive environments (the main principles of the KLA). To encourage such reflectivity during student teachers' practicum, we therefore must monitor, and perhaps alter, the traditional power relationships which have shaped practica in the past.

A student teacher can be considered as a tertiary student who is undertaking an initial teacher education program, whether it be a one-year diploma at the end of a degree or integrated within a degree program. What is distinctive about a student teacher's university experience is their study of pedagogy and, more particularly, the undertaking of practica or fieldwork in educational settings (e.g. schools, outdoor education centres, coaching clinics). Teaching practica is central to a student teacher's professional development and the National Standards and Guidelines for Initial Teacher Education (Australian Council of Deans of Education 1998) suggest that practica should occupy at least 100 days of a teacher education program with students working under the supervision of an experienced teacher and perhaps a university supervisor.

Many areas of professional preparation require a practicum or fieldwork component. Its purpose is to initiate a student into the traditions of a community of practitioners in terms of their conventions, constraints, language, values and repertoire of practices and knowledge bases: 'A practicum is a setting designed for the task of learning a practice. In a context that approximates a practice world, students learn by doing, although their doing falls short of real-world work' (Schon 1987, p 37). The implicit claims of a practicum therefore include that a practice exists, it is worth learning, it can be learned by the student teacher, and that it is represented in its essential features by the practicum. On a teaching practicum a student may undertake tasks that simplify or focus practice, perhaps without some of the pressures or distractions of the real one, and most often under close supervision.

The centrality of the practicum therefore posits the practicum performance of, and the relationship between, both the student and the supervising teacher as central to the student teacher's development. Cooperating or supervising teachers, or mentors, are frequently considered part of the teacher education partnership between universities, employing authorities and school systems. Talk of partnerships raises such questions as: Do all those involved share the same view of the partnership? Who is responsible for what? Who in the partnership has the most appropriate knowledge, skills and resources directed towards what, how and at what time in the program?

Given the complexity of factors which shape the practicum, no two school-based field experiences are the same. Each experience will differ in its context, the nature of the learners, the subject matter to be taught, and the student/supervisor expectations and relationships. The student teacher also brings with them to the practicum the richness of their own biography with a range of skills, experiences, understandings, orientations and expectations which are profoundly important in shaping how the student teacher will approach the practicum and beyond. Posner (1996, p 9) advises student teachers that their challenge is to 'bloom where you are planted', which suggests making the most of the opportunities presented. These may range from that of an observer, sporting team coach, camp leader, to those of a beginning teacher. The balance of these tasks and experiences will depend on negotiation between you, your university and your school supervisor.

The role of a student teacher on practicum can therefore be fairly complex. You are in some senses and contexts restricted in your responsibilities and experimentation, while in another sense expected to be responsible and innovative. You are not autonomous, yet you are expected to show initiative. A successful practicum is therefore usually shaped by the student teacher's ability to understand their own needs and meet these while being sensitive to the context of the school and their supervisor's expectations.

Why do a practicum?

Policy directions

Increasingly, the practicum is becoming central to Australian teacher education as it has done in other countries. There are instances in Canada and England where the entire teacher education program is done 'on-site' in schools. The driving forces behind this arise from conservative discourses which favour the decreased input of the universities' 'theoretical' knowledge and the increased input of the 'practical' and efficient school-based education. As Tinning (1996) observes, there have not been such direct calls for the dismantling of university-based teacher education in Australia as elsewhere, but there have been shifts in which the practicum has gained in relative importance although not necessarily in terms of the resources it attracts. For example, it may be that the number of days spent in schools has increased within a PETE program but the amount of support offered by the university through the provision of university tutors has dwindled. Consequently, while some university personnel continue to visit student teachers in schools, others act as merely a liaison should problems arise.

The National Standards and Guidelines for Initial Teacher Education (1998), if introduced, will confirm the centrality of the practicum in PETE in Australia. The Guidelines (1998, p 23) suggest that 'there will normally need to be at least 100 days of field experience, with a minimum of 80 days of supervised in-school experience' allowing for field experience to be under-taken in non-school settings. Clearly, these Guidelines value the contribution of the practicum to a student's professional development through the provision of well-coordinated and collaborative experiences organised between universities, schools, teachers and student teachers.

Learning opportunities

Posner (1996, p 16) suggests the following as generic goals for a student teacher undertaking their practicum:

- to find out what teaching is really like (i.e. career exploration)
- to see if I like teaching (i.e. personal preferences)
- to see if I can really do it (i.e. self-testing)
- to learn some skills and modify certain habits (i.e. training)
- to develop my own approach or style (i.e. personal style)
- to apply what I have learned in (university) to real students and to real classrooms (i.e. theory into practice).

Can you see yourself in this list? Some of the goals are related to professional development while others focus on self- and career exploration.

With respect to professional development during the practicum, you 'practice' in a double sense. In a delimited school environment you will undertake many of the responsibilities of a teacher, and you will also experiment with and refine a range of skills and behaviours (Schon 1987). Research suggests that this practice has the potential to play a powerful role in learning to teach. This can be understood in part by looking at how we learn. Contemporary cognitive psychologists emphasise the situated nature of cognition (Lave & Wenger 1991; see Chapter 10). This suggests that the context of learning is crucial and that what is learned cannot be separated from how and where it is learned. For student teachers learning opportunities must therefore be grounded in the school contexts in which they will be used. In this way student teachers learn in the contexts of what Lave & Wenger refer to as 'communities of practice', in which experienced practitioners induct newcomers to the community.

Interestingly the Lave & Wenger theory raises some questions regarding the value of the practice of micro-teaching with peer groups which is popular in some teacher education courses. How useful are the teaching skills learned in the context of micro-teaching, which is actually a different community of practice from that encountered in a practicum? This obviously connects with the concept of transferablity of skills from one context to another.

One concern with practicum experiences is that they tend to encourage the student teacher to reproduce the teaching modelled by the supervising teacher. According to Tinning (1987) this tends to reproduce a utilitarian teaching practice where 'going with what works' is the main objective. It seems, therefore, that student teachers benefit from:

- multiple opportunities for school-based practica during their teacher education;
- gradual and systematic lead into teaching practices;
- teaching pupils of various year levels and in groups which gradually increase in size;
- planned interactions with carefully selected and briefed school supervisors;
- ongoing campus-based seminars in which student teachers are guided to critically examine their school experiences; and
- extended periods of time in the practice school in order to enhance understanding of the school organisation and increase student teachers' sense of ease with their colleagues.

Negotiating the practicum

Potential concerns and conflicts

If you are feeling a bit anxious about your practicum, you are not alone. The practicum can be an extremely demanding time, physically and emotionally. You can be staying up late at night planning your lessons for the following day, have an early start the next morning to attend athletics training, and be surrounded by strangers throughout the day. By necessity, you may also try to maintain part-time work, thereby adding a pressure that will potentially undermine the quality of your performance. Without wanting to be discouraging, it is important that prior to your practicum you consider potential problems and conflicts that may arise in order that you can anticipate, avoid or alleviate them.

Sue Capel (1992) found that student teachers in the United Kingdom were moderately anxious about their forthcoming practicum experiences. In particular they were most anxious about being observed in the act of teaching by the supervising teacher and the university lecturer and about having their teaching evaluated and assessed.

A number of researchers have identified the different concerns of student teachers in terms of stages of development. For Fuller & Bown (1975) the first stage for student/beginning teachers is the survival or self-concern stage in which the teacher is preoccupied with being in control, being liked, and their supervisors' opinions. The second stage concerns when teachers are trying to perform well in terms of their methods, materials and mastery of skills while coping with often difficult conditions. The third and final stage shifts to a focus on the impact of teaching and the teachers' efficacy in meeting the needs of pupils as individuals. While Fuller & Bown have argued that these stages are sequential, other research suggests that they are not pure, invariant or common across all teaching contexts, reinforcing the influence of cultural contexts for interpreting both research and teaching outcomes.

Building on Fuller and Bown's work, Maynard & Furlong (1993) identified five stages in the develpment of student teachers. After early idealism prior to the practicum, students focus on survival with respect to class control and management, and on fitting into the school. After their initial adjustment they report that students begin to recognise difficulties associated with competing demands and the expectations of their supervisors. In the fourth stage students are found to plateau, staying with methods and approaches which have worked. Student teachers have difficulties shifting their focus to the needs of pupils. Students then move on to the final stage, when their attention turns to the pupils' needs and they experiment with their teaching.

In summary, research on PETE students' concerns on entering their practicum include:

- pupil commitment and behaviour;
- meeting the needs and maintaining the interest of all pupils;
- inadequate knowledge about the content to be taught;
- being observed and evaluated by the supervising teacher;
- not correctly adopting the routine or methods of the school; and
- feeling like a stranger within the school.

You should discuss your concerns with your supervisors, your university tutors and your peers in order to shift your concerns beyond those of survival to those which are more broad-ranging and educational.

In addition to being aware of how your concerns or preoccupations might shift during your practicum experiences, it is important to recognise that there may be some enduring conflicts or deeply felt tensions that occur throughout a practicum (Hardy 1997). Some student teachers report a perceived sense of animosity towards themselves as student teachers or individuals as outsiders moving into the established professional practices and social networks of a school or staffroom. Furthermore, the school teachers may have different beliefs and values about physical education and the teaching profession from those held by the students. As teachers develop their own routines, habits and areas of expertise, their teaching practices and attitudes towards teaching become highly personal. Anecdotal and research evidence suggests that student teachers are often advised to 'forget what they told you at university . . . this is the real thing!'. Consequently there is pressure on student teachers to adopt the supervising teachers' advice, where possible, in order to 'get along' and 'fit in' (Rikard & Knight 1997). This is not only a point of tension for the student teacher—it can also undermine what are important theoretical frameworks which can inform their current and future practices, and does little to assist the student teacher to develop their own style.

Not surprisingly, there is abundant research which demonstrates that student teachers are usually chiefly concerned with complying with what works. The research of Iannaccone (1963) almost 40 years ago still reflects the situation of most student teachers. Iannaccone found that when student teachers followed the advice of the supervising teacher 'it worked', and 'getting through the lesson' became the primary objective. It was claimed that in the final analysis the rationale of 'does it work to solve the immediate problem at hand?' became the chief criterion for student teachers in accepting or rejecting a particular teaching procedure. Ziechner (1986) called this feature 'the development of a utilitarian teaching perspective' and similar practices have been noted by Tabachnick et al (1978), Popkewitz (1977) and Zimpher et al (1980).

Research in the PETE context found that student teachers in physical education behave similarly (see Tinning 1984 and Schempp 1983). Tinning described it as a 'pedagogy of necessity' and it is a major source of tension for student teachers who might be expected by the university to use the practicum as a time to experiment with different teaching methods and ideas. As the manifestation of a utilitarian teaching perspective, a pedagogy of necessity is not conducive to experimentation. Moreover, Macdonald & Tinning (1995) have found that PETE students' preference for utilitarian-type knowledge extended beyond the practicum and in fact characterised their preference in the entire PETE program.

Conflicts may also occur with respect to administrative expectations and misunderstandings surrounding the practicum. For example, supervising teachers may complain that they have not received sufficient guidelines from the university or perhaps the university is concerned that the supervisor is not fulfilling their reporting requirements. In each case the student teacher is often left to resolve these communication difficulties. Finally, as suggested above, pressure may arise from the opposing demands and expectations of the school, the university, and the private life of the student in the form of time demands. Students might be balancing paid work with school expectations as well as university lectures and assignments.

Each practicum experience is idiosyncratic in terms of the challenges it presents. However, the above conflicts may be avoided, or at least reduced, through each stakeholder (university, school, supervisor and student) understanding and sharing the purpose of the practicum, and establishing effective and ongoing systems of communication.

Working with your supervisors

When student teachers are placed in a school for the practicum it is assumed that they are there to learn not only about teaching in particular, but also about schooling and education in general. In most practica there is a hierarchical relationship between the student teacher, the supervising teacher and the university supervisor. This triad (as it is sometimes known) usually works out its own interpersonal relations within an overall framework in which the student is usually at the bottom of the hierarchy. In a sense, the supervising teacher and the university lecturer are seen as the experts and the student teacher as the novice. In most situations the power rests with the supervising teacher and the university lecturer. Power to determine what will be taught and when rests with the teacher (although the 'privilege' of choosing what to teach is at times delegated to the student teacher), and the power to judge teaching competence most often rests with the teacher and the lecturer. The asymmetrical power relations of the triad is a fundamental ingredient in most student teaching situations. Although members of the triad are supposed to cooperate with respect to the common task of improving your teaching, tensions sometimes exist between teacher and lecturer which can make life difficult for the student teacher.

In the context of the practicum, the student teacher is often caught in the middle of the tension between teacher as expert and university lecturer as expert. Whose knowledge is correct? Where is the truth? Typically, there is an artificial dichotomy created between practical knowledge and theoretical knowledge. In this dichotomy teachers are considered to be practitioners and university supervisors to be theorists. This classification of theorist/practitioner is, however, rather limited and certainly a gross over-simplification. Viewing teachers as practitioners (only) gives the impression that they operate in atheoretical ways and that their daily practice is an incoherent set of actions which are unrelated to any considered notion of teaching and learning. But this is certainly not the case. It has long been recognised that teachers do operate on the basis of their own theories-of-action (see Schon 1983; Smyth 1987; McCutcheon & Burga 1990).

Importantly, however, these theories-of-action are usually part of the teacher's tacit world. They tend to be invisible in much the same way as the hidden curriculum is invisible. They are seldom articulated and are most often unrecognised by the teachers themselves. Often it needs considerable reflection on one's own teaching to begin to bring to the surface these theories which underpin our teaching. As McCutcheon & Burga (1990) claim, the theories-of-action are the product of experience, intuition, reflection, and to a lesser extent the theories of the theorists. Generally the ideas of the theorist will become only part of the teacher's belief system when they have been seen to work in the practical context. Teachers are, in the words of Doyle & Ponder (1977), 'pragmatic sceptics' when it comes to incorporating the ideas of theorists.

So, from our point of view, while teachers may be pragmatic sceptics, they are also theorists. Their theory is not the nomothetic, law-like type but rather the idiographic, particularistic type. Another important point concerning the artificial dichotomy between teacher/practitioner and lecturer/theorist is that it reinforces a hierarchy in which the theorist is placed above the practitioner. Such a hierarchy severely limits the ability of those responsible for the education of student teachers to work collaboratively together. It is another dimension of the triad relationship which often causes stress for the student teacher trying to make sense of whose knowledge is most important.

Support and feedback from your supervisory teacher

Many studies indicate that a supervising teacher has a strong influence over the learning of student teachers. Supervisors need to have a clear vision of what are good teaching practices and these should be those shared by the university. The supervisors' key role is to steer students' practice through reflective conversations towards these practices and understandings. In order to do this the supervisor needs the time and authority to prioritise their supervisory responsibilities, together with knowledge of the students' university program, assessment expectations and procedures, and how to assist students to develop their knowledge and skills (Shenton & Murdoch 1996). Although a practicum might also be supported by university tutor visits, the supervising teachers know more about the school, the people in it, and can provide consistent, regular and continuous feedback.

Perhaps the degree of support given by the supervising teacher relates to motivation to take on a student teacher in the first place. One of the more altruistic rewards for having student teachers includes teachers expanding their learning as they attempt to share their knowledge and the professional satisfaction of knowing they have helped a potential colleague. One of the more instrumental rewards is money. Payments are made by the university to the school department or individual teacher, and this is a strong motivation for some teachers to be involved. However, even when the university or college is paying for the privilege of having a student placed at a particular school, the extent to which the training institution actually has much control over the practicum setting is highly problematic. Unfortunately, universities often find it difficult to place all their student teachers and therefore they cannot be choosy with respect to placing the student in an appropriately supportive practicum site.

Some of the specific supervisory tasks which may be required of a teacher include (Taylor & Stephenson 1996):

- demonstrating and modelling teachers' work (within and beyond the classroom);
- guiding student teachers in the values, customs and routines of the school and profession;
- interpreting curriculum guides;
- liaising between the student teacher and other staff, and parents;
- providing alternative ideas and materials;
- supporting student teachers emotionally and making them feel part of the team;
- monitoring student teachers' planning and preparation;
- observing and critiquing lessons, and communicating progress verbally and in written reports; and
- evaluating student teachers' performance.

Things to help negotiate the practicum

Acknowledging the range of tasks, dilemmas and concerns that you and your supervisor may bring to the practicum leads to the following questions:

- How can you work most effectively with your supervising teacher?
- What do you expect from your supervisor?
- What might you need?
- How will you express your needs to your supervisor?
- What might the supervising teacher be thinking and feeling about having you as a (temporary) colleague?

As a student teacher you need to try to view your practicum from the perspective of the supervisor, the pupils and the school, as well as your own. The relationship between you and your supervisor is not only reliant on the articulation of clear goals and expectations—both people must be ready to listen and respond to the changing circumstances of the practicum. Most importantly you need to *carefully watch* the supervisor and their patterns of interaction with the staff and pupils of the school:

- What are the routines which they expect?
- What methods do they use to gain the students' attention and promote learning? How do they spend their breaks?
- What other tasks are they responsible for apart from teaching classes?
- What appear to be the time pressures on the teacher?
- What are 'hot' issues within the school?

While you may not always agree with the supervising teacher, it is essential that you seek to understand the factors which shape their perspectives and practices.

Establish a pattern for how you will communicate with your supervisor. Will this be: after each lesson? at the end of each day? verbally? free written comments? completion of a proforma addressing aspects of your teaching? Perceived ineffective lessons can have a strong impact on your confidence, especially if it is related to pupils' off-task behaviour and lack of motivation. This confirms the importance of student teachers receiving positive as well as corrective feedback about their lessons, and you may need to remind your supervisor of this.

As you appraise the context in which you are working, consider what way you can maximise your experience. Clearly, early in your practicum you need to discuss with the supervising teacher what they are hoping you will demonstrate and achieve. Many supervising teachers are known to sum up their expectations in two words, 'Enthusiasm' and 'Initiative'.

Your university should assist supervising teachers as much as possible in performing their role through providing clear administrative guidelines and educational expectations. With respect to further practicum support, universities differ greatly. Research suggests that university tutors' conversations with supervising teachers are frequently too rushed and too based on insufficient data/observation to be significant. Rather than try to give feedback on specific lessons, university tutors' time might be better utilised in helping supervising teachers in their teacher education role and encouraging student teachers to integrate theoretical and research ideas into their practices, thereby helping student teachers to move beyond the status quo.

Developing expertise

Foundation knowledge and skills

Student teachers do not enter schools with no knowledge of schooling and teaching. As discussed in Chapter 6, while you may lack experience as a teacher, you have a wealth of knowledge, skills and interests generated from your schooling, university and general life experiences, as well as enthusiasm and energy to contribute to the life of the school. Remember, it was Lortie (1975) who maintained that your apprenticeship of observation from your own 12 years of schooling is powerful in shaping your patterns of learning to teach. This early socialisation into teaching is then modified and extended through university experiences.

Shulman (1987) has outlined a framework for the types of knowledge which underpin teaching. When you undertake your practicum, you may already have acquired some of this knowledge; some will be best developed during your practicum, while more will be developed subsequently in your PETE program and throughout your professional life.

Given that physical education has learning outcomes which we can consider as 'theoretical' and 'practical', PETE students have special demands placed on them. With respect to *subject matter knowledge*, PETE students are typically exposed to a range of knowledge which embraces both physical activities and the socio-cultural and biophysical sciences. PETE students also learn about the curriculum in order that they understand the principles and processes for planning programs and selecting materials and resources (see Chapter 13). In addition, PETE students need:

- knowledge of the learners (see Chapter 7);
- general pedagogical knowledge related to management and organisation (see Chapter 18);
- knowledge of educational contexts ranging from the characteristics of specific classrooms to local communities and wider cultures; and
- knowledge of educational ends, purposes, values and philosophies such as those which address questions like 'What does it mean to be physically educated?'.

Pedagogical content knowledge in campus-based components of PETE may well cover the theory of how to teach particular subject matter in physical education but it is in the authentic context of a school in which you can best develop and refine the practical knowledge associated with this knowledge. Let us suppose that you were requested to teach a unit on (field) hockey to a class of year 8 children at your practicum school. The first thing you would need to assess is your *subject matter content knowledge* of hockey:

- Do you know the concept of the game?
- Do you know what 'offside' is?
- Do you know the composite skills of the game?
- Do you know the rules of the game and could you umpire a game?
- Can you physically demonstrate the various skills of the game?

The second thing to assess is your *pedagogical content knowledge* of teaching hockey:

- Have you taught hockey before?
- Do you know the best way(s) of teaching the skills?
- Do you know the best ways of teaching the offside rule?
- Do you know the best drills and practices for each skill?
- Do you know the best analogies, illustrations and demonstrations to use to teach the skills of the game?
- Can your supervising teacher supply you with some ideas?

Finally you would need to assess your *curriculum content knowledge* for hockey:

- What are the best resources for teaching the game and its skills?
- Are these resources available in your school library or perhaps back at university?
- What are the sources of knowledge about hockey that are made available through the Australian Sports Commission and the Australian Coaches Council?
- Where can you get access to these resources?
- What other activities have the class done that might relate to hockey in any way—for example, other hitting skills?

Some of the content knowledge required to teach hockey, and the other activities that make up a physical education syllabus, will be 'provided' to you in your teacher education course at university. Often 'human movement labs' or 'practical activities' will provide you with practice of, and knowledge about, how to perform and teach the movement skills necessary in a variety of games like hockey. But it would be exceptional if in the course of your training you covered every possible game skill or movement activity you might ever have to teach. Accordingly, for some activities you will most likely have to acquire the relevant content knowledge in the field. That is, you will need to know where to get the information you require and how to develop it so that you can learn to teach the activity. Obviously this is a part of your professional development as a teacher and it will continue long after you graduate from your PETE course.

Your ability and opportunity to demonstrate and develop your general pedagogical knowledge and specific pedagogical content knowledge while on the practicum will be contingent on a number of factors. Of utmost importance is the context of the practicum, including the support and cooperation of the supervising teacher and the pupils, the school curriculum and its match to your knowledge and skills, and access to facilities and resources. A student's preparation for teaching can also be highly influential. Well-planned lessons can influence your instructional behaviours in terms of providing more clear explanations and detailed feedback. So, too, can your familiarity with the subject matter knowledge to be taught. Where student teachers are less confident with subject matter knowledge, they seem to have difficulty planning more challenging pedagogical approaches, and additional planning time is required (Rovegno 1994). Rovegno concluded that the goals and capabilities of the student teacher combined with sedimented aspects of the school context supported students teaching within a 'curricular zone of safety' (1994, p 279). Through ongoing participation in the practicum and the development of subject matter knowledge, student teachers alter their zones of safety and, in turn, the possibilities for practice.

It seems that knowledge acquired within the context of a university campus is not easily applied to the culture of classrooms. We have discussed how the knowledge valued by teachers is different in kind from that usually privileged by university lecturers (see 'Working with your supervisors', above). Notwithstanding this potential different emphasis on valued knowledge, the most positive learning environment in a practicum exists where:

- schools and universities share a strong sense of commitment to the professional development of student teachers;
- schools reinforce the PETE program messages;
- universities make realistic and negotiated expectations on student teachers regarding assessment tasks to be completed during the practicum;
- student teachers are supervised by university and school staff who share a common set of criteria and expectations;
- there is a commitment to the development of reflective teaching attitudes and skills;
- student teachers are held accountable for their learning; and
- PETE staff and supervising teachers model quality teaching behaviours themselves.

Being evaluated

Tensions between evaluation and diagnosis

Two of the major purposes of teaching rounds are: diagnosis of things a student teacher needs to work on to improve their teaching competence, and evaluation of the performance of the student teacher. These things themselves are often difficult to reconcile. For a long time it has been known that many student teachers experience a good deal of confusion in trying to reconcile these two contradictory functions (see Fitzclarence 1983), and the confusion is also experienced by the supervising teacher and the lecturer, for they are expected to both diagnose and evaluate.

Because of the hierarchical relationship within the triad (with the student teacher at the bottom), most students are not in a good position to contest or disagree with the diagnostic comments presented by the teacher or lecturer. Of course it is often claimed that the triad should operate in a collaborative manner but the extent to which a more collaborative endeavour is pursued depends very much on the players in the triad and the philosophy of the teacher education program itself. Where power relations keep the student teacher 'in their place' as a novice and the teacher and lecturer are perceived (perhaps by themselves or the student) as experts, then the tension between diagnosis and evaluation is less obvious. In each case judgments are made by the experts about the teaching of the novice. All the student teacher needs to do is to heed the advice and attempt to carry it out.

Problems arise, however, when the advice of the experts is conflicting. If, as we have seen earlier, the advice of the teacher is of an idiographic nature pertaining to particularistic-type knowledge, and the university supervisor's advice is of a more nomothetic or generalistic type, then the potential for confusion and tension is high. This is compounded when the student teacher is expected to heed the advice (the diagnosis) of both teacher and lecturer. 'Going with what works' in the particular context and modelling the teacher's ways of doing things most often wins out, and this can have problematic consequences if the judgments of their teaching competence are made on a normative basis—that is, normative in the sense that the performance of one student teacher is judged against (in relation to) the performance of the other student teachers, who are in different schools with different supervising teachers.

Although some PETE courses use descriptive assessment rather than normative ratings, the problem of who makes the judgment remains an issue. In a study of Deakin University student teachers Henry et al (1986) found that the distribution of ratings across student teachers was most plausibly explained by differences associated with the sex of the student who supervised them (from the university), the school in which they taught, and the specific grade level. To be placed in particular classes, in particular schools, with particular teachers and university supervisors seemed to significantly influence the chances of receiving good ratings for a particular teaching round. The study clearly demonstrated that the claimed objectivity of ratings of student teachers' competence was in fact untenable. Of course, student teachers have long known this. After each practicum some student teachers can always be heard complaining about having a particular teacher who 'never gives an "outstanding" rating', or having a particular supervisor who knows nothing about physical education, or being placed in a certain school in what is considered a 'difficult area', and so on. They recognise the inconsistencies and unfairnesses in the system because they experience them.

oty over to you

Discuss the findings of Henry et al's (1986) research study in your tutorial. To what extent do they reflect the experiences of members of the tutorial? What could be done to improve the situation and make evaluations fairer?

In trying to execute these sometimes conflicting tasks, supervisors may face a number of dilemmas. Teachers report that simultaneously acting as guide, tutor, counsellor, friend and assessor can detract from the task of facilitating the student's learning (Capel 1996).

Appraising performance

Assessment of performance should not dominate your practicum experience, yet students have frequently reported their concern about being observed by the supervising teacher, the supervisor's reaction to unsuccessful lessons, and how the assessment would be made. This raises the question of why you have to be assessed.

In the new times outlined in Chapter 2, appraisal of the standards of a performance is linked to the discourses of quality assurance and accountability. Quality assurance suggests that the 'consumers' of a service such as teaching can be confident of its reliability, consistency and safety, whereas accountability suggests that teachers should be able to justify their activities to the public and respond to advice. While the expectations for accountability and quality assurance in the case of teachers is problematic— as governments are largely the producer of teachers, consumers of their services, and provide the conditions under which teachers must work—there is an international trend for teachers to have to demonstrate minimum standards of performance. Assessment of practicum performances provides some of this assurance. The Senate Inquiry into the Status of Teachers (1998) therefore recommended that registration standards for those entering teaching must be developed. While acknowledging that the defining of standards is difficult, it 'insists that establishing such standards of professional teaching practice is possible, unavoidable and absolutely necessary' (p 16).

The American National Association for Sport and Physical Education is instructive in this regard, with their framework for beginning teacher competencies in which dispositions ('the beliefs and attitudes that teachers would need to hold to implement the standard') (NASPE 1995, p 4) are outlined alongside the knowledge and skills.

NASPE

Beginning Physical Education Teacher Standards

Standard 1 Content knowledge
The teacher understands physical education content, disciplinary concepts, and tools of inquiry related to the development of a physically educated person.

Standard 2 Growth and development
The teacher understands how individuals learn and develop, and can provide opportunities that support their physical, cognitive, social and emotional development.

Standard 3 Diverse learners
The teacher understands how individuals differ in their approaches to learning and creates appropriate instruction adapted to diverse learners.

Standard 4 Management and motivation
The teacher uses an understanding of individual and group motivation and behavior to create a learning environment that encourages positive social interaction, active engagement in learning, and self-motivation.

Standard 5 Communication
The teacher uses knowledge of effective verbal, nonverbal, and media communication techniques to foster inquiry, collaboration, and engagement in physical activity settings.

Standard 6 Planning and instruction
The teacher plans and implements a variety of developmentally appropriate instructional strategies to develop physically educated individuals.

Standard 7 Learner assessment
The teacher understands and uses formal and informal assessment strategies to foster physical, cognitive, social and emotional development of learners in physical activity.

Standard 8 Reflection
The teacher is a reflective practitioner who evaluates the effects of his/her actions on others (e.g. learners, parents/guardians, and other professionals in the learning community) and seeks opportunities to grow professionally.

Standard 9 Collaboration
The teacher fosters relationships with colleagues, parents/guardians and community agencies to support learners' growth and well being.

Source: NASPE 1995, pp 5–6. Reprinted from National Standards for Beginning Physical Education Teachers, with permission from the National Association for Sport and Physical Education (NASPE).

oty over to you

Perhaps you have noticed that the meaning of 'reflection' implicit in Standard 8 is somewhat different from that which we use to orient this book.

Find out what we mean by 'reflection' (see Chapters 1 and 16) and write some notes on the differences (and any similarities).

Discuss this within your tutorial group.

In terms of personal transformation or growth of student teachers, there are questions as to how articulating a set of competencies or criteria for the assessment of performance can be both an educative tool and an instrument for appraisal (Hattam & Smyth 1995). One response is to approach assessment as collaborative and ongoing. Rather than having formal 'one off' judgments of performance, assessment should be integral to practicum experience. Having clear targets or goals for the students' performance can be helpful in focussing students' development and relieving the pressure of assessment through explaining what is important throughout their practicum. It should also be recognised that contextual factors such as the subject matter, class size, pupils' level of schooling or dispositions, and the school's expectations and behaviour management policies shape what could be construed as competent practice.

Following is a list of criteria used in one PETE program to monitor student teacher progress in the practicum and to evaluate practicum performance.

1. Using and developing professional knowledge and values.
2. Planning for optimal learning.
3. Facilitating the learning process.
4. Communicating, interacting and working with students.
5. Reflecting, evaluating and planning for continuous improvement.

Furthermore, those involved in the assessment process should acknowledge that the assessment of your performance will be a subjective process. First, your competence or ability cannot be absolutely known but rather there may be evidence which more or less strongly indicates the presence (or absence) of ability (Preston & Kennedy 1995). The collection of evidence raises questions of what should be collected, in what form, how much, and by whom. It is suggested that combinations of types of evidence should be recognised in the making of judgments. Reference to evidence is made easier and more concrete where there are naturally occurring 'products' in the course of your work, such as lesson plans. Eraut (1994) also suggests, as does Whitty (1994), that direct observation should be accompanied by discussion with you to ascertain your analyses of how and why you chose a course of action and your responses to it. Second, it should be recognised that the assessment process will be shaped by the supervising teacher's expertise, values and experiences. Given this subjectivity, it is important for the language of assessment to be accessible and meaningful to all those involved with the process or, as Louden & Wallace (1993, p 50) suggest, to 'ring true' to teachers. In summary, assessment resides with the prudent, flexible and appropriate application of professional appraisal and should recognise the constraints and opportunities of the practicum context.

Regulating performance

As suggested earlier, in practising as a teacher in a school you are being enculturated not only into the knowledge and skills of the community of teachers through a formal system of instruction, observation and feedback, but also into the values, beliefs, attitudes and comportment (physical presentation) associated with the professional group of physical educators. Therefore, we argue that apart from the formal appraisal processes there are also *social regulatory* mechanisms at work which act to shape your self- and social identities in the school context. Subtle surveillance becomes a secondary mechanism of power which may act to constrain and shape what you wear, say and do. Personal struggles associated with this surveillance are often evident in the process of being socialised into the social identity of 'physical education teacher'.

Social regulation refers to practices which sustain identities by condoning some behaviours and outlawing others—in the case of physical education teachers, focussing in particular on their bodies, physical comportment and appearance. To meet the expectations for a physical education teacher, a particular body shape, particular styles of dress and comportment, and particular professional and physical competencies effectively identify the teachers as 'normal'. To be 'overweight' or even 'non-athletic' would be regarded as abnormal for physical education teachers. As discussed more fully in Chapter 4 we have observed that strong messages are conveyed to women in particular with respect to their presentation. Social regulation also embraces practices which measure an individual against more or less established, though perhaps unarticulated and certainly arbitrary, social expectations. These social expectations can be particularly powerful in shaping how you interact in the staffroom and at staff functions. Will you join the group for drinks at the pub on Fridays? Will you participate in conversations deriding particular pupils? Will you join the morning tea roster? While none of these social 'rituals' may be central to your performance on practicum, your responses will be noted and pressures exerted.

When an identity embedded in a particular social position—for example, as a phyiscal education teacher at Bonnybrook High School—is significantly at odds with how an individual sees and feels about themselves, there is a serious risk of dissonance. A challenge for the student teacher is to resolve what may be tensions between their social identity in this context and their self-identity. They also may need to reflect on the regulatory mechanisms at work and consider whether they will embrace, acquiesce to, or resist them.

Summary

- The practicum is an essential part of all PETE. There is a required number of days' teaching that you will need to complete in order to register as a teacher.
- Successful practicum experiences require that the student teacher can effectively communicate with the supervising teacher. We suggest that you can be active in shaping the nature of your experience.
- Negotiating the expectations of your practicum is important.
- Being evaluated on your teaching performance while on the practicum is a standard feature in most PETE courses and it involves more than judging your in-front-of-class skills.
- You will develop your skills across various practicum experiences and you should see your practica as a series of developmental opportunities.

References

Capel, S. (1996). 'Anxieties of physical education students on first teaching practice'. *European Physical Education Review*, 2(1), pp 30–40.

Doyle, W. & Ponder, G. (1997). 'The practicality ethic in teacher education', *Interchange*, 8(3), pp 22–28.

Eraut, M. (1994). *Developing Professional Knowledge and Competence*. London: Falmer Press.

Fitzclarence, L. (1983). 'When the crunch came: A two dimensional view of school experience'. *Australian Journal of Teaching Practice*, 3(2), pp 11–17.

Fuller, F. & Bown, O. (1975). 'Becoming a teacher'. In K. Ryan (ed.), *Teacher Education*. Chicago, IL: Chicago University Press.

Hardy, C. (1997). 'Sources of conflict during the school experience of pre-service physical education teachers'. *European Physical Education Review*, 3(2), pp 116–128.

Hattam, R. & Smyth, J. (1995). 'Ascertaining the nature of competent teaching: A discursive practice'. *Critical Pedagogy Networker*, 8(3&4), pp 1–12.

Henry, J., Pateman, N. & Tinning, R. (1986). 'A dilemma in teaching practice assessment: The lottery of competitive assessment'. *The South Pacific Journal of Teaching Practice*, 14(2), pp 82–90.

Iannaccone, L. (1963). 'Student teaching: A traditional stage in the making of a teacher', *Theory into Practice*, 19(3), pp 73–80.

Knight, J., Lingard, R. & Bartlett, L. (1993). 'Re-forming teacher education: The unfinished task'. In Knight, Bartlett & E. McWillaim (eds), *Re-forming Teacher Education: The Unfinished Task*. Rockhampton: UCQ Press.

Lave, J. & Wenger, E. (1991). *Situated Learning: Legitimate Peripheral Participation*. Cambridge: Cambridge University Press.

Locke, L. (1979). 'Supervision, schools and student teaching: Why things stay the same'. Presented at *American Academy of Physical Education*, New Orleans.

Lortie, D. (1975), *Schoolteacher: A Sociological Study*. Chicago, IL: University of Chicago Press.

Louden, W. & Wallace, J. (1993). 'Competency standards in teaching'. *Unicorn*, 19(1), pp 45–53.

McCutcheon, Gail & Burga, Jung (1990). 'Alternative perspectives on action research'. *Theory into Practice*, 24(3), pp 144–151.

Macdonald, D. & Tinning, R. (1995). 'Physical education teacher education and the trend to proletarianization'. *Journal of Teaching in Physical Education*, 15(1), pp 98–118.

Maynard, T. & Furlong, J. (1993). 'Learning to teach and models of mentoring'. In D. McIntyre, H. Hagger & M. Wilkins (eds), *Mentoring; Perspectives on School-Based Teacher Education*. London: Kogan Page, pp 69–85.

NASPE (1995). *National Standards for Beginning Physical Education Teachers*. Reston, VA: National Association for Sport and Physical Education, pp 5–6.

Popkewitz, T. (1977). 'Ideology as a problem of teacher education'. Presented at *Annual meeting of the American Educational Research Association*, New York.

Posner, G. (1996). *Field Experience: A Guide to Reflective Teaching*. New York: Longman.

Postman, N. (1989). *Conscientious Objections: Stirring up Trouble about Language, Technology and Education*. London: Heinemann.

Preston, B. & Kennedy, K. (1995). 'The national competency framework for beginning teaching: A radical approach to initial teacher education'. *Australian Educational Researcher*, 22(2), pp 27–62.

Rikard, G.L. & Knight, S. (1997). 'Obstacles to professional development: Interns' desire to fit in, get along, and be real teachers'. *Journal of Teaching in Physical Education*, 16, pp 440–453.

Rovegno, I. (1994). 'Teaching within a curricular zone of safety: School culture and the situated nature of student teachers' pedagogical content knowledge'. *Research Quarterly for Exercise and Sport*, 65, pp 269–279.

Schempp, P. (1983), 'Learning the role: The transformation from student to teacher'. Presented at *AAHPERD Annual Convention*, Minneapolis, Minnesota.

Schon, D. (1983). *The Reflective Practitioner: How Professionals Think in Action*. New York: Basic Books.

Schon, D. (1987). *Educating the Reflective Practitioner. Toward a New Design for Teaching and Learning in the Profession*. San Francisco: Jossey-Bass.

Senate Employment, Education and Training References Committee (1998). *A Class Act: Inquiry into the Status of the Teaching Profession*. Canberra: Commonwealth of Australia.

Shenton, P. & Murdoch, E. (1996). 'Partnerships in school-based training: The implications for physical education'. In M. Mawer (ed.), *Mentoring in Physical Education*. London: Falmer Press, pp 9–21.

Shulman, L.S. (1987). 'Knowledge and teaching: Foundations of the new reform'. *Harvard Educational Review*, 57(1), pp 1–21.

Smyth, S. (1987). *A Rationale for Teachers' Critical Pedagogy: A Handbook*. Geelong: Deakin University.

Spodek, B. (1974). 'Teacher education: Of the teacher, by the teacher, for the child'. In K. Ziechner (ed.), 'Alternative paradigms of teacher education', *Journal of Teacher Education*, 31(6) pp 45–55.

Stenhouse, L. (1975). *An Introduction to Curriculum Research and Development*. London: Heinemann.

Tabachnick, B., Popkewitz, T. & Ziechner, K. (1978). 'Teacher education and the professional perspective of teachers'. Presented at *Annual Meeting of the American Educational Research Association*, Toronto, Canada.

Taylor, M. & Stephenson, J. (1996). 'What is mentoring?'. In M. Mawer (ed.), *Mentoring in Physical Education*. London: Falmer Press, pp 22–37.

Tinning, R. (1984). 'The student teaching experience: All that glitters is not gold'. *Australian Journal of Teaching Practice*, 4(2), pp 53–62.

Tinning, R. (1987). 'Beyond the development of a utilitarian teaching perspective'. In G. Barrett (ed.), *Myths, Models and Methods in Sport Pedagogy*. Champaign, IL: Human Kinetics.

Tinning, R. (1996). 'Mentoring in the Australian physical educaiton teacher education context: Lessons from cooking turkeys and Tandoori chicken'. In M. Mawer (ed.), *Mentoring in Physical Education: Issues and insights* (pp 197–217). London: Falmer Press.

Whitty, G. (1994). *Deprofessionalising Teaching: Recent Developments in Teacher Education in England. Occasional Paper No. 22*. Canberra: Australian College of Education.

Ziechner, K. (1986). 'The practicum as an occasion for learning to teach', Presented at *Third National Conference on the Practicum in Teacher education*, Geelong.

Zimpher, N., de Voss, G. & Nott, D. (1980). 'A closer look at university student teacher supervision', *Journal of Teacher Education*, 31(4), pp 11–15.

chapter sixteen

objectives

By the end of this chapter you should be able to:

- understand the significance of learning to reflect;
- appreciate that reflective practice is not what teachers normally do when they merely think about a particular lesson or day's activities;
- see how action research uses systematically collected data as a basis for reflection;
- distinguish between types of data (information) collected as a basis for reflection;
- apply a reflective orientation to your own PETE course.

The reflective (student) teacher

According to John Dewey (1933, p 3), 'turning a subject over in the mind and giving it serious and consecutive consideration' was indicative of reflective thinking or reflection. For teachers this involves analysing their beliefs and attitudes and monitoring the effects of their actions and attitudes, and it is therefore central if you hope to improve, refine, adjust or adapt your practices and, in time, those of the school. Donald Schon (1987) in *Educating the Reflective Practitioner* described what he considered was a crisis in confidence in professional knowledge arising from all too few professional practitioners, such as teachers, being prepared or able to 'descend to the swamp' (p 3) of the messy, confusing yet important human concerns, preferring to remain on the high ground of manageable, technical preoccupations. In HPE teaching we could liken this analogy to a teacher who is preoccupied with getting the sports carnival to run smoothly without questioning the educational and social outcomes of it for the schools' pupils and the associated sporting authorities.

As suggested by Schon, teachers can reflect-in-action (thinking and reshaping action as you do it) and reflect-on-action (thinking back on what you have done). With experience and reflection-on-action during the practicum your ability to reflect-in-action in order to respond to the simultaneous, unique and uncertain situations which arise will develop. Professional (and personal) growth is not based merely on experience. In order to change and grow it is necessary to reflect on the experiences and assess whether they have been productive or unproductive of moving you towards your personal or professional goals. An unreflective teacher with 20 years' experience may be considerably less competent than a reflective teacher with considerably less experience in terms of years.

Van Manen (1995) identified three levels of reflectivity in which student teachers might engage. The first level suggests student teachers are concerned with considering what works in a lesson to maintain peace and order. Only at the second level do the student teachers engage in debate over educational goals and the associated principles of implementation. At the third level they might begin to consider issues beyond the classroom, such as concerns for equity. He argued that each level of reflection can contribute to the refinement of educational practice and therefore reflection at all levels should present as dimensions of reflection and thereby learning to teach. You will note that these are somewhat consistent with what may be your concerns on entering the practicum (see Chapter 15). While such conceptions of reflection may be criticised for being too focussed on the individual teacher, they do provide a framework from which you may work.

Learning to reflect

It is not so easy to learn to reflect. Inez Rovegno (1992) gives an insightful account of the difficulties of learning to reflect on teaching. From her case study of a student teacher, Rovegno concludes that in relation to learning to reflect, 'students who prefer to rely on authority to direct their lives, work, play, actions, relationships, and the very way they conceive of the world and their place in it are at a disadvantage' (p 507). Her claim is that students who are what she calls 'received knowers' (i.e. those who come to know by listening to others) 'trust authority to name the task and the solution' (p 507). These students are not disposed to be sceptical of the prejudices of their elders.

Rovegno also claims that 'reflection is a personal act of constructing knowledge based on confidence in one's inner voice' (1992, p 508). She identifies that the unequal power relationship between student and teacher limits the possibility for development of such confidence. Rovegno then goes further in saying: 'I suspect what may be at the heart of reflection is coming to value and trust the self as part of knowing and recognizing the subjective nature of knowledge' (p 509).

There are limitations, however, with this conception of reflection, as it is essentially individualistic and fails to produce an understanding of the macro social/structural influences on schooling and teaching. Learning to value one's own inner voice might well be important, but so, too, is learning to recognise the relationships between knowledge, power and language and vested interests in particular versions of truth cloaked in the authority of teacher and text.

An Australian study into the development of reflection with PETE students is revealing here. As a result of student responses to reflection in the classes Jennifer Gore (1990) taught, she classified students on the basis of their openness to develop reflection. There were the *recalcitrants* (i.e. those for whom reflection was seen as peripheral or irrelevant), the *acquiescents* (i.e. those for whom reflection was a means to an end in that it was expected of them) and the *committed reflectors* (i.e. those who saw the value in reflection about teaching and schooling more generally). Students differed in how they reflected and what they reflected on, but essentially her study confirms students' preference for Van Manen's first level of survival questions.

It is important to note that while questions addressing teaching practices are important, asking these alone does not account for the broader consequences of physical education and schooling. For example, after a lesson you may wonder: 'Could everyone see my demonstration?', 'Were my instructions clear?', and your answers could well be positive thereby suggesting a successful lesson. However, if you asked yourself: 'Was the javelin lesson relevant to all the pupils?', the answer might well be no. Thus, reflective questions should be broad and cover the range of:

1. ethical, social, political and moral issues (e.g. Did I make assumptions about the interests and abilities of the Asian pupils?);
2. values, goals and relevance of the program (e.g. Are my teaching strategies too focussed on the competitive?);
3. instructional methods, strategies, and materials (e.g. Could I employ more methods which are learner-centred?).

During your practicum, reflection-on-action can be encouraged through a range of approaches. The keeping of logs and journals, doing videotape commentaries, making clearly focussed teaching observations, and conducting in-depth discussions with supervisors and colleagues provide avenues for reflection. Professional conversations should encourage you to describe what is occurring, why, whether change should occur and, if so, what it should look like. Many student teachers are required by their university to keep a journal or log of reflections addressing such questions within the particular context of their practicum.

What are the benefits of reflecting on a range of questions? We suggest that in asking questions concerning ethics, relevance and instructional methods you may:

- become more inclusive of the backgrounds, needs and interests of the pupils;
- introduce more meaningful, focussed and engaging learning experiences;
- empower pupils;
- find your role more challenging and rewarding; and
- come to better understand the values and beliefs which shape your practice and what influences these.

Professional development through reflection is based on deconstructing and reconstructing knowledge over time. Ideas, beliefs, professional theories and values about teaching are modified, changed, rejected or reframed as new information becomes available and circumstances change. Through reflective thinking, you can question behaviours that are guided by impulse, tradition or authority, and acknowledge and build on your own experiences.

Herein is an important distinction that we would make between being a (reflective) teacher and being an *instructor*. Instructors know technique, they know how to do something and they have instructional skills to show others how to do it. Think for a moment about an army drill instructor. He (or she) knows the techniques of marching and can instruct others (under the sanction of a strict discipline code) in those skills. His job is not to evaluate or question the purpose of marching or whether it is a worthwhile educational pursuit. Similarly an aerobics instructor can demonstrate the moves and lead the class in those moves. Her (or his) job is essentially a technical one, even if it is done with considerable enthusiasm and panache. It is not their responsibility as an instructor to raise questions relating to the commodification of the body or the cult of slenderness (see Tinning 1985).

A physical education teacher, however, *does* have a moral responsibility to ask such questions. The teaching of aerobics within a physical education class should be not only for the development of aerobic moves and perhaps fitness benefits, but also to educate students about the way in which aerobics actually works as a cultural practice. At least this is our position with respect to what it would mean to be a reflective teacher rather than merely an instructor.

Becoming a reflective teacher

Habitual teaching and intentional reflection

Improving your own educational practice is an intentional activity. But much day-to-day teaching is habitual in the sense that little time is spent in conscious reflection or analysis with respect to the key questions of: 'What are the implications of what I teach and the way I teach?' and 'How can I teach in a better way?'. It is important to recognise that some of our teaching is, of necessity, habitual in a similar way to how it is important that the technical skills of driving a motor vehicle (such as operating the clutch and changing gears) become automated (habitual). When these skills are automated, a driver can then concentrate on what is happening with the traffic while driving.

Similarly, in teaching, when the technical skills are mastered and become habitual in the sense that they no longer require conscious effort, then attention can be directed to other issues of classroom practice. However, habitual teaching practices should be able to be defended or justified and this means that although habitualised, at some stage each and every aspect of teaching practice should be open to scrutiny in order that it can be analysed.

For the majority of student teachers, less of their teaching will be habitual because most of it is new and hence requires conscious attention. As a consequence you will probably reflect more on technical issues (such as: Am I giving feedback equitably around the class?) than on issues relating to the educational purpose of the activities themselves. But as you develop the technical skills you should 'free' yourself up to reflect on broader issues.

But habitual teaching practices should be able to be defended or justified, and this means that although habitualised, at some stage each and every aspect of teaching practice should be open for scrutiny in order that it can be analysed. In this sense the task of reflection might be easier for a student teacher than for an experienced teacher, who does things habitually without any conscious thought.

It is important to realise that when we talk of reflective teaching we are *not* refering to what teachers *normally do* in the act of teaching. Being a reflective teacher is more than simply thinking about one's work. The concept of reflecting on one's practice requires a commitment to the notion of *extended professionalism.* According to Stenhouse (1975, p 144), extended professionalism is characterised by:

- a commitment to systematic questioning of one's own teaching as a basis for development;
- the commitment and the skills to study one's teaching; and
- the concern to question and to test theory in practice by the use of those skills.

Applied to the context of learning to teach, reflective teaching should:

- enable the student teacher to recognise patterns of behaviour in their teaching (and with the teacher education course itself) which otherwise would go unnoticed;
- involve the student teacher in giving conscious attention to issues relating to pedagogical practice and curriculum decisions; and
- involve the student teacher in recognising the potentials and limitations of individual power in the broader institutional constraints of all teaching situations.

The process of reflection can be approached through:

- some form of systematic collection of information (data) which in many cases extends beyond the limits of one individual lesson (most meaningful learnings take more than one lesson); and
- some form of journal keeping in which the patterns of everyday events and practices are documented and subsequently subjected to reflection with the benefit of hindsight and with the possible addition of understandings gained from certain relevant readings, discussions and the like.

In relation to the practising teacher, reflection will most likely:

- occur after rather than during a specific teaching episode. This is recognition of the fact that teaching is too totally engaging to allow reflection-*in*-action (while teaching), and realistically it can occur only as reflection-*on*-action some time after the lesson has ended; and
- recognise the fact that in the normal course of events reflection-*on*-action will not be an ongoing aspect of teachers' lives. Rather, because it involves systematic collection of data (often by an observer) it will most likely be an occasional, but regular, practice (perhaps once or twice a term) rather than a frequent practice.

An action research approach to reflective teaching

Action research, as defined by Kemmis (1982), is a process which fosters a 'reflective orientation which informs and influences practice' (Henry 1980). Although action research has had a long and somewhat tortured history in education (see McTaggart 1991), and it suffers from commonly held perceptions of research as entailing white coats, controlled variables, statistics and the like, it has become a major form of developing extended professionalism. *It is a formal approach to systematic self-study.* According to Grundy & Kemmis (1981, p 84), action research aims at educational improvement in three areas:

1. the improvement of practice;
2. the improvement of the understanding of the practice by its practitioners; and
3. the improvement of the situation in which the practice takes place.

In essence, educational action research involves practitioners (teachers or student teachers) in cycles of *planning, acting, monitoring* and *reflecting* with respect to their educational practice. Action research may be used to address a variety of issues.

Example

You are teaching a unit on soccer to a year 9 mixed sex class in a suburban high school. You observe that a number of pupils seem rather uninterested in the activity and are trying to opt out of participation. After discussions with your supervisor, you agree that together you should survey the pupils to ascertain what physical activities they most enjoy. Your first action step is to prepare the survey, administer it and collate the results. On analysis of the survey results it appears that the group is divided in terms of those who would like to do activities such as gymnastics and dance and those who do prefer ball sports. Where to from here?

You discuss the next cycle with your supervisor and pupils and conclude that, with the students' cooperation and by drawing on the new learning outcomes indicated in the syllabus documents, each class will have a common concept to be addressed (e.g. momentum of objects) and then the class will divide to explore it (the concept) with respect to their preferred activity.

You teach the next lesson(s) and your supervising teacher collects data on the involvement of all the pupils with the activities. In reflecting on the data you find that while the concept (e.g. momentum) seemed to interest some of the pupils, still the same group of pupils who were not interested in soccer proved disruptive. After all, the concept was still being explored through ball game activities and it was these activities that were less than reinforcing for some pupils. You discuss with the teacher the impracticality of having all students choosing exactly what they felt like in class. You discuss whether you could explore the concept (of momentum) via some gymnastics and dance lessons.

The steps in the cycle are seen as a dynamic process which aims to bring together practice and ideas about practice. Improvements in understanding and in practice can be made systematically, responsively and reflectively. Through this process a rationale for practice (for doing certain things in certain ways) can be both defined and tested. This cycle of planning, acting, monitoring and reflecting is deceptively simple but it can represent a radical shift in terms of a view of professional development. It has the potential to help teachers move beyond the taken-for-granted of their everyday practice and to bring to a conscious level that which has been habitual. It embodies the notion of reflective teaching which is an essential feature of extended professionalism.

Monitoring and reflecting

In order to systematically study and analyse one's teaching it is necessary to monitor the teaching and collect information (data) on what happens. For our purposes we will assume that data collection is part of the monitoring process. But it is not possible to monitor everything. Useful monitoring demands a focus and learning to reflect on teaching in a systematic manner requires that selection of a *particular issue or feature* of the teaching act as the focus for reflection.

Experience has shown us that for many student teachers (and practising teachers as well) finding a focus for reflection is a difficult task. There are so many things happening at once in any lesson and it is sometimes hard to know where to start to find an issue to focus on. The focus of reflection is that aspect of practice which you want to improve and/or better understand.

David Hamilton (1973) suggests that there are eight propositions which are important to all who set out to observe (and monitor) teaching. We have adapted his suggestions so that they refer specifically to observation of physical education teaching. They are as follows:

1. In physical education classes students and teachers never learn nothing. (Equally, nothing never happens.)
2. Students (or for that matter teachers) are never ignorant or know nothing.
3. Collectively the participants of any physical education class comprise an interactive social nexus.
4. As knowledge is unevenly distributed (and redistributed) in the physical education class, life in the class is inherently unstable.
5. Within the physical education class context, the relationship between teacher and pupils is best understood as a refracting medium rather than a transmitting medium. (Thus, for example, different individuals learn different things from the same event.)
6. The learning milieu in physical education classes is not a pre-determined setting, but instead is socially constructed.
7. Within the physical education class context time is a potent influence, suffusing all that takes place.
8. In physical education lessons, communication is not merely verbal. Participants, materials and objects are transmitters of a range of additional 'messages'.

Hamilton's eight propositions can provide a useful beginning point in trying to identify an issue of practice which can serve as the focus for systematic reflective study. Examples of issues which some of our students (both student teachers and inservice teachers) have used as the focus for their observation and reflection are listed below.

- Is my teaching more characteristic of direct or indirect teaching methods? How would I know?
- How can I shift the decision making in my lessons more towards

giving the children a greater say? What are the results of trying to do just that?

- In relation to sexism, what is the nature of my interaction with boys and girls in their classes? To what extent does my chosen curriculum have a gender-interest bias?
- What is the class reaction to different competitive and cooperative games experiences? Is there any link between gender and preference for competitive or cooperative games?
- Do the assessment tasks link to the learning experiences of my unit?
- How much time do the children actually get to practise skills in my lessons? To what extent does my teaching reflect the proportions of lesson time spent in management, waiting, receiving instructions and activity shown in the literature?
- How can I improve the quality of my teaching?
- What is the nature of the feedback which I give the children in my physical education teaching? What are the implications for such feedback? Can it be improved?

Let us look at examples of two of the ideas listed above which student teachers have used as their focus. In both cases the student teacher got the supervising teacher to collect data for them on the issue of focus.

Example

'What is the nature of the feedback which I give children in my class?'

For feedback, one student teacher asked her supervising teacher to record each student's name and the number and type of feedback comments which she directed to each pupil. After the lesson she met with the teacher and discussed the data. Why did some particular children get the lion's share of feedback? Why did a small group of boys receive nearly all the negative behaviour feedback? How might she distribute the feedback more evenly around the class in the next lesson? These and other questions formed the basis of her systematic self-study. She was reflecting in a way which was informed by evidence rather than guesses, and the process involved both her and the teacher in a collaborative endeavour in their attempt to devise strategies which could be tested out in the next lesson.

Example

'How much time do children actually spend practising the required skills in my lesson?'

For time on task, that student teacher asked her supervising teacher to record the time intervals during which the pupils were engaged in the actual movement activity they were requested to do. The teacher was also requested to record how much time the children spent waiting for a turn and waiting for instructions. In the post-lesson discussion the teacher was able to show what percentage of the total lesson time was spent by the children on task and also how much time was spent waiting. Reasons why this occurred were then discussed and strategies for improving time on task and reducing waiting time were planned for trialling in the next lesson.

While these two examples relate specifically to teacher behaviour, one could also focus attention specifically on student learning. Either way, in reflecting on your work as (student) teacher you will be confronted with the inter-connectedness of teacher behaviour and student learning.

Getting good data

Unfortunately, gathering 'good data' about teaching is not all too easy. It requires practice in order to do it proficiently. But that actually begs the question of what exactly we mean by 'good data'. To use phrases like 'it should be reliable and valid' may well confuse more than it illuminates but those terms do actually contain the essence of what good data means. For example, if you wish to determine the nature of the feedback given to the class and you arrange for the supervising teacher to observe your lesson and record all instances of feedback (say, positive, neutral, corrective, negative), it is essential that the supervising teacher clearly understands what is meant by the definitions of feedback to be classified and that they are sufficiently skilled at recording identical instances as the same category. If on one occasion a teacher tells a child to 'Bend your arms more when you catch the ball' and your observer categorises that instance of feedback as 'corrective', then it is vital that the next time the teacher says 'Bend your arms more when you catch the ball', the same categorisation is made. That is actually the issue of reliability. It is also necessary to make valid interpretations of the nature of the feedback used.

In the example overleaf, the teacher claimed that the feedback was neutral in its effect. Feedback is generally categorised as positive, negative or neutral in its effect (see Chapter 17); however, in this instance the teacher's claim seems unsupportable in the light of the other teachers' reactions. His judgment was, in this instance, not a valid one. Perhaps in this example the only way to be sure of the validity of the classification of feedback would be to find out how the actual pupil felt about the comment.

Different types of data

Data can be of many different types. They may take the form of a number or frequency of events which occurred during a lesson: for example, the frequency of corrective feedback statements; the number of practice trials a child received in the lesson; or the number of times a particular child asked a question. They may take the form of time measurements of certain dimensions of the lesson (e.g. the percentage of lesson time the children were

> ## Example
>
> At a conference for physical education teachers some years ago, a teacher told a seminar that he constantly used terms like 'turkey' and 'unco' in his interaction with his classes. He claimed that he used them equally when addressing all children—the low-skilled and the high-skilled. He argued that all the children accepted those comments as perhaps mildly humorous but with a neutral effect. Some other teachers in the seminar challenged him by claiming that the terms would have different impact on different children. To label a child who is having real problems learning physical skills an 'unco' may well have a negative impact on their self-image. Moreover, it was pointed out that the frequency of use might also have differential effects. One such comment to the uncoordinated child might be far more damaging than five such comments to the high-skilled child.

on task; the percentage of lesson time the children spent waiting for a turn; or the percentage of lesson time the teacher spent talking to the class when they were not active). They may take the form of an illustration of teacher movement throughout the lesson so that it is possible to determine which children in the class received little close attention from the teacher. They may also take the form of a record of which children received verbal feedback from the teacher and the nature of that feedback. They may take the form of transcripts made from an audiotape of the lesson from which it would be possible to analyse the nature of the teacher's verbal interaction in the lesson. They may take the form of a record of pupil interactions: Which children interact with which children? What is the nature of their interaction?

To collect such data it is possible to use systematic observation instruments which were designed specifically for the task. *Analysing Physical Education and Sport Instruction* (1989) edited by Darst et al or Siedentop's *Developing Teaching Skills in Physical Education* (1991) are worthwhile sources of such instruments. However, the use of such formal data-gathering instruments requires a good deal of practice by the collector before you can expect good data to be collected. It is usually beyond the realm of practicality in most student teaching situations but it is certainly possible to develop your own version of an instrument for your particular purposes.

In most student teaching situations you may find that information on your issue of focus is best obtained by devising your own way of collecting it. Perhaps it will be something that you work out with your supervising teacher or university lecturer. However you go about determining how the data are to be collected, the fact remains that you should try to make them 'good data'.

Sometimes it is possible to collect data for yourself, although such practice does not discount the necessity for work with a colleague (your supervising teacher, lecturer or even another student teacher) in discussing the data and the possible future actions you plan to take based on analysis of the data. Probably the simplest way of obtaining data about your own teaching is to have the lesson recorded on videotape. Perhaps one of your students could operate the camera for you. Once you have the lesson taped then you can replay it over and over in your own time and take data from your observations.

In the absence of a videotape recording of your lesson(s) you can still record some of the events and happenings by simple methods. One example of how to collect frequency-type data (e.g. the number of practice trials a particular child gets during the lesson) is to use a hand-held event recorder of the type that cricket umpires use to count the number of balls each over. In general it is more difficult to collect data for yourself in physical education lessons than it is in the classroom. That said, however, it is still important to understand that self-collecting data is a possibility and can provide useful information for analysis of your teaching.

Keeping a journal for reflection

Importantly, data or information which is relevant to your educational practice are not all contained in the actual lessons you teach. There are aspects of your professional lives which go beyond individual lessons. One useful tool for tapping the wider aspects of your teaching is the use of the professional journal. This is more than simply keeping a diary, although the concept is not dissimilar. Journals resemble diaries insofar as they contain a chronologically ordered sequence of written reflections on events. The difference between them is in the fact that the journal is intended as a record which is used for the purposes of learning from experience, often in collaboration with at least one other person. We have used a method of organised reflection with our student teachers where they have recorded their reactions to their teaching experiences on the practicum, to required readings, to class tutorials, to practical sessions and to lectures. Subsequent analysis of the journal can reveal patterns of concern or interest which might otherwise go unnoticed in the hustle and bustle of daily life.

Keeping a personal professional journal can be a very rewarding experience in terms of gaining new insight into your own professional practice. As Mary-Lou Holly (1984, p 6) points out, the journal is more than a diary of events:

> In a journal, the writer can carry on a dialogue between and among various dimensions of experience. What happened? What are the facts? What is my role? What feelings and senses surround the events? What did I do? What did I feel about what I did? Why? What was the setting? The flow of events? What preceded it? Followed it? What might I be aware of if the situation arises again? This dialogue, traversing back and forth between objective and subjective views, allows the writer to become increasingly more accepting and perhaps less judgmental as the flow of events takes form. Independent actions take on added meaning.

Because the journal has the capacity to help you determine patterns in what might appear to be unrelated events in your own daily practice as a student teacher, it is possible to gain new insight which provides the catalyst for attempts to better understand and/or change something about your practice.

Reflective practice

We consider that, in its broadest sense, *reflective practice* is an intellectual disposition which functions like a set of lenses through which to view all educational and cultural practices. Reflective practice will be 'applied to' more than the act of teaching. It will have a broader function than merely what happens in specific lessons. Reflective practice will also engage issues relating to schooling and education as inherently political and ideological social structures. In this sense we consider the term 'reflective practice' to be a broader and more appropriate notion of reflection than 'reflective teaching'.

Such conscious reflective practice is a feature of extended professionalism and needs to be an essential ingredient in all 'methods' courses of PETE programs. By 'essential ingredient' we mean something which must be embedded within the pedagogy of the course itself. It should be embedded in the pedagogical processes through which student teachers acquire pedagogical and curriculum knowledge, and it should facilitate a reflexivity not only towards the student teacher's own teaching but also of the 'methods' course and teacher education program.

Playing the game of reflection

Student teachers are not mere functionaries doing everything that is expected of them in their teacher education program. Also, we do not expect that you will embrace all our ideas or even agree with some of them. While there is sometimes conflict between the expectations of a supervising teacher and university lecturer, in most cases student teachers have reasonably well-developed behaviours which they employ to progress through the program within what they feel to be an acceptable balance between effort and success (reward). Such behaviours are collectively called 'studentship', and it is as much a part of learning to be a teacher as it is in learning to be a doctor or a lawyer.

Reflecting on one's own practice through action research or other reflective processes is something which may be explicitly required in your university course, though this would be the exception rather than the rule. If such reflection is required then you can still go through the motions and satisfy the formal accountability system and receive a grade, only to subsequently forget about it as a form of professional development. Remember Gore's (1990) recalcitrants, acquiescents and committed reflectors. However, regardless of the specific requirements of the practicum, our hope from this book is that you might learn to embrace the notions of extended professionalism and build reflective practice in your understanding of what it means to be a good teacher.

Reflecting on PETE programs

Some educators have criticised teacher education for perpetuating the view that learning to teach is merely a personal challenge to acquire a range of technical skills (e.g. giving clear directions and providing accurate feedback). It is argued that PETE courses which focus on (or privilege) technical aspects of teaching fail to prepare teachers who are reflective and able to appreciate the social and political complexities of teaching and schooling.

A nice way to begin to think about PETE pedagogies is to ask the question: What is considered to be the *central problem* of teacher education? The choice of pedagogy is part of the operationalisation of a solution (or way to tackle) the perceived central problem. For some physical education teacher educators the central problem is: How can we train student teachers to become effective teachers? and How can we best develop the teaching skills of student teachers? For others it is: How can we train teachers to be reflective of their work in ways which embody a critical social perspective?

over to you

Discuss in your tutorial groups what you consider to be the central problem of PETE. What should PETE be actually arranged to do?

In our view there is little doubt that within PETE the dominant form of pedagogy is 'performance pedagogy' (Tinning 1993). This pedagogy is based on structured discourses which foreground utility and which are concerned with the problem of *how* to teach physical education. The main structuring questions in this discourse centre around techniques and strategies which are concerned with the most efficient ways to achieve essentially non-problematic ends.

Within this pedagogy there is a heavy emphasis on management and class control skills because, in sympathy with the Fuller & Bown (1972) developmental model for student teachers, 'that's where student teachers are at'. Smith, in his much quoted *Model for a School of Pedagogy*, reveals very clearly what he considers to be the principal concern of teacher education:

> *The pre-service student should not be exposed to theories and practices derived from ideologies and philosophies about the way schools should be. The rule should be to teach thoroughly, the knowledge and skills that equip beginning teachers to work successfully in today's classrooms. (1980, p 23)*

This begs the question of what knowledge and skills are actually necessary in today's classrooms and gymnasia. Also, as Beyer (1984) has claimed, 'Just because teachers appear to develop in a particular way under present circumstances does not imply that this is the way we ought to help teachers grow' (p 23).

As advocates of critical pedagogy we argue that the *central problem* for PETE courses should be the relationship of school to society—the way in which knowledge is created, disseminated and legitimised, and the nature of teaching itself. Schools and PETE programs should be considered as sites of cultural production and reproduction, and a key problem for teacher education is to engage the power relations which mediate these processes.

A critical pedagogy questions the role of schools in society with an agenda for change and social action. Of course, we realise that this is not a universally popular thing to do, and there are many within (and without) education who argue vehemently against this agenda (see, for example, Education Forum 1998).

If you are in a typical PETE program then it is likely that most of your experiences of pedagogy will be of a didactic nature, in which the lecturer has the knowledge (about something) and proceeds to impart it to you via lectures, vidoes, small group discussions and the like. Most often you will be given no voice in deciding what it is you desire to learn. The curriculum is predetermined and you simply follow the course outline to complete the work. Knowledge is received. The lecturer is the expert and you are the novice. The epistemological shortcoming of many PETE programs is that 'essential knowledge' is produced, determined, validated, legitimised and implemented by the lecturers and merely 'received' by student teachers (see Lawson 1993). In some subjects this is indeed the case. When learning about the protocols of exercise testing or about the action of quadriceps femoris in an anatomy class, you are the novice and what is to be learnt is relatively straightforward (though not necessarily simple or easy). But there are other times when your own experiences are valid and need to be sought in the learning process.

In practice a critical pedagogy of PETE may involve some of the following subject matter and approaches.

Socially critical subject matter recognises that what is taught and learned is a reflection of traditions, biases and priorities at a particular place and time and, as such, has social, ethical and political implications for pupils, teachers and schooling. Therefore, subject matter may range from why the movement sciences approach the study of the human body using the male body as the reference point (and what impact this then has on physical education) to why is there a revival of 'the basics' in school curricula (and what its impact is on physical education). Examining textbooks, videotapes, films and newspapers in terms of their underlying messages is a method through which critical skills can be developed.

Negotiation suggests regular and respectful communication in which staff and students have a share of power in the decision-making and communication processes. It is a worthwhile principle to pursue, not just between teaching staff and students but between students themselves. Negotiating what is to be learned and how it might be assessed respects PETE students as self-managing learners and is likely to increase commitment to learning.

Reflection, as mentioned in Chapter 1, suggests the asking of a range of questions which should include challenging the taken-for-granted in physical education and constantly questioning why physical education is approached in this way and who it is that benefits.

Praxis has many interpretations, but in this context it is taken to mean the junction of theory and practice, and thought and action. Rather than relying on didactic lecturing to encourage learning, class-based and practicum-oriented tasks, group work, inclusive discussions, debates and life histories are some methods through which learning becomes engaging, meaningful and relevant.

While we have argued that socially critical subject matter and pedagogies are essential if PETE is to contribute to contemporary, rigorous and inclusive physical education (see, for example, Tinning 1993, Hickey & Glover 1996, Macdonald 1997), there is evidence that PETE students resist these approaches.

As mentioned earlier, most PETE students enter their programs with expectations that they will be studying biophysical sciences (e.g. exercise physiology, biomechanics), participating in traditional physical activities, and practising teaching in 'real life' contexts (Macdonald et al 1999). Therefore, subject matter which is not scientific or practical/vocational may initially be seen as irrelevant.

There is evidence that a strong thematic approach to teacher education or, to use Lortie's (1975) terminology, 'a shared culture' can result in changes to student teachers' beliefs and practices. It needs to be consistently reinforced across all learning contexts, including the practicum, and, we would add, implemented in line with a critical pedagogy. What could be considered the shared culture of your program?

Unofficial discourses

The previous discussion has focussed on the overt or official curriculum of PETE. However, just as with the school curriculum there are hidden, unexamined and unintentional discourses which shape students' learning and experiences. The pattern of privileging certain discourses invests particular groups with social energy and voice, while other groups or individuals may be silenced, constrained or resistant.

Privileging of certain kinds of scientific knowledge is not a neutral act but one intricately entwined with powerful men's voices who have been most interested in the study of elite sport. Whitson & Macintosh (1990) claimed that this discourse of performance, in turn, prioritises the performance qualities of speed, strength and power rather than, for example, flexibility or rhythm. Where success in assessment and status is linked to the demonstration of masculine 'predispositions', such as in many physical activities undertaken by PETE students, it is most likely that the 'competence' of the male student is reinforced in the eyes of all students.

over to you

What discourses are privileged in your PETE program?
What are the examples of privilege?

The gendering of PETE is inevitably multidimensional. It occurs through the subject matter, class interactions and behavioural expectations to name a few. Flintoff (1993) observed in PETE programs overtly masculine behaviours comprising of demonstrations of physical prowess, competitiveness, sexual innuendo, excessive drinking, and distancing from stereotypically feminine and homosexual traits in very public displays. Many female students therefore negotiate PETE within a narrow sphere of acceptability—the sphere demarcated through the description of body shape and presentation proscribed by dominant male culture, through sport defined as a male domain, through an exposure to scientific and thus masculine knowledge, and through a socialisation process in which men and women accept male domination in their endeavours as normal. We are not saying that female PETE students are subservient 'dopes' but rather that hegemonic processes have rendered most female PETE students active in producing and reproducing those discourses which position them as disempowered.

Staffing patterns also shape a PETE context in terms of who students see on the academic staff, what seniority they see a faculty as holding, and in what content areas the faculty members teach and research.

over to you

Examine the staff profile of your PETE department. Discuss the possible influence of gender on male/female achievements as measured by promotion success.

Summary

- Developing as a reflective student teacher is the first step in the journey to become a teacher whose work is characterised by reflective practice.
- Learning to reflect is not as easy as it might seem, and some student teachers actively resist becoming reflective.
- Reflection is an intentional act and not one that is a normal part of habitual teaching.
- Action research is a form of reflective teaching which requires the systematic collection of data (information) as a basis for reflection.
- A reflective orientation can be applied to the PETE course that you are now studying. It is informative to consider the discourses which might be privileged in your course and the extent to which certain other useful discourses are marginalised.

References

Beyer, L. (1984). 'Field experience, ideology, and the development of critical reflectivity'. *Journal of Teacher Education*, 25(3), pp 36–41.

Darst, P., Mancini, V. & Zakrajsek, D. (1989). *Analysing Physical Education and Sport Instruction* (2nd edn). Champaign, IL: Human Kinetics.

Dewey, J. (1933). *How We Think: A Restatement of the Relation of Reflective Thinking to the Educative Process*. Chicago, IL: Henry Regnery Co.

Education Forum (1998). *Health and Physical Education in the New Zealand Curriculum: A Submission on the Draft*. Auckland: Education Forum.

Flintoff, A. (1993). 'Sexism and homophobia in physical education: The challenge for teacher educators'. *Physical Education Review*, 17(2), pp 97–105.

Fuller, F. & Bown, O. (1972). 'Becoming a teacher'. In K. Ryan (ed.), *Teacher Education*. Chicago, IL: Chicago University Press.

Gore, J.M. (1990). 'Pedagogy as text in physical education teacher education: Beyond the preferred reading'. In D. Kirk & R. Tinning (eds), *Physical Education, Curriculum and Culture: Critical Issues in the Contemporary Crisis* (pp 101–138). Basingstoke: The Falmer Press.

Grundy, S. & Kemmis, S. (1981). 'Educational action research in Australia: The state of the art' (an overview). Paper presented at the *Australian Association for Research in Education*, Adelaide.

Hamilton, D. (1973). 'At classroom level'. Unpublished PhD, Edinburgh University, Edinburgh.

Henry, J. (1980). 'Teachers as researchers: An action research model applied to inquiry teaching'. Unpublished manuscript, Deakin University.

Hickey, C. & Glover, S. (1996). 'National curriculum and physical education in Australia: New horizons or false hopes'. *Journal of Physical Education New Zealand*, 29(1), pp 3–6.

Holly, M.L. (1984). *Keeping a Personal Professional Journal*. Geelong: Deakin University Press.

Lawson, H. (1993). 'Dominant discourses, problem setting, and teacher education pedagogies: A critique'. *Journal of Teaching in Physical Education*, 12, pp 149–160.

Lawson, H. (1993b). 'Teaching as a moral calling: Induction, reflection, action and renewal'. Address to the AIESEP International Conference on Training Reflective Teachers, University of Quebec, Quebec, Canada, July.

Lortie, D. (1975). *Schoolteacher: A Sociological Study*. Chicago, IL: University of Chicago Press.

Macdonald, D. (1997). 'Teacher attrition'. Commissioned paper for the *World Education Report*. Paris: UNESCO.

Macdonald, D., Kirk, D. & Braiuka, S. (1999). 'The social construction of the physical activity field at the school/university interface'. *European Journal of Physical Education*, 5(1), pp 31–51.

McTaggart, R. (1991). *Action Research: A Short Modern History*. Geelong: Deakin University.

Rovegno, I. (1992). 'Learning to reflect on teaching: A case study of one pre-service physical education teacher'. *The Elementary School Teacher*, 92(4), pp 491–510.

Schon, D. (1983), *The Reflective Practitioner: How Professionals Think in Action*. New York: Basic Books.

Schon, D. (1987). *Educating the Reflective Practitioner*. San Francisco: Jossey-Bass.

Siedentop, D (1991). *Developing Teaching Skills in Physical Education*. Palo Alto, Mayfield Publishing Company.

Smith, B.O. (1980). 'On the content of teacher education', In E. Hall, S. Hord & G. Brown (eds), *On the Content of Teacher Education*. Austin, TX: University of Texas Research and Development Centre for Teacher Education.

Stenhouse, L. (1975). *An Introduction to Curriculum Research and Development*. London: Heinemann.

Tinning, R. (1993). 'We have ways of making you think, or Do We?'. *Reflections on 'training' in reflective teaching*. Paper presented at the training of teachers in reflective practice of physical education, Trois-Rivieres.

Tinning, R. (1985). 'Physical education and the cult of slenderness: A critique'. *ACHPER National Journal*, 107 (Autumn), pp 10–14.

Tinning, R. (1998). 'Performance and participation orienting discourses in the field of human movement: Implications for a socially critical physical education'. In J.-M. Fernandez-Balboa (ed.), *Critical Aspects in Human Movement: Rethinking the Profession in the Postmodern Era*. New York: Suny Press.

van Manen, M. (1995). 'On the epistemology of reflective practice'. *Teachers and Teaching: Theory and Practice*, 1(1), pp 33–51.

Whitson, D. & Macintosh, D. (1990). 'The scientization of physical education: Discourses in performance'. *Quest*, 42(1), pp 40–51.

Further reading

Fernandez-Balboa, J-M. (1997). 'Knowledge base in physical education teacher education: A proposal for a new era'. *Quest*, 49, pp 161–181.

Ennis, C. (1984). 'A future scenario for physical education: A movement for life curriculum'. 2017-2035. *JOPHERD*, September, pp 4–5.

Kirk, D. (1997). 'Thinking beyond the square: The challenge to physical educators in new times'. *Quest*, 49, pp 181–185.

Kirk, D. (1998). 'Educational reform, physical culture and the crisis of legitimation in physical education'. *Discourse*, 19(1), pp 101–112.

Siedentop, D. (1994). 'Curriculum innovation: Toward the 21st century'. *ICHPER Journal*, Winter, 11–14.

chapter
seventeen

objectives

By the end of this chapter you should be able to:

- appreciate something of the limitations of research attempts to find the essence of good teaching in physical education;
- explain the significance of 'time management' in definitions of effective teaching;
- recognise the shortcomings of some physical education teaching as represented by descriptive studies;
- understand the difference between what is *intended* and what is *learned*;
- appreciate how defining good teaching is inherently a political process in which different vested interests place different emphases on what they consider important and necessary.

Quality teaching

Judging your teaching performance

Like it or not, judgments will be made about your teaching competence (or, as we prefer to say, about the quality of your teaching) by many people for many reasons throughout your career as a teacher. The judgments made in your school experience rounds as student teacher will have a significant bearing on your chances of gaining employment when you graduate.

There are many people with vested interests in the competence of teachers. Administrators (especially principals) will judge teacher competence on the basis of peer reports (the opinion of colleagues), on folklore, discipline and achievement, together with their interpersonal relationship with a teacher. They will do so for reasons relating to promotion, tenure, transfer and general accountability to parents and the employing authority.

Politicians and the business world will also have their say about teacher competence. All will have particular 'axes to grind'. The politician (especially of the conservative persua-sion) will be interested in the cost-effectiveness of education: is it supplying a skilled workforce, can a particular claim about teachers or schools enhance their reputation within the voting community? The business world will be interested in the ability of graduates from the school system to turn up (on time), add up, be able to read what they are required, problem-solve, and do as instructed. To the extent that schools provide such graduates, they (and the teachers who teach in the schools) will be judged as successful. In general, when schools are deemed to be delivering what certain interest groups in society deem to be important outcomes (not necessarily educational), the teachers who teach in them will be judged as competent. When these same interest groups feel the school system is not delivering certain outcomes, then it will be teachers who are judged to be incompetent.

In the case of many physical education teachers, the principal and other school administrators will often judge quality teaching by the success or otherwise of school sporting teams in competition. Winning teams may tend to reflect well on the physical education teacher but we now understand that this says very little about the quality of physical education teaching in a school.

On the other hand, because physical education is considered to be a 'non-academic' part of the school curriculum, there is a good chance that the only judgments made of physical education teaching will be related to whether the class causes no disruptions (noise, in particular) to other classes (academic), that there are no injuries (and hence no litigation), and that children seem to enjoy the experience. In this sense teaching quality in physical education might be less in the public eye in some schools than is the case with an academic subject. Notwithstanding this, there has been considerable research into the nature of 'good' teaching in physical education.

'The right stuff': looking for the essence of good teaching

Early research efforts attempted to reveal a *common set of characteristics* which were considered to be widely accepted as the qualities of a good teacher. The researchers found that people disagreed on the 'essential' qualities. What was vitally important or essential to one individual seemed to be trivial or even irrelevant to others. Even the 'experts' disagreed!

The 'experts' used in most studies were usually school principals or university lecturers and they were asked to rate certain teachers as effective or ineffective. Comparisons between these teachers were then made on the basis of such variables as personality traits, mental abilities and academic achievement. The results were inconclusive. Individual teacher characteristics like personality and IQ failed to distinguish between the effective and ineffective teachers as rated by the 'experts'.

Although there were many methodological shortcomings in these early research studies the significant fact is that the results were inconclusive largely, and most importantly, because people disagreed with respect to what they *believed* to be the characteristics of good teaching.

The best method of teaching

Research to find the essence of good teaching continued in earnest through the 1950s; however, the focus moved from the search for characteristics to the search for the best method of teaching. The aim of this 'methods research' (as it became known) was to find which teaching method was superior. Of course, superior in what sense seems to be a key issue. Again, there were many methodological problems with these studies, not the least of which was the fact that, as Siedentop (1991) claims, 'the researchers often set out to "prove" that the innovative method was better' (p 39). In the final analysis little was learned from this line of study except perhaps that we should be guarded in accepting claims that any *one* particular teaching method is best for all children in all settings and in all subject or activity areas.

Looking at the lessons

One of the most powerful criticisms of the early research in teaching physical education was that the researchers had treated the classroom or gymnasium as if it were a 'black box' (Locke 1977). What this meant was that researchers did not actually go out onto the playing field or into the gym to view real lessons. In the 1960s, however, researchers in education, and shortly afterwards in physical education, began to investigate what teachers and pupils actually *do* in their classes. They designed a multitude of instruments (see Darst et al 1989) which were used to collect systematic and objective data about what happens in physical education lessons. The question of what *really* happens in these lessons came some time later, as we shall explore shortly.

Equipped with these instruments the researchers began to describe events in physical education based on the measurements that these instruments provided. The effort of a decade or more of systematic description of the behaviour of teachers and pupils in physical education classes has been very productive. We now know a good deal about the nature of physical education in terms of the behaviours of the main actors—namely, teachers and pupils.

Armed with ways to systematically record behaviour in classes, researchers began another phase of investigations which came to be called 'process–product' research. In essence, what researchers attempted to do was to collect data on teacher behaviour in the gym and then to determine the correlation between certain of those behaviours (process) and some measure of pupil learning (product). This approach worked well in the classroom, and one of the most influential reviews of this teaching effectiveness research by Rosenshine & Furst (1971) identified five key variables which were claimed to be consistently related to pupil academic achievement. These variables were:

1. clarity of presentation;
2. teacher enthusiasm;
3. variety of activities;
4. task-oriented and business-like teacher behaviour; and
5. the content covered by the class.

There have been, however, relatively few studies done in physical education using true process–product procedures, largely because the 'products' (the performances, the behaviours) of physical education usually take much more time to record. For example, measuring/judging and recording every pupil's performance in a dance lesson will take considerably longer than a pencil and paper test in mathematics. Moreover, some of the outcomes of physical education, such as the development of good sporting behaviours, are more difficult to measure than many classroom-based outcomes. Accordingly, teaching effectiveness researchers in physical education have tended to generalise from the available classroom research findings (e.g. using the five key variables mentioned above) to the physical education context. While this may be appropriate in certain contexts, the limits of such generalisations are definitely not known and we therefore need to be cautious in making the jump from classroom research findings to solutions for physical education teaching.

In synthesising the relevant classroom and physical education research, Daryl Siedentop (1983) claimed that the following *eight strategies for effective teaching* are confirmed by research in the classroom *and* the gymnasium.

1. Devote a large percentage of time to content.
2. Minimise management/wait/transition time in class routines.
3. Devote a high percentage of content time to practice.
4. Keep students on task.
5. Assign tasks that are meaningful and matched to student abilities.
6. Keep the learning environment supportive and set high but realistic expectations.

7. Give lessons smoothness and momentum.

8. Hold students accountable for learning.

A more recent account of the research supported strategies of effective teaching is presented by Mick Mawer (1995).

Effective teachers of physical education appear to:

PLAN their work more effectively and

- have a clear idea of what they intend to accomplish and how they will accomplish it;
- analyze and diagnose pupil levels of skill, knowledge and understanding, and are aware of pupil developmental characteristics in order to be able to design and prescribe appropriate learning experiences to 'match' pupil ability, thus ensuring high levels of success in practice and learning;
- progress work to be done in sequence and in appropriate small steps linked to clear instructional goals, thus minimizing frustration and failure and achieving greater continuity of progression;
- provide meaningful, realistic, challenging and appropriate, attainable goals for individual pupil learning and success;
- develop effective sequences of appropriate questions to enable pupils to develop understanding of concepts;
- design effective class management procedures, anticipate situations and have contingency plans prepared in case of unforeseen problems with lesson administration.

Effective teachers of physical education appear to:

PRESENT new material well and

- explain new concepts and pupil tasks with clarity and effective communication skills;
- make good use of modeling/demonstrations.

ORGANISE AND MANAGE pupils and learning experiences by

- planning for preventative management through quickly established management structures, routines, and class rule/contracts, therefore providing more time and opportunity to learn;
- making the lesson task expectations clear, monitoring pupil progress and ensuring that pupils are clearly accountable for what they are learning;
- creating a business-like learning environment and class atmosphere;
- effective use of resources.

Effective teachers of physical education are:

ACTIVE TEACHERS because they spend more time actively involved in teaching pupils and they

- have highly developed observation skills to be able to diagnose pupil learning difficulties;
- offer task intrinsic and positive, specific, augmented feedback related to lesson objectives;
- demonstrate skills and explain concepts clearly and concisely;
- monitor pupil progress to maximize pupil time for practice, and minimize inappropriate pupil inactivity and waiting;
- sustain lesson momentum;
- utilize more lesson time in the presentation of material and performance feedback.

Effective teachers appear to provide:

A POSITIVE, SUPPORTIVE AND WARM LEARNING ENVIRONMENT [and]

- they individualize feedback and guidance for personal levels of mastery and understanding and do not make comparisons between pupils;
- they are enthusiastic, pleasant and positive;
- they plan interesting lessons, allowing pupils to share in decision making;
- they provide pupils with greater time and opportunity to learn;
- they are aware of teacher expectancy effects.

Effective teachers of physical education have a repertoire of:

TEACHING STYLES and know how and when to use them to facilitate pupil learning and understanding.

Also, effective teachers of other subjects appear to:

TEACH FOR UNDERSTANDING by

- planning appropriate sequences of questions to facilitate pupil understanding of concepts and lesson content;
- the use of a variety of skills and strategies to develop discourse and discussion;
- providing learning experiences and opportunities to apply understanding;
- providing support and task simplification strategies and other forms of 'scaffolding'. (Although it has been noted that there is at present a lack of research support for this variable in PE.) (Mawer 1995, *The Effective Teaching of Physical Education*. Essex: Longman, pp 51–53)

The importance of time management

Reviewing both Siedentop's and Mawer's summaries we can see that the management of time has been a major focus of much of the research into teaching effectiveness. Neil Postman (1989) claimed that what we know about something will depend on the questions we ask of it. The same is true of effective teaching, and it just so happens that many of the questions which drove research were related to time management. Indeed, the most prolific forms of research relating to physical education teacher effectiveness has been what is called 'academic learning time' (ALT) research.

ALT-PE is a particular version adapted from the general education context for specific use with physical education classes. It is a unit of time in which a pupil is engaged with the task set by the teacher which they can perform successfully. To gather these data an observer must watch the class and make decisions concerning whether or not a majority of the class are engaged in doing the task which has been set by the teacher within a certain time interval. A judgment is also made concerning the difficulty of the set task with respect to the ability of the class. Siedentop et al (1986) claim that: 'The concept of ALT-PE provides a simple, convenient criterion by which to judge teaching effectiveness in physical education' (p 376). For the supporters of this claim, ALT-PE is the 'essence' of teaching effectiveness in physical education. As McLeish (1985, p 84) argued: 'It was our conclusion that the ALT-PE system supplies the mission element, or indeed major component, needed to evaluate effective teaching in physical education. Time-on-task, academic learning time, opportunity to learn—call it what you will, and measure it if you can—this is the vital component of an effective lesson'. It is strong praise indeed for this concept adapted from classroom research. We have some strong reservations about the claims made for ALT but these will be discussed later. Let us now consider some of the ideas which have been gleaned from the many studies into the nature of physical education classes.

Some not so flattering research findings

Reading the recent literature on physical education teaching effectiveness reveals that most studies did not use pupil achievement as a dependent variable but instead used the notion of academic learning time (ALT) as a proxy measure of pupil achievement. These studies, and the purely descriptive studies which proceeded them, have told us a great deal about what is happening in physical education classes, at least from one perspective. Descriptive research in different countries (such as France, Canada, Australia, New Zealand and the United States) has revealed patterns of teacher and pupil behaviour in physical education classes which appear to be (taken on average) more similar than dissimilar. Remembering that averages are made up of highs and lows, we know that pupils in physical education classes spend:

- somewhere in the vicinity of 28 per cent of their lesson time waiting for something to happen (waiting in line, waiting for a turn, waiting for equipment etc.);
- up to 20 per cent of their time involved in managerial tasks like choosing teams, moving from place to place or being organised for practice;
- around 20 per cent of their lesson time receiving information from the teacher about such things as how to play the next game, how to perform a skill better; and

- about 25 per cent of the time in actual physical activity—and even some of that time they might be performing activities which are either beyond their current ability, in which case they may learn little except perhaps to feel inadequate, or beneath their ability, in which case they may become bored.

We also know that physical education teachers spend:

- something in the vicinity of 20 per cent of their time managing the class (i.e. organising, giving directions, arranging for things to happen);
- about 30 per cent of their time instructing (conveying information to the class about the physical activity itself—giving coaching points, if you like); and
- between 20 and 40 per cent of the time monitoring (i.e. just watching the class without interacting).

If we believe, as McLeish (1985) and Siedentop et al (1986) have claimed, that ALT-PE is the best measure of teaching effectiveness then we could only conclude that most physical education lessons are woefully ineffective. However, let us not rush to conclusions before we learn what other things have been 'discovered' by research.

 over to you

In tutorial time, work in small groups and view a videotape of a physical education lesson. Record all the above-mentioned time dimensions for teacher and pupils. Compare your findings with those of the research literature. How do they match up? Discuss whether the lesson you analysed would be judged as a good lesson on the basis of the data you collected concerning the use of time. The videotaped lessons can be those of student teachers recorded on a recent teaching round.

 let's reflect

Think back to your own school days. Can you remember a particular incident which you think represented an example of good or bad teaching in physical education? Write a brief account of the incident. Include something of the context (where, when, who etc.) and detail of what happened and why you consider it to be either good or bad. Compare some of the incidents in your tutorial. Discuss any similarities and differences.

For all of us, our history in physical education classes (both as participants or observers) has much to do with forming our position with respect to what we consider to be good teaching. It may also be the case that some of our experiences help us to identify what it is we think to be inappropriate in relation to good teaching, and that is useful as well.

 author reflection

When I trained to become a physical education teacher in the 1960s the dominant characteristics of good teaching were represented as maximum pupil activity, firm class control and detailed lesson planning. A good teacher was expected to have a loud voice and an authoritative manner. In some sense the child was an object to be moved about in such a manner as to 'make good' the lesson plan. Spontaneity and enjoyment were not seen as essential; on the contrary, they often led to unpredictability and unplanned outcomes.

I became a better teacher as I improved at implementing my carefully planned lessons. Such was the emphasis on following the lesson plan that we had to plan (and write into our lesson plan) the actual words which we would use for the entire lesson. This included describing activities to the class, offering coaching points, and even giving management and class control prompts. My lesson plans were more like scripts of a play in which the lead actor delivered lines which were rehearsed and predetermined.

It is probably obvious that such detailed planning hardly characterises the daily work of today's practising teachers; nonetheless, some of these values are still influential in informing notions of good teaching. In our view, however, to plan well and to keep the class active for the optimal time each lesson is merely a *necessary but not sufficient* condition for good teaching.

Other findings

Descriptive research has also revealed something of the nature of the interactions between physical education teachers and their pupils, and the findings are hardly cause for much celebration. We know that physical education teachers do provide feedback to their pupils but that it is not all too abundant. Data from a (now dated) study by Cheffers & Mancini (1978) claim that the typical pattern is something like 45 feedback comments in a 30-minute lesson. Whether a rate of 1.5 feedback episodes per minute is considered sufficient or not is of course the significant issue. Perhaps, rather than the number of episodes, it is the nature of the feedback that is more important.

The feedback which is most common in physical education is that which is evaluative in nature rather than descriptive or prescriptive. Statements like 'nice work'and 'good effort' are typical. Siedentop (1983) claims that the most predominant form of feedback which teachers give to skill performance is what he terms 'corrective'. Moreover, when teachers give feedback to pupils about their performance of managerial or organisational tasks (like getting out the equipment or arranging themselves into certain formations for the playing of a game or practice of a skill), the predominant form is what he terms a 'nag'. A nag is defined as a low-intensity reprimand such as 'Listen to me when I'm talking' or 'I told you all to be quiet'. According to Siedentop: 'The combination of corrective feedback and nagging represents over 80 percent of the total interactions—what that means is that the teacher tends to react to what students do incorrectly. The environment does not appear to be a heavily negative one, but it just as obviously is not a positive one' (p 58). Considering that creating a supportive environment is one of the factors necessary for effective teaching, Siedentop's evidence is less than encouraging.

Other research studies such as those by Griffin (1981), Macdonald (1990) and Wright (1997) have also used descriptive analyses of what is happening in physical education classes and they have revealed other information which is important when considering the nature of good teaching. Pat Griffin found that teachers tend to praise girls more for effort and boys for performance. Teachers also give girls less instructional feedback than boys. Doune Macdonald's research on the nature of the interaction patterns between teachers and students in coeducational and single-sex physical education classes in Queensland secondary schools revealed different interaction patterns for boys and girls. Boys had a greater proportion of verbal interactions with the teacher than girls did, and a higher proportion of positive interactions were either directed to or initiated by boys.

Jan Wright's (1997) research into the nature of the language used by teachers in physical education classes revealed that girls are encouraged to perform physical activity, yet are often simultaneously restrained and constrained by the manner in which they must perform. They are encouraged to be conscious of their appearance, to be careful and to generally limit their performance. These restrictions are consistent with societal sex stereotypes which effectively limit the opportunities for girls. Boys, on the other hand, were limited only by safety factors. Unlike the girls, they were not faced with the ambiguities between femininity and physicality. Significantly, the teachers themselves were unaware of the subtle way in which the language they used in their teaching actually treated boys and girls differently and accordingly perpetuated sex stereotyping which restricted girls compared with boys.

Looking for Mars while pointing at Jupiter

These research findings add further complexity to the task of defining good teaching. Importantly, knowledge of such subtle discrimination has only recently been forthcoming from the research literature. It is a bit like using a telescope to view the heavens. You can see more with a telescope than the naked eye, and improvements in the power and sophistication of the telescope enable us to see things previously unnoticed. However, no matter how powerful the telescope, it will not yield information on the planet Mars if it is pointing at Jupiter. While the research reported by Siedentop (1983) gave a good deal of information about one particular planet in the heavens of good teaching, other researchers (such as Griffin 1981, Bain 1990, Macdonald 1990 and Wright 1997) have pointed their telescopes at different planets. Taken together, these studies help us to get a better understanding of the complexity of the subject. To make judgments on the nature of the subject we should therefore recognise that we will need to take the various aspects into consideration.

Certainly the research mentioned above raises more questions than it answers. If we are to learn from what the research has already found out then we need to factor into the good teaching equation answers to such questions as:

- Is it possible to claim to be a good teacher if your classes are characterised by high levels of activity (ALT perhaps) but children hate attending class and do things to avoid participating?
- Is it possible to be a good teacher if you privilege boys over girls?
- Can good teaching exist in a climate which is essentially a negative one in which criticism and nagging represent the dominant forms of teacher–pupil interaction?

What is intended and what is learnt

Siedentop et al (1986) claimed that 'effective teaching can only be judged in terms of the goals of the teacher' (p 374). But is it enough to claim that a teacher who achieves clearly specified learning goals (like the improvement in levels of physical fitness) is therefore an effective teacher? Of course, we should have a clear notion of what it is we expect pupils to learn (*learning outcomes*) from our teaching (or more particularly from engagement in our classes) and we should be able to articulate these learnings in terms of a purpose for our teaching. But the problem with such a definition is that it too readily slips into conceiving of good teaching in a predominantly technical way. When attention is focussed only on the question: Were the learning outcomes achieved? there can be a tendency to leave unasked such questions as: What is the purpose and value of a particular outcome?; What is learned in physical education lessons which was not part of the teacher-identified program outcomes?; What if the children learned sex-stereotyped limitations on their own potential'?; and Is a teacher effective if they achieve trivial or even inappropriate goals?

In considering what is learned it is useful to think of the following framework for what has been called the 'functional curriculum'.

for your information

Pat Dodds (1985) outlined the notion of the functional curriculum in an attempt to provide a conceptual categorisation of all the things which were learnt (or might be learnt) in physical education. There are four levels of the functional curriculum.

The first or *overt* level includes the explicit formal curriculum that the teacher defines in work programs and lesson plans. This is public knowledge in that the program is made available to the school principal for 'perusal'. It states what is intended for children to learn.

The second level is more difficult to identify, for it exists at the *covert* level. These are learnings which are not formally stated in lesson plans or work programs but which teachers would 'readily agree are consciously and intentionally communicated to students in the act of implementing the explicit curriculum' (Kirk 1992). Such things as 'learning to obey authority', 'applying themselves to a task', and 'students trying hard' would represent such covert curriculum.

Things which are *not* included in the curriculum represent the third level, called the *null* curriculum. Those activity areas, ideas, concepts and values which are either knowingly or unintentionally omitted from the explicit and covert curriculum represent the null curriculum. For example, javelin throwing may not be included in the curriculum because it is considered dangerous, and swimming is not included in the program because the school has no access to a nearby pool. In this case javelin and swimming would represent parts of the null curriculum. A curriculum for a coeducational class which did not include activities such as netball, gymnastics and dance might give stong messages to girls that boys' activities are most important and that their interests are little valued. The messages would be contained in the null curriculum.

At the fourth level is the *hidden* curriculum, which is composed of the learnings which result from reflexive aspects of what teachers do and say. (Note that this definition is probably a more restrictive one than is normally associated with the term.) For instance, a teacher might spend the bulk of the lesson time interacting with the most able physical performers in the class while virtually ignoring the 'battlers'. Such differential attention leaves its own messages with pupils and it is not what is written in the teacher's lesson plan as a learning outcome. Similarly, a teacher's tone of voice or non-verbal communications may convey a message which is quite different from the actual words spoken. Such unconscious influences, while in and of themselves perhaps rather trite or non-significant, are often extremely powerful and negative. Like the silt in a river bed which eventually hardens to form mudstone, many of the subtle, unnoticed learnings from the hidden curriculum can have a powerful cumulative effect.

The hidden curriculum, together with the null and covert curricula, can be collectively thought of as representing opportunities for not-so-obvious or beneath-the-surface student learning.

A teacher who achieved desired fitness outcomes but ignored the other learnings which were consequent on the process of getting fitter in that particular class setting could hardly be regarded as effective. In this sense school physical education programs are (or should be) different from, for example, army physical training programs. In the army there is no educational intention. The sole purpose of a particular training program would be to get the soldiers 'fit to fight'. Whether or not they enjoy the process of becoming fit is irrelevant. Only the product, the fitness goal, matters. Not so with school physical education.

When we ask only 'Were the teacher's goals met'? there is a tendency to ignore some of the learnings which are difficult to assess or evaluate—certainly measure! Improvements in fitness, motor skill performance, knowl-edge of game rules and strategies are all relatively easy to measure and hence more likely to be used as the measure of effectiveness than, for example, improvements in attitude, cooperation, good sporting behaviours, or the desire to participate in physical activity beyond the school setting. Surely our considerations of the nature of good teaching should include more than is typically included in considerations of effective teaching.

Don Hellison (1985), who has spent many years teaching 'high-risk' youth from detention centres and inner city schools in the United States, has used physical education to develop certain social skills. Dissatisfied with the relevence of fitness and skills as the major goals for physical education, he developed an alternative set of goals which focussed on human needs and values. His claim that physical education goals can be portrayed as developmental stages which represent a progression from irresponsibility through self-control to caring is discussed in Chapter 3. However, for the purposes of conceiving what might characterise quality teaching, Hellison's goals would demand a *different focus* for the judgments of quality teaching. The extent to which pupils moved through the stages towards caring would be the basis for the judgment of quality in such a physical education program. Learning outcomes would be related to the developmental stages. Obviously such developmental stages would be more difficult to 'measure' than the level of fitness reached, the proficiency of performing certain new physical skills, or the amount of lesson time the children spend on task.

Seeing individuals and not just the class

As we see in Chapter 9, the way in which young people experience physical education is certainly not homogeneous. Yet for all our rhetoric about treating pupils as individuals, many physical education programs still treat them as if they were a single pupil. This is where some observations of physical education classes can be misleading. It would be possible to observe a class and conclude that a lesson was a success based on the students' apparent involvement in the task set by the teacher. However, using *individual* pupils as the unit of analysis rather than the entire class can reveal a very different picture. Some pupils become skilled at avoiding participation: they are the competent bystanders (Tousignant 1982) who keep slipping to the back of the line, who assist others rather than perform themselves, and who generally get lost in the business of the entire class. Some pupils actually find physical education lessons an unsafe environment in which their feelings of vulnerability relating to their physical competence are readily on display. So although the class as a whole might appear to be enjoying 'itself' there will probably be some individuals who go through the motions in terms of participation and obedience but would, given half the chance, sooner be doing anything but physical education. With such pupils in our class, would we be entitled to claim that our teaching was effective?

For us, then, no matter how much some members of the class liked physical education and how much they identified with the teacher and how much they may have learned, if there are pupils who leave each physical education class feeling inadequate or alienated then we could not defend it as a successful lesson. Perhaps it is now time to begin to use the individual pupil as the unit of analysis for making judgments about teaching quality. By concentrating on the whole class as the unit of analysis we continue to get preoccupied with the issue of efficiency and miss much of how physical education is *actually experienced*. Perhaps this view is rather idealistic, but research evidence and our experience reveal that it is more than the isolated pupil who progressively feels turned off physical education. We do, however, recognise that there will always be some children who are not turned on to physical activity and who, given the chance, would rather not do physical education. If such young people do not enjoy physical education for idiosyncratic reasons, that is very different from having some children turned off *because* of the particular teacher and their teaching.

Keeping them entertained

Neil Postman (1985), an American social analyst and critic, claims that within the United States (and we might argue within Australia also) television has so influenced social life that every major social concern has been reduced to entertainment. News is entertainment, politics is entertainment, religion is entertainment and education is entertainment. Through their engagement with the world through television, young people have learned to expect to be entertained and those expectations reach into the school curriculum as well as the lounge room. Education which fails to entertain is written off as 'boring'. How many times do we hear secondary school children in particular refer to school as boring? How many times have you said it yourself?

Put in the context of a physical education lesson or program, we find that unless the class experiences their involvement as entertaining, they will, in various ways, withdraw their cooperation from the teacher and make the lesson more like 'off-task, bored, and indifferent' than 'busy, happy and good'. Siedentop (1982) and many others have claimed that there was a motivational problem with adolescent youth in school physical education in the United

States. Australian research (see Tinning & Fitzclarence 1992) reveals that the same problem existed here in Australia in the 1990s.

In the early 1980s Siedentop argued that the solution to the motivational problem in physical education lay in teachers 'teaching better'. We now realise that it is more complicated than that. As we have already seen, what it means to teach better is a contested notion. Would keeping the children 'busy, happy and good' with entertaining activities satisfy the motivational problem? Would it satisfy as good teaching? If a teacher set out to entertain the class and achieved such a goal would we be happy to judge that teacher to be effective? From our perspective there must be some judgment with respect to the *educational value* of the curriculum. It seems the 'essence' of good teaching requires more than merely the achievement of keeping the 'class' participating, enjoying the lesson and remaining obedient.

Placek (1983) claimed that it was apparent that teachers and student teachers (in the United States) 'apparently view success very differently than do researchers who design studies to tease out variables of effective teaching'. She found that for most teachers and student teachers the dominant concerns in teaching physical education are to keep the children 'busy, happy and good'. She interviewed teachers and student teachers to determine how they conceived successful and unsuccessful lessons and concluded that, although almost half considered success related to student learning: 'Success, in many cases, is not Sharon or Bob learning to jump shot correctly. Success is related to the immediate, observable happenings in the gym. Are the students participating (busy), enjoying themselves (happy), and doing what the teacher directs (good)?' (p 54).

Good teaching, effective teaching and quality teaching: What is the difference?

You may have noticed in the above section that we have used the terms 'good', 'effective' and 'quality' with regard to teaching. Are these terms synonymous or do they have particular meanings which should be recognised to differentiate between them? In research terms, the search for the characteristics of *good* teaching became the search for the characteristics of *effective* teaching. More recently, in Australia, Britain and the United States, there have been a number of government inquiries into the nature of *quality* teaching. So why the difference in terminology? Is there some good reason why the terminology related to the issue of good teaching has changed over time?

The first important shift to understand is the introduction of the term 'effective teaching'. As we said, it was associated with the research movement which sought links between what teachers do in class (or in the gym) and what pupils learned. It made judgments concerning the degree to which the intentions of the teacher, in terms of achievement, were actually attained. An effective teacher was one who could achieve their stated objectives (usually expressed in behavioural terms). Effectiveness is part of the language of a more technical view of teaching which, within the United States at least, was associated with greater attempts to hold schools and teachers accountable for the academic achievement of pupils. The language of effectiveness was part of the discourses of accountability and school reform in the 1970s and 80s. The language of effectiveness was part of a broader social trend towards what has become known as 'technocratic rationality', in which technical answers (through the application of science) are sought to solve social problems, and efficiency and productivity are the dominant values.

Wilf Carr (1989) from Sheffield University has argued, along with many others, that when teaching and education are conceived in technocratic terms, the main focus becomes efficiency. Attention is drawn towards *how* particular goals can be achieved without adequate attention being given to the worthiness of these goals.

The teacher effectiveness movement was a result of this form of technocratic thinking and it had the tendency to position teachers as more like technicians than professionals. All a teacher needed to do to be judged effective was to successfully implement a curriculum designed by a specialist or curriculum 'expert'. Consideration of the worthiness, the educational purpose, of a curriculum activity was not necessary or even expected.

We share the concern with the use of the term 'effectiveness' in relation to the issue of good teaching. We prefer 'quality teaching' as a term which has the potential to move our attention beyond a focus merely on issues of effectiveness relating to the achievement of pre-specified objectives. However, 'quality' itself is not a word which solves the problem of technocratic thinking.

For Carr, 'identifying quality teaching requires making explicit whether the criteria being employed derive from intrinsic or instrumental values' (1989, p 3). In physical education it has been the pursuit of the instrumental values, such as improvement in fitness, which has been the focus of attention concerning good teaching. In the teacher effectiveness research within physical education little attention has been given to the intrinsic, educational values of physical education. As Carr argues, we need to bring these issues back into the debate over the nature of what quality in teaching actually means.

Notwithstanding this particular issue with respect to professionalism and intrinsic educational values, we believe that the term 'quality teaching' has the potential to move the debate beyond concern over 'mere' efficiency. It has the potential to represent a more comprehensive account of good teaching which serves the interests of all concerned with the issue. However, whatever term is used, there will always be contestation and disagreement as different interest groups emphasise aspects of teaching which they consider most important.

From our perspective, quality teaching is not an end-point but a *process*. Quality teaching should be a reflective process with respect to two fundamental questions: What are the implications for what I teach? and What are the implications for the way that I teach? In addition to the strategies that Siedentop (1991) and Mawer (1998) outlined, quality teaching should involve:

- the search for ways to make your lessons more meaningful, purposeful, just and enjoyable; and
- the conscious search for contradictions in our practice. These contradictions will be manifest in the difference between what we think we are doing and what we are actually doing; between what we think (or hope) students are learning and what they are actually learning.

Summary

- People will always make judgments regarding the nature of your teaching. Such judgments will be influenced by many factors, some of which will not be explicit.
- Over the years researchers have tried to identify the essence of good teaching. A variety of research measures have been used, ranging from rating scales to observation of actual lessons and systematic recording of teacher and pupil behaviour.
- Much of the descriptive research of what happens in lessons reveals a rather bleak picture of the general quality of physical education teaching.
- Time management (especially academic learning time, or ALT) has received considerable research attention in physical education. In general terms teachers are judged to be more effective when they use time wisely (i.e. they do not waste it) and the class gets plenty of activity.
- It cannot be assumed that what is intended to be learnt is what actually *is* learnt. The notions of the hidden, covert and null curriculum are important in this context.
- Notions of good, effective and quality teaching usually foreground certain teaching attributes while marginalising others. As such, these terms carry political assumptions and cannot necessarily be considered to mean the same thing.

References

Bain, L.L. (1990). 'Research in sport pedagogy: Past, present and future'. Paper presented at the AIESEP World Congress, Loughborough, UK.

Carr, W. (1989). *Quality in Teaching: Arguments for a Reflective Profession.* London: Falmer Press.

Cheffers, J. & Mancini, V. (1978), 'Teacher–student interaction'. In W. Anderson & G. Barrette (eds), *What's Going on in Gym? Motor Skills: Theory Into Practice* (Vol. Monograph 1,). New York: Teachers College Columbia.

Darst, P., Mancini, V. & Zabrajsek, D. (1989). *Analysing Physical Education and Sport Instruction* (2nd edn.). Champaign, IL: Human Kinetics.

Dodds, P. (1985). 'Are hunters of the functional curriculum seeking quarks?' *Journal of Teaching Physical Education*, (4)2, pp 91–100.

Griffin, P. (1981). 'One small step for personkind: Observations and suggestions for sex equity in coeducational physical education classes'. *Journal of Teaching in Physical Education*, Introductory Issue, pp 12–18.

Hellison, D. (1985). 'Goals and strategies for teaching physical education'. Champaign, IL: Human Kinetics.

Kirk, D. (1992). 'Physical education, discourse, and ideology: Bringing the hidden curriculum into view'. *Quest*, 44, pp 35–56.

Locke, L. (1977). 'Research on teaching in physical education: New hope for a dismal science'. *Quest*, 28, pp 2–16.

Macdonald, D. (1990). 'The relationship between the sex composition of physical education classes and teacher/pupil verbal interaction'. *Journal of Teaching in Physical Education*, 9, pp 152–163.

Mawer, M. (1995). *The Effective Teaching of Physical Education*. Essex: Longman.

McLeish, J. (1985). 'An overall view'. In B. Howe & J. Jackson (eds), *Teaching Effectiveness Research*. Victoria, BC: University of British Columbia.

Placek, J. (1983). 'Conceptions of success in teaching: Busy, happy and good?'. In T.T.J. Olson (ed.), *Teaching in Physical Education*. Champaign, IL: Human Kinetics.

Postman, N. (1986). *Amusing Ourselves to Death: Public Discourse in the Age of Show Business*. New York: Viking.

Postman, N. (1989). *Conscientious Objections: Stirring up Trouble about Language, Technology and Education*. London: Heinemann.

Rosenshine, B. & Furst, N. (1971). 'Research in teaching performance criteria'. In B. Smith (ed.), *Research in Teacher Education*. Englewood Cliffs, NJ: Prentice Hall.

Siedentop, D. (1982). 'Movement & sport education: Current reflections and future images'. Paper presented at the VII Commonwealth and International Conference on Sport, Physical Education, Recreation and Dance, Brisbane.

Siedentop, D. (1991). *Developing Teaching Skills in Physical Education* (3rd edn.). Mountain View: Mayfield Publishing Co.

Siedentop, D.M., Maud, C. & Taggart, A. (1986). *Physical Education Teaching and Curriculum Strategies for Grades 5–12*. Palo Alto: Mayfield.

Tinning, R. & Fitzclarence, L. (1992). 'Postmodern youth culture and the crisis in Australian secondary school physical education'. *Quest*, 44(3), pp 287–304.

Tousignant, M. (1982). 'Analysis of task structures in secondary physical education classes'. Unpublished PhD, Ohio State University, Columbus.

Wright, J. (1997). 'The construction of gendered contexts in single sex and co-educational physical education lessons'. *Sport, Education and Society*, 2(1), pp 55–92.

Further reading

Tinning, R., Kirk, D. & Evans, J. (1993). *Learning to Teach Physical Education*. Sydney: Prentice Hall.

chapter eighteen

objectives

By the end of this chapter you should be able to:

- recognise that pedagogy exists in a broader context than the specific lesson environment;
- appreciate how school demographics affect lesson delivery;
- understand how the ethos of the PE department is lived out in the lessons taken by teachers;
- comprehend how issues of class management are related in complex ways to teacher curriculum choices, personal circumstances for pupils and teachers, and a range of other non-technical issues;
- appreciate how teaching quality can be influenced by a range of factors, including the context.

Postcards from the field (a fictitious case study)

Before the observational practicum, Dr Sue Daniels had given every student teacher a handout which comprised three table-like pages that she called her 'cascading context'[1] framework. The three frameworks were meant to make explicit some of the contextual factors that cascade down from the broader social influences to individual physical education lessons. More specifically, the proposition that the model attempts to represent is the 'fallout' from economic, political and social arrangements as they affect education. Her model suggests that the fallout can be traced to school demographics, PE department ethos and purpose and, eventually, through programs and lessons to the actual quality of interactions between teachers and students.

Although there are limitations to linear representations of such complex phenomena, Figure 18.1 is an attempt to map the cascading context.

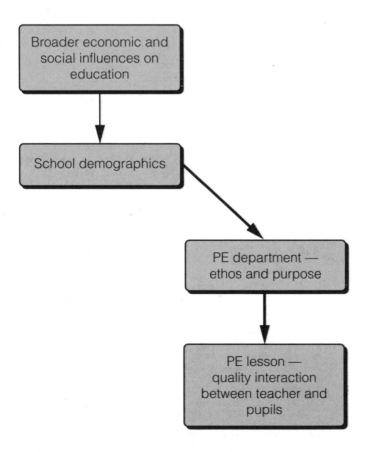

Figure 18.1 Cascading context of PE pedagogy

With the cascading context as the model, Dr Daniels presented the class with the following framework for guiding their observations on the practicum and recording what she called the 'pedagogy in context'.

What to look for at different levels of context

1. the school
- demographics/SES
- description of the school environment
- leadership (principal)
- parent/children demographics
- school mission/ethos?

2. the PE department
questions to ask of the PE teachers ... to observe:
- sense of enthusiasm for their work
- participation in decision making
- opportunities for professional development/nature of professional interaction
- goal congruence
- policy and practice?
- sense of efficacy (we can do this)
- resources to carry out the job?
- after-school commitments?
- interaction with non-PE staff?

3. the lesson
- what happened? (This can be done as a small story.)
- who made the decisions?
- where did the lesson fit?
- what strategies did you notice re class control/management?
- was there a lesson plan?
- what was the nature of the interaction between teacher and pupil ... feedback?
- was the lesson meaningful, purposeful, enjoyable and just? Was there a supportive environment?
- was there any assessment of achievement?
- was the lesson outcomes-based?
- was there any form of teacher reflection on the lesson?
- catering for inclusivity and difference
- opportunities to learn/time on task
- connection to key outcomes of KLA?

Dr Daniels suggested that although they would be collecting information on all dimensions of the framework simultaneously, they would be required to present their findings to the tutorial in the form of an account of the school context, the lesson processes, and then the PE department context. Also, when describing one of the lessons, they should take particular note of the participation of two pupils—one a top-level performer and the other a low-level performer.

Now, in the post-practicum tutorial, Philip, Mary and Rebecca got together as a group for the purposes of the tutorial task. Along with the other groups in the class, they spent the first 20 minutes discussing what they had observed from their particular practicum school.

Factors affecting practice: school demographics

Philip was first to give his account.

Seaview High

Background/SES

Seaview High was a relatively well-resourced government school in a middle class eastern suburb. The suburb developed in the 1950s and could generally be described as leafy. The school was on a major arterial road but was well set back behind the main ovals and the gymnasium. The grounds and buildings were well maintained and the impression was one of order and control. Nothing seemed out of place and the kids all wore uniforms that looked somewhat like those of the neighbouring private schools.

Leadership

Philip said he had a meeting with the principal in which he talked mainly about the DoE's policies and the difficulties of providing a comprehensive curriculum with decreasing funds. The principal was also at pains to highlight the 'exceptional' (his words) performance of the school in the Senior School Certificate results. Maintaining a strong academic performance he said was essential if the school was to compete with the private schools and other state secondary colleges in the surrounding region. If they failed to attract sufficient numbers of students then they would lose staff and be unable to offer a competitive range of subjects, thus further limiting their competitiveness.

In his two weeks at the school Philip never saw the principal outside the administration building. Teachers remarked that he was seldom ever seen in a classroom and certainly never took a walk down to see what was happening in the gym.

Parents/kids

From what Philip could ascertain most of the families were two-income households with the man (usually) in full-time employment and the mother (often) in part-time employment. Philip was surprised to hear that Seaview had a large proportion of first-generation Asian students (about 14%). The bulk of the school population was, however, of Anglo/European background, and all families (except for a few) spoke English at home. The kids did seem rather well behaved but Philip sensed that the school was 'keeping the lid on' by means of rules and sanctions. It did not have a relaxed, enjoyable feel to it.

Mary gave her account next.

Stonemeadows Secondary College
Background/SES

There was little doubt that Stonemeadows represented the other side of the track from Seaview. Stonemeadows was a rather down-at-heel collection of drab grey prefabs on a rocky, plain landscape in the developing western suburbs. Not a very inspiring setting was Mary's summation. The school had a large ethnic population with some 23 per cent of Asian origin (mainly Vietnamese), 45 per cent European (mainly Turkish, Serbian and Greek) and a smaller proportion of South American (mainly Chilean). Well over half of the kids did not speak English in their home. Unemployment in the region was very high and most families had at least one male adult unemployed.

Leadership

Mary told how she was personally briefed by the principal at Stonemeadows. She explained to Mary what her expectations for the school were and the leadership style that she preferred. Mary said that she talked a lot about the importance of providing a supportive and encouraging environment for all staff as she considered that this was a necessary (but not sufficient) ingredient for overall school effectiveness with respect to pupil achievement and development. The principal admitted that she believed physical education and sport was a very important curriculum vehicle for the socialisation of these children, for whom the English language academic curriculum was difficult and challenging.

Parents/kids

With so many of the parents being recently arrived migrants with little or no English language, their involvement in the life of the school was negligible. While many parents might have had expectations that their children would do well at school and then perhaps gain a good job, in practice they really didn't engage with the school or the expectations with regard to homework. Those parents who had found work tended to be doing menial factory or other manual work such as labouring. The disconnectedness between school life and home life was something that the children just had to live with. It was something that the school was trying to change. The range of experiences (some absolutely horrific) that some of these migrant (and refugee) kids brought to school as their 'background' was mind-boggling.

Rebecca gave her report last.

Church Girl's Grammar
Background/SES

Church Girl's Grammar (called Church for short) was off the scale in terms of resources. The overall impression was one of privilege. As an old established private school (founded in the early 1920s), Church had everything from a full-sized swimming pool (indoor!), two gyms, ivy covered cloistered classrooms, lush green playing fields, and specialist arts, music, drama, science, and info-tech complexes (more than just rooms).

Parents who sent their girls to Church would have had a combined household income in the top 5 per cent of the country. In most cases that income was earned by the father, who was a professional of some sort or who owned his own business. Accordingly, the school had a very high proportion of mothers that did not work outside the home. School drop-off and pick-up times saw the carpark packed with more than the odd Volvo, BMW or Range Rover. When some of the mothers of the senior students shared their experiences as Church mums, they jokingly (but also seriously) said they were really research assistants to their girls in the Senior School Certificate.

The girls who went to Church all seemed to have the sort of cultural capital that privilege and money provide. Obviously there were exceptions but, at least in Rebecca's eyes, all the girls seemed to be so . . . she struggled for the right word . . . sophisticated? No that's not quite it. (Frustrating how language lets you down sometimes.)

Leadership
Rebecca never met the principal (sorry, the headmistress) of Church but she was acutely aware of her influence in the school. Apparently the PE staff never saw her either (outside special assemblies and the like) but she was well respected and had high expectations of all staff.

Factors affecting practice: the PE department

Seaview High

* Craig was the most experienced of the four PE teachers at Seaview. He had been there for 12 years and was head of department. While Philip considered him to be still enthusiastic about his work, he definitely wasn't enthusiastic about new ideas and especially about the new KLA. The other three teachers, two women and a man, were much younger, having only been teaching for about three years each. They all seemed to know what they were doing but there wasn't much evidence that they talked much as a department. Craig tended to handle all the communication from above and merely reported to the others on the latest edit from 'headquarters', as he disparagingly called the admin. building.

    The PE staff at Seaview seemed to have relatively independent lives in terms of their teaching. In the two weeks that Philip was there they didn't have one staff meeting and he witnessed very little professional interaction between the four staff. Each teacher just got on with organising and teaching their classes and didn't (seem to) connect with what was going on in the other classes.

* Philip interviewed each of the PE staff separately and they all gave a similar story with respect to Craig's leadership. He led and they followed. Craig made most of the significant decisions regarding curriculum and usually defended it by saying that that was the way the school had always done it. The lack of participation in decision making was certainly an issue for the teachers but they seemed

resigned to just getting on with their work and not challenging Craig.

- It seemed that the staff were keen to attend professional development activities and openly discussed their participation in ACHPER short courses, school curriculum days and the annual state ACHPER physical education conference. Craig was less enthusiastic but did attend curriculum days, and always went to the ACHPER conference more to catch up with some of his old mates than to engage with some of the new ideas.

- There was a PE policy for the school, but when Philip asked to see it Craig gave it to him with a rather dismissive 'This is the sort of crap that we have to do for headquarters'. The other teachers were quick to say that they had no input into its development nor was there an explicit expectation from Craig that the policy actually guide their day-to-day practice.

- All the PE staff considered that they had sufficient resources at the school to do their job but, of course, there were additional things they had on their 'wish list'. Frank wanted to get a full class set of rollerblades, for example, and Jenny said she wished they had a separate dance/aerobics studio. Overall most of them considered that it was time rather than equipment or facilities that was the greatest impediment to their work.

Stonemeadows Secondary College

- According to Mary the PE staff at Stonemeadows were constantly engaging one another both formally in meetings and informally about their work. They often team-taught and had a very interactive/collaborative relationship.

- Probably the most visible thing about the PE department was its individual and collective enthusiasm for the work and the kids at Stonemeadows. Annie, the head of the department, had been at Stonemeadows for the past six years and each of the other three teachers for four, three and two years respectively. Annie was even learning Vietnamese at the local TAFE. It seemed to Mary that unperpinning their positive enthusiasm was a genuine love for their subject, a belief in the value of their subject for children in this particular context, and a deep belief in a 'fair go' for all these kids.

- From what Mary could ascertain, this department had a very democratic decision-making process. For example, three years ago when Eddie was first appointed to Stonemeadows, they all went to a seminar on sport education in physical education given by representatives of a project started in Western Australia. They were impressed by the account given of SEPEP by two of the WA teachers and they returned to Stonemeadows with a collective commitment to giving it a go next term. This was no HOD decision or edict—it was a genuine collective agreement and it was followed by considerable collaborative planning. When Mary talked to each of the staff separately, they all commented that they each had a say in the decisions of the department and that their contributions were taken seriously.

The SEPEP seminar was just one of the professional development activities that the PE department did as a team. But even when one of the staff attended an inservice there was always a reporting back discussion session that followed.

Importantly, some of these discussions occur at the pub after work on Fridays. Eddie is even doing his Masters via distance education and his assignments and readings are often the focus of discussion and argument among the four teachers of the PE department. One of Annie's frustrations is that in an increasingly busy context, time to interact professionally is increasingly hard to find.

- The PE policy was a nice example of the collaboration and shared decision-making process at Stonemeadows. Not only did the PE staff collectively write their policy, they did so in collaboration with the head of curriculum for the school and the principal. They all talked about how they felt that the PE program genuinely fitted in with the school curriculum and reflected the ethos of the school. The PE program goals were congruent with those of the school not only in policy but also in practice.

- There was no doubt that resources at Stonemeadows were average at best. Yes the PE department was always bidding for more equipment and, yes they did need another indoor teaching space for wet and inclement weather days. But the whole school needed more funding, not just PE, and there was a sense of being in it all together and coping with what they had. There were plans for a new school to be built but they were not holding their breath for that political promise to materialise. Importantly, there was an understanding that, although more resources would be great, what they had and the support they received from the principal was at least adequate to achieve their goals.

Church Girls Grammar

At Church the PE department (all seven of them) seemed to be constantly communicating about their teaching, particular children, and other general professional matters.

- One of the most impressive features of Church from Rebecca's perspective was the sense of enthusiasm that the teachers displayed for their work. The more sceptical side of her thought that it was probably due to the fact that their performance was constantly on the line in the private system but that didn't quite seem to gel with what she saw and heard. These teachers were committed to the children and the school. Rebecca did wonder if they had a life beyond school.

Significantly all the teachers were relatively young. Tracey was the HOD and she must have been in her mid-30s. All the other teachers, except Gabby, were in their 20s. Gabby was 32. Rebecca thought of the stereotype of enthusiasm and youth. She remembered Mr Jessie at her school and he was so enthusiastic and he must have been almost 50, for goodness sake. Also, there was Ms Falmer who, although only in her mid-20s, displayed no real enthusiasm for her teaching.

- In the two weeks at the school Rebecca sat in on two of the weekly debrief sessions held during a common spare period on Monday before lunch. Most of the major curriculum decisions had been made at the end of the previous year (they had a staff retreat for two days to work though some of those decisions), so Rebecca didn't see any shared decision making in that respect. However, there were many ongoing issues that required decisions and she did witness a collaborative spirit in the meetings. Tracey chaired the meetings and had a couple of matters 'from above' to raise before they got on to other matters. Overall the meeting was less reflective of their teaching (quality or purpose) and focussed mainly on dealing with admin. stuff. Notwithstanding this focus, there was a sense of collegiality that impressed Rebecca. She thought that she would like to work in this school.

- Tracey told Rebecca that they were all encouraged to do PD and their department received funding for teacher release of up to one day per term to attend PD seminars or activities. One particular inservice that they had recently attended as a staff was a workshop on 'Litigation and the PE teacher'.

- There was little doubt that the way in which the PE program was conducted at Church was congruent with their PE policy. Their policy, which was developed as a collaborative exercise with all the PE staff and the director of curriculum for the school, was explicitly related to the school policy and mission statement and also to the outcomes of the KLA.

- The resources to carry out the policy were abundant and reflected the central place of PE and sport in the ethos of the school. About the only thing that PE teachers seemed to want more of was time. That is, more lesson time for each student.

- One of the features of Church, and most other private schools of its status, is the extensive school sports program. Huge resources are committed to fielding teams in competition with other private schools. One Queensland boys' school is reported to spend in the order of $300,000 each year on rugby coaching and competition alone! At Church, all the PE staff coached at least one team and had out-of-school commitments to the teams, which occupied most of Saturday. With at least two nights a week training and Saturday competition, the commitment to the school was heavy to say the least. Rebecca wondered whether she could keep enthusiastic for years on end under such a demanding schedule.

Factors affecting practice: the lesson processes

Philip described the following lesson as somewhat representative of others he observed. In describing the lesson Philip also provided an insight into how two pupils with different abilities engaged with the lesson pedagogy.

At 11 o'clock on Wednesday morning coed class 7B made their way in an orderly manner to the netball court where Mr Rowe was finishing some minor arrangement of equipment.

The class was enthusiastic because they like Mr Rowe and their PE sessions with him. Well, most of them anyway. Craig began the lesson with a game of ball tag (one of the class 'favourite' games), in which two kids (a boy and a girl) are chosen as the throwers.

On a signal from Craig the class ran around inside the netball court (Craig knew to define the boundaries) attempting to avoid the balls which were thrown at them by the throwers. Some of the slower-moving children were the first to be hit by a ball and they then joined the team of throwers. David, who is somewhat overweight and less physically able than others in the class, was actively pursued as an easy early target. Craig noticed this but said nothing. As the game progressed it was only the most agile, like Sonia, who continued to avoid the ball until at last Greg called an end to the game with a shrill blast on his whistle. The class had been taught to stop immediately on the sound of the whistle.

Skill practice in pairs using soccer balls followed. Craig had the children pair off with a partner and then, on a signal from him, one person from each pair ran over to the nearest equipment basket and collected a ball. There was much pushing and shoving because the children all wanted to get the best balls. Some of the slower or less assertive children finished up with the oldest balls, which were coloured dull brown (instead of nice bright-coloured patches) and which didn't bounce as well as the newer ones. David got one of the oldest balls.

Equipped with their own ball the pairs practised passing the ball to one another from a distance of about 3 metres apart. Wendy was doing fine until Dave ran across her path in pursuit of his mis-kicked ball. Dave continued to have difficulty accurately directing the ball to his partner. Craig told him to use only the inside of his foot to pass because you get better control that way. Craig eventually stopped the class with the whistle blast and told them of the next activity. In this activity Sonia managed 15 accurate passes, Wendy 11 and Dave 6.

More paired ball-passing activities followed. During all the activities Craig gave some coaching points to the kids he saw doing the skill incorrectly (in terms of what might be defined as competent by an elite performer as a model). After these activities, the class were arranged into groups of four for a modified game of soccer passing. The object of the game was for three of the group to pass the ball from one to another while the fourth group member attempted to intercept the pass.

Craig let the kids pick their own fours and most of the groups were composed of either boys or girls. Only the kids who were left out of the choice teams were 'forced' to participate in coed groups. David finished up in a group with three girls. During this activity some of the groups failed to change over if the centre person could not intercept a pass, with the result that some children spent the entire time in the middle chasing and never got to actually practise the passing skill. Those children soon tired of chasing and just stood in the middle watching the ball being passed around them.

Craig walked around the groups and gave verbal 'encouragement' to the chasers: 'Come on, really try hard to get the ball', 'Don't give up when you miss it once', 'Mary, don't take so long to get your pass away' etc. In this activity, Sonia successfully intercepted the passed ball on each of the three times she was in the centre and had none of her foot passes intercepted. Wendy intercepted the ball twice and had the ball intercepted from her pass on two occasions. Dave had his first pass intercepted immediately and spent the rest of the time as chaser in the centre. He could not intercept the passes and the drill served to expose his lack of skill.

Following this activity Craig chose four team captains and asked them each to pick teams for relays. Craig chose Sonia and Dave as two of the captains. When the four teams were arranged he explained the rules of the relay race. Each kid was required to run and dribble the soccer ball around the obstacles, around the cone at the end and then back to the next kid in line.

When the relay began two boys failed to weave in and out of all the required obstacles. Craig noticed immediately and sent them back to repeat their run. Most kids took the requirements seriously and dribbled around all the obstacles. Dave was berated by some of the boys (the same two who previously cheated) in his team for taking too long. Throughout the entire relay, Craig stood to the side and encouraged the children to 'Go as fast as you can' 'Hurry up, he is catching you' etc.

The winning team was the first team finished and all sitting down. The fact that the first team to be seated had one less runner than the other team was completely overlooked by Craig. The other team members were at pains to point this out but their plea went unrecognised. Following the relay Craig instructed the class to have a quick shower, change and head out to lunch.

In analysing the lesson from the framework given by Dr Daniels, Philip made the following assessment:

• It seemed that the lesson was part of a unit on the development of soccer skills. Later in the unit they were to play some six-a-side games. Craig's explicit curriculum concerned giving the class practice at passing and trapping with a soccer ball, improving their skills at trapping and passing a soccer ball under pressure from opposition, and at dribbling a ball on the run as well as in a competitive situation. Probably Craig would admit that, although not in his formal plan, he also wanted the lesson to contribute to learnings in team work, cooperation, and good sporting behaviour. These aspirations are mostly covert rather than explicit.

- Craig didn't have any major control problems except when the kids were fighting over getting the best ball from the basket. He seemed to have done all the right things (at least those that Philip had been taught). He defined the area clearly, he kept all the class in view all the time, he arranged for plenty of activity so there generally wasn't a lot of waiting around, his voice was strong and he used a whistle to stop the class. For the children's part they generally did cooperate with each other and the teachers in the lessons.

- There was no doubt that Graig made all the significant decisions in the lesson. Kids got a say in who they grouped with but essentially that was all.

- The interactions between Craig and the class were underpinned by a tone of authority and the kids (mostly) did as they were told. Craig did give feedback but it certainly wasn't all positive (see Siedentop's comments on feedback in Chapter 17).

- Although Philip didn't see any lesson plan, he had seen Craig's work program and saw where this lesson fitted into the unit.

- Philip asked Craig about the connection of the lesson to the outcomes of the KLA and his response was rather casual: 'Yeah, all the things they are doing in the soccer unit can be connected with the human movement strand outcomes but I certainly don't bother to list them all for each lesson'.

- There didn't appear to be any form of ongoing recording of individual performance that might be connected to assessment. From what he had learned about outcomes-based education, it didn't seem to him that the lesson fitted that description, at least not in any explicit way. Craig did say that 'When you have been teaching as long as I have you just know what level the kids are at'.

- Philip wasn't exactly sure what teacher reflection would look like in practice and he had to ask Craig later whether he did reflect on the implications of what he taught and how he taught. 'When the lesson goes well I don't usually think much about it again . . . it's just on to the next lesson. But when something goes wrong or some kids really muck up then I think about why that happened', said Craig. Philip didn't think that was exactly what was meant by reflection but he didn't know what else to ask.

- In considering whether the lesson was meaningful, purposeful, enjoyable and just for all the children, Philip thought long and hard. He hadn't actually talked to all the kids about their experience of the lesson but he did get to talk to David, Wendy and

Sonia—the ones he 'tracked' in the lesson. From what he had observed he thought that David would have found the lesson unenjoyable whereas Sonia and Wendy would have enjoyed it. It didn't seem so simple. David, while recognising the frustrations he felt at certain times in the lesson (as in the passing skills practice), overall said that physical education was OK. Sonia on the other hand said she was bored in the lesson, while Wendy said she just loved PE. The extent to which the lesson was meaningful and purposeful was hard to judge. Although the children knew that the lesson was about soccer skills they were vague about the actual purpose of doing the selected activities. As to whether the lesson overall was just, Philip reckoned that there were quite a few instances when, for some kids like David, it was just plain unfair. He wondered whether Craig would have seen it that way.

Stonemeadows Secondary College

Before giving her account of a lesson she had observed, Mary said that she had expected that the kids at Stonemeadows would be 'off the planet' when it came to discipline and control. She admitted to preconceptions when judging the school. To her surprise, things were very different.

SEPEP

Mary was waiting at the basketball courts when the class arrived with their PE teacher Annie Constansi. A small group of kids were carrying the equipment which included basketballs, team bibs, timing clocks and even some chairs and a small fold-up table.

Annie gathered all the kids together and reminded them of their duties and responsibilities. Children readily volunteered information about what their roles were and then set off in their groups. In a very short time there were two six-a-side basketball games in progress with kids doing all the referring, scoring, team management and coaching. Annie, for her part, stood on the sidelines and occasionally offered some coaching advice.

As the games progressed the enthusiasm of the players increased. It was obvious to Mary that these kids were actually taking the game seriously. This wasn't the normal PE pick-up team with no-one really caring who won or lost. There was something important about the game and, more significantly, something very important about the teams. The kids really identified with their team and there was a sense in which even the gun players were supportive of the less skilled because it was in the team's best interest to have EVERYONE play to the best of their ability.

Mary watched the participation of two kids: Chin-Lo was a talented sportsperson with good ball skills and Tran was a low-skilled boy much smaller in stature than the other boys of the class. As the game progressed Chin-Lo gained many possessions and was generally effective in passing the ball to a team mate. On two occasions she scored a goal by a running layup technique that was practised in the drill sessions earlier in the term. Tran on the other hand continued to have difficulty with dribbling and often would pass the ball off in a panic rather than attempt to run and dribble. Mary saw Annie take Tran aside (there was always a substitute player ready to take to the court) on two occasions to give him some specific coaching on how to dribble. Most of the coaching was in demonstration form as Tran's English was still rather poor. Each time Tran returned to the game after coaching his fellow team members made a fuss of his return.

When the timing bell sounded both games ceased and Annie called all the players and officials together for a debriefing. Annie reminded the scorers to record the scores on the sport ed. board inside the gym. She then praised the class for their work and informed them that next week's class would be cancelled because of the excursion to ScienceWorks. There were some mumblings of discontent but she did remind them that their team could arrange to have their own practice after school and it was up to the sports board to arrange it if that's what they wanted. Annie reminded the equipment monitors to hang the bibs up on the hanger in the storeroom as they had found them. She then dismissed the class to shower and change and followed them over to the change room to monitor 'activities'.

- Mary was amazed by this lesson. It seemed that all the day-to-day decisions in the lesson were made by the children. They decided on their teams (in earlier sessions) and they stayed in their team for the entire 10-week SEPEP segment. Of course, the decision to do sport ed. and to focus on basketball for this term was made by Annie.
- This particular lesson was part of the 10-week sport ed. unit. The kids knew that they would be playing basketball for the entire term and that at the end of term there would be a series of play-offs against teams from other classes also doing sport ed. basketball. The season would end with considerable festival and excitement and this was a highlight of the term for many children.

This organisation was based on the requirements of the Sport Education in Physical Education Program as outlined in the *SEPEP Teachers' Manual* (Alexander et al 1995). SEPEP differs from what happens in conventional PE. The sport participation is organised in seasons rather than the short three-week block which typifies the multi-activity curriculum (see Siedentop et al 1986). It involves affiliation with a team for the duration of the season, it has formal schedules of competition, the keeping of records and a festive culminating event. Importantly, it is not seen as inter-school sport transposed onto the physical education timetable. Rather it is intended to be a true 'sport for all' experience.

- Annie didn't have a lesson plan as such. Instead she had a detailed outline of the sport ed. unit with key events, possible coaching points, and the major social and performance outcomes she had listed in the form of the KLA outcomes from the human movement, physical activity and the community, and social relations strands.
- Class control and management were actually transferred to the class. For example, those students who were refereeing (apparently they all rotated such positions so that during the term they each had a turn at all roles) were responsible for applying the rules of the game. When disputes occurred it was the sports board committee that considered what decision was needed. Annie acted as an adjudicator only when the sports board could not reach agreement.
- One of the most obvious features of the lesson for Mary was the interaction between the teacher and the class. The teacher had set up a context in which she didn't have to be 'centre stage', as she called it. Instead, students were given responsibilities and these responsibilities were taught. Annie was the overseer to whom students would report if they had a problem that they couldn't deal with. But then that was one of the chief outcomes that Annie was working on developing—a sense of responsibility along the lines of Hellison's (1985) model (see Chapter 14).
- It certainly seemed that the lesson was meaningful and purposeful for the class. The kids did enjoy SEPEP and this was obvious in their enthusiasm. The environment was supportive in that team members were encouraging of each other no matter what their skill level. Of course, as Annie admitted, things were far from perfect. This was the first season and there was much to learn.

 ## for your information

Data from a study by Terri Carlson (1995) suggest that the three components that distinguish SEPEP from regular PE (namely time, team affiliation, and increased student responsibility) were clearly linked: 'Time was needed for students to develop a team commitment and an acceptance of the strengths and weaknesses of individual team members. Time was needed for the less skilled player to improve and the others to realise that it was worth investing energy into their team members. The teacher no longer had sole responsibility for improving students' performance. Students began to realise that blaming a low skilled player for their loss would not help the team. They began to coach and encourage. Lower skilled players began to realise that, with practice and coaching, they could make a contribution to the team' (p 8).

However, Curnow & Macdonald (1995) warn that 'a sport education unit can simply provide the opportunity for many students to live out their stereotypical understandings, particularly given the student-centred pedagogy' (p 9).

- It was clear that Annie had planned her lesson(s) in relation to the progressive attainment of key learning outcomes from the KLA. Apparently the PE department at Stonemeadows had been chosen to trial the KLA back in the mid 1990s when it was being developed and they had since been committed to the idea of using learning outcomes as the major orienting focus for their work.

- Although Annie recorded some notes on the participation of a few pupils at the end of the lesson, actual reflection on the lesson in terms of the implications for what was taught and how it was taught wasn't obvious to Mary. Of course, when she thought about it she realised that these two reflective questions were in fact implicit driving questions which got their PE department to engage in SEPEP in the first place. Moreover, they did meet as a department at the end of each week and collectively reflect on the week's lessons.

- When Mary considered the extent to which the lesson catered for inclusivity and difference, she concluded that the very nature of SEPEP seemed to offer something for everyone. The different roles were not gendered and they did demand a variety of skills and abilities, not all of which were physical performance. The fact that the focus was on basketball rather than a non-ball game activity was perhaps an issue but she realised that the time frame of the yearly curriculum was more appropriate as a unit of analysis for that issue. If over the entire year they did only team ball games then that would become an issue.

- Athough Mary didn't record the actual time-on-task (or more specifically the ALT-PE) for Chin-Lo and Tran she was confident that they both received plenty of activity in the lesson. Annie's withdrawal of Tran from the game to give specific skill practice seemed most appropriate for his level of skill development. On the other hand Chin-Lo was active throughout the entire game in both offensive and goal-shooting moves and also in defensive strategies. Mary had the impression that all the class was similarly engaged in its tasks throughout the game.

Church Girls Grammar
Rebecca seemed rather captivated by her observations of Church. The lesson she observed and recorded for this tutorial task was an aerobics/fitness class in the dance studio.

Gabrielle entered the dance room from the door which led from her office and the gym. Everything was close to hand at Church. This group of girls, 18 in all, had chosen to do aerobics as their fitness unit and were in their second week of a six-week unit. There were two sessions per week. Other girls from year 8 were in one of three other groups. One group was doing power-walking/jogging on the beach (Church has access to a long stretch of the bay). Another group worked in the school cardio-room doing conditioning work on bicycle and rowing ergometers, walking on treadmills and lifting light weights. The remaining group was doing an aquatics fitness program in the school pool.

As they entered the room Gabrielle reminded them of their warm-up routine and asked Margo to lead a group warm-up. After the first few stretches Gabrielle interrupted to emphasise a point about correct technique and then asked Tan to take over. Each girl seemed to take the responsibility seriously and the rest of the class performed the stretches with purpose.

Rebecca remarked that the uniform of the girls in PE intrigued her. There was a wide range of apparel including baggy board shorts, tight bicycle shorts, baggy t-shirts, singlets, leotards and even tracksuits. The common link was that they were all in the school colours of purple and gold and the girls mixed and matched as they liked. The main deal was that they felt comfortable.

After the 5-minute warm-up each girl took her own resting pulse rate (they had been taught how to do this in the previous session) and recorded it on a green card which was to be used across all the sessions to chart their progress. Six of the girls actually wore a new heart rate monitor belt which automatically recorded their heart rate. The PE department had invested in half a dozen of these new gadgets to test their efficacy for use in the fitness sessions.

Gabby asked Jane to select a CD and the 20-minute aerobics session began. From Rebecca's perspective there was nothing special about the aerobics itself. The girls were well spaced around the floor and Gabby led the class from a raised platform at the front. Like all good aerobics instructors Gabby did everything in the mirror image of the class. When the girls were to move to the right, she moved to her left (which was the left for the class). She constantly shouted enthusiastic comments to the girls as a class ('Push your hands up high and it's up, up, down, down') and she even gave some encouraging comments to individual girls ('That's great Imira, you are really in tune').

Rebecca had decided to focus attention on one girl in a leotard outfit and one in a tracksuit. She figured that they might be at different ends of the performance spectrum. She was right. Natasha was energetic, lithe and extremely well coordinated. Belinda was a rather reserved, big girl who had some trouble keeping up with the speed of coordinated movements. Rebecca followed the two girls intently. Both girls worked hard throughout the session but at times Belinda let the rhythm and pace *of the movements go on without her. She just slowed down and joined back in when she was ready. Gabby directed a couple of encouraging comments specifically at Belinda and Rebecca sensed that Belinda felt good about the encouragement. Natasha for her part could have been out the front leading the session. She knew all the moves and was genuinely enthusiastic throughout the entire session.*

When the music stopped all the girls lay on their backs and took their pulse. The girls with the HR monitors simply pressed a button to reveal their pulse rate. They recorded the figure on their green chart and then rested for a few minutes as Gabby walked around them praising them for their effort. It was obvious to Rebecca that the fitness levels of the girls ranged widely as within a few minutes some of the girls had completely recovered while others were still visibly red-faced and puffing. Another pulse check and recording after 5 minutes and then Gabby instructed them to have a shower and go to their next class.

- After the lesson Gabby explained how the aerobics sessions and the activities done by other groups fitted into the fitness unit. All the girls had to chart their progress over the six-week program to measure their improvement. They also had to keep a journal in which they recorded their feelings about the exercise program and notes on the discussion sessions (separate from the practical sessions) they had had in the first, third and sixth week. The class discussions were about the value of fitness, the commodification of the (female) body, the myth of the perfect body and the problem of excessive exercising. Gabby said the girls were very candid in their journals and they were also encouraged to include stories of their experiences and clippings from newspapers and magazines to add to their discussion.
- There was no doubt that this was a teacher-directed lesson. Gabby made most of the important decisions. Choice of music was left to the girls. Although the pace of the aerobics was set by Gabby, she had made it explicit that girls were to make their own rest periods throughout if they were getting fatigued. Gabby did explain that for the last two sessions she was going to get the girls to run the entire session and she was giving them some more responsibility each week.
- As seemed to be the case generally at Church, discipline and class control didn't seem to be an issue. Typically the classes were enthusiastic and well behaved. Gabby did explain that there is a discipline strategy that is implemented if someone misbehaves. The strategy is consistent throughout the school and consists of warnings and detentions. Rebecca thought that a detention on Saturday morning was a powerful deterrent . . . for the teachers who supervise the detention as well as the students!
- Gabby did say that they are very big on preventive management

strategies. That is, they plan strategies to minimise the chances of misbehaviour. Giving the girls some choices in the activities they do and planning for the avoidance of long waiting periods during any activity are two such strategies. Of course, increasing choice and personal responsibility is not just a management strategy. It is fundamentally a philosophy about what educational outcomes are worth pursuing.

• Rebecca asked Gabby if she did lesson plans for such sessions. 'Not in a formal sense', was her reply. Rather, she did have a detailed outline of the unit of work in terms of the activities and the outcomes she wished to develop. She described her teaching as outcome-focussed but not specifically outcome-based. In other words, she identified certain outcomes from the KLA (in particular outcomes in the human movement, physical activity and community strands) and she worked towards their attainment by the end of the unit. She didn't use the lesson as a unit of analysis in the sense that she checked to see whether particular outcomes were developed in specific lessons.

• The record cards were a measure of achievement in relation to improvements in fitness for the girls. But Gabby did realise that girls like Natasha had already came to the class with a high level of aerobic fitness and the two sessions per week weren't likely to improve this at all. On the other hand, for the Belindas of the class they would see marked improvements over the six-week period. The journals also provided a record of the way in which the girls were engaging with the issue of fitness. Gabby collected the journals for a progress check at the end of the third week and then for assessment at the end of term.

• Even though all girls were doing the same activity, Gabby did provide both class and individual feedback to the girls. Typically the feedback was in the form of encouragement. Rebecca wondered whether what they had learnt earlier in the tutorial on quality teaching about the nature and type of feedback given to girls (see Jan Wright's 1997 research mentioned in Chapter 17) was happening in Gabby's class. One thing was certain, however: the lesson did seem to be enjoyable for all the girls. Indeed, Mary looked hard at each and every girl to see if there were signs that they were not enjoying the session. She noted that Belinda, even when she struggled to keep up, was generally smiling and laughing. There was a strong sense that the girls all liked Gabby and it was obvious that she cared for them. Rebecca found Gabby's enthusiasm and commitment to 'her girls' as she called them to be genuinely inspirational.

• There was no doubt in Rebecca's mind that Gabby had created a supportive environment in which the activities were both enjoyable and just. Discussions with some of the girls during recess confirmed that they could see the purpose in the fitness unit and the activities they chose were meaningful for them in working towards the purpose. There was no sense in their just doing the activities for their own sake—they were all done with specific intent.

- Gabby didn't sit down at the end of each lesson and consciously reflect on her teaching. Rather, she and the other PE teachers met each week on a formal basis to discuss their work in general. With seven teachers in the department there wasn't really any time to get into the details of particular lessons but they did reflect on the extent to which there were factors which were limiting the possible achievement of their stated outcomes. Judgments, for example, about the implications for what they taught were made at the department level when they set out the curriculum.

Observations in the BIG picture

For the next tutorial task Dr Daniels arranged everyone into small groups of three for discussion. Mary sat down around a small table with Philip and Rebecca. Dr Daniels asked them to come up with a framework that they could agree on for judging the quality of the lessons they had observed and recorded.

Rebecca was quick to explain that, in her opinion, Gabby's teaching was 'fantastic'. She defended the claim by saying that Gabby was so enthusiastic and encouraging of the students and, from what she saw, the students all enjoyed physical education and there were no hassles or class behaviour problems. She wrote down on their shared overhead transparency (which they would have to reveal to the class in the plenary time) three descriptors which she said summed up her judgment: enthusiasm, class control, and pupil enjoyment.

Philip was less than effusive in his judgment of Craig's performance. Although he had basically managed the class OK, with the exception of the fiasco of distributing the balls, Philip said that Craig's lesson seemed to lack enthusiasm. It was as if Craig was just going through the motions. So when Rebecca asked him what he reckoned were the three main things that would define a good teacher of physical education, Philip agreed with what Becki had already written.

Mary's judgment, however, of Annie Constansi's teaching was rather more sophisticated. In the first instance she agreed that there had to be a level of class management and control or else 'everything would be chaos'. But she did say that she thought that what the kids learnt in and from the lesson seemed to be a necessary consideration for a judgment on quality of teaching. She asked: 'What if the teacher was enthusiastic, say, about fitness, but the enthusiasm was seen by some students as more gung ho and that turned those kids off fitness? That would hardly be good teaching, would it?'. Philip and Becki agreed but decided that that was taken for granted in their judgments.

After more discussion they were happy enough to record enthusiasm (but not zealotry), class management and control, pupil enjoyment and pupil learning as the Big Four for consideration in judging quality teaching. In the class plenary that followed a number of other groups identified the same dimensions. A couple of groups claimed that the teacher needed to be a role model in terms of their physique (not fat or out of shape) and in terms of their demonstration of what they wanted the class to do. There was considerable argument over that point.

Note

1 This conceptual framework was devised by Ken Alexander from Edith Cowan University (1999).

References

Alexander, K. (1999). The 'cascading context of pedagogy': Thoughts on a conceptual model. Unpublished paper, Edith Cowan Unverisity, Perth.

Alexander, K., Taggart, A. & Thorpe, S. (1995). 'Government and school contexts for the development of sport education in Australian schools'. *ACHPER Healthy Lifestyles Journal*, 42(4), pp 4–6.

Carlson, T. (1995). ' "Now I think I can". The reaction of eight low-skilled students to sport education'. *ACHPER Healthy Lifestyles Journal*, 42(4), pp 6–9.

Curnow, J. & Macdonald, D. (1995). 'Can sport education be gender inclusive? A case study in an upper primary school'. *ACHPER Healthy Lifestyles Journal*, 42(4), pp 9–12.

Hellison, D. (1985). *Goals and Strategies for Teaching Physical Education*. Champaign, IL: Human Kinetics.

Siedentop, D.M., Maud, C. & Taggart, A. (1986). *Physical Education Teaching and Curriculum Strategies for Grades 5–12*. Palo Alto: Mayfield.

Wright, J. (1997). 'The construction of gendered contexts in single sex and co-educational physical education lessons'. *Sport, Education and Society*, 2(1), pp 55–92.

Further reading

Mawer, M. (1995). *The Effective Teaching of Physical Education*, Harlow: Longman.

chapter nineteen

objectives

By the end of this chapter you should be able to:
- appreciate some of the legal responsibilities that confront the teacher of physical education;
- understand the notions of legal duty of care and foreseeability;
- comprehend the limitations and precautions necessary in situations where physical contact with a pupil is necessary or warranted;
- recognise potential instances in which a teacher might be deemed to be negligent.

Duty of care

The teacher–pupil relationship has a built-in legal duty requiring teachers to care for their pupils (Tronc 1996). When an accident should not have happened and where injury was preventable, then it is likely that claims of teacher negligence will be made.

> *Negligence is a tort, or civil wrong, where the injured person usually claims compensation from the other party who has caused the injury. Normally a court action is contemplated, liability is alleged and damages are sued for. (Tronc 1996, p 4)*

What the teacher has neglected is their *legal duty of care*. The legal concept of negligence has these main components: there is a duty of care; there is a breach of that duty of care; and there is a resultant injury which should have been foreseen.

The level of care which teachers must exercise is escalating under the pressure of an increasingly litigious society. The level of care required is affected by factors such as: the age and capacity of the pupil, the pupil's prior reputation for trustworthiness, and the nature of the activity.

> *The most common kinds of negligence in our schools are those where the teacher fails to intervene when any reasonable person would perceive and foresee a danger and would step in to stop the risky activity. (Tronc 1996, p 22)*

Teachers should therefore be aware that doing nothing can be negligent. In order to prevent dangerous behaviours, teachers need to make class rules for safety well known, consistently enforce them and repeat them when necessary. When doing so, teachers need to pay particular attention to ascertain that the students understand the instructions. The students' age, ability to comprehend and levels of English need to be considered.

A legal duty of care exists during school hours and these extend to school activities before or after school, at weekends, and both on and off the school campus (i.e. it exists on camps, excursions, sporting fixtures and the like). For excursions teachers must take into account a range of additional factors such as: reliable and safe transport; supervision of students during transportation; the use of private cars; parental permission notes. In seeking permission for students to participate in an excursion, teachers must provide all significant information in order that the parent can make an informed decision.

Foreseeabiltiy is particularly important for teachers of physical activity. They need to step back from their practices and try to envisage what accidents could possibly occur and institute routines or practices which should avoid all foreseeable accidents. Obviously the skills of monitoring and reflecting (see Chapter 16) and of lesson planning (see Chapter 13) would be useful here. Also, the state education authority safety manuals would be of value. On the basis of foreseeable injuries the manuals outline in detail what precautions

should be taken. It is the school's responsibility to ensure those manuals are accessible and the teachers' responsibility to use them in planning activities.

The area of teachers' and schools' liability for pupil safety is complex, constantly shifting. However, it is essential that student teacher and teachers are fully informed with respect to school procedures for punishment, excursions, safety etc. We should also be aware that there are differences across the Australian states and across school systems within states. For example, teachers in non-government schools are more likely to be judged as acting *in loco parentis* (receiving authority by direct delegation from parents) than those teachers in government schools in which the state is responsible for the provision of schooling (Tronc & Sleigh 1989).

Limited research

To date there has been very little research conducted into the issue of physical education teachers' legal responsibilities. One useful exception is the honours thesis of Kate Middleton (1999). According to Middleton physical education teachers are required to respond to many demands in their work. One of the most problematic demands on them has been the recent increase in the standard of care they are expected to provide for their students. This increase has changed physical education:

> *Overall, participants displayed a basic understanding of their fundamental legal obligations such as duty of care, the duty to foresee dangerous*

conditions, the duty to provide adequate supervision and instruction, and the duty to provide safe equipment and facilities. (p 149)

Three major findings of her study were that:

- most of the teachers were found to have a basic but sometimes superficial and incomplete understanding of their legal obligations;
- most of the teachers could have improved the safety of their daily practice by obtaining a deeper understanding of legal concepts and best professional practice; and
- teachers' legal obligations were found to affect curriculum decision making by contributing to the elimination of particular activities.

Child abuse and neglect

Teachers are often in a position to detect child abuse—physical, emotional, sexual and that caused by neglect. Consequently teachers are one group that has a *mandatory* obligation to report suspected cases of abuse although the specifics vary across states and territories. Child protection documents in most states clearly outline teachers' responsibilities in this area.

Teachers should note, however, that abuse can occur in schools. Teachers can be part of this abusive system through belittling comments, and from refusal to intervene where students are being teased or victimised. In other words, through erring by omission.

Dangerous liaisons

Sexual contact

Anecdotal evidence suggests that young HPE teachers, predominantly male, are particularly vulnerable to sexual innuendo regarding relationships with female students. Upper secondary school classes are usually more relaxed and personal than other teaching/learning contexts. Furthermore, young teachers are frequently posted to schools away from their families and friendship systems in isolated communities where their social relationships develop in and around school life. In these circumstances, it is tempting for young teachers to form friendships with students. However, this is fraught with danger. At all times a teacher needs to be in a position to instruct, assess or reprimand all students without favour or the perception that favouritism may emerge.

Teachers must take the greatest care not to place themselves in compromising situations where allegations can made against them. Where teachers receive 'love letters' from students, these are best ignored. It is illegal for a teacher to be alone with a student.

Physical contact

Should you avoid ever touching a child? No, but in doing so teachers need to be cognisant of where one touches, for what reason and for how long. In physical education, the need to touch children is increased in the instructional process. This may involve physically positioning a student in order to refine a skill or supporting a student during a performance such as spotting in gymnastics. It is generally advised that students be informed of the necessity of physical contact in some activities (e.g. spotting in gymnastics) and that they be permitted to choose not to participate if that is their wish.

While teachers can be sued as individuals for negligence in the course of their work, it is far more likely that teachers are supported through vicarious liability arrangements whereby employers take general responsibility for the actions of their employees.

Contact sport is clearly a site for potential injury, more so in a competitive situation. However, the same principles apply; the teacher must:

- give appropriate duty of care;
- foresee danger points/activities;
- provide adequate support and instruction; and
- provide safe equipment and facilities.

 over to you

In your tutorial discuss the following case histories and the court judgments made in each case. Identify the main issue of negligence (if negligence is claimed) and what could/should have been done about it.

Discuss the way in which you might modify or change your teaching on the basis of concerns regarding injury and litigation.

Case 1

A warning unheeded

A case illustrating the foreseeability principle was *Watson v Haines* 1987 (Australian Torts Reports 80-094), often referred to as the *Longnecked Footballer Case*.

This was a case involving quadriplegia suffered by a 15-year-old schoolboy when a rugby scrum collapsed. The New South Wales Minister for Education, Mr Paul Landa, had been warned of the risk. The danger had been foreseeable and yet nothing had been done. The Honourable Mr Justice Allen of the New South Wales Supreme Court scathingly attacked the incompetence of the educational bureaucracy.

Dr Yeo, an internationally recognised expert in spinal injuries, had become aware of numerous cases of footballers with long, thin necks becoming victims of spinal injuries. He produced a high-quality audiovisual guide warning schools of the potential foreseeable dangers. The Minister for Education had previously spent many years as an advocate in workers' compensation cases and would have been able to understand the significance of a warning of this kind from a medical expert.

The Minister for Education gave Dr Yeo nine minutes of his time in 1980 to look at the audiovisual materials, together with the head of the department's materials and information division. The Minister said the audiovisual materials were excellent and told his divisional head to arrange for their distribution to schools. Dr Yeo had 300 of the kits to give to schools.

The departmental official regarded the matter as low-priority and did not distribute the kits to schools. Because there were more than 300 schools, he came to the conclusion that the 300 gift kits were of little use to the department. As a compromise, he placed 100 of the kits in resource centres, available for borrowing by schools. The advertising of the kits' availability was not more than an ineffective token gesture. Teachers were unaware of the kits, no schools borrowed them, and they lay forgotten and unused.

The victim, Watson, had a long, thin neck and, therefore, to the explicit knowledge of the Department of Education, was a person foreseeably at serious risk of spinal injury if he were to play in the front row of a football scrum.

If the audiovisual kit had been used and the message had been promulgated, the boy would very likely have been saved from life in a wheelchair.

The education department attempted to offload responsibility, blaming its teachers. It argued that the teachers would have ignored any warnings had they been given. There was not any evidence to support this, and the judge was withering in his criticism of the education department for its efforts at buck-passing.

The judge described the case as extraordinary. High-level bureaucrats had ignored clear expert advice of foreseeable danger, and had failed to understand the urgency of a warning about likely impending injury. They had been warned, and the foreseeability was clear, that permanent paralysis could be the result of a failure to act.

Case 2

The trampoline

This case involved a busload of secondary school students with their two teachers arriving at a weekend camping venue where the activities centred on physical education and science.

As the students alighted from the bus they were confronted with a row of trampolines, which generated much excitement. The teachers warned the students off, however, telling them that trampolines were dangerous if you did not know what you were doing and they would therefore be out-of-bounds until the next afternoon. At that time, formal instruction would be provided and the teachers would be available as catchers and supervisors. And so to bed.

The next morning the teachers woke to the sound of much activity around the trampolines. As the students appeared to be competent—and, anyway, breakfast was imminent—the teachers chose not to intervene. A girl lost control, her head made heavy contact with the metal frame, and she was turned into an instant quadriplegic.

This was teacher negligence. They had breached their duty of care. Injury—foreseeable injury—had directly resulted. They had failed to intervene when they saw the students doing the very thing that they had told the students was dangerous a few hours earlier. They had failed to follow up their own rule. They had foreseen danger and turned a blind eye. The girl had disobeyed instructions, but the liability was primarily theirs, although the injured girl lost some of her compensation claim because of her own contributory negligence.

Case 3

The line in the ground

This case involved a teacher who very sensibly spent some time warning students playing a game of softball under her supervision not to encroach on the batting area when they were waiting their turn to bat. Otherwise, she said, they could be hit by a swing of the bat, or perhaps by a flung ball. To reinforce her point, she drew a line on the ground with a cricket stump and hammered the stump into the ground on that line, warning the students that they must stay behind the stump and behind the line.

Time passed. From where the teacher was standing, she could see all the class except one, the scorer. When she turned to ask the score, a boy waiting his turn to bat was hit between the eyes with a bat and suffered serious injury.

Was this an 'out-of-the-blue' incident and, therefore, not negligence? No, it was negligence. The teacher had not sufficiently intervened to ensure her students' safety.

Over a series of batting-side changes, the waiting teams had progressively moved forward, knocking over the stump, crossing the line and sitting where the teacher had previously foreseen danger. She did not send them back often enough. A teacher must keep on intervening, keep on telling students, as often as is necessary.

Telling students just once does not provide ongoing legal protection for a teacher. Young, willful, curious or disobedient students have to be protected from the folly of their often dangerous inexperience, whenever and wherever the need for intervention arises. As it often does.

Case 4

Gymnastics assessment

Jodie Bowen, a year 12 student at St Dymphna's Secondary College, suffered a fracture to her right elbow when she fell while performing a gymnastic manoeuvre (vaulting over a vaulting horse) during a physical education period at school. At the time, she was practising the manoeuvre in readiness for a formal assessment. She had protested to the teacher about having to take the test, having been away on the day that class instruction had been given on the manoeuvre. Two other students with a similar lack of knowledge and skill also protested and were excused. Jodie Bowen, by contrast, was required to prepare and practise for the test.

Formal instruction in the manoeuvre was not provided by the teacher, who delegated this role to another student. The teacher did not supervise the vaulting practice but sat with her back to the vaulting horse, supervising another class in tumbling exercises. The mats provided for the vaulting exercise were not the thick type normally used for vaulting manoeuvres, but tumbling mats with less protective capacity. The teacher did not direct any 'catchers' to support Jodie as she completed the execution of the manoeuvre.

Although Jodie Bowen was not the 'immature' child described in some of the cases, being beyond the age of compulsory schooling, and present at the college of her own choice, nevertheless the duty of care remained in the general instructor–learner relationship. There was a foreseeable risk of injury associated with a hazardous activity (as acknowledged in safety handbooks for physical education); and there was demonstrable causality in the teacher's requiring Jodie Bowen, against her protests, to undertake an unsupervised, dangerous activity without prior adequate training.

On the basis of the reported cases and the summary of Jodie Bowen's accident, you should be of the opinion that Jodie has good prospects of success in an action for negligence against the school authority and the teacher concerned.

Summary

- Teachers can be held to be negligent if they do not exercise adequate duty of care with respect to their pupils.
- Legal duty of care is a complex notion which involves recognition of such factors as: the potential danger of a situation; avoiding danger where possible; providing appropriate instruction; consideration of contextual factors such as a pupil's age and experience; and providing safe facilities and equipment.
- Teachers have a legal responsibility to report instances of physical, emotional, sexual abuse and/or neglect.
- Teachers should avoid circumstances in which possible sexual innuendo might be attributed to a liaison with a pupil.

References

Middleton, K. (1999). 'Physical education teachers' understanding and concerns regarding their legal obligations and implications for practice'. Unpublished B.Ed (Phys Ed) Honours thesis, University of Ballarat, Ballarat, Vic.

Tronc, K. (1996). *You, Your Schools and the Law: Legal Advice and Guidance for Teachers and Administrators in Today's Schools*. Brisbane: Fernfawn Publications.

Tronc, K. & Sleigh, D. (1989). *Australian Teachers and the Law*. Sydney: Butterworths.

Further reading

Christiansen, M. (1986). 'How to avoid negligence suits: Reducing hazards to prevent injuries'. *Journal of Physical Education, Recreation and Dance*, 57(2), pp 46–52.

Clement, A. (1988). *Law in Sport and Physical Activity*. Dubuque, IA: Benchmark Press.

Conn, J. (1993). 'The litgation connection: Perspectives of risk control for the 1990s'. *Journal of Physical Education, Recreation and Dance*, 64(2), pp 15–61.

Brown, S. (1993). 'Selecting safe equipment: What do we really know?'. *Journal of Physical Education, Recreation and Dance*, 64(2), pp 33–35.

Swan, P. (1997). 'Could gymanstics "as activity and as teaching" be the litmus test of a changing profession?'. *ACHPER Healthy Lifestyles Journal*, 44(2), pp 14–18.

chapter twenty

In his book *The Art of the Long View*, Peter Schwartz (1998) wrote that at a time when the world's major oil companies were adopting a siege mentality towards future oil production issues, the Shell Oil Company employed futurists to help them work on 'what-if' scenarios. In discussing the implications of one of the scenarios, company directors were able to set in motion changes which meant that when the 'unthinkable' oil crisis of the 1970s actually happened, it was the only company to be prepared. In our view, contemplating future scenarios may be just as significant for our profession.

According to Richard Slaughter (1996), how we think about the prospects of the future is very much a product of our history. Guessing the type of professional world you will work in at the start of the new century is an exercise in crystal ball gazing. But there are trends for which we can witness and project possible (though not necessarily likely) scenarios. Some of the trends include:

- government cost-cutting in education;
- downsizing in schools and universities;
- outsourcing as a strategy for cost-cutting;
- the increased significance of fitness as a major component of health;
- the rise of sport education as a concept;
- the privatisation of school physical education delivery;
- the increasing use of computer technologies in fitness monitoring;
- the increasing use of video surveillance in schools; and
- the increasing connection between the TAFE sector and universities.

One way or another you will need to develop an *informed* position with respect to the potential impact of such trends on the practice of physical education in schools and universities. A siege mentality—that is, pretending such scenarios will never happen or that it will be business as usual for physical education in the first few decades of this century—will not work. Remember that many of our field's senior professionals have expressed concern over the survival of physical education in secondary schools (see Locke 1998, Siedentop 1993 and Kirk 1996). Many have called for a radical rethink of the subject.

According to Stephen Covey (1990), 'our paradigms affect the way we interact with other people' (p 28). Moreover, 'if we want to make relatively minor changes in our lives, we can perhaps appropriately focus on our attitudes and behaviours. But if we want to make significant, quantum change, we need to work on our basic paradigms' (p 31).

In talking about paradigms, Deepak Chopra (1993) suggests that what is holding us back from envisioning new possibilities (for example, in physical education) is 'our conditioning, our current collective worldview that we were taught by our parents, teachers, and society. This way of seeing things—the old paradigm—has aptly been called "the hypnosis of social conditioning", an induced fiction in which we have collectively agreed to participate' (p 3). We, like you, are a product of our experiences (and our genes), so when we conjure up scenarios for the future of physical education we naturally construct them from our particular ways of seeing the world (paradigms).

Keeping that limitation in mind, here are three scenarios that we have constructed which pick up on (or play out) some of the trends mentioned above.

Scenario 1: circa 2001

The screen Oliver is watching suddenly goes blank. 'Computer on', he shouts, 'Computer on'. The time appears on his monitor and his worst fears are realised. It's 3 pm and Oliver's afternoon education session is about to come online. Frantically, he pushes the buttons on his remote control and his mother appears on the screen, 'Can we override today please mum, I don't want to . . .'. 'No Oliver', interrupts his mother, 'we can't override, you have to do your classes. I'm not making any more excuses for you. You're going to sit there and you're going to do it'. The screen goes blank once more. Oliver curses the day that he had his override privileges rescinded. Whenever a student's rating drops by three percentage points or more, the removal of the override privilege is automatically invoked. The dilemma for Oliver is whether to endure the six months of 'override exclusion' or work to get his grades back above the 72nd percentile. The screen bursts to life and the details of the afternoon's sessions are announced. 'Oh no', says Oliver aloud. As a desperate last act Oliver brings his mother back on the screen. 'Mum it's okay, it's not important. It's only phys ed.', he pleads. 'No Oliver', comes an emphatic reply, 'I don't care if it's origami, you're going to sit there and do it'. Oliver's face drops in defeat. 'It's not fair', he pouts, 'it's just a crock of bullsh-', and his mother's screen goes blank.

Oliver begins to surf the afternoon's offerings. Channels 1 and 3 have got 'boring' Mr Thomas giving the tutorial titled *The Body as a Lever System*. Oliver realises that Channel 3 is running a couple of minutes in front of Channel 1 and contemplates the incentive of a shorter session. Still, the thought of another 46 minutes with Mr Thomas is too much. Feeling disgruntled and running against the clock Oliver opts to search. A broad smile appears on his face when he sees Melinda Cathright appear on Channel 37. Somehow Melinda seems to make it a little more bearable. And there's always the promise of her exercise routine where she will remove her tracksuit to do stretches and calisthenics. These, of course, are done with the utmost dignity and postural deportment. For Oliver, Melinda's session is not only satisfying visually but, more importantly, he will be able to participate in the debriefings that are bound to take place among his friends. When one of his mates asks, 'Who saw Melinda's leg routine the other night?', he will be there.

Oliver endures the session that also focusses on the body as a lever system and has the usual segments on 'Nutritional advice' and 'Exercising at home'. He lies on the floor in front of his monitor reading magazines during the session while maintaining enough attention to respond to the prompts that sporadically appear on his screen throughout the session. Melinda's exercise circuit is oriented to shoulder and neck flexibility. Despite this aspect of muscular development being of increasing concern among the now computer-dependent population, it has little interest for Oliver who is disappointed in the static nature of the circuit. He pays little attention to the substantive issues that are discussed and workshopped in the session and is overwhelmingly unconcerned when he dutifully submits his attendance and comprehension details at the end of the session. He realises that physical education is not too important in the breakdown of his overall education profile. The infrequent nature of online physical education sessions is testimony to this view. Melinda bids her viewers well with a bit of advice about the importance of staying healthy and performing a daily exercise regimen. She concludes with the promise of more exciting programs soon and an overview of her next session that among other things will include hamstring and lower back flexibility. Oliver immediately feels some redemption. Melinda disappears from view and is replaced by an older woman Oliver has never seen before, introducing the subject of Art. 'No way', exclaims Oliver. 'Mum, Mum', he yells to bring his mother back on screen, 'It's Art mum, I don't do it any more. CAN I PLAY A GAME?'.

Scenario 2: circa 2020

In no school is there a subject called 'Physical Education'. In most secondary schools physical activity classes are of two separate types. First there are the fitness sessions which all pupils participate in three times per week. These are largely self-organised with the students working on prescribed fitness task cards designed and marketed by Pyke, Flemming and Telford Fitness Incorporated. No teachers are involved in these sessions. The pupils are supervised by community sport volunteers (actually unemployed young adults) who monitor the sessions by merely recording the participation (number of laps run etc.) of each student. This record is used by the school health specialists to hold students accountable for their fitness maintenance and development. The community sport volunteers have to participate in some form of community project in order to collect their youth allowance payments, and school fitness monitoring is considered an easy option compared with helping out in an old person's home, joining the Clean Up Australia project, or working in the government 'Dob in a Smoker' vigilante unit.

The other activity session in the timetable of most secondary schools is a one-hour sport education class per week. These sessions are conducted by a sport education instructor who is hired by the school to conduct the weekly sessions.

Apparently, following the performance of Australia at the Sydney 2000 Olympics, the federal government formally acted on the most controversial recommendation of the *Millenium Inquiry into Health & Physical Education as a Key Learning Area*. It converted all physical education teacher education programs in universities (most of which were then located in Schools of Human Movement and Sport Science) into sports education programs within the TAFE sector. In the government's eyes, a sports education instructor required no more than a two-year associate diploma, and this could be accomplished within the TAFE sector at a much reduced cost. Stripped of their teacher education programs and staff, the now considerably smaller university Schools of Human Movement and Sport Science were renamed Departments of Sport Science, and their focus was solely on the study of elite sports performance.

In concert with the federal government's privatisation philosophy, the *Aussie*

Sport programs, so well known in the late 1980s and early 1990s, were privatised in 2001. Under the new arrangements, the franchised firm *SportEd Inc* had cornered the market throughout Australia and offered to schools a program of sport education on a one-hour-per-week basis. *SportEd Inc* provided the instructors (graduates of the new TAFE Sports Education programs) and all the necessary equipment. All that schools are required to do is to timetable the Sports Education sessions and apply for a federal government Sports Education school subsidy.

It is no surprise to learn that *SportEd Inc* is sponsored by McDonald's, Coke and Pizza Hut and that the activities in Sports Education classes feature regularly in advertisements on commercial television and in the print media as well. No-one seems to recognise, or at least be bothered by, the contradiction between those sponsored messages to consume and the media-induced cultural 'imperative' to have trim bodies. Besides, Diet Coke, McDonald's light burger and the 'Sport It' pizzas were a major marketing success story.

The new Sports Education replaces what were the remnants of the physical education programs located in the old Key Learning Area of Health and Physical Education. The state governments have welcomed this initiative because it means that they no longer have to fund the salaries of physical education teachers or find money for equipment. For its part, the federal government claims that new arrangements for school sport education save the taxpayer an estimated $127 million each year as it no longer has to support large departments of staff in universities or the four-year degree programs in which they teach. The new TAFE arrangements are truly reflective of 'world's best practice'.

Scenario 3: circa 2030

There is a small television monitor high up on the east wall of the gym. The students come in and immediately follow the instructions from the voice coming from the large television on the western wall (placed neatly between the old wall bars). The voice belongs to Mitchell Glasson, the teacher in charge of human movement for the school. Mitchell has prerecorded a set of instructions which are used for all class management. In the next half hour the class will be led through a workout which systematically exercises different body parts and maintains an appropriate intensity of training. Cardio-funk music provides the rhythm and backdrop for the sessions. Each student in the school must attend three of these sessions a week.

Mitchell is the only physical education person on staff at Granview Grammar. He is a graduate of the degree program Human Kinetics from the University of Dunedin. He has no teacher training. The government, taking the lead from Britain, decided that, in order to reduce the cost of education, teachers needed only to possess a good degree in the relevant subject field and could learn to teach 'on the job'.

Mitchell, with his Human Kinetics degree, was snapped up by Granview because it has for many years (since the early 2000s) been at the forefront of Senior Physical Education. There were a few changes to this course during the 1990s. The major ones being that its name was changed to Senior Human

Movement Studies and physical activity was eliminated from its syllabus to maintain its academic credibility. Mitchell is well versed in all the latest research on sports performance enhancement and technologies but he knows little about teaching movement. However, this is not much of a problem because physical education as we knew it has not existed at Granview since Mitchell's appointment.

Actually it was Mitchell's innovative ideas which impressed the Board of Trustees at his interview. The Board was keen to reduce the staff numbers in the school and his ideas allowed the school to meet the government requirements set out in the *School Fitness Bill 2010* while shedding the three other physical education staff. The only activity requirement now at Granview is the fitness maintenance class. Mitchell teaches only Senior Human Movement Studies and manages the fitness maintenance classes. He does not even own a whistle.

Having studied computer technologies at Dunedin, Mitchell conceived a way to eliminate face-to-face teaching in these fitness maintenance classes. In addition to the use of video instruction, and surveillance for kids mucking around, each student is required to wear a special exercise monitor belt which contains a small computer to record the heart rate. At the end of each class the student is responsible for downloading their recorded information into the data bank.

The sessions are run in the gym every hour on the hour and each student chooses the appropriate session according to timetable options relating to their academic studies. Mitchell has a profile of every student in his computer. He has assessed their heart-rate threshold for training effect and he has developed a program which automatically graphs each student's HR for each session. The program also identifies students whose HR has fallen below threshold and issues a warning to the student. Two warnings and the student is required to pick up extra classes.

Mitchell's ideas represent the cutting edge of school practice for the year 2030.

Perhaps you find some of these scenarios agreeable with your philosophy for physical education. However, if you find them disturbing it is probably because they disrupt your taken-for-granted beliefs about the nature and purpose of physical education, and/or your sense of comfort in the ways in which things are currently done. Just remember, these scenarios reflect trends that are *already* in practice. Remember also that we are not suggesting that these scenarios will eventuate in their entirety. Our purpose is to get you to think beyond the present so that you can make strategic choices and decisions with respect to the sort of physical education teacher you wish to become and the career aspirations you wish to pursue.

At the interview: What if?

At a very practical level, it is probable that when you apply for a teaching job you will be asked to attend an interview. Among the many questions that might be asked of you are: Explain your personal educational philosophy with regard to physical education.

In answering this question you might wish to consider:

- the purpose of physical education in the curriculum;
- the role of the physical education teacher;
- the contemporary relevance of PE in the context of young people's lives; and
- the importance of reflective practice for ongoing professional development.

There are a myriad enduring and contemporary issues that you might be asked to speak about in an interview. However, one way or another most of them will be underpinned by the four philosophical issues mentioned above.

Perhaps as you engage the ideas contained in the pages of this book, you will begin to think differently about the physical education and your role as a teacher. Perhaps the ideas of this book will help you become the sort of teacher who can understand how your practice connects with the major social trends of these 'new times'. One thing is certain, however: your ability to understand physical education as a cultural practice will better equip you to cope with the demands and changes of teaching. It will help you with the enduring and contemporary issues of your future career in physical education.

References

Chopra, D. (1993). *Ageless Body, Timeless Mind*. Sydney: Random House.

Covey, S. (1990). *The Seven Habits of Highly Effective People: Restoring the Character Ethic*. Melbourne: The Business Library.

Kirk, D. (1996). 'The crisis in school physical education: An argument against the tide'. *ACHPER Healthy Lifestyles Journal*, 43(4), pp 25–28.

Locke, L. (1998). 'Advice, stories, and myths: The reactions of a cliff jumper'. *Quest*, 50(2), pp 238–248.

Schwartz, P. (1998). *The Art of the Long View: Planning for the Future in an Uncertain World*. Chichester: Wiley.

Siedentop, D. (1993). 'Curriculum innovation: Toward the 21st century'. Paper presented at the ICHPER, Yokohama, Japan.

Slaughter, R. (1996). *New Thinking for a New Millennium*. London: Routledge.

Further reading

Slaughter, R. (1996). *New Thinking for a New Millennium*. London: Routledge.